D0153177

CONDUCTORS AND COMPOSERS OF POPULAR ORCHESTRAL MUSIC

CONDUCTORS AND COMPOSERS OF POPULAR ORCHESTRAL MUSIC

A Biographical and Discographical Sourcebook

REUBEN MUSIKER
AND NAOMI MUSIKER

FOREWORD BY
DAVID ADES

GREENWOOD PRESS
Westport, Connecticut

Library of Congress Cataloging-in-Publication Data

Musiker, Reuben.
Conductors and composers of popular orchestral music : a biographical and discographical sourcebook / Reuben Musiker and Naomi Musiker ; foreword by David Ades.
p. cm.
Includes bibliographical references (p.) and index.
ISBN 0-313-30260-X (alk. paper)
1. Popular music—Bio-bibliography. 2. Orchestral Music—Bio-bibliography. 3. Popular music—Discography. 4. Orchestral music—Discography 5. Composers—Biography. 6. Conductors (Music)—Biography. I. Musiker, Naomi. II. Title.
ML105.M92 1998
784.2'164'0922—dc21 97-1714
[B] MN

British Library Cataloguing in Publication Data is available.

Library of Congress Catalog Card Number: 97-1714
ISBN: 0-313-30260-X

First published in 1998

Greenwood Press, 88 Post Road West, Westport, CT 06881
An imprint of Greenwood Publishing Group, Inc.

Printed in the United States of America

The paper used in this book complies with the Permanent Paper Standard issued by the National Information Standards Organization (Z39.48-1984).

10 9 8 7 6 5 4 3 2 1

Every reasonable effort has been made to trace the owners of copyright materials in this book, but in some instances this has proven impossible. The authors and publisher will be glad to receive information leading to more complete acknowledgments in subsequent printings of the book and in the meantime extend their apologies for any omissions.

Cover photo: Robert Farnon and his orchestra.

In memory of
Rollo Scott
(1925-1995)

Who single-handedly kept
popular orchestral music alive on Radio South Africa
(South African Broadcasting Corporation)
for fifteen years until its demise in 1995

Contents

Foreword

In many respects, popular orchestral music can be considered the Cinderella of the music scene. It is rarely taken seriously, yet appeals to millions who seldom realize that it is a clearly distinguishable art form in its own right. It is a sad fact that musical snobbery still exists to an astonishing degree and, for some inexplicable reason, popular orchestral music is often on the receiving end of such bigotry.

Perhaps one reason is that many so-called classical composers have, at times, written music that might be considered part of the light and popular music repertoire. This particular aspect of their work would be regarded as something akin to worthless by those musical elitists who seem to think it criminal to write music that can be appreciated by the masses. Light music could be described as 'serious music that is approachable'; in other words, it can be enjoyed for what it is, rather than endured, the lasting impression created by some of the more obscure classical works.

By now, you will have realized that I have an axe to grind and it is simply this: music in all its forms is to be enjoyed by us all and none of us should feel ashamed, or indeed guilty, if our choice of listening pleasure fails to meet with the approval of others. It is self-destructive to suggest that a particular type of music is beneath one's dignity. It is equally astonishing that anyone could state that a particular style of music was the only kind to be enjoyed, to the exclusion of others. A highly respected critic (respected, that is, by his own blinkered colleagues), recently admitted that he knew little of the works of George Gershwin. Such an attitude can only have resulted from a self-imposed exclusion from the enjoyment of the music of a twentieth-century genius.

Happily, people who appreciate and understand popular orchestral music seem mercifully free of such petty and stupid hang-ups. They are usually music lovers who embrace catholic tastes, often reflecting their mood at a particular time; sometimes revelling in the glorious sounds created by Frederick Delius, Claude Debussy and Maurice Ravel, yet on other occasions equally appreciative of Duke Ellington and his contemporaries.

The twentieth century has given music lovers a wonderful choice of material to sample. Never before have we all had the opportunity to listen to such a wide variety of performers; the greatest singers, musicians and orchestras and, equally, the talented writers whose compositions they bring to life.

Popular orchestral music is difficult to define. It also goes under the heading 'concert music' and, in German-speaking countries, it has the wonderful title 'Gehobenes Unterhaltungsmusik'. People who love popular orchestral music have no problem in identifying it; other music lovers may be aware that it falls somewhere between classical and popular music.

By the time the reader reaches the end of this book, it will be clear that popular orchestral music is the province of the most talented composers, arrangers and conductors of this century. It is no criticism to describe it as 'popular' simply because it appeals to millions. In the early years of long-playing records, albums of popular music sold in vast quantities, making conductors such as Mantovani, Percy Faith and George Melachrino household names around the world.

Light music was, however, around long before the 1950s. In Britain, Eric Coates, Edward German and Haydn Wood were creating music to enliven public concerts that conveniently transferred to one side (and occasionally two), of a 78 rpm record. Some analysts of the genre, consider that the 78 record was largely responsible for imposing a discipline on composers and arrangers, forcing them to develop their ideas concisely and without waste of time.

Whatever the reasons, it is a fact that we have witnessed the emergence of a kind of music that encompasses original works, (Robert Farnon and Leroy Anderson being the preeminent examples) and also clever arrangements of popular songs. I hesitate to use the once common phrase 'popular symphonic', but some readers will understand that description.

Thanks to sound recording, music lovers are no longer restricted to current fads. Anything that has ever been recorded during the past 100 years can be enjoyed whenever we wish, and there is no doubt that the invention of the compact disc has been beneficial in extending the available repertoire to a degree unobtainable during the LP era.

Popular orchestral music can take its place as an important art form of the twentieth century. Many musicians famous in other spheres have at times contributed to the vast quantities of riches to be discovered. More importantly, many gifted writers have established their own distinguished careers in this fertile area of the music scene.

They have long deserved the kind of tribute which this book provides. Professor Reuben Musiker has made a lifelong study of this style of music, and there is no one better qualified to take an overview of popular orchestral music as a worldwide phenomenon. Indeed, it has been my pleasure to count him as a friend and to witness his diligent researches over a forty-year period, even though we have been separated by two continents, half a world apart. His painstaking studies will delight music lovers already familiar with the famous names whose work he describes. Others will be encouraged to investigate this area of the music scene, which is happily seeing a significant resurgence of interest as this exciting century draws to a close.

David Ades
4 November 1996

Preface

ORIGINS

This book was born out of a passion for popular orchestral music, which has lasted for half a century, from the mid-twentieth century onward. It has been reinforced and abetted by an equally strong passion for collecting 78s, long-playing records and more recently, compact discs, an assemblage which now totals some 2,500 records, all in the popular orchestral field and gathered from all over the world. At the same time, an extensive library of literature of popular music was built up to support the music collection.

As it proved impossible to achieve comprehensiveness, however, the compilation of the present work has necessitated intensive use and consultation of a number of discographical sources. It is primarily a book about records, that is, long-playing 33⅓ rpm discs (LPs), as well as compact discs (CDs) but not 78 rpm and 45 rpm records.

As far as the authors are aware, this is the first work of its kind, bringing together biographies and discographies in a single tool. No collector or librarian has the time to consult half a century of such important discographical sources as the Schwann catalogues (U.S.A.) or the Gramophone catalogues (U.K.). Although the discographies in the present work are selective, they nevertheless span half a century in a single sequence. It is the authors' hope that the book will be useful to collectors, music and record librarians, disc jockeys and radio stations throughout the world.

SCOPE

In this book, the terms 'light' and 'popular orchestral music' are used in a generalized way, to cover many aspects of popular music for orchestra. Included are the various forms of popular music that stem from folk and jazz sources and which include such forms as palm court music, music excerpted from operettas and musical comedies, as well as theater and show music, in fact, almost anything in an undemanding mode of musical address.

The term 'operetta' is defined as a light opera with spoken dialogue. Nowadays operetta has become almost synonymous with musical comedy, which is the term applied to any sentimental-humorous play containing plenty of light music. The music is generally light and lively (never serious) and frequently interrupted by dialogue.

'Palm court music' is the term applied to authentic arrangements of salon, theater and dance orchestra music, popular in the first half of the twentieth century. The music was generally sweet and sentimental but could also be robust, syncopated, sparkling and even humorous. The music frequently included singing, whistling, tap dancing, fox trotting and 'wicked' tangoing.

The term 'middle-of-the-road' is generally and loosely applied to any genre of music falling between serious classical music and popular music.

The concept certainly includes the serious composer writing in a lighter vein than normal. However, the best and most typical popular orchestral music is that which is written by composers specializing in the idiom. The concept of popular orchestral music, as employed in the making and writing of this book, is seen to be derived from various types of music and musical activity.

The focus of the present work is on the 1940s, 1950s and 1960s. Popular orchestral music, as it is understood in this book, reached its zenith in these years. In the case of the United States, the first half of the twentieth century was a golden age for popular music, and it was a period dominated by great composers of popular song.

In the 1970s and beyond, 'pop music' largely took over the popular music scene and this influence immediately became apparent in film and 'mood' music. On the other hand, the 1970s also witnessed a great vogue for the use of so-called classical themes. The period from 1930 to 1960 relates to more 'middle-of-the-road' music, which is the trend followed in this book. Unfortunate terminology has crept into music literature, especially among purveyors of light orchestral music, namely the term 'easy-listening' music.

In *Elevator Music*, his entertaining book on Muzak, easy-listening and mood music, Joseph Lanza draws attention to the widespread but wrongly held belief that this kind of music has frequently been condemned by many critics as boring, dehumanized, vapid, cheesy, elevator-type music. Such reactions, he states, appear to be based more on cultural prejudice than honest musical appraisal.

> After decades of rock, rhythm and blues, folk, heavy metal and rap, a desensitized population seems to assume that if music is not hot, heavy, bubbling with jackhammer rhythms and steaming with emotion or anger, it is somehow less than good, or (worse), less than art. (2)

This ill-deserved reflection, held by so many regarding popular orchestral music, is a myth that needs to be dispelled. It is one of the principal reasons that this present book came into being, for as Lanza asserts:

> Muzak and mood music are, in many respects, aesthetically superior to all other musical forms: they emit music the way the twentieth century is equipped to receive it. They have so successfully blended genres and redefined music appreciation that they have become the music world's Esperanto. (5)

Popular orchestral music as we know this genre today, may be said to have been derived from a number of very different streams of musical forms and activities, including the following distinct categories:

1. The activities of the select group of classically trained conductors who devoted themselves to the promotion of popular music in the symphonic idiom. Notable examples of such maestros are Morton Gould and Andre Kostelanetz, who are dealt with comprehensively in their respective sections of the book. They did not abandon classical music but operated in both genres.
2. The role played by conductors and arrangers who emanated from dance band, 'big band', swing and even jazz environments and formed large orchestras while continuing to play band music. Many of these conductors and arrangers did the backing arrangements for leading popular singers but also went on to make orchestral arrangements in their own right.
3. The contributions of composers who wrote music for films. Film music is background music that has become an integral part of the film's sound track and which includes the work of specialist composers. Some of these composers were trained in a classical tradition, while others came from the Broadway theater. Film music included major orchestral themes that were subsequently extracted from the film score for performance by individual orchestras. An-

other type of score included the use of a brief but persistent theme, which became a continuing motif throughout the film.

In the 1950s, film theme songs became almost as important as the films themselves and often outlasted the original film. There are numerous examples of this trend because in the 1950s, the film theme song became more or less mandatory, the screen becoming one of the main outlets for quality songs and music.

4. The activities of composers who composed mood music in the specific context of the term. Mood music has come to be known as easy-listening music; however, it does have a far more exact connotation. In the strict sense of the term, mood music means background music written for radio and television programs (including 'commercials'), as well as feature, documentary and newsreel films. Mood music originated in the era of silent movies, when cinema pianists were required to accompany silent films. Commercial libraries of sheet music were established before World War I by the De Wolfe Organization in Great Britain and Giuseppe Becce in Germany. Subsequently, mood music was publicly performed (with copyright permission) on gramophone records and more recently on compact discs. In the years 1936–37, Decca manufactured mood music discs for the English music publishers Bosworth and Boosey and Hawkes. Smaller firms in Germany and Australia established similar libraries, as did Brunswick in the United States. Later, in England, His Master's Voice issued a mood music catalogue. Chappell & Co. established what was to become one of the finest mood music libraries, described in the main body of the text (see p. 42). By the mid-1950s, an increasing number of mood music publishers had entered the field. More recently the genre has come to be known as production music.
5. Composers who wrote for the musical theatre, including Broadway, and for musical comedies. Their contributions were not always focused specifically on the orchestra, but this book deals with their work in terms of the orchestra. The authors feel that this is an original contribution, not well covered in the extensive literature on these composers.

A central theme of this book is the role of the conductor in the development of popular orchestral music through the years. In the 1930s, the 'symphonic-pop' tradition was continued on network radio by classically trained arranger-conductors, such as Arthur Fiedler, Morton Gould, Andre Kostelanetz and Percy Faith, all of whom explored the abundant resources of strings. The big string orchestras were used to accompany the new school of crooners after World War II. In the late 1940s and 1950s, lush arrangements of popular songs by large, concert-sized orchestras came into vogue. These orchestras were prolific in record terms. Much of this type of light orchestral music survived beyond the eras of the 78 rpm records and 33 ⅓ rpm long-playing records into the current compact disc era. Only a small fraction of the LP popular orchestral repertoire, however, has found its way onto compact disc.

The authors have attempted to adhere to the theme that forms the main trend of the book, which is popular music as seen through orchestral interpretations. Consequently, discographies appended to composers' biographies are limited largely to popular orchestral repertoire. Vocal sound tracks and classical works of popular composers such as Gershwin are excluded.

It was the authors' original intention to confine the book to conductors. However, it soon became apparent in the course of compilation that many conductors were also composers and that the work of composers arranged for orchestra could not be ignored. Consequently, a selection of leading American and British composers in the popular field has been included. In the case of conductors, a broader, more universal selection was made. There has been an attempt to maintain a balance between British and American varieties of popular music and their composers.

EXCLUSIONS

The following genres of music are, as a general rule, excluded from the scope of the book:

Classical and serious music

Light classical music, such as Viennese waltzes, palm court and salon music

Military and brass band music

Jazz

Dance band music, except in those instances where the dance band was enlarged by the addition of strings to create a light orchestral texture and effect

Vocal music, including jazz, popular and classical, written for individuals and chorales

ARRANGEMENT

The book is arranged in two sequences:

1. Biographies and select discographies, both arranged alphabetically, of the well-known and better-known conductors and composers about whom biographical information could be obtained. The birth and/or death dates of some conductors could not always be ascertained, even in the case of those in the main biographical sequence, despite intensive reference searches. It has taken many years to assemble this information, particularly in view of the fact that biographical information is more often than not elusive and covered only to the barest, minimal extent by the existing encyclopedias of popular music, such as Faber, Guinness, Oxford and Penguin (see Select Bibliography).
2. Select discographies of conductors about whom little or no biographical information could be found. It has not always been possible or feasible to provide record numbers, although these are given wherever possible.

Many of the records and CDs listed in the discographies are available in different parts of the world, even though not always included in catalogs. The authors have access to these resources and will readily assist collectors in obtaining elusive records and CDs mentioned in the book.

All the conductors and composers mentioned throughout the book are brought together in a single, combined name index, to facilitate information retrieval. A select bibliography is appended to highlight the principal sources used to compile the information given in this book.

A book of this nature will inevitably be found to have omissions of both conductors and composers. There was a time, particularly in the 1950s, when the pages of the Schwann record catalogue were overflowing with the names of conductors, many of whom made only a few records. Quantity, however, has not been a criterion for selection. The authors hope that they have succeeded in including nearly all the popular orchestral conductors who made their mark in the United States and in Europe.

In a sense this is a pilot edition of the book. The authors hope that readers throughout the world will write to them with suggestions for improvement, as well as information, which will be incorporated into a subsequent edition, if such a development is necessitated.

The music world changes frequently; new compact discs appear constantly and the authors look forward to updating the present text as soon as circumstances warrant it.

Reuben Musiker and Naomi Musiker
P.O. Box 44163
Linden, Johannesburg
2104, South Africa
Fax: 2711-782-0986

Acknowledgments

In the course of preparing this work for publication, the authors received invaluable help from many quarters and they wish to express their sincere thanks to the following persons:

David Ades, secretary of the Robert Farnon Society, for contributing the foreword and for his friendship, support and encouragement over many years; also for his enthusiastic and ready willingness to publish numerous articles by the authors in the *Journal into Melody* ever since its inception in 1956.

Henry (Hank) Steele for making available a list of his extensive record collection and for keeping the authors informed of many records of which they, living in Africa, would otherwise have been unaware.

Gary Haberman for providing record numbers from his impressive collection of popular orchestral music.

Ron Cowley for searching the Internet for relevant compact discs in the fields covered by this book.

Sydney Becker, Alan Bunting, Serge Elhaik, Bill Halvorsen, Carlos Ribeiro, Gene Tipton, Malcolm Powell, Robert Van Camp and Sune Walfridsson for assistance with various aspects of record and tape collecting through the years, as well as their unfailing friendship.

Alicia Merritt, Acquisitions Editor, Music, Greenwood Publishing Group, for overseeing this book to fulfillment and for her inspired editorship.

Wanda Giles, copyeditor, whose impeccable work and professionalism, as well as her interest in, and knowledge of, the subject matter, made it a pleasure for the authors to correct the many inconsistencies and imperfections which she noted. She also made many invaluable suggestions which greatly enhanced the final text. A true *rara avis* in this field of musical reference book publishing!

Key to Record Symbols

Record manufacturers' names and numbers have been included in the discographies wherever possible and wherever known. This has not always been feasible. All LP records are 12" unless otherwise indicated. Mono refers to monaural or monophonic sound recordings. Stereo refers to stereophonic sound recordings. The discographies appended to the biographies of conductors and composers are orchestral only, not vocal.

Record Symbols	Name of Record Company
ABC (Mono), ABCS (Stereo)	ABC Paramount
ACL	Ace of Clubs (Decca)
AFSD	Audio Fidelity
B	Richmond (Mono)
B	Warner Brothers (Mono)
BBL	Philips
BS	Warner Brothers (Stereo)
BT	Bainbridge
CAL	RCA Camden (Mono) (U.S.)
CAS	RCA Camden (Stereo) (U.S.)
CDS	Command
CL (Mono), CS (Stereo)	Columbia
CLP	His Master's Voice

CRL	Coral
DL	Decca (U.S.)
DLP	Design
E (Mono)	Dot
ECS	Eclipse
EK, LN	Epic
FCS	Roulette
GGL	Golden Guinea (Pye)
H	Capitol (10")
INTS (Stereo)	RCA Camden
K, KL (Mono), KS (Stereo)	Kapp
L	Lion
LCS, LM (Mono)	RCA Victor
LK	Decca (U.K.)
LL	London
LMM (Mono)	Liberty
LPBR (Mono)	Everest
LPHM (Mono)	Polydor
LPM	RCA Victor (Mono) (U.S.)
LRP	Liberty
LSC (Stereo)	RCA Victor (Stereo)
LSP (Stereo)	RCA Stereophonic (U.S.)
LSS (Stereo)	Liberty
LST (Stereo)	Liberty
LX	Vik
LXA	RCA Victor
MC	MCA
MFP	Music for Pleasure
MG(Mono)	Mercury
MGM	Metro Goldwyn Mayer
MGV	Verve
ML (Mono), MS (Stereo)	Columbia
MS	Reprise
NPL	Pye
PC (Mono)	Pickwick
PDL	Felsted
PHM	Philips

PPS (Stereo)	Mercury
R	Roulette
RD	RCA Monaural (U.K.)
RDM (Mono)	Reader's Digest
RDS (Stereo)	Reader's Digest
REB	British Broadcasting Corporation (BBC)
RLP	Riverside
RM	Oriole
RS	Reprise
S	Alshire
S	Richmond (Stereo)
SCX (Stereo)	Columbia (U.K.)
SDBR (Stereo)	Everest
SDL	Felsted
SE (Stereo)	MGM
SF	RCA Stereo Fidelity (U.K)
SFL	Fontana
SKL (Stereo)	Decca
SLPHM (Stereo)	Polydor
SML	Mercury
SP (Stereo)	Decca
SP, ST (Stereo), STAO, T (Mono)	Capitol
SPC (Stereo)	Pickwick
SR (Stereo)	Mercury
SRS	Regal
SRW	Mercury Wing
SS	United Artists
SW	Capitol (Stereo)
33SX (Mono)	Columbia (U.K.)
S	Time
UAL	United Artists (Mono)
UAS	United Artists (Stereo)
VL	Vocalion
VLP	Varsity
W	Capitol (Mono)
WB	Warner Brothers (Mono)
WDL	Disneyland

WGS	Westminster (Stereo)
WP	Westminster (Mono)
WS	Warner Brothers (Stereo)
WWS	United Artists
ZS	Rediffusion

BIOGRAPHIES AND DISCOGRAPHIES OF CONDUCTORS AND COMPOSERS

ADDINSELL, RICHARD (13 January 1904–14 November 1977)
Richard Addinsell was born in Oxford, England, and studied at the Royal College of Music, London. He commenced his career by contributions to the Andre Charlot revues. In 1929, he wrote the incidental music for the Old Vic production of *Adam's Opera* and in 1930 left to study music in Europe. He returned to England in 1932 and wrote the music for the stage production of *Alice in Wonderland*. Shortly after that, Addinsell was contracted to write film music for RKO in Hollywood. During the 1930s, he also continued to write incidental music for shows and radio plays. For many years, he served as accompanist and cocomposer to the distinguished artist and film actress Joyce Grenfell. Their best-known work was probably 'I'm Going to See You Today'.

Addinsell scored for about fifty films, the first being *The Amateur Gentleman* for Alexander Korda in 1936. He achieved fame in 1941, when he wrote 'Warsaw Concerto' for the film *Dangerous Moonlight*. He wrote the 'Prelude and Waltz' for *Blithe Spirit* (1945) and the theme music for *The Passionate Friends* (1948). Other notable compositions included 'Ring Round the Moon' and 'Festival'. In 1957, he composed 'I Found a Dream' (lyrics by Christopher Hassall) for *The Prince and The Showgirl*.

ADDISON, JOHN (b. 16 March 1920)
John Addison was born in West Cobham, Surrey, and studied oboe, clarinet and piano at the Royal College of Music, London, where he won an

award for composition. He served in World War II in the 23rd Hussars. Subsequently, he became a professor of harmony and composition at the Royal College of Music. His early works included various classical works; a ballet, *Carte Blanche* (1953); and incidental music for plays, *Othello*, produced by Laurence Olivier, the London revue *Cranks* and John Osborne's *Luther* and *The Entertainer*, for which he later scored the film version.

Addison wrote the music for about ninety film scores, including *Seven Days to Noon* (1950); *The Man Between* (1953); *The Maggie* (1954); *Reach for the Sky* (1956); *Lucky Jim* (1957); *Carleton-Browne of the F.O.* (1958), *A Taste of Honey* (1962), *Tom Jones* (1963), for which he won an Academy Award; *Torn Curtain* (1966) and *Sleuth* (1972). His most recent work is the theme music for Angela Lansbury's TV series *Murder She Wrote*.

ALWYN, WILLIAM (7 November 1905–12 September 1985)
William Alwyn was born in Northampton and graduated from the Royal Academy of Music, where he was appointed professor of composition. He composed various classical works and was a founder member of the Composers' Guild of Great Britain, serving three terms as chairman. He was awarded the C.B.E. in 1978.

He scored some sixty feature films, including *Desert Victory* (a 1943 documentary), *The Rake's Progress* (1945), *Green for Danger* (1946), *Odd Man Out* (1946), *The Fallen Idol* (1948), *The History of Mr Polly* (1949), *A Night to Remember* (1958), *Carve Her Name with Pride* (1958) and *Swiss Family Robinson* (1960).

AMBROSE (born Bert Ambrose) (1897–12 June 1973)
Ambrose was born in London and learned the violin as a child. He went to New York in his teens and played in cinema orchestras for silent films. He made his debut as violinist in a band led by Emil Coleman. From 1917 to 1920, he led the band at the Palais Royal, New York. He then returned to London to form an orchestra at the Embassy Club, Bond Street. In 1927, he moved to the Mayfair Club, where he stayed for six years, assembling one of the finest dance bands in the United Kingdom. This band earned a worldwide reputation that lasted for more than twenty years. The band broadcast regularly from the club and recorded for Decca, United Kingdom. His theme tune was 'When Day Is Done'.

In 1933, Ambrose returned to the Embassy Club and for the rest of the 1930s played at Ciro's, the Café de Paris and other London nightspots. In 1940 he toured the Variety theaters with a small group. He led a band throughout World War II and into the 1950s but disbanded in 1956.

He subsequently became an artist's manager and was responsible for promoting the careers of Joe Crossman, George Chisholm, Max Goldberg, Lew Davis, Tommy Mcquater, Tiny Winters, Danny Polo, Billy Amstell and singer Kathy Kirby in the 1960s. He also played an important role in the careers of band leaders such as Ted Heath, STANLEY BLACK, George Shearing, Sidney Lipton, GEORGE MELACHRINO and arrangers Lew Stone and Sid Phillips. Vocalists who worked with him included Sam Browne, Elsie Carlisle, Evelyn Dahl, Vera Lynn, Anne Shelton and Denny Dennis.

Select Discography

Starlit Hour—The Music of Peter De Rose MGM E 3350

Compilations

Ambrose 1928–32 (1974); **Recollections** (1981); **1929 Sessions** (1982); **Happy Days 1929–30** (1982); **Tribute to Cole Porter** (1983); **Soft Lights and Sweet Music** (1983); **Hits of 1931** (1984); **Swing Is in the Air** (1984); **The Golden Age of Ambrose and His Orchestra** (1985); **Body and Soul** (1986); **Faithfully Yours 1930–32** (1986); **I Only Have Eyes For You** (1986); **S'Wonderful** (1987); **Ambrose 1935–37** (1988); **The Sun Has Got His Hat On** (1988); **Champagne Cocktail** (1988).

ANDERSON, LEROY (29 June 1908–18 May 1975)

Biographical Details

Leroy Anderson was born in Cambridge, Massachusetts. He showed musical promise from an early age and mastered the organ and double-bass. While in high school he wrote the school's graduation songs for three years running.

He studied at the New England Conservatory of Music and at Harvard University, graduating in 1929. He obtained his master's degree in 1930. He served as organist and choirmaster of the East Congregational Church in Milton, Massachusetts, from 1929 to 1935. In 1935, he became a freelance musician. He composed and arranged music for the BOSTON POPS ORCHESTRA, directed by ARTHUR FIEDLER, and began to establish himself as a composer of light orchestral works. One of his first successes was 'Jazz Pizzicato', composed in 1939. After a period of active service in the U.S. Army, from 1942 to 1946, he resumed his musical career, producing popular compositions, most of which were introduced by the Boston Pops Orchestra. Around 1950, American Decca engaged him to record his works with a fifty-piece orchestra.

Musical Achievements

Some of his works included titles such as 'Fiddle-Faddle', 'Syncopated Clock', 'Sleigh Ride', 'Blue Tango', 'Belle of the Ball', 'The Typewriter', 'Plink, Plank, Plunk', 'Serenata', 'Bugler's Holiday', 'Sandpaper Ballet', 'The Waltzing Cat', 'Song of the Bells', 'Promenade', 'Phantom Regiment',

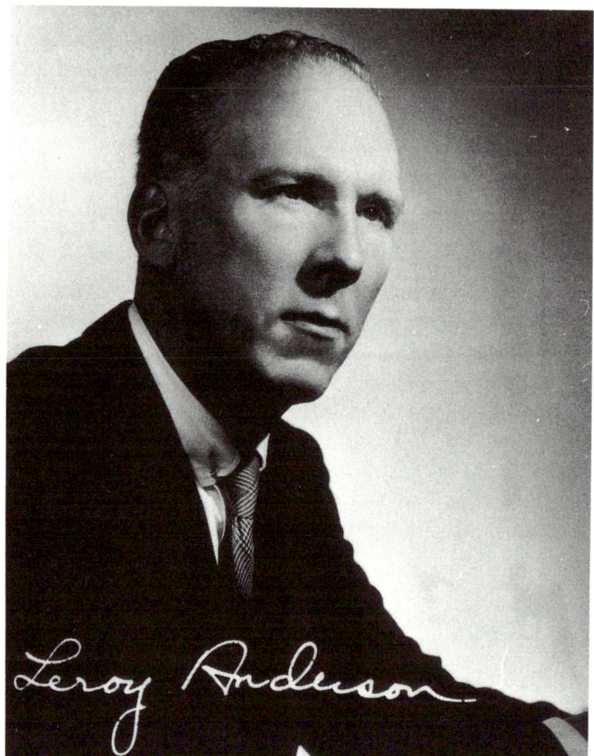

Leroy Anderson

and 'Forgotten Dreams'. He also composed the music for the 1958 Broadway musical *Goldilocks*.

Anderson was a versatile musician, able to capture many moods and rhythms in his music. He was extremely fond of string arrangements, particularly violin pizzicato.

'Blue Tango' sold over two million records and became the first strictly instrumental number to top the American Hit Parade. 'Fiddle-Faddle' is reminiscent of the 'perpetual motion' compositions of the nineteenth century, e.g., the 'Moto Perpetuo' of Paganini. 'The Typewriter' was used to good effect in the 1959 motion picture *But Not for Me*, starring Clark Gable. 'Sandpaper Ballet' conjures up a picture of the once very popular soft shoe shuffle, featured in the world of variety theater. 'Serenata' contained lively Latin-American rumba rhythms and was recorded by vocalists such as Sarah Vaughan and Nat 'King' Cole.

Select Discography

Greatest Hits BMG 1993

Leroy Anderson Conducts Leroy Anderson MCA Records MCL 1690

New Music of Leroy Anderson Decca DL 74335

Pops Concert Decca DL 9749

Compact Discs

Blue Tango—Leroy Anderson's Greatest Hits Pro Arte 8011

Fennell, Frederick. Conducts Leroy Anderson Polygram 32013

Fennell, Frederick. Conducts Leroy Anderson and Eric Coates Polygram 34376

Fiddle-Faddle Vanguard 6008

Kunzel, Erich. Syncopated Clock and other Favorites by Leroy Anderson Proarte 264

Leroy Anderson Collection MCA 9815

Leroy Anderson Collection MCA 1988, 2-CD set

Pro Arte Orchestra. Leroy Anderson's Greatest Hits. Maxiplay 8011

Slatkin, Leonard. The Typewriter: Leroy Anderson Favorites (With Saint Louis Symphony Orchestra) RCA 09026–68048–2

Steinberg, Pinchas. Blue Tango: Symphonic Pops by Leroy Anderson (With Kolner Rundfunk Orchestra) Capriccio 10299

APPLEWAITE, STANLEY (b. 1925)

Stanley Applewaite was born in Sheffordshire and began his professional career as a pianist. He later turned to composing, conducting and arranging and became conductor of the Norton Green Symphonia in the 1950s.

Select Discography

'All The Things You Are': The Music of Jerome Kern Design Records DLP 35

ARLEN, HAROLD (born Hyman Arluck) (15 February 1905–23 April 1986)

Harold Arlen was born in Buffalo, New York, the son of a cantor in a local synagogue. He gained musical experience in the synagogue choir and was taught by his mother. As a teenager, he earned a living as a pianist on lake steamers and in nightclubs. He formed his own band, the Buffalodians, with whom he recorded in 1926. In New York, he worked as a jazz band singer, pianist and arranger and led his group in a Broadway cafe. He was given a vocal part by VINCENT YOUMANS in the show *Great Day* (1929). During this period he composed a song in collaboration with lyricist Ted Koehler, entitled 'Get Happy'. This song was used in *9.15 Revue* and made famous by singer Ruth Etting. He was employed for some time by the publisher J. H. Remick and in the 1930s, recorded as a singer with Red Nichols, Benny Goodman, Joe Venuti and Eddie Duchin.

Arlen wrote 500 songs, many in collaboration with Koehler, for revues at the Cotton Club, one of which was Lena Horne's famous song 'Stormy

Weather'. The distinctive Arlen touch was the jazz-based, blues-rooted quality of his music, which placed him in the same category as DUKE ELLINGTON. The basic elements of his musical style were a strong, flowing melodic line and a subtle, but marked feeling for improvisation.

Arlen moved to Hollywood in the 1930s but continued to write songs for Broadway, working with lyricists such as Dorothy Fields, Leo Robin, Johnny Mercer, Yip Harburg and Ira Gershwin, in addition to Koehler. Some of his great songs included 'Between the Devil and the Deep Blue Sea', 'Stormy Weather', 'I Gotta Right to Sing the Blues', 'I've Got the World on a String,' 'Blues in the Night', 'That Old Black Magic', 'Happiness Is a Thing Called Joe', 'It's Only a Paper Moon' and 'Fancy Free'.

He was a prolific composer for films, including *Take a Chance* (1933), *Star Spangled Rhythm* (1942) and *The Sky's the Limit* (1943). His most successful effort in this respect was *The Wizard of Oz* in 1939, with Judy Garland. Songs from this score included 'Somewhere over the Rainbow', 'We're Off to See the Wizard' and 'Follow the Yellow Brick Road'. He also composed tunes for the plays *Earl Carroll Vanities, Rhythm Mania* and *St. Louis Woman.*

Additional Readings

Ewen, David. *Great Men of American Popular Song*. Englewood Cliffs, NJ: Prentice-Hall, 1970, pp. 251–271.

Hemming, Roy. *The Melody Lingers On*. New York: Newmarket Press, 1986, pp. 1–28.

Jablonski, Edward. *Harold Arlen: Happy with the Blues*. New York: Doubleday, 1961. Reprinted with new introduction and revised bibliographies, New York: Da Capo Press, 1986.

Jablonski, Edward. *Harold Arlen: Rhythm, Rainbows and Blues*. Boston: Northeastern University Press, 1996.

Select Discography

Cordell, Frank. Suite Based on the Music of Harold Arlen Reader's Digest RDS 6057

Kostelanetz, Andre. Harold Arlen Columbia CL1099

Ornadel, Cyril. I've Got the World on a String: Music of Harold Arlen World Record Club

Poliakin, Raoul. Music of Harold Arlen and Richard Rodgers Everest LPBR 5066

Rose, David. Let's Fall in Love: Music of Harold Arlen MGM E3101

ARLT, HANS-GEORG

Hans-Georg Arlt was born in Berlin. His mother was a well-known pianist and his grandfather a repetiteur. He studied the violin and completed his musical education at the Berlin High School for Music.

From 1946 to 1950, he was concertmaster of the Berlin Radio. He then took up the position of concertmaster and violin virtuoso with the RIAS Dance Orchestra. In 1958, he formed his String Orchestra, which became a household name to radio and television audiences throughout Germany.

Select Discography

Ein Neuer Sound Geht Um die Welt Ariola 32721T

Musik Klingt Durch Die Nacht Ariola S712311T

Musik Zum Tanzen Und Traumen Ariola 317191

The Sound of Strings Oriole Records RM143 [A monaural reissue of Ariola 32721T, see above]

ARNOLD, MALCOLM (b. 21 October 1921)
Malcolm Arnold studied trumpet, conducting and composition at the Royal College of Music, London. He played principal trumpet in the London Philharmonic Orchestra from 1942 to 1948 and subsequently became a full-time composer, combining his film work with serious compositions.

His best-remembered film scores are *Badgers Green* (1949), *The Sound Barrier* (1952), *Hobson's Choice* (1954), *The St Trinian's* series (1954–66), *Trapeze* (1956), *The Bridge over the River Kwai* (1957, which won an Academy Award for the scoring of Kenneth Alford's 'Colonel Bogey March'), *Dunkirk* (1958), *The Inn of the Sixth Happiness* (1958), *Tunes of Glory* (1960) and *Whistle Down the Wind* (1962).

B

BACHARACH, BURT (b. 12 May 1928)
Burt Bacharach was born in Kansas City. He was the son of a journalist and at first wanted to be a footballer. At high school his interest in music grew, and he appeared in shows with Dizzy Gillespie and Charlie Parker. He had his own band for a while and then studied music at McGraw University. Later he attended courses given by Darius Milhaud, Bohuslav Martinu and Henry Cowell at the New School for Social Research in New York. He won a scholarship to the Music Academy of the West, Santa Barbara. After 1952, he conducted and arranged for various record companies and accompanied singers such as Vic Damone, Polly Bergen, Steve Lawrence and the Ames Brothers. From 1956 to 1960, he accompanied Marlene Dietrich before her return to Germany in 1961.

His own compositions began to attract notice. They included the hits 'The Story of My Life' and 'Magic Moments' (1957). Bacharach achieved great success collaborating with lyricist Hal David to produce some of the most sophisticated popular songs of the 1960s. These included 'Wives and Lovers', 'Walk on By', 'What the World Needs Now Is Love', 'Reach Out for Me', 'Trains and Boats and Planes', 'Blue on Blue', 'Always Something There to Remind Me', 'The Look of Love', and 'Do You Know the Way to San Jose?'

He wrote the title songs and music for the films *Wonderful to Be Young* (1962), *What's New, Pussycat?* (1965), *After the Fox* (1966), *Promise Her Anything* (1966), *Alfie* (1966), *Casino Royale* (1967), *Butch Cassidy and the Sundance Kid* (1969, Academy Award for 'Raindrops Keep Falling on my Head'), *The April Fools* (1969). Singer Dionne Warwick made hits with songs such as 'Alfie' (1966), 'The Look of Love' (1968), 'I'll Say a Little Prayer' and 'This Girl's in Love With You' (1969). Bacharach made many recordings under his own name in the 1970s. His successful musical, *Promises, Promises* (1968) with lyrics by Hal David and book by Neil Simon, was highly acclaimed. He was also involved in two film musicals, *Lost Horizon* (1972) and *Together* (1980).

Bacharach's songwriting partnership with Hal David ended in the early 1970s. He remained inactive until the 1980s, when he scored major hits with 'Arthur's Theme', 'On My Own', and 'That's What Friends Are For'.

Throughout his career, Bacharach recorded a series of solo albums, but these achieved limited success. His reputation rests firmly on his fine songwriting.

Select Discography

Chacksfield, Frank. **Burt Bacharach** Decca PFS 4230.

Ron Goodwin and His Orchestra Play Burt Bacharach Columbia TWO 373

Compact Discs

Classics, Vol. 23 A&M 2521 (Collection of hits other artists had with Bacharach's songs)

Greatest Hits A&M 3321 (Collection of hits Bacharach had as a recording artist)

Hayman, Richard. **Best of Burt Bacharach** NAXOS 8 990051

BARBER, FRANK

Frank Barber was born in London. He had a classical training in music and conducted a small ensemble known as the Salon Strings and also a full orchestra. He himself was able to play the piano, violin, viola and flute.

Select Discography

Deep Percussion 24–4508

Dinner Music Capitol T 10082

Hello London Columbia 33 SC 1193

Hi-Fi Dinner Music Capitol T 10082

Melodic Percussion Capitol ST 2794

Room Five-Hundred-and-Four: The Music of George Posford Columbia 33 SX 1233

BARCLAY, EDDIE (born Edouard Ruault) (b. 26 January 1921)

Eddie Barclay was born at Verseau in France. He earned his living as a waiter in his parents' cafe. He commenced his musical career in the late 1930s after winning a prize in a competition organized by the Hot Club de France. His small piano-and-rhythm combination became well known in the Parisian cabaret world, and Barclay founded 'Le Club' with one of his old friends, Pierre-Louis Guerin, who later became famous as producer of music-hall entertainment. Barclay's group recorded for some leading Continental labels and met with considerable success in this field too.

The outbreak of the Second World War and the German occupation of France affected Barclay's career. After the liberation of France in 1945, his love for jazz music was stimulated by contact with the American forces. He became a jazz pianist and then turned to the record business, becoming one of the forerunners of the LP record industry. For the first session, he gathered together a group of musicians who were all personal friends of his, including Jerry Mengo, Jack Dieval and Hubert Rostaing. The record label was named Blue Star and specialized in jazz. Barclay worked tirelessly, and the company became one of the major European recording concerns. In this venture, he was assisted by his wife, Nicole.

Barclay was also an exponent of light music and assembled an orchestra of forty-five instruments for which he arranged and also conducted.

Select Discography

BOUM! The Music of Charles Trenet Felsted PDL 85007

Cherchez La Femme Felsted PDL 85029

Confetti Felsted PDL 85065

Dial D for Dancing Felsted SDL 86032

Eddie Barclay and Orchestra Felsted L 86004

Eddie Barclay Plays Paris MLP 8055, SLP 18055

Film Favourites Felsted PDL 85045

Film Festival at Cannes Mercury MG 20188

Meet Mr Barclay Felsted PDL 85024

Memories of Our Prom Mercury MG 20486, SR 60165

Moulin Rouge Felsted 10" SDL 86006

Music for Dinner Felsted 10" SDL 86007

Music for Dreaming Felsted PDL 85003

Music for Relaxing Felsted SDL 86008

Music from the Movies, Vol. 1 Felsted SDL 86005

Music from the Movies, Vol. 2 Felsted SDL 86012

Music to Make Her Yours Felsted PDL 85014

Musical Bouquet Felsted PDL 85025

Musique d'Ambiance: 12 Themes de Michel Legrand et Eddie Barclay Barclay 920377

Paris for Lovers Mercury MG 20190

This Is Paris, Vol. 1 Felsted PDL 85009

This Is Paris, Vol. 2 Barclay 82106

Twilight Time Mercury MG 20488, SR 60167

BARKER, WARREN

Barker was educated at the University of California in Los Angeles and worked steadily as an arranger for radio and television programs, on scores for motion pictures and recordings for various record companies. He also conducted for night club acts in Las Vegas. For six years he did the famous Railroad Hour on NBC, familiarizing himself with many operettas and musical comedies.

Select Discography

As I Hear It Warner BS 1247 (Arranged by Warren Barker and conducted by Matty Melneck)

Broadway Compleat Warner BS 1253

Far Away Places Warner WS 1308

Hawaiian Eye Warner WS 1355

The King and I Warner WS 1205

Music of Desire WS 1364

77 Sunset Strip Warner W 1289

Strings '66 Warner W 1631 (Contents identical to Music of Desire)

Top TV Themes Warner WS 1289

Waltzing down Broadway Warner BS 1218

Warren Barker Is In Warner WS 1331

BARRY, JOHN (b. 3 November 1933)

John Barry was born in York, England. His father owned theaters, and this awakened his interest in film music at an early age. His interests lay in both classical and jazz music. His earlier scores for popular films leaned toward jazz, notably the theme from the first James Bond movie *Dr. No* (1962). He went on to do most of the Bond films, including *From Russia with Love* (1963), *Thunderball* (1965), *You Only Live Twice* (1967) and *On Her Majesty's Secret Service* (1969). He is equally well known for his lush scores, which include *Out of Africa* (1985) and *Dances with Wolves* (1990); scores for historical settings such as *The Lion in Winter* (1968) and *Mary Queen of Scots* (1971); and scores for contemporary films such as *Midnight Cowboy* (1969), *Body Heat* (1981) and *Indecent Proposal* (1993).

Select Discography

Alice's Adventures in Wonderland Warner BS-2671

Day of the Locust London PS 912

The Deep Casablanca NBLP 7060

Diamonds Are Forever United Artists UAS 5220

The Dove ABC ABDP-852

Greatest Movie Hits Columbia C 3 9508

King Kong Reprise MS 2260

Last Valley Dunhill DSX-50102

Mary Queen of Scots Decca DL 79186

Compact Discs

Beat Girl/Stringbeat Play It Again Play 001

Best of James Bond EMI CDBOND007

Best of John Barry Polydor 849 095–2

Classic John Barry, Vols. 1 and 2 Silva Screen FILMCD141/169

Dances with Wolves Epic 467591–2

From Russia with Love EMI CDP7 95344–2

Goldfinger EMI CDP7 95345–2

Music of John Barry Pickwick 983379–2

BASS, SID

Sid Bass was born in New York City. He majored in music at New York University. He spent three years in the Army Air Corps, where he conducted bands which entertained hospital patients and played for Officers' Club dances and radio shows.

He subsequently arranged for several orchestras and supervised and arranged for radio and night club acts. His compositions include 'The Old Soft Shoe', 'Greatest Feeling in the World' and 'Pine Tree Pine Over Me'.

Select Discography

Common Ground RCA LSP 2141

From Another World Vik LX-1053

Sound and Fury Vik LX 1084

With Bells On RCA Camden CAS 501

BAXTER, LES (14 March 1922–15 January 1996)

Les Baxter was born in Mexia, Texas, and studied piano at Detroit Conservatory and Pepperdine College, Los Angeles. He gave up a career as a concert pianist and played in dance bands for a while. At the age of twenty-three, he joined Mel Tormé's Mel-Tones as a saxophonist and vocalist. He also worked with the Artie Shaw Band.

After an initial struggle, he began to get commissions for background music and arrangements for record sessions. He obtained radio work with Bob Hope, Ronald Coleman and Abbott and Costello and also was musical director for *Halls of Ivy*. A recording contract followed in 1950 with Capitol Records, which involved making arrangements for singers like Margaret Whiting. Baxter was responsible for the hits, 'Mona Lisa' and 'Too Young', sung by Nat 'King' Cole. With FRANCK POURCEL conducting, he and David Dexter composed the album for Capitol Records entitled *La Femme*.

With his own orchestra, he released a number of hits, including 'April in Portugal', 'Ruby', 'Unchained Melody' and 'Poor People of Paris'. He also achieved success with albums of his own orchestral suites *Le Sacre du Sauvage, Festival of the Gnomes, Taboo, Ports of Pleasure, Love Is a Fabulous Thing, Teen Drums, Miracles* and *Brazil Now*. The first three of these were recorded on Capitol, the latter on Gene Norman's Crescendo label.

Baxter completed a series of film scores which included Roger Gorman's Edgar Allan Poe films *House of Usher* and *The Pit and the Pendulum; Black Sabbath*; *Comedy of Terrors*; *Muscle Beach Party; The Dunwich Horror* and *Frogs*.

Musical Achievements

Baxter achieved a distinctive sound by means of his creative arrangements. He was able to enhance and enlarge the qualities of a good piece of music because he had a clear knowledge of its atmosphere, theme and background. He had a special interest in the instruments of foreign countries, and this involved him in a lot of travel. He drew on new and exotic instrumental sounds to give his arrangements a special flavor.

Select Discography

Academy Award Winners R9–6079

African Jazz Capitol ST 1117

Baxter's Best Capitol T 1388

Brazil Now!

Broadway '61 Capitol ST 1480

Caribbean Moonlight Capitol T 733

Confetti Capitol T 1029

I Could Have Danced All Night SPC 3048

Jewels of the Sea Capitol ST 1537

Kaleidoscope Capitol T 594

Les Baxter Visits South Pacific World Record LP T 397

Love Is a Fabulous Thing Capitol ST 1088
Midnight on the Cliffs Capitol T 843
Music Out of the Moon Capitol 10" H 2000, T 390
Ports of Pleasure Capitol ST 868
Primitive and Passionate RS 6048
Quiet Village Capitol ST 1846
Ritual of the Savage DT 288
Round the World Capitol T 780
Sacred Idol Capitol ST 1293
Sensational Capitol ST 1661
Sounds of Adventure (2) S-90984
Space Escapade Capitol ST 968
Taboo Capitol T 655
Teen Drums Capitol ST 1355
Thinking of You Capitol H 474 (10")
Voices in Rhythm RS 6036
Wild Guitars Capitol T 1248

Compact Discs

African Blue: Brazil Now GNP 2036
Baxter's Best Capitol CDD 7243 83702824
By Popular Request Bacchus BA 0014
Exotic Moods Capitol 37025 (2 CDs)
For Dancers Only: Favorite Tangos CEMA 57010
Les Baxter's Best Capitol 37028
Que Mango l (With 101 Strings) SCAMP SCP 9718
Ritual of the Savage Capitol
Skins! Capitol 774
Taboo Capitol 655

BENJAMIN, ARTHUR (1893–1960)

Arthur Benjamin was born in Sydney but spent most of his life in England. He studied piano and composition at the Royal College of Music beginning in 1911. After serving in World War I, he returned to Australia as a teacher of piano at Sydney Conservatory. He returned to Britain in 1921, where he took up a post at the Royal College of Music, London.

His compositions cover a wide span, from his more serious operas such as *A Tale of Two Cities* (1950) and *Tartuffe* (1960), orchestral works, chamber music, songs and piano music to music in a lighter vein.

An example of the latter is *Two Jamaican Pieces* for small orchestra published in 1938. These consist of 'Jamaican Song' and the more popular 'Jamaican Rumba', which became so successful that it earned for the composer an annual barrel of rum given by the Jamaican authorities in recognition of the fame he had brought to the island.

BENNETT, ROBERT RUSSELL (15 June 1894–17 August 1981)
Bennett was born in Kansas City, Missouri. His father, George Robert Bennett, played the trumpet and violin in the Kansas City Philharmonic Orchestra and his mother, May Bradford Bennett, taught piano.

At the age of three Robert contracted polio, and the family moved to a farm south of Kansas City. There his mother taught him to play the piano; his father taught him band instruments well enough for him to be able to substitute for absent members of the local band organized by his father. By the age of ten Robert Russell Bennett was giving piano recitals.

In 1909, the family moved back to Kansas City and Bennett began to study harmony, counterpoint and composition with the Danish musician Carl Busch. He was already becoming interested in lighter music. To support his classical career, he played in dance halls, cinemas and pit orchestras in the town.

In 1916, Bennett set off for New York. At first he played the piano in dance halls and restaurants. Eventually he found work as a copyist at George Schirmer, the music publisher. In 1917, when the United States entered World War I, Bennett enlisted in the infantry. He was transferred to a headquarters unit because of a crippled foot and organized and conducted army bands, scoring the arrangements.

After the war Bennett applied for the position of orchestrator at T. B. Harms and Company. As a trial, he was given COLE PORTER's 'An Old-Fashioned Garden' to orchestrate. The song became the hit of the year, and Bennett was hired. By 1922, he was orchestrating full-length musicals and had started on a career that was to bring him recognition as the master of his craft and earn him the title 'the Beethoven of modern orchestration.

His orchestrations for notable Broadway shows included RUDOLF FRIML's *Rose-Marie*, JEROME KERN's *Show Boat, Roberta* and *Very Warm for May* and ARTHUR SCHWARTZ's *The Bandwagon.* He did the arrangements for *Of Thee I Sing* and *Porgy and Bess* for GERSHWIN, and for Cole Porter he scored *Kiss Me, Kate.* His most productive period was probably with RICHARD RODGERS, for whom he orchestrated *Oklahoma!, Carousel, South Pacific, The King and I, Pipe Dream, Flower Drum Song* and *The Sound of Music.* He also scored FREDERICK LOEWE's musicals *My Fair Lady* and *Camelot.*

Despite his success as a Broadway arranger, Bennett considered this work as the worst kind of potboiling. In 1926, he gave up his Broadway career to study classical composition in Paris with Nadia Boulanger. Under her instruction, he composed his *Symphony* and *Endymion*, an Operetta Ballet. Between 1927 and 1930 he wrote the *Abraham Lincoln Symphony*, an opera, *An Hour of Delusion*, and *Sights and Sounds*, an orchestral piece. In 1931, he was awarded a joint prize, sponsored by the Radio Corporation of America, for his *Abraham Lincoln Symphony* and *Sights and Sounds*. In 1932 Bennett collaborated with Robert A. Simon on an opera entitled *Maria Malibran*.

From 1936 to 1940, Bennett was stationed in Hollywood, contributing original music as well as orchestrations to more than thirty films. These included *Show Boat* (1936), *Hunchback of Notre Dame* (1939), *Brigham Young, Frontiersman* (1940) and *Rebecca* (1940). His major compositions during this period were *Eight Etudes for Symphonic Orchestra* (1938).

He returned to New York City in 1940 and introduced his own program, entitled *Russell Bennett's Notebook*, on radio station WOR. In 1941, WOR commissioned him to write a symphony on baseball which he entitled *Symphony in D—for Dodgers*. His fourth symphony, *On College Themes*, was commissioned by a radio station for performance on Football Day. His most popular work was the fifth symphony, *The Four Freedoms*, commissioned by the *Saturday Evening Post* in 1943. Other works composed by him included an opera, *The Enchanted Symphony* (1946); his *Sixth Symphony; Overture to the Mississippi*; and chamber music *Toy Symphony* and *Water Music* for string quartet. Bennett also created a number of 'symphonic pictures' based on his musical comedy scores. These included *Porgy and Bess, Carousel, Finian's Rainbow, Lady in the Dark* and *Kiss Me, Kate*.

In 1952, Bennett undertook his first important television assignment when he orchestrated RICHARD RODGERS' music for *Victory at Sea*, a naval history of World War II, originally presented in twenty-six half-hour episodes. A series of RCA Victor recordings were made based on this score. *Victory at Sea* was also condensed into a feature film lasting 100 minutes.

From 1954 onward, Bennett was associated with NBC-TV's *Project 20*. He also returned to Hollywood periodically to work on films. He won an Oscar for his score of the movie version of *Oklahoma!*, produced in 1955. He wrote the music for the television programs *The Real West* (1960) and *The Valiant Years* (1961). He died in New York in 1981.

Select Discography

By Special Arrangement (Original Broadway orchestrations) AEI 2106

Broadway Hits of Yesterday Varsity VLP 6011 (10")

Highlights from Richard Rodgers' Victory at Sea (Arranged by Robert Russell Bennett; conducted by Reinhard Linz) Pye Golden Guinea GGL 0073

Porgy and Bess Suite. West Side Story Suite (Robert Russell Bennett conducting RCA Victor Orchestra) Camden CAS 1044

Robert Russell Bennett's Symphonic Pictures (Robert Ashley conducting the MGM Orchestra) M.G.M. E3131

Victory at Sea 2 vols. RCA LSC 2226, 2335 (LPs) [Also on CD]

BERLIN, IRVING (born Israel Baline) (11 May 1888–22 September 1989) Irving Berlin was born in Temun, Siberia. His family emigrated to the United States when Berlin was four. By the time he was fourteen, he was earning a living by singing popular songs in cafes and on street corners. Subsequently, he became a song plugger and singing waiter. In 1906, he began writing songs, his first published song being 'Marie from Sunny Italy' in 1907. Berlin had no formal musical training and was unable to read or write musical notation. His hunt-and-peck piano technique was confined to the key of F.

His early work was strongly influenced by ragtime music. 'Alexander's Ragtime Band', written in 1911, became a big hit. He continued to write ragtime hits until 1913. In 1914, he commenced writing scores for Broadway revues. From 1916 to 1918, Berlin worked primarily in the musical theater. In 1918, after a short spell in the army, he resumed his musical career and became America's leading songwriter. In 1919, he founded his own music publishing company and contributed to the famous *Ziegfeld Follies*. For several years he also wrote his own *Music Box Revue* for the Music Box Theatre, which he owned in partnership with Sam H. Harris.

Some of his best theater shows were produced from the 1930s onward and include *Face the Music* (1932), *As Thousands Cheer* (1933), *Louisiana Purchase* (1940), *This Is the Army* (1942), *Annie Get Your Gun* (1946, filmed in 1950), *Miss Liberty* (1949), *Call Me Madam* (1950, filmed in 1953) and *Mr. President* (1962).

Berlin made a major contribution to film music, including *Puttin' on the Ritz* (1929), *Top Hat* (1935), *Follow the Fleet* (1936), *On the Avenue* (1937), *Alexander's Ragtime Band* (1938), *Holiday Inn* (1942), *Easter Parade* (1948), *White Christmas* (1954) and *There's No Business like Show Business* (1954).

Songs by Berlin include the following titles: 'Piano Man' (1910), 'Play a Simple Melody' (1914), 'When I Leave the World Behind' (1915), 'You Forgot to Remember' (1925), 'Blue Skies' (1926), 'Because I Love You' (1926), 'The Song Is Ended' (1927), 'Marie' (1928), 'Coquette' (1928), 'Say It Isn't So' (1932), 'How Deep Is the Ocean?' (1932), 'I Never Had a Chance' (1934) and 'God Bless America' (1938).

Additional Readings

Barrett, Mary Ellin. *Irving Berlin: A Daughter's Memoir.* New York: Simon and Schuster, 1994.

Bergreen, Laurence. *As Thousands Cheer: The Life of Irving Berlin.* New York: Viking Press, 1990.

Ewen, David. *American Songwriters.* New York: H. W. Wilson, 1987. pp. 29–41.

Ewen, David. *Great Men of American Popular Song.* Englewood Cliffs, NJ: Prentice-Hall, 1970. pp. 100–115.

Freedland, Michael. *Salute to Irving Berlin.* Comet, 1990. First published New York: Stein & Day, 1974.

Green, Benny. *Let's Face the Music.* London: Pavilion Books, 1989. pp. 153–182.

Hemming, Roy. *The Melody Lingers On.* New York: Newmarket Press, 1986. pp. 29–54.

Hyland, William G. *The Song Is Ended.* New York: Oxford University Press, 1995. pp. 17–32, 146–59, 195–206, 260–74.

Whitcomb, Ian. *Irving Berlin and Ragtime America.* New York: Limelight Books, 1988.

Select Discography

Black, Stanley. Music of Irving Berlin London LL811

De Vol, Frank. Columbia Album of Irving Berlin Columbia C2L12 [2 LPs], W2K75042 [2 CDs]

Gleason, Jackie. Irving Berlin's Music for Lovers Capitol SW106

Goodman, Al. Salutes Irving Berlin Promenade 2079

Kostelanetz, Andre. Music of Irving Berlin Columbia CL768 [Also on CD]

Mantovani. Waltzes of Irving Berlin London LL1452

Melachrino, George. Ballads of Irving Berlin RCA LPM/LSP 2817 [Also on CD]

Melachrino, George. Waltzes of Irving Berlin RCA LPM/LSP 2561 [Also on CD]

Melachrino, George. Music of Irving Berlin RCA Camden CAS 2220 (Abridged versions of ballads and waltzes)

Ornadel, Cyril. Always: Music of Irving Berlin (Arrangements by Bruce Campbell) World Record Treasures SC18

Poliakin, Raoul. Irving Berlin: Great Man of American Music Everest 6058 (Monaural)/3058 (Stereo)

Stott, Wally. There's No Business Like Show Business: A Tribute to Irving Berlin Philips B10106 R

Yorke, Peter. Melody Lingers On: The Music of Irving Berlin and Victor Herbert Decca DL8240

BERNSTEIN, ELMER (b. 4 April 1922)

Elmer Bernstein was born in New York City. His first ambition was to be a concert pianist. While in service during World War II, he scored many radio programs for the Armed Forces Radio Service. His first film assignments were for *Saturday's Hero* (1951) and *Boots Malone* (1952). This was followed by *The Man with the Golden Arm* (1955), which was an innovation in the introduction of jazz and other idiomatic writing. In 1956, he took over the score of *The Ten Commandments* from VICTOR YOUNG, who was too ill to continue the work. Bernstein had a novel approach to film music and made use of typically American themes, as is evident in the score of *The Magnificent Seven* (1960). His score for *To Kill a Mockingbird* (1962) popularized the use of intimate, more personalized music in films, while *Animal House* (1978), and *Airplane!* (1980) introduced the element of humor.

Other films he scored include *The Comancheros* (1961), *Walk on the Wild Side* (1962), *Birdman of Alcatraz* (1962), *The Great Escape* (1963), *Hawaii* (1966), *Thoroughly Modern Millie* (1967), *True Grit* (1969), *Trading Places* (1983), *Ghostbusters* (1984), *My Left Foot* (1989), *Rambling Rose* (1991), *The Age of Innocence* (1993). His theater production was entitled *How Now, Dow Jones?*

In 1970, Bernstein became president of the Composers and Lyricists Guild of America and championed the right of film composers and lyricists to retain ownership rights to their film works.

Select Discography

The Age of Innocence Epic EK57151

The Comancheros. True Grit Varese Sarabande VCD47236

Elmer Bernstein Conducts Elmer Bernstein Denon CO75288

Genocide Intrada FMT8007D

Magnificent Seven. The Hallelujah Trail (Phoenix Symphony Orchestra. Conductor James Sedares) Koch International 37222–2

The Ten Commandments MCA MCAD42320

BERNSTEIN, LEONARD (25 August 1918–14 October 1990)

Leonard Bernstein was born in Lawrence, Massachusetts, and educated at the Boston Latin School and Harvard University. He became a distinguished classical conductor with the New York Philharmonic Orchestra. He composed the film background score for *On the Waterfront* and also wrote the music of *On the Town* (1944), *Wonderful Town* (1953), *Candide* (1956) and the television production of *Peter Pan*. He is best known for his music for the score of *West Side Story* (1957), with lyrics by Stephen Sondheim. His songs from this show include 'Maria', 'I Feel Pretty', 'A Little Bit of Love', 'America', 'Tonight' and 'Something's Coming'. His other well-known songs are 'New York, New York' (from *On the Town*) and 'A Quiet Girl' (from *Wonderful Town*). In both the latter shows the lyricists were Betty Comden and Adolph Green.

Additional Readings

Burton, Humphrey. *Leonard Bernstein.* Garden City, NY: Doubleday; London: Faber & Faber, 1994.

Burton, William Westbrook (ed). *Conversations about Bernstein.* New York: Oxford University Press, 1995.

Ewen, David. *American Songwriters.* New York: H. W. Wilson, 1987. pp. 41–45.

Freedland, Michael. *Leonard Bernstein.* London: Harrap, 1987.

Gottlieb, Jack, ed. *Bernstein on Broadway.* New York: Amberson, 1981.

Peyser, Joan. *Bernstein: A Biography.* New York: Morrow; London: Bantam Press, 1987.

Secrest, Meryle. *Leonard Bernstein: A Life.* London: Bloomsbury, 1995.

Select Discography

Pourcel, Franck. Franck Joué Pour Les Amoureux: West Side Story Pathe Marconi EGF 700 (France) (45 rpm disc)

Terry, David. Bernstein's Broadway: The Great Show Music of Leonard Bernstein Warner WS 1325

Compact Discs

Bennett, Robert Russell. West Side Story: Orchestral Selections (With RCA Victor Symphony Orchestra) RCA 09026–68334–2

Bernstein, Leonard. Bernstein Conducts Bernstein (With Los Angeles Philharmonic Orchestra, Israel Philharmonic Orchestra, Vienna Philharmonic Orchestra) Deutsche Grammaphon 447952

Bernstein, Leonard. Candide/On the Town/On the Waterfront/Funny Face/West Side Story (With Royal Philharmonic Orchestra) Belart 4611432

Bernstein, Leonard. Music of Leonard Bernstein (With New York Philharmonic Orchestra) CBS MLK 39448

Bernstein, Leonard. New York, New York: Best of Leonard Bernstein Deutsche Grammaphon 4231982

Mauceri, John. American Classics: Symphonic Dances from West Side Story. Philips 4386632 [CD] (Also contains **Gershwin, An American in Paris; Ellington: Harlem**)

BINGE, RONALD (15 July 1910–6 September 1979)

Ronald Binge was born in Derby, the eldest of three children. His father died in 1920, leaving the family in poor financial circumstances. Fortunately Ronald was assisted by family and friends and at the age of seven became a chorister in St. Andrew's Church, Derby. He received piano lessons from the organist and choirmaster of the church, William James Baker, who provided him with insight into the art of music.

Binge also studied organ, harmony and counterpoint but was unable to complete his studies at a music college. At the age of seventeen, he obtained employment as organist at a local cinema. He also tried his hand at composing music for the local cinema orchestra, as an accompaniment to the silent films of the era. With the arrival of talking films, the orchestra became redundant, and Binge was left alone to play the organ during intervals. He also played for local functions in restaurants, at dances and as a pianist and accompanist at concerts.

In 1931, Binge obtained employment as pianist in the orchestra at the east coast resort of Great Yarmouth. Here he was expected to play more than one instrument, and he took up the piano accordion. Unfortunately, all the musical instruments in the concert hall were destroyed by a fire on the pier, and he had great difficulty in acquiring another piano accordion.

At the end of the season, he moved to London, where it took time and persistence on his part to find work. He became extremely proficient in his performance on the piano accordion and won several awards. On accordion and piano he had a wide and varied experience, playing with orchestral combinations of many kinds. He took every opportunity that he was offered for orchestrating and composing.

In 1935, Ronald Binge's association with MANTOVANI began. Mantovani formed the Tipica Orchestra, and Ronald Binge did all the arrangements. He also composed during this period and wrote his first film score for *Thirteen Men and a Gun*, originally made in Austria, with dubbed English dialogue.

In 1940, Binge joined the Royal Air Force and was posted to Blackpool, the Lancashire seaside resort. Here he came into contact with SIDNEY TORCH, who had formed an orchestra from military personnel. Binge was asked to take charge of the station choir, also formed from recruits. He directed this for the next two years, with fortnightly joint concerts with Sidney Torch's orchestra. Around this time, Binge wrote a piece called 'Spitfire', after the famous fighter plane of that name. He also studied German, after coming across some music books in that language. His tutor was an Austrian refugee called Maryan Friedman. In 1944, he entered a Royal Society of Arts examination in German, held at Newcastle-upon-Tyne. Here he met his future wife, Vera.

After demobilization in 1945, Binge found work as an orchestrator. His work was acclaimed by John Ireland and also NOËL COWARD, when Binge scored *Pacific 1860*, a musical staged at the Theatre Royal Drury Lane in December 1946. This work was done at the request of Mantovani, who conducted the musical and with whom Binge renewed acquaintance at the end of the war. At this time, Binge had some of his most successful pieces published and broadcast. The publisher who most encouraged him in his composing achievements was Walter Eastman, head of the London firm of Ascherberg, Hopwood and Crew. In 1951, he was made a member of the Royal Philharmonic Society, whose membership was limited to 150 musicians.

Binge was responsible for the reorganization of the Mantovani orchestra in 1951, on the invitation of Henry Sarton of Decca Recording Company. Binge created an orchestra consisting of a few wind instruments and a large string section. With this, he was able to produce the 'cascading strings' effect that became famous as the Mantovani sound. In this, Binge was influenced by the reverberations produced by sacred music performed in great cathedrals, such as the music of Claudio Monteverdi. The song that best showed off this effect was 'Charmaine'. Other hits were 'Some Enchanted Evening', 'Diane', 'Ramona' and 'Greensleeves'. In the two radio series that followed, Mantovani broadcast several Binge compositions, including 'Andante Cantabile', which was destined to become one of the most successful pieces of British orchestral music written in the 1950s. It was republished under the title 'Elizabethan Serenade' in 1952 and was subsequently performed by many broadcasting light orchestras of the time. It became the signature tune for the BBC's series *Music Tapestry*, a favorite of the 1950s. It won AN IVOR NOVELLO Award in 1957 and was published as a song version, 'Where the Gentle Avon flows'.

After the two 1951 radio series, Binge ended his association with Mantovani. He composed music for many films, including *Desperate Moment, The Runaway Bus, Dance Little Lady* and *Our Girl Friday*. He also wrote music for more than fifty films for American television.

Among his later works were a 'Festival Te Deum', a symphony and many songs. He also wrote music for brass and military band, such as 'Flash Harry', 'Old London', 'Cornet Carillon', 'Duel for Conductors' and 'Trumpet Spectacular'.

The BBC International Festival of Light Music in 1956 commissioned Binge to compose his 'Concerto for Saxophone', which received its first performance with Michael Krein as soloist. Another major work was 'Saturday Symphony' (1966–68). Binge conducted them both in a recording by the South German Radio Orchestra.

His love of light orchestral music found outlet in a genre called 'library music', which consists of recordings made by music publishers for promotion in broadcasting and films and not primarily for sale to the public. One such recording made by Binge was called *Sailing By*, and it became very popular.

Binge served for several years on the councils of the Songwriters' Guild and the Performing Rights Society. He always attempted to advance the cause of British light music. He died in September 1979 at his home at Ringwood in Hampshire.

Musical Achievements

Binge was an extraordinarily versatile composer, arranger and musician receiving equal acclaim in the fields of classical and mood music performance. One of Binge's most noteworthy achievements in the field of light music was the creation of the 'cascading strings' for the Mantovani Orchestra. This was done purely by clever scoring, dividing the violins into several parts, each allotted a different melody note in turn. Binge adopted this 'cascade' effect with solo cornets for his 'Concert Carillon'.

Many of his compositions achieved great popularity, particularly 'Elizabethan Serenade' and 'Sailing By', which was for many years the concluding music on BBC Radio 4. 'Elizabethan Serenade' is original in its accompaniment pattern on lower strings, with two contrasting melodies in which effective use is made of two flutes and clarinet.

He also demonstrated extreme ingenuity in his arrangements. For example, he composed two 'palindromic' compositions, 'Vice Versa' and 'Upside/Downside'.

His career as a conductor commenced at a rather late stage with the late-night BBC radio series of 1955 to 1963 called *String Song*. He enjoyed this phase of his career tremendously and was invited to conduct his own music throughout Europe.

Musical Compositions

'Caribbean Calypso', 'Concert Carillon', 'Concerto for Saxophone', 'Dance of the Snowflakes', 'Elizabethan Serenade', 'Faire Frou Frou', 'Fire God', 'High Stepper', 'Madrugado', 'Man in a Hurry', 'Miss Melanie', 'Red Sombrero', 'Sailing By', 'Saturday Symphony', 'Song of Canterbury', 'Tales of the Three Blind Mice', 'Thames Rhapsody', 'Trade Winds', 'Venetian Carnival', 'Watermill'.

Scores for the Cinema

Desperate Moment (1953), *Our Girl Friday* (1953), *The Runaway Bus* (1954) and *Dance Little Lady* (1954).

Select Discography

Concerto For Saxophone and Orchestra/Saturday Symphony Rediffusion 1971

Girl of My Dreams RCA LPM 1458 [Also on CD]

If You Were The Only Girl Gold Star 1500003

Say It with Flowers RCA LPM/LSP 1890

Summer Madness RCA LPM/LSP 1737

Compact Discs

British Light Music—Ronald Binge Marco Polo 1994

BLACK, STANLEY (b. 14 June 1913)

Stanley Black was born in London and started piano lessons at the age of seven. He studied at the Tobias Mathay School of Music. He started composing at the age of twelve. In 1929, he won an arranging contest sponsored by *Melody Maker*, a weekly jazz periodical. He became a jazz pianist recording with American bands such as Coleman Hawkins, Louis Armstrong and Benny Carter and also British musicians such as Lew Stone and Harry Roy. In 1938, while recording with Roy's orchestra, he visited South

America and developed a lifelong fascination for Latin-American music, on which subject he became an expert.

After serving with the Royal Air Force from 1939 to 1944, he became house conductor and arranger for the Decca Record Company. From 1944 to 1952, he also served as conductor of the BBC Dance Orchestra. He participated in numerous radio shows, including *Hi Gang*, *Much Binding in the Marsh*, *Black Magic* and *The Musical World of Stanley Black*. He appeared in numerous Royal Command Performances in 1951 and thereafter. He composed for numerous BBC documentaries and wrote the theme tune for 'The Goons' and *Double Top*. He also worked on over one hundred films, either as score composer and/or musical director.

His credits include *It Always Rains on Sunday* (1948), *The Long and the Short and the Tall* (1961), *The Young Ones* (1961), *Summer Holiday* (1962), *City Under the Sea* (1965) and *Crossplot* (1969). He also composed the musical score for comedies such as *Laughter in Paradise* (1951), *The Naked Truth* (1957) and *Too Many Crooks* (1958).

Black is one of the most widely travelled conductors in Great Britain, and has undertaken numerous concert tours in Europe, the United States, Canada, Australasia, and the Far East.

In 1994, he performed with Vincent Grappelli in a Charity Gala Performance in the Barbican Hall, London. He has been awarded an OBE and Life Fellowship of the International Institute of Arts and Letters. In 1987 he was awarded a British Academy of Songwriters, Composers and Authors Gold Award. In 1988 he was given the Freedom of the City of London award. In 1995 he became Life President of the Celebrities Guild of Great Britain.

Select Discography

Accent on Romance Richmond B 20024

All Time Top Tangos PS 176

Black Magic

Bolero/Polovtsian Dances

Broadway Blockbusters Decca PFS 34114

Broadway Spectacular Decca PFS 34077

Capriccio

Carnival in the Sun Decca LK 4108

Cash Box Instrumentals PS 158

Cole Porter Symphonic Suite London LL 1565

Cuban Moonlight PS 137

Dancing in the Dark London LL 1099

Digital Magic

Dimensions in Sound

Exotic Percussion Decca PFS 34008

Festival in Costa Rica London LL 1101

Film Spectacular Decca PFS 34025
Film Spectacular, Volume Two Decca PFS 34031
Film Spectacular, Volume Three: James Bond Decca PFS 34088
Film Spectacular, Volume Four: The Epic
Film Spectacular, Volume Five: The Love Story
Film Spectacular, Volume Six: Great Stories from World War II
Film World of Stanley Black Decca PA PA/SPA 60
Flamingo (Mantovani Orchestra, conductor Stanley Black) Bainbridge BT 6239
Focus on Stanley Black
For Latin Lovers London LL 1681
France
Friml and Romberg London PS 191
Gershwin Concert
Gershwin Goes Latin London PS 206
Girls, Girls, Girls London LL 3012
Grand Canyon Suite
Great Film Themes London PS 113
Great Love Stories
Great Rhapsodies for Orchestra
Grieg Concert
ITV Themes
Kern and Berlin Richmond B 20011
Latin World of Stanley Black
Melodies of Love Richmond B 2004
Moonlight Cocktail London LL 1709
Music for Romance London LL 1149
Music of a People [Jewish music] London SP 44060
Music of Irving Berlin London LL 811
Music of Lecuona Decca SKL 4049
The Night Was Made for Love Decca LK 4130
Place Pigalle London LL 1742
Plays for Latin Lovers
Red Velvet London LL 1592
Richard Rodgers London LL 1209
Russia Decca PFS 34084 [LP], London 452492Z [CD]
Satan Superstar
Showcase LB 251
Soft Lights and Sweet Music Richmond B 20031
Some Enchanted Evening London LL1098

Sophisticat in Cuba London LL 1781

Sounds Wide Screen

South of the Border Richmond B 20003

Spain (2 volumes) SP 44016 SP 44149

Spectacular Dances LCL 75020

Sputniks for Orchestra

Summer Evening Serenade London LL 1332

S'Wonderful

Symphonic Suite: Jerome Kern London LL 579

Tchaikovsky Concert

Tribute to Charlie Chaplin London SP 44184

Tropical Night London LL 1615

Tropical Moonlight

Twelve Top Tangos

Compact Discs

Broadway Magic (With London Festival Orchestra) Polygram 314520 233–2, Rebound 20233

Film Spectacular Deram 844–763–2

Great Love Stories (With London Festival Orchestra) Decca 417.850–2

Great Movie Themes (With London Symphony Orchestra) Pickwick PWKS 4203, PWKMC 4203 CD/Cassette

Symphonic Suite: Jerome Kern (With Kingsway Promenade Orchestra)

BLISS, SIR ARTHUR (1891–1975)

Sir Arthur Bliss was born in London and studied at Rugby and Pembroke College, Cambridge. He received his musical education at the Royal College of Music and was involved in staging concerts and writing incidental music. His contributions to lighter orchestral music resulted from his film scores for Alexander Korda's *Things to Come* (1936) and for *Christopher Columbus* (1949), *Men of Two Worlds* (1946) and *Seven Waves Away* (1956).

Select Discography

Bliss Conducts Bliss Dutton Laboratories CDLXT2051

Christopher Columbus. Seven Waves Away. Men of Two Worlds (Slovak Philharmonia Male Choir; CzechoSlovak Radio Symphony Orchestra. Conductor Adriano) Marco Polo 8.223315

Things to Come Suite (Conducted by Bernard Herrmann) London SPC 21149

BLOCH, RAY (b. 3 August 1903)

Ray Bloch was born in the United States of emigrants from Alsace-Lorraine. His father was a chef who encouraged his musical ambitions. He started singing in choirs at the age of eight and at the age of twelve, conducted his first chorus at a Christmas festival. This led to a lifelong profession of choral group conducting.

His first important employment was as a piano player for a leading music publisher. In the early 1920s he played with ballroom bands in New York and with an orchestral quintet that was billed opposite the famous original Dixieland Jazz Band. He formed a jazz quintet which toured from New York to California. In the late 1920s, he became a radio performer, playing the piano at several stations.

In 1931, he became arranger-accompanist for the quartet known as the Eton Boys. He subsequently led several choral groups, the most notable of which were the Swing Fourteen. He was employed to take charge of the choral group for the CBS show *Johnny Presents*. Later he was promoted to orchestra leader of this show. This was the turning point in his career, as he moved on to other shows including Ed Sullivan's *Toast of the Town*, Steve Allen's *Songs for Sale*, CBS-Radio's *Big Time* and NBC-TV's *Kate Smith's Evening Hour*. He launched into an energetic schedule of conducting, coaching, orchestrating and choral directing. He was able to promote the singing careers of many soloists who formed part of his vocal groups, including Jack Smith, Gordon MacRae, Genevieve Rowe, Benay Venuta, Alan Dale and Sally Sweetland.

Select Discography

American Waltzes Coral CRL 56069 (10")

Easy Listening Coral CRL 56052 (10")

BONFA, LUIS (b. 1922)

Luis Bonfa was born in Brazil and collaborated with the composer, author, pianist and singer, ANTONIO CARLOS JOBIM in popularizing indigenous Brazilian music. Through their score for *Black Orpheus*, the bossa nova gained worldwide popularity.

Bonfa's haunting main themes 'Samba de Orfeu' and 'Manha de Carnaval' (English version: 'A Day in the Life of a Fool') were the highlights of this score.

Select Discography

Black Orpheus Verve 830 783–2 [CD]

BONNEAU, PAUL (14 September 1918–8 July 1995)

Paul Bonneau was regarded as one of the leaders of the French style of light music. He was born at Moret-sur-Loing and trained at the Paris Superior National Conservatory of Music, where he won several prizes.

In 1945, he began to do arrangements for Ray Ventura, Paul Misraki,

Marc Lanjean and Jean Faustin. He also wrote some orchestrations for the orchestra of Jacques Helian.

At this period his attention was drawn to light music. In 1944, he wrote 'Westminster Chimes'. This was his most famous piece of music and was recorded for Radio Diffusion Française, for whom Paul worked, as composer and conductor until the end of his career in the 1980s. Other compositions included 'A Frenchman in New York' (in memory of George Gershwin), 'Tic Tac Pompadour', 'The Riviera Suite', 'Sparrows of Paris' and 'The Schoenbrunn Waltz'. In addition, he recorded the works of other French composers such as Pierre Petit and Vincent Dy Muy (Paul Aliprandi) and occasionally performed lesser-known works of English light music composers such as Albert W. Ketelby.

Bonneau also composed more serious music. The Lamoureux Concerts performed his 'Concerto for Saxophone, Alto and Orchestra' and the Cologne Concerts presented his 'Overture for a Tragedy' and his 'Rhapsody for Piano and Orchestra.' From 1951 onward he scored more than fifty-one films, often in collaboration with Francis Lopez, Henri Betti and Fred Freed. He also wrote music for plays, ballets and light operas. He collaborated with Francis Lopez in the Parisian Temple of Light Opera to produce scores such as *The Singer of Mexico, The Golden Fleece, The Mediterranean Sea, The Three Musketeers* and *Volga*. Many of the eighteen light operas orchestrated by Bonneau were performed at the Chatelet Theatre. He also orchestrated the familiar versions of *The White Horse Inn, Viennese Waltz* and *Christmas Rose*.

In 1958, Bonneau began recording with the Great Orchestra of Paris, (later the Light Symphonic Orchestra of Paris), for the Ducretet Thomson record company. Their long-playing records included *Waltzes of France—The Belle Epoque, The Most Famous Waltzes from Light Operas* and *The Most Famous Waltzes from Films*. He also wrote arrangements for the Radio Diffusion Française choir of sixty female voices, known as the Djinns. These recordings met with great success and resulted in the award of a prize from the Charles Gros Academy and an appearance on American TV with Pat Boone in 1960.

From 1964 onward, Bonneau recorded for the Paris office of CHAPPELLS. He also recorded the *World Landscapes* by French composer Pierre Duclos and the *Great French Light Opera Revue* in 1980. Two compact discs followed: *The Famous Great Operatic Arias* and *The Overtures and Music of Famous Operatic Ballets*.

After a long illness, Bonneau died at Conflans-Saint-Honorine at the age of 75.

BOSTON POPS ORCHESTRA

The Boston Pops Orchestra was founded in July 1885 by Henry Lee Higginson, who in 1881 had started the Boston Symphony Orchestra. Higginson wished to establish summer concerts of a lighter type of music, after the style of the Austrian concert gardens in Vienna. Billed as Promenade Concerts, the Boston series combined light classical music, tunes from the musical theater and humorous novelty numbers.

Almost all of the early conductors were selected from the membership of the Boston Symphony Orchestra, apart from the first conductor, German-born Adolf Neuendorff. After the turn of the century, the Promenade Concerts were renamed the 'Pops' and were performed in the Symphony Hall. For many years, from 1930 onward ARTHUR FIEDLER served as conductor. He established a series of free outdoor 'Esplanade Concerts' in 1929.

The Orchestra has broadcast nationally since 1962. From 1969 onward, the television series *Evening at the Pops* made the orchestra famous throughout America and beyond. After Fiedler's death in 1979, JOHN WILLIAMS was appointed conductor in 1980 and retained much of the format of the original programs.

Note: For recordings made by the Boston Pops Orchestra, see FIEDLER, ARTHUR, and WILLIAMS, JOHN.

BOWEN, WILLIAM HILL. See HILL-BOWEN, WILLIAM

BRODSKY, NICHOLAS (1905–24 December 1958)
Nicholas Brodsky was born in Odessa. He learned piano as a child and studied in Rome, Vienna and Budapest. His first musical compositions were contributions to Viennese operettas and European popular songs. In 1937, he came to England to write the songs for C. B. Cochrane's revue *Home and Beauty*. He was solely a songwriter and incapable of scoring incidental music for films. Collaborators such as CHARLES WILLIAMS and PHILIP GREEN were employed to assist him with the scores attributed to him, notably *French Without Tears* (1939), *Freedom Radio* (1941), *The Way to the Stars* (1945), *Carnival* (1946) and *A Man About the House* (1947).

His later Hollywood career revealed his talent as a songwriter in *The Toast of New Orleans* (1950, 'Be My Love'), *Because You're Mine* (1952, title song), *Love Me or Leave Me* (1955, 'I'll Never Stop Loving You').

BROWN, NACIO HERB (22 February 1896–28 September 1964)
Nacio Herb Brown was born in Deming, New Mexico, but grew up in Los Angeles. He was educated at the Musical Arts High School, Los Angeles. His earliest songs were 'When Buddha Smiles' and 'Doll Dance' (both 1921).

As an adult he worked for a time as a vaudeville pianist but subsequently took up merchant tailoring and the real estate business. He wrote songs as a pastime until 1928, when he was asked to write the score of *The Broadway Melody*, for which he produced the hit songs 'The Wedding of the

Painted Doll' and 'You Were Meant for Me'. He wrote for various revues, but his most important work was with MGM Studios, producing and writing, usually in partnership with Arthur Freed. Other collaborators were Buddy De Sylva, Gus Kahn and Leo Robin. He wrote hit songs for films and also scored the music. His credits include *Broadway Melody* (1929); *Marianne* ('Blondy, 1929); *Hollywood Revue* ('Singin' in the Rain', 1929); *Untamed* ('Chant of the Jungle', 1929); *The Pagan* ('Pagan Love Song', 1929); *Lord Byron of Broadway* (1930); *Montana Moon* ('The Moon Is Low') (1930); *Whoopee* (1930); *A Woman Commands* (1932); *The Barbarian* (1933); *Going Hollywood* ('After Sundown', 'Temptation', 'We'll Make Hay when the Sun Shines', 1933); *Hold Your Man* (1933); *Peg o' My Heart* (1933); *Broadway Melody of 1936* ('You Are My Lucky Star', 'I've Got A Feelin' You're Foolin', 'Broadway Rhythm'); *A Night at the Opera* ('Alone', 1935); *San Francisco* (1936); *Babes in Arms* ('Good Morning', 1939); *Ziegfield Girl* ('You Stepped Out of a Dream', 1941); *Greenwich Village* (1944); *The Kissing Bandit* ('Love Is Where You Find It', 1948) and *Singin' in the Rain* (1952).

His only Broadway show was *Take a Chance* in 1932. He retired in 1943, leaving California to live in Mexico, but he returned in 1948 to write again for the movies. He continued writing songs until well into the 1960s. Other songs by Brown were 'Should I?' (1930); 'You're an Old Smoothie' (1933); 'Eadie Was a Lady' (1932) and 'All I Do Is Dream of You' (1934).

Additional Readings

Ewen, David. *American Songwriters*. New York: H. W. Wilson, 1987. pp. 67–72.

Select Discography

Chacksfield, Frank. Broadway Melody: Compositions of Nacio Herb Brown Decca LK 4151 (UK); London LL 1509 (USA) [Also on CD]

BURT, JOHN E.

John E. Burt was a Canadian-born conductor, arranger and composer who wrote music and toured with Paul Whiteman and Ray Noble. He spent considerable time in London, working as a pianist and was also employed in commercial music publication. He spent three years in the Canadian Navy, during which he wrote a considerable amount of music for naval bands. Subsequently he was appointed recording director and supervisor of the Canadian Talent Library. He wrote and directed many shows for the CBC, including a series with Giselle MacKenzie.

Select Discography

And His Orchestra. Canadian Talent Library S5014

Around the World. Johnny Burt and His International Strings RCA Victor PCS-1199

The Strings of . . . . Canadian Talent Library S5001

C

CAMARATA, (TUTTI) SALVATORE

Camarata was born in Verona, New Jersey, and studied violin in his childhood. He later took up trumpet playing. He attended New York's Juilliard School of Music, where he studied composition and orchestration.

In London, Camarata organized the Kingsway Symphony Orchestra, which included seventy trained musicians from the Royal Philharmonic and other British orchestras. For Decca Record Company, he made recordings of operatic highlights from the operas of Giacomo Puccini, Giuseppe Verdi and Georges Bizet, as well as his own arrangement of Edward MacDowell's 'Woodland Sketches'.

Select Discography

Autumn Disneyland WDL 3021

I Want to Be Happy: Music of Vincent Youmans Everest

Deep Purple: Music of Peter de Rose Everest LPBR 5079/SDBR 1079

Music for a Lazy Afternoon Decca DL 8112

Rendezvous Vocalion VL 3660

Spring Disneyland WDL 3032

Summer Disneyland WDL 3027

Tutti's Trumpets S Time Records 2106

Winter Disneyland WDL 3026

CARAVELLI **(real name Claude Vasori)** (b. 12 September 1930)
Claude Vasori was born in Montmartre, Paris. His father was Italian and his mother, French. He began to play the piano at the age of six and studied at the Rheims Conservatory. In 1950, he obtained work as a pianist in various bars in Paris. In 1952, he met the singer John William and became his accompanist. When William began recording for Pathé Marconi, Vasori was asked by the manager of the record company, Pierre Hiegel, to arrange and conduct the backup music for the singer. In this way, Vasori became the accompanist for many artists.

When Hiegel was dismissed, Vasori left Pathé Marconi. In 1957 he was engaged by Decca, where he began to record under the name of Claude Vasori and His Orchestra. From 1958 to 1959, he worked for the record company Ducretet-Thomson. He also recorded many LPs as Cucio Ermino and His Orchestra, playing in the Latin style.

In 1959, Vasori met Ray Ventura, who asked him to record a version of the music from the Gina Lollobrigida film *Where the Hot Winds Blow*. The recording was completed in Brussels and was such a great success that Ventura engaged Vasori to work under his Versailles record label. Christian Deffes, the manager of Versailles, conceived the idea of providing Vasori with the pseudonym of Caravelli and His Magical Violins. The first album released in 1960 was entitled *Dance Party*.

The Caravelli Orchestra was composed of a strong rhythm section, four trombones, eighteen violins, six altos and four cellos. Sometimes trumpets or oboes would be added. There was also a chorus. Caravelli strove to obtain a distinctive sound, by using strings and other instruments in the lower register. For twenty years his recordings were done in Brussels. In 1979, he returned to Paris, because the Brussels recording equipment had become outdated.

At the same time, he continued to write film music under his original name, Vasori. These included *Le Pont Elevateur* in 1960 and *La Vitesse Est A Vous* in 1961.

In 1963, Ventura was forced through financial problems to sell his Versailles recording company to CBS, and Caravelli worked from that time onward under the CBS label. His last albums in the late 1980s and the very last one entitled *Romantic World* in 1991 were recorded at the Palais des Congres Studios at the Porte Maillot in Paris.

Select Discography

Caravellissimo Versailles (10")

Carnet de Bal Versailles (10")

Dites Le Avec Caravelli Versailles (10")

Dites Le Avec Des Fleurs Versailles (10")

Dites Le Avec Des Notes Versailles (10")

La, La, La Columbia CS 9690

Michelle Columbia CS 9324

Parisian Strings S Time Records 72028

Portrait of Paris Columbia CS 9407

San Remo Greatest Hits Columbia CS 9613

Si J'avais des Millions Canadian Columbia FS 679

Compact Discs

Orquestras Spectaculares CBS (Brazil)

Rainbow CBS 26259

Tenderly CBS 463226 Z

CARMICHAEL, HOAGY (born Howard Hoagland Carmichael) (22 November 1899–28 December 1981)
Hoagy Carmichael was born in Bloomington, Indiana. He studied the piano with his mother and with a black ragtime pianist, Reggie Duval, after the family's move to Indianapolis. He graduated as a lawyer from Indiana University and played jazz part-time. He was acquainted with many jazzmen. In 1926, one of his early compositions, 'Riverboat Shuffle', was published by Irving Mills. This was followed by 'Washboard Blues' and 'Barnyard Shuffle' in 1927, which was later modified to become his greatest hit, 'Stardust', in 1929, with lyrics by Mitchell Parish. In the late 1920s, Carmichael gave up his legal career to become a full-time musician and composer. He played and recorded with artists such as Bix Beiderbecke, the Dorsey Brothers, King Oliver and Louis Armstrong. He also made records under his own name.

His songs include 'One Night in Havana' (1929), 'Georgia on My Mind' (1930), 'Rockin' Chair' (1930), 'Lazy River' (1931), 'New Orleans' (1932), 'In the Still of the Night' (1932), 'Lazybones' (1933), 'Snowball' (1933), 'Two Sleepy People' (1938), 'The Nearness of You' (1938), 'Skylark' (1942), 'In the Cool, Cool, Cool of the Evening' (1951) and 'My Resistance Is Low' (1951). Many of these songs were written for or appeared in films. Carmichael performed many of these songs himself and he appeared in many films as singer/pianist and as a character actor. He wrote one musical comedy, *Walk with Music*, in 1940.

Additional Readings

Carmichael, Hoagy. *The Stardust Road.* New York: Rinehart, 1946. Reprinted Bloomington: Indiana University Press, 1983.

Carmichael, Hoagy, and Stephen Longstreet. *Sometimes I Wonder: The Story of Hoagy Carmichael.* New York: Farrar, Straus and Giroux, 1965.

Ewen, David. *American Songwriters.* New York: H. W. Wilson, 1987. pp. 77–86.

Select Discography

Farnon, Robert. Hoagy Carmichael Suite London LL623

101 Strings. Hits Written by Hoagy Carmichael Alshire S5008

Sharples, Bob. Hoagy Carmichael's Ballads For Dancing Coral CRL 57034.

CARSTE, HANS

Hans Carste was born in the Palatinate but grew up on the Danube, in the Austrian province of Wachau. He studied music in Vienna and gained experience at the Vienna Volksopera. He spent a short time as conductor of Breslau's Opera House and then moved to Berlin, where he worked as composer and conductor for film and theater. During World War II he saw service in Russia, where he was severely wounded. He returned from the war in 1948 and was employed as head of the music department of Berlin Radio RIAS. He composed an operetta, which was performed successfully at Nuremberg and on several occasions subsequently.

He became a conductor of large string orchestras and achieved fame with his series called *Musical Treasures*.

Select Discography

Das Grose Georg Gershwin Album Eurodisc-Ariola 78 333 XK

Das Wiener Lied mit Hilde Guden Polydor 2371 057

Die Schonste Lieder der Welt (Singer Felicia Weathers) Decca SLK 16 472-P

Eine Unvergessene Stimme Polydor 249 190

Konig Walzer Polydor LPHM 46534

Leichtes Blut. In an Old World Ballroom Polydor SLPHM 237072

Musical Promenade Polydor 249 328

Musical Treasures 7 volumes. Polydor [This series of seven albums is an English retitled issue of *Zwischen Tag Und Traum* (see below), identical in every respect, including the same record numbers.]

Musicale Polydor 222 101

Primaballerina Polydor LPHM 46 343

Spaziergang mit Musik Polydor 249 328

Unser Sonntags-Konzert Polydor LPHM 46 891

Unter sudlicher Sonne Polydor LPHM 46 571

Zwischen Tag und Traum (7 albums) Polydor 237 135, 237 373, 237 379, 237 477, 249 155, 249 289, 2371 058, CD Polydor 109 581/83

CESANA, OTTO

Cesana was a classical musician with a deep appreciation of popular music. His early musical studies included piano, organ, music theory and composition. He also gained a knowledge of all orchestral instruments. Cesana worked as arranger and composer for various Hollywood motion picture studios and on many radio programs. In 1941, he gave a j[illegible] concert in New York's town hall with his own band, playing a program of original music. He composed six symphonies, four overtures, numerous suites, concertos for instruments such as piano, clarinet, trumpet and trombone, as well as many short pieces, including sonatas, trios and songs.

Select Discography

Autumn Reverie Audio Fidelity AFSD 6170

Brief Interlude Capitol T 1032

Devotion Audio Fidelity AFSD 6182

Dream, Dream, Dream Audio Fidelity AFSD 6162

Enchantment Audio Fidelity AFSD 6191

Ecstasy Columbia CL 631 [Also on CD]; Columbia GL 103 (10")

For My Love Columbia CL 2583 (10")

Leaves in the Wind Audio Fidelity AFSD 6188

Lush and Lovely Audio Fidelity AFSD 6176

Night Magic Audio Fidelity AFSD 6179

Sheer Ecstasy Warner WS 1390

Sound of Rome RCA LSP-2600

Sugar and Spice Columbia CL 6261 (10")

Velvet Touch Audio Fidelity AFSD 6167

Voices of Venus Columbia CL 971

CHACKSFIELD, FRANK (9 May 1914–9 June 1995)

Frank Chacksfield was born at Battle, Sussex, England. He started piano lessons at the age of seven and also learned to play the organ. He took particular interest in the theory of music, passed Trinity College Music Examinations and performed in Hastings Music Festivals before the age of fourteen. By the age of fifteen, he was organist at Saleshurst Church, near Robertsbridge in Sussex.

Frank gave up a career in a solicitor's office to devote himself to music. He formed his own dance band in 1936 and held a resident engagement at Hilden Manor Road House at Tonbridge, Kent, for three years.

In 1939, he volunteered for the Royal Army Service Corps. Ill health caused him to be transferred to an entertainment unit, where he became arranger for the *Stars in Battledress*, produced by the War Office under the direction of George Black. His first radio broadcast was *Original Songs at the Piano*, at the BBC's Glasgow Studios.

On his return to civilian life, Frank became musical arranger and adviser

Frank Chacksfield

to comedian Charlie Chester, accompanying Chester's resident singer, Frederick Ferrar, in the *Stand Easy* programs. Chacksfield also conducted the Henry Hall and GERALDO orchestras. Later BBC contracts as arranger/conductor involved shows such as *Up the Pole, The Frankie Howard Show* and *Puffney's Post Office* with Jon Pertwee.

Chacksfield formed his own band, The Tunesmiths. He played for variety shows as well as appearing many times on BBC Radio's *Music While You Work*, in the early 1950s. At the same time, he became arranger/conductor for several recording companies, such as Polygon, Columbia, Parlophone and Decca.

In 1953, he joined Decca and stayed with that company for twenty-six years. In the same year, he conducted the hit novelty number 'Little Red Monkey', with composer Jack Jordan playing the clavioline. Later that year, with a forty-piece orchestra, Chacksfield recorded the CHARLIE CHAPLIN theme 'Limelight', which gave him his first gold disc. In 1954, he surpassed this achievement with the release of 'Ebb Tide', which earned a second gold disc. He developed his own lush string sound using thirty-two violins and broadcast and recorded with large orchestras for the rest of his life. 'On the Beach' made the charts in 1954, and he had further successes with versions of 'Flirtation Waltz' and 'Memories of You'. Other mood pieces such as 'In Old Lisbon' and 'Donkey Cart' (1956) and the Chaplin theme 'Smile' established the easy-listening style that became his hallmark.

Chacksfield had achieved the distinction of producing the first British nonvocal disc to reach number one in the best-selling charts in the United States. He had his own weekly radio shows for a time, such as *Limelight* and *Melody Hour* and in later years broadcast regularly on programs such as *Friday Night Is Music Night*. In 1954, he introduced his BBC television shows, which ran on and off until 1964. The last of his TV productions were four shows in the series *Best of Both Worlds*, which were shown throughout the world.

In the 1960s and 1970s, Chacksfield was occupied with radio and television shows in southern Ireland. From 1965 to 1966, he and the French conductor ROGER ROGER hosted a light music series, each spinning their own and other artists' discs.

In 1972, Chacksfield toured Japan with a forty-piece orchestra, presenting fifteen shows in twelve cities in sixteen days, in addition to a TV recording session and two radio shows.

He also appeared regularly on radio and television in the United States and performed in concerts in other parts of the world. He continued recording until the end of the 1980s. Among his later albums were *Love Is in the Air* (1984) and *A Little More Love* (1987), which included arrangements of Abba's 'Dancing Queen' and Paul McCartney's 'Silly Love Songs'.

Musical Achievements

Chacksfield succeeded in achieving distinctive arrangements of popular music, as is evident in the recording of 'Ebb Tide', in which use is made of the natural sound of the sea and of sea gulls to achieve a highly atmospheric background. Another example is his 1975 recording of 'Wandrin' Star' from the show *Paint Your Wagon*. This is a richly orchestrated version, slightly humorous in style and immediately attractive to the listener.

The 1977 LP *Vintage 52* was made as a contribution to the twenty-fifth anniversary of Queen Elizabeth II's accession to the throne. This represented the best and most popular range of that year's music. His highly skilled and professional arrangements kept him in the forefront of popular easy-listening conductors. The range of his interests in music were very broad, ranging from swing to romantic and concert hall aspects. Chacksfield has, by means of his popular appeal, made his contribution to British light musical entertainment.

Musical Compositions

'Autumn in Capri', 'Autumn Island', 'Blue Train', 'Bossa for Bess', 'Candid Snap', 'Clouds', 'Colonial Cup', 'Coming Home', 'Cuban Boy', 'Fête des Jardins', 'Fifi Moulin', 'Goo Goo Eyes', 'Hop Scotch Hop', 'Innishannon Serenade', 'I Don't Know Where to Start', 'It's Just a Daydream', 'K. O. Corral', 'Love Is Forever', 'Midway Magic', 'My Autumn Love', 'My Blue Dream', 'On the Smooth Side', 'Prairie Moon', 'Rather Shy', 'Rosella', 'Seamist', 'Silk and Gold', 'Summer Serenade', 'Sunny Isle', 'Tambola', 'Tamoretta', 'Two Summers Ago', 'Via Veneto', 'Web of Dreams'.

Select Discography

All Time Top TV Themes Decca PFS 4087

Broadway Melody Decca LK 4151, London LL 1509 [Also on CD]

Close Your Eyes Decca LK 4138, London LL 1440

Cole Porter Decca PFS 4250

Dinner at Eight-Thirty Decca LK 4160

Ebb Tide Ace of Clubs ACL 1034, BSP 23, London PS 322, London SPC 3231

Evening in London London PS 135

Evening in Paris Decca LK 4081

Evening in Paris-Rome London PS 126

Evening in Rome Decca LK 4095, London LL 1205

First Hits of 1965 London PS 416

Focus on Frank Chacksfield Decca 505 23/24

Foreign Film Festival London SP 44112

Frank Chacksfield—Volume 1 Decca LK 4084

Globetrotting Decca PFS 4061

Glory That Was Gershwin Decca PFS 4287

Golden Sounds Ace of Clubs SCL 1253

Great Country and Western Decca PFS 4080

Gypsy Violins Ace of Clubs SCL 1212

Happy Talk: Music of Rodgers and Hammerstein Ace of Clubs SCL 1244

Hawaii Decca PFS 4112

Hello Young Lovers Ace of Clubs SCL 1210

Herbert and Romberg Richmond S 30086

Hollywood Almanac (2 records) PSA 3201

If I Had a Talking Picture of You Decca LK 4135

Immortal Serenades SKL 4018

King of Kings London PS 246

Love Letters in the Sand London PS 145

Lovely Lady Decca LK 4172

Magic Strings London PS 304

Mediterranean Moonlight Decca LK 4168, London LL 1588

Million Sellers S 30045

Music of George Gershwin Decca LK 4113 [Also on CD]

Music of Noel Coward Decca LK 4090, LL 1062 [Also on CD]

New Ebb Tide London SPC 44053

New Limelight London SPC 44066

On the Beach London LL 3158

Opera's Golden Moments London SPC 21092

Play to Me, Gypsy Ace of Clubs ACL 1060

Presenting London LL 1041

Romantic Europe Eclipse ECS 2150

Showboat and Porgy and Bess ECS 2090

South Pacific Richmond B20046

South Sea Island Magic Decca LK 4174, Eclipse ECS 2002

Tango Eclipse ECS 2042

Waltzes to Remember Decca LK 4198

World of Immortal Classics SPA 5, SPA 176

World of Immortal Classics, Vol. 2 SPA 51

Velvet London LL 1443

'You' London LL 1355

Compact Discs

Feelings Hallmark 301692

Million Sellers Eclipse 8441882

Music of Cole Porter Polygram 314520344 2

Thanks for the Memories: Academy Award Winners: 1934–1955 Eclipse 8440632

CHAILLE, PIERRE

Pierre Chaille commenced his musical career by playing the violin in Paris clubs on the Left Bank. In the late 1930s, he organized a successful small orchestra. During World War II, he served as band director in the French armed forces. He subsequently formed a large orchestra, known as the Grande Orchestre, that became internationally famous. He recorded for ABC-Paramount record company.

Select Discography

Romance a la Mood ABC-Paramount ABC 280

CHAPLIN, CHARLIE (born Charles Spencer) (16 April 1889–25 December 1977)
Chaplin was a British actor, author, composer and film director. He started his career in the British music hall as part of Fred Karno's company. He accompanied the company to Hollywood in 1914 and stayed on to become the most famous of all silent film comedians, a legend in his own time. Chaplin was perhaps less successful in the era of the talkies, but this did not diminish his remarkable reputation.

His major films included *Easy Street* (1917), *The Immigrant* (1917), *The Kid* (1921), *The Gold Rush* (1925), *City Lights* (1931), *Modern Times* (1936), *The Great Dictator* (1940), *Monsieur Verdoux* (1947) and *Limelight* (1952).

Chaplin wrote the music for most of his films and some of his themes and songs became standards.

Select Discography

Black, Stanley. Tribute to Charlie Chaplin London SP44184

Douglas, Johnny. Music from Charlie Chaplin Movies (With Living Strings) CA Camden CAS 2581

Kostelanetz, Andre. Music of Charlie Chaplin and Duke Ellington Columbia PC 34660.

Villard, Michel. Music From the Films of Charlie Chaplin Vogue VGC 7096 (English edition); SLD 837 (French edition)

CHAPPELL MOOD MUSIC LIBRARY
The Chappell Recorded Music Library in England was created in 1942, in order to meet the ever increasing demand for background music for radio and television programs, for television commercials, feature, documentary and newsreel films. All the material was specially recorded under the Chappell label and commissioned from some of the finest contemporary composers. Two orchestras, the Queen's Hall Light Orchestra (thirty-eight players) and the Telecast Orchestra (twenty-three players) were employed, in addition to many other combinations and soloists. The aim was to provide a musical background to literal and imaginary situations. The Chappell Library is one of the most extensive in Europe. At one time it consisted of 1,500 sides. Many of the most popular pieces by ROBERT FARNON, SIDNEY TORCH and CHARLES WILLIAMS originated in the Chappell Library. The Chappell Mood Music Library became one of the finest in the world. In

recent years, Chappell's have issued a number of compact discs of their archival recordings, and these have become available to the public.

Select Discography/Compact Discs

Famous Themes: Remember These Grasmere CD 10

Life in the 1940's Chappell 202

London Calling Grasmere ALP 30

More Famous Themes Grasmere ALP 30

Nostalgia Themes Chappell 120

Pastoral Themes Chappell 159

Robert Farnon: More Famous Themes Chappell 201

Vintage Recordings Chappell 203/204

CLEBANOFF, HERMAN (b. 1917)

Clebanoff was born in Chicago. His father was a distinguished cantor, born in Kremenchug in the Ukraine, who was forced to flee to England to escape Russian persecution of the Jews. The family subsequently emigrated to the United States.

Clebanoff started studying the violin at the age of five and commenced recitals at the age of seven. He was educated at Lane Technical High School, Chicago, where he acted as concertmaster of the school orchestra. He frequently played in string quartets. On leaving high school, he joined the Chicago Civic Orchestra, where he became concertmaster. In 1937, he became the youngest member of the Chicago Symphony Orchestra.

Clebanoff joined the WPA Illinois Symphony Orchestra in 1940, to further his experience in a wide range of classical and contemporary music. He also performed gypsy music in cafes. In that same year, he married Helen Margoyle, soprano with the Chicago Civic Opera Company.

In 1941, he accepted a post as staff musician at NBC in Chicago, where he played all types of music, in many cases acting as soloist. He obtained leave of absence from NBC in 1945 and went to New Orleans as concertmaster and assistant conductor of the New Orleans Orchestra. On his return to NBC in 1947, he was appointed concertmaster. By this time, he had gained familiarity with all types of music, both classical and popular. He was active in chamber music, organizing the resident string quartet for Roosevelt University in Chicago and playing in the violin-cello-piano group known as the Pro Music Trio. At the same time, during his ten-year stint with NBC, he evolved ideas for his own type of orchestral mood music and was tremendously active in recording and conducting.

In 1957, he formed the Clebanoff Strings and made his first album for Mercury Records called *Moods in Music*. This album was immediately acclaimed, and Mercury signed him to a long-term contract. Following this, he did a concert tour, playing selections of classics and popular music from his Mercury albums. He collaborated with two arrangers, Wayne Robinson, former head arranger at NBC, and Caesar Giovanninni, musical director and distinguished pianist.

The Clebanoff Strings toured widely, and Clebanoff took up residence in Sherman Oaks, California, where he reformed his string group for concert performances and recordings. For his own use, he acquired a violin made by J. B. Guadagnini in 1786 and performed on this instrument as a solo voice with his Strings.

Musical Achievements

Clebanoff was acclaimed as a brilliant musician and a skilled specialist in sound. He had a full knowledge of the different types of microphones for each instrumental section and firmly believed in the special use of recorded sound. One of the outstanding features of the Clebanoff Orchestra was the maestro's own articulate and expressive violin solos. The tone of his violin was presented with a unique muted echo recording sound. Occasionally he would make use of instruments in addition to strings to vary his music. This is evident in the album *More Songs from Great Films*, in which brass instruments are added.

Select Discography

Accent On Strings MGD 16 [A promotional sampler record featuring previously issued items.]

Exciting Sounds Mercury PPS 6012

Film Concert Mercury SR 60887

Great Operettas Mercury SR 60148

Great Songs from Great Films Mercury SR 60162

Great Women of Film Mercury Wing SRW 16399

Love Themes from Great Films Mercury MG 20578, SR 60238

Moods in Music Mercury SR 60005

More Songs from Great Films Mercury MG 20483

Once upon a Summertime DL 74956

Songs from Great Films Mercury SR 60017

Songs from Great Shows Mercury SR 60065

Strings Afire Mercury PPS 6019, Mercury Wing SRW 16357

Strings Afire in Spain Mercury PPS 6032

Twelve Great Movie Themes Mercury SR 60640

Twelve Great Songs Mercury SR 60720

World's Great Waltzes Mercury SR 60237

CLEBER, JOS (b. 1916)

Jos Cleber was born in Maastricht in the Netherlands. He studied at the Conservatory of Music in Maastricht and started his professional career in 1939 as arranger, violinist and trombonist with the AVRO Light Music Orchestra. He also played with the world-famous Concertgebouw Orchestra, the Metropole Orchestra and a dance orchestra called the Ramblers.

In 1948, he went to Indonesia, (then the Dutch East Indies), to form a new orchestra. On his return, the AVRO Broadcasting Company asked him to set up a light music orchestra called 'De Zaaiers' comprising some twenty-three musicians, occasionally augmented to forty-five, performing under the name The Cosmopolitan Orchestra. Economic stringency forced the disbandment of this orchestra. Cleber continued to work for AVRO as musical adviser for radio and television programs. This included a TV program designed to provide opportunity for young musicians to perform before a large audience.

Jos Cleber worked in South Africa for a while in the early 1960s, at the invitation of the South African Broadcasting Corporation. He retired in 1981.

Musical Achievements

During his long career, Cleber made some recordings for the CHAPPELL Recorded Music Library. He appeared with his Cosmopolitan Orchestra on the Epic label of CBS in the United States. This included one LP, *Golden Violins*, which he shared with his colleague DOLF VAN DER LINDEN. This album was compiled from material originally released in Europe.

Select Discography

Music of the City . . . Amsterdam. Columbia CL 1169

COATES, ERIC (27 August 1886–21 December 1957)

Eric Coates was born in Hucknall, Nottinghampshire, of a musical family. His father was a doctor, and his mother both played the piano and sang. While still a teenager, Coates became the leader of a student orchestra conducted by John Munks in Hucknall Public Hall. His rapid progress led to his taking classes with Georg Ellenberger and theory and harmony with Ralph Horner. At the age of sixteen he took up the viola in addition to his violin playing in order to play chamber music for the Nottingham Sacred Music Society, whose concerts were conducted by Sir Henry Wood. At this period, he also learned to play the flute.

He won an academy scholarship and studied at the Royal Academy of Music, specializing in viola with Lionel Tertis and composition with Frederick Corder. While still a student, he wrote a setting for Shakespeare's 'Who Is Sylvia?', which became a favorite song of Dame Nellie Melba. He played in various theater orchestras, including the opera orchestra conducted by Sir Thomas Beecham. He subsequently joined the Queen's Hall Orchestra under Henry Wood and became lead viola in 1912. In 1911, he wrote the successful 'Miniature Suite,' which was conducted by Wood in the Promenade Concerts. He left the orchestra in 1919 to concentrate on composing and conducting. After a few difficult years, he had further success with the 'Merrymakers' overture in 1922.

After a brief stay in Sussex, he returned to Baker Street, London, where he and his wife stayed until 1939. His compositions during this period included 'By the Sleepy Lagoon' (1930), 'London' (1932) and 'London Again' suites of music. The 'Knightsbridge March' from the 'London' suite became famous as the signature tune of the BBC program *In Town Tonight*. During World War II, Coates composed 'Calling All Workers', which was first broadcast by the BBC Orchestra conducted by Stanford Robinson in 1940. The 'Three Elizabeths' suite followed in 1944.

Coates returned to London at the end of the war (1945) and continued writing and conducting his own works. He became established as England's most famous composer of light music. His compositions include 'Stonecracker John' (1909), 'A Dinder Courtship' (1912), 'The Green Hills of Somerset' (words by Fred E. Weatherly, 1916), 'I Pitch My Lonely Caravan' (words by Annette Horey, 1912), 'Thinkin' of You' (words by Dorothy Dickson, 1922) and 'Bird Songs at Eventide' (words by Royden Barrie, 1926).

Select Discography/Compact Discs

Boult, Adrian. Music of Eric Coates BBC RD9106

Coates, Eric. Conducts His Own Music: Historic Recordings HMV CDP 799255–2

Groves, Sir Charles. Music of Eric Coates EMI CDB 762557

Lanchberry, John. Music of Eric Coates (With Sydney Symphony Orchestra) HMV ESD 7062

Music of Eric Coates. Vol. 1. Conifer CDHD 211/212 [2 CDs]

Music of Eric Coates. Vol. 2. Conifer 75606 62390 2 [2 CDs]

Nabarro, Malcolm. Music of Eric Coates ASV WHL 2069

COLLINS, ANTHONY (1893–1962)

Anthony Collins studied violin and composition at the Royal College of Music and began his career as an orchestral player. From 1926 to 1936, he was principal viola with the London Symphony Orchestra and Covent Garden Orchestra. In 1939, he went to Hollywood, where he wrote film scores for RKO. He was also in demand as a conductor, in which role he attempted to promote interest in British music. He returned to Britain during World War II and conducted for numerous concerts and recordings.

Collins wrote many classical works but occasionally attempted light orchestral music. One of his best known compositions in the lighter sphere was 'Vanity Fair', associated with William Thackeray's famous novel of the same name. This has been recorded by Ernest Tomlinson and the RTE Concert Orchestra (MARCO POLO 8.223522).

COLLINS, MICHAEL

Michael Collins was born in Liverpool to parents who were professional musicians. He began his musical studies of piano and cello playing in Liverpool at the age of seven. At the age of ten, Collins was playing piano and cello in variety at the London Coliseum. He appeared later as soloist with various orchestras throughout the north of England. At the age of twenty-one, he was appointed principal cellist in the BBC Orchestra, London, a post he held for six years. He was tutored in the art of conducting by Constant Lambert and Sir John Barbirolli. He subsequently conducted some of the finest orchestras in Britain, including the BBC, the Scottish Symphony, and the Halle.

Collins was particularly skilled at directing English and Italian opera companies, such as the world famous Carl Rosa Opera Company. He also enjoyed an enviable reputation in musical comedy. He was musical director for Sir Charles B. Cochran and also directed performances of *Kiss Me, Kate, Fanny* and *Where's Charley?*

His career in recording started when he attracted the attention of Norman Newell, Artists and Recording Manager at the EMI Recording Organization in Britain. The successful recording of the LP *Where's Charley?* earned him a long term contract as musical director of show albums. *Bitter Sweet, Desert Song, Chu Chin Chow, Song of Norway* and *Show Boat* were recorded subsequent to this first meeting. Collins also produced a superb Tchaikovsky selection, *None but the Lonely Heart*, and an LP of *Famous Hymns*, with a magnificent fifty-piece string orchestra.

Select Discography

Abide with Me (Hymn Tunes) Columbia 33 JSX 1123

Melodies That Will Last Forever Columbia 33JSX 1371

None but the Lonely Heart (Themes of Tchaikovsky) Columbia 33JSX 1154

Waltzing Through the Years Columbia 33 JSX 1194

CONNIFF, RAY (b. 6 November 1916)

Ray Conniff was born in Attleboro, Massachusetts. He received his first musical tuition from his father, a trombonist with the Attleboro Jewelry City Band and his mother, who played piano. While at high school, Ray joined a local band and taught himself arranging, with the aid of a mail-order tuition course.

After graduation in 1934, Ray went to Boston and got his first professional arrangement with Dan Murphy's society orchestra, the Musical Skippers. In 1936 he moved to New York, where he was employed as a trombonist-arranger with Bunny Berigan. Two years later, he became trombonist-arranger for Bob Crosby's band, the Bobcats. In 1939, he went to work for Artie Shaw, where he became known for his trombone solos, and also appeared with the band of Vaughn Monroe. He took part in many radio shows and studied at the Juilliard School of Music, New York.

He worked with Glen Gray's orchestra until 1944, when he became arranger for various groups on the Armed Forces Radio, and played in Artie Shaw's U.S. Navy Band. After the war, he arranged for the band of Harry James and was later with Jerry Wald, Sonny Burke and FRANK DE VOL. In the late 1940s, Conniff became a freelancer and also made an intense study of hit records in order to discover the key to successful recording.

In 1953, he met Columbia's Mitch Miller and became musical director for Columbia Records. He was invited in 1954 to arrange for their artist Don Cherry. The lucky disc was *Band of Gold*, a million seller. This was followed by a string of arrangements for Johnnie Ray, Guy Mitchell, Frankie Laine, Marty Robbins and Johnny Mathis. Conniff was eventually allowed to produce his own album, *'S 'Wonderful* (1956), which sold half a million copies. More albums followed and he became a top-selling artist on the Columbia label.

Conniff made many LPs that developed the swing-era formula he had used with Shaw, James and others, starting a trend that was widely copied. He continued into the 1970s, toured England in 1973, and cut an album in Moscow in December 1974 entitled *Ray Conniff in Moscow*. He was the first American to record in the Soviet Union.

The key to Conniff's success was the use of skillfully blended, mixed choruses as an orchestral instrument. His orchestra consisted of eighteen musicians, with choruses of four girls and four boys. The Conniff Singers were a group of twenty-five, consisting of twelve girls and thirteen boys, usually backed by eight musicians. By 1970, he had won nine Gold Discs from R.I.A.A. for million-dollar-selling albums. One of these albums was *Somewhere My Love*, issued in 1966, the title taken from the vocal version of 'Lara's Theme', from the film *Doctor Zhivago*. This theme became one of the most famous successes in the history of film background music.

Ray Conniff's conducting of his arrangements in the late 1950s and early 1960s resulted in twenty-eight of his albums reaching the top forty of the Pop Album charts. One of the albums that proved successful in 1962 was *Rhapsody in Rhythm*. His last appearance on the chart came with *Harmony* in 1973.

The Ray Conniff International Fan Club has published *'S Conniff: The*

Ray Conniff Newsletter: A Publication for Collectors and Admirers of the Music of Ray Conniff, June 1992–. The address of the club is Manfred Thonicke, Haynstrasse 8, D2000 Hamburg 20, Germany.

Select Discography

Alone Again Columbia 31629

Bridge over Troubled Water Columbia 1022

Broadway in Rhythm Columbia 1252

Christmas with Conniff Columbia 1390

Concert in Rhythm Columbia 1163

Concert in Rhythm—Volume 2 Columbia 1415

En Espagnol Columbia 9408

Friendly Persuasion Columbia 9010

Happiness Is Columbia 9261

Happy Beat Columbia 8749

Harmony Columbia 32553

Hawaiian Album Columbia 9547

Hollywood in Rhythm Columbia 1310

Honey Columbia 9661

Invisible Tears Columbia 9064

I Can See Clearly Now Columbia 32090

I Love How You Love Me Columbia 9777

It Must Be Him Columbia 9595

It's the Talk of the Town Columbia 1334

Jean Columbia 9920

Love Affair Columbia 9152

Love Story Columbia 30498

Love Theme from The Godfather Columbia 31473

Memories Are Made of This Columbia 1574

Music from Mary Poppins Columbia 9166

Ray Conniff's Greatest Hits Columbia 9839

Ray Conniff's World of Hits Columbia 9300

Rhapsody in Rhythm Columbia 1878

'S Awful Nice Columbia 1137

'S Continental Columbia 1776

'S Marvelous! Columbia 1074

'S Wonderful! Columbia 925

Say It with Music (A Touch of Latin) Columbia 1490

So Much in Love Columbia 1720
Somebody Loves Me Columbia 1642
Somewhere My Love Columbia 9319
Sound of Music, My Fair Lady and Other Great Movie Themes
Speak to Me of Love Columbia 8950
This Is My Song Columbia 9476
Turn Around, Look at Me Columbia 9712
We Wish You a Merry Christmas Columbia 1892
We've Only Just Begun Columbia 30410
You Are the Sunshine of My Life Columbia 32376
Young at Heart Columbia 1489

Compact Discs

Always in My Heart Sony 44152
Broadway Rhythm Sony 8064
Campeones Sony 80319
Christmas Album Sony 38300
Christmas Caroling Sony 40167
Concert in Rhythm Sony 8022
Conniff Meets Butterfield Sony 8155
Essence of Ray Conniff Sony 53574
40th Anniversary Sony DISCOS/GLOBO 81650
Friendly Persuasion Sony 9010
Greatest Hits Sony 9839
Happiness Is Ray Conniff Sony 64688
Happy Beat Sony 8749
Hawaiian Album Sony 47990
Hollywood Rhythm Sony 8117
Homenaje A. Sony Discos, Orfeon 506
Invisible Tears Sony 9064
Just Kiddin' Around (With Billy Butterfield) Sony 8822
Latinissimo Sony DISCOS/GLOBO 81161
Love Affair Sony 64686
Many Moods Sony 15903
Mary Poppins Sony 64687
Memories Are Made of This Sony 8374
Plays Broadway Sony 47990
Rhapsody in Rhythm Sony 8678

'S Awful Nice Sony 8001

'S Continental Sony 8576

'S Marvelous Sony 8037

'S Wonderful Sony 925

Say It with Music Sony 8282

16 Most Requested Songs: Encore Sony 66129

Somewhere My Love Sony 9319

Speak to Me of Love Sony 8950

Supersonico Sony DISCOS 80257

This Is My Song Sony 65018

World of Hits Sony 65017

You Make Me Feel So Young Sony 8918

Young at Heart Sony 8281

CONTI, BILL (b. 1942)

Bill Conti first came to prominence for his musical score for the film *Rocky* (1976). This production marked the beginning of Conti's association with producer John G. Avildsen, for whom he scored *The Karate Kid* trilogy (1984, 1986 and 1989). Other film scores include *The Right Stuff* (1983), *North and South* (1985) and *The Adventures of Huck Finn* (1993). Conti was also responsible for the title themes for television series *Dynasty* and *Cagney and Lacey.*

Select Discography

Adventures of Huck Finn Varese Sarabande VSD5418

Masters of the Universe Silva Screen FILMCD095

North and South. The Right Stuff Varese Sarabande VCD47250

Rocky Liberty 46081-2

Rocky II Liberty 46082-2

Rocky III Liberty 46561-2

Year of the Gun Milan 873 025

COPLAND, AARON (14 November 1900–2 December 1990)

Aaron Copland was born in Brooklyn, New York. He is often described as the first important composer from the United States. LEONARD BERNSTEIN called him 'the best we have.' The son of Russian immigrants, Copland was a pupil of Nadia Boulanger in Paris, before making his mark with such challenging avant-garde works as a symphony for organ and orchestra (1925). Subsequently, he produced works that had more popular appeal, although he never compromised his musical ideals. His most popular pieces included *El Salón Mexico* (1936), which incorporated Mexican folk music; *A Lincoln Portrait* (1942); the Pulitzer prize-winning *Appalachian Spring* (1944); *Fanfare for the Common Man* (1942); and the opera *The Tender Land* (1954). Several of his most celebrated early works achieved a highly successful fusion of classical structures with jazz motifs. Copland was a Kennedy Center honoree toward the end of his life. He brought his interest in American folk music to films, as he had also done in ballets such as *Billy the Kid* (1938) and *Rodeo* (1942). His film scores included *Of Mice and Men* (1939), *Our Town* (1940), *The Red Pony* (1949) and *The Heiress* (1949), for which he received an Academy Award.

Select Discography

Music for Films (Saint Louis Symphony Orchestra. Conductor Leonard Slatkin) RCA 09026 61699–2 [CD]

CORDELL, FRANK (1918–August 1980)

Frank Cordell was born in Wimbledon, England. By the age of fourteen, he was a competent pianist. He won a London jazz contest at seventeen. He was offered an apprenticeship at the Warner Brothers Film Studios and received a thorough grounding in the various technical aspects of film production. He also ran a semiprofessional band, writing all their scores and playing in professional jazz groups in the West End of London.

At the outbreak of war in 1939, he became a musician with the Royal Air Force. He toured as far as Cyprus, Palestine (now Israel) and Syria. Later, in Cairo, he conducted a *Music for Moderns* weekly radio program.

In 1947, he returned to London, where he arranged and conducted for the British Broadcasting Corporation. He also worked on motion picture sound tracks and as a conductor on records.

In about 1952, Frank Cordell was approached by Walter Ridley of His Master's Voice Records to become the musical director for all HMV contracted artists, a post he held until 1962. During the 1950s, he provided the backings for a number of popular singers on His Master's Voice. He developed a distinctive style which became a trademark of the rhythmical output of singers such as Alma Cogan and Ronnie Hilton. He also made some light orchestral records of his own for HMV. On several records, the composer is named as Meillear, which may be a pseudonym for Frank Cordell. They included 'Happy Horn Blowers', 'Chiquita' and 'Big Ben Waltz'. He also recorded an unusual arrangement of 'Delicado'.

In 1962, he decided to become a full-time composer of film music. He obtained employment through Noel Rogers of United Artists Music, Hollywood. Cordell spent twenty-five years writing for films, television and records and subsequently concentrated on writing his own compositions for publication and performance. The LP *Music by Frank Cordell* shows his ability as a composer of great imagination.

Select Discography

Best of Everything United Artists UAS 6590, ULP 1175, SULP 1175

Great Epic Film Themes SLS 50243

Hear This CLP 1611, CSD 1475, Capitol ST 10346

Melody Lingers On CLP 1153, Capitol ST 10180 [Also on CD]

Mixed Moods SM 214

Music by Frank Cordell CLP 1064

Suite Based on the Music of Harold Arlen Reader's Digest RDM/RDS 6057

Sweet and Dry CLP 1341, Capitol T/ST 10262 [Also on CD]

COURAGE, ALEXANDER (b. 1919)

Alexander Courage was born in Philadelphia and educated at the Eastman School of Music, Rochester, New York. He served as Air Force Band leader during World War II. After the war he composed and conducted for CBS Radio and collaborated with ANDRÉ PREVIN and Adolph Deutsch as arranger for MGM. From 1957 onward, he scored for television shows including *Lost in Space, The Waltons* and *Voyage to the Bottom of the Sea* and films including *The Left-handed Gun* (1958) and *Tokyo After Dark* (1959). Courage is best known as composer of the famous main title music for the original *Star Trek* series. He has orchestrated and arranged the scores of musical films, including *Guys and Dolls* (1955), *Dr. Doolittle* (1967) and *Hello, Dolly* (1969). His most recent collaborators have been JOHN WILLIAMS *(Jurassic Park)* and Jerry Goldsmith *(Bad Girls)*.

COWARD, NOËL (16 December 1899–26 March 1973)

Noël Coward was born in Teddington, Middlesex. He received little formal education but came from a musical family. His parents were amateur dramatic operatic singers, and his father worked for a firm of piano manufacturers.

At the age of ten Coward won a prize for singing at a seaside concert and was composing by the age of fifteen. He wrote for romantic operetta scores, as in *Bitter Sweet* and *Conversation Piece*, and also produced witty, satirical songs, such as 'Mad Dogs and Englishmen' and 'The Stately Homes of England'. The best of his music was produced in the 1930s with artists such as Gertrude Lawrence, Beatrice Lillie and Jack Buchanan. After 1945, his style of music lost its popularity. He was knighted in 1972, and in 1973 a revue, *Cowardy Custard*, comprising his songs and sketches, was produced at the Mermaid Theatre.

His principal scores include *London Calling* (1932); *Andre Charlot's London Revue of 1924* ('Parisian Pierrot, 'Poor Little Rich Girl); *On with the Dance* (1925); *This Year of Grace* ('A Room with a View', 'Dance

Little Lady, 'World Weary', 1928); *Bitter Sweet* ('I'll See You Again', 'Zigeuner', 'If Love Were All', 1929); *Private Lives* ('Someday I'll Find You', 1930); *Cavalcade* ('Twentieth Century Blues', 1931); *Words and Music* ('Mad about the Boy', 'Mad Dogs and Englishmen', 'The Party's Over', 1932); *Conversation Piece* ('I'll Follow My Secret Heart', 'Nevermore', 1934); *Tonight at Eight Thirty* ('Has Anyone Seen Our Ship?', 'You Were There', 1936); *Operette* (1938), *Set to Music* ('I'm so Weary of It All', 'The Stately Homes of England' 1939); *Sigh No More*, (1945); *Pacific 1860* (1945); *Ace of Clubs* (1950); *After the Ball* (1954); *Sail Away* (1961); *The Girl Who Came to Supper* (1963).

His films include *Cavalcade* (1933); *In Which We Serve* (1942); *This Happy Breed* (1944). He wrote a ballet, *London Morning*, in 1959. Other well-remembered songs include 'Forbidden Fruits', 'Don't Put Your Daughter on the Stage, Mrs Worthington', 'London Pride', 'I Wonder What's Happened to Him' and 'Matelot'.

Coward was buried in Jamaica, where he had lived since 1949 and where he built a fascinating home.

Additional Readings

Briers, Richard. *Coward & Company*. London: Robson Books, 1989.

Castle, Charles. *Noël*. London: W. H. Allen, 1972.

Citron, Stephen. *Noël and Cole: The Sophisticates*. New York: Oxford University Press, 1993.

Cole, Stephen. *Noël Coward: A Bio-Bibliography*. Westport, CT: Greenwood Press, 1994.

Fisher, Clive. *Noël Coward*. London: Weidenfeld & Nicolson, 1992.

Green, Benny. *Let's Face the Music*. London: Pavilion Books, 1989. pp. 73–94.

Hoare, Philip. *Noël Coward: A Biography*. London: Sinclair-Stevenson, 1995.

Lesley, Cole. *The Life of Noël Coward*. London: Jonathan Cape; New York: Knopf, 1976.

Morley, Sheridan. *Noël Coward: A Talent to Amuse*. London: W. H. Allen; New York: Doubleday, 1972.

Morley, Sheridan. *Noël Coward and His Friends*. London: Weidenfeld and Nicolson, 1979.

Select Discography

Chacksfield, Frank. Music of Noël Coward Decca LK 4090 [Also on CD]

Paramor, Norrie. Magnificence of Noël Coward Polydor 2310279

D

DALE, SYD (1924–15 August 1994)
Syd Dale was a British arranger, conductor and composer. For many years he was a well-known broadcaster with his various ensembles. In the 1970s, he founded the Amphonic Sound Stage company, which was active in the music production business.

His compositions include 'Until Love Songs End', 'No Time to Dream', 'Never Saw a Girl So Pretty', 'Those Wasted Years', 'Starting All Over Again', 'Summer Serenade', 'Making the Changes', 'Winter Sunshine', 'Ready to Play', 'Passing Fancy', 'Play for Keeps', 'Japanese Water Garden', 'Japanese Jumble', 'Ophelia', 'Velvet Blue', 'Together Again' and 'Misty Moments'.

Select Discography

Set of six albums produced by Syd Dale, recorded at Lansdowne Recording Studios under the Go Ahead Records Label

Volume 1. **Love Isn't Just for the Young** GA 103 Stereo

Volume 2. **Love Isn't Just for the Young** GA 104 Stereo

Volume 3. **Where Our Love Began** GA 106 Stereo

Volume 4. **Once Upon a Summertime** GA 107 Stereo

Volume 5. **When I Fall in Love: A Musical Tribute to Nat 'King' Cole** GALP 108 Stereo

Volume 6. **Sentimental Journey** GALP 109 Stereo

Compact Discs

Orchestral Backgrounds: A Tribute to Syd Dale. Amphonic/Sound Stage AVF 122 CD

D'ARTEGA (ALFONSO ARMANDO ANTONIO FERNANDEZ)

D'Artega was born in Spain and came to the United States as a child. He studied orchestration and composition under Boris Levenson, a former pupil of Nikolay Rimsky-Korsakov. He was a classical musician who developed a distinctive style in the playing of popular music.

He gained employment with broadcasting networks and conducted on the *Jell-O Program, Your Hit Parade, Ripley's Believe It or Not Show* and the *Cavalcade of Music.* He became the director of concerts for the Buffalo Philharmonic Orchestra. He frequently conducted the Pop Concert Orchestra at Carnegie Hall and was appointed its permanent conductor.

His most famous composition was 'In the Blue of Evening' (1943), which held a spot on the *Hit Parade* for twenty-one weeks. His works for symphony orchestra include 'American Panorama', 'Dream Concerto', 'Niagara' and the 'Fire and Ice Ballet'. He has written and conducted sound tracks for motion pictures, and portrayed Peter Tchaikovsky in the movie *Carnegie Hall.*

Select Discography

Breeze and I: The Music of Lecuona Universal UP539 (Australia)

George Gershwin Story (With Symphony of the Air Orchestra) EPIC LN 3651

Pop Concert in Manhattan Mercury MG 20060

Songs to Remember (With the Living Strings) RCA Camden CAL/CAS-857

DAVIS, CARL (b. 1936)

Carl Davis was born in Brooklyn and began studying music at the age of seven. He was educated at Queen's College in New York and at the New England College of Music. He learned composition from Paul Nordoff and Hugo Kauder. His first important commission was music for the revue *Diversions*, which was staged in Greenwich Village in 1959. Before moving to London in 1961 Davis spent some time studying with Per Norgard in Copenhagen and working with the Royal Danish Ballet. Following the success of *Diversions* at the Edinburgh Festival in 1961, Davis was asked by Ned Sherrin to write music for the series *That Was the Week That Was.*

Davis composed for television, stage and screen. He was associated with a project to write scores for classic silent movies, particularly the Thames Silents, a scheme initiated by Jeremy Isaacs. These silent films include *Intolerance, The Thief of Baghdad, Ben-Hur, Napoleon* and *The Wind.* His scores for modern films include the BBC production of *The Trial* (1992) and *Pride and Prejudice* (1995).

Select Discography

Ben Hur Silva Screen FILMCD043

French Lieutenant's Woman DRG CDRG106

Intolerance Prometheus PCD105

Napoleon Silva Screen FILMCD149

Pride and Prejudice EMI CDEMC3726

The Trial Milan 873 150

West Side Story, Porgy and Bess, The King and I (With Royal Liverpool Philharmonic Orchestra) EMI 077776748726

DE LOS RIOS, WALDO (b. 7 September 1934)
De Los Rios was born in Buenos Aires. His mother was the well-known folk singer Martha de Los Rios. He began his musical studies at the age of seven. His professional career began at thirteen, when he accompanied his mother on the piano, along with a band composed of guitars and instruments typical of Argentine folk music. He also toured with his mother and developed an interest in the music of the countries that they visited. He graduated from the National Conservatory of Music and Scenic Art with the degree of professor in music. The turning point in his career came when his mother asked him to make special orchestrations for some music she was planning to record. As a result of this work, he was signed up by the directors of Columbia Argentina, who brought him to the attention of Columbia Records. His initial records in Argentina were enormously successful and helped to rekindle an interest in that country's musical heritage.

Select Discography

Kiss of Fire Columbia CL 965

DE VOL, FRANK (b. 20 September 1911)
Frank De Vol was born in Moundsville, West Virginia. His father was conductor of a theater orchestra in Canton, Ohio. At fourteen he made his appearance as a violinist and later occasionally substituted for his father as conductor. De Vol studied conducting with Albert Coates and arranging with Mario Castelnuovo-Tedesco.

The orchestras with which he played included those of George Olsen and Alvino Rey; he was acclaimed for his appearance at the Hollywood Bowl. In the 1940s, he conducted his orchestra for the Mutual Radio Network show *California Melodies*. He was active in radio and television work and composed scores for movies such as *The Big Knife* (1955), *Pillow Talk* (Academy Award nomination, 1959), *Guess Who's Coming to Dinner?*

(1967) and *The Longest Yard* (1974). De Vol wrote 'Hush, Hush, Sweet Charlotte', for the movie of the same name.

With his famous Rainbow Strings, he recorded with vocalists such as Tony Bennett, Johnny Ray, Doris Day ('Que Sera, Sera') and Nat 'King' Cole ('Nature Boy'). He also made many successful orchestral albums for Columbia records, including *Portraits.*

He was nominated for television's Emmy Award for his music on the Rosemary Clooney Show, in which he also acted. He contributed the score for the TV series *My Three Sons, Alcoa Theatre* and *Bus Stop*. De Vol also did some acting in the film *Boys' Night Out* and appeared in the television comedy series *I'm Dickens . . . He's Fenster*. Singing was another of his accomplishments.

Select Discography

Big Beat Special US Columbia 2003/8803

Classics in Modern Capitol H 185 (10")

Columbia Album of Irving Berlin (2 records) Columbia C2L 12; also issued as CS 8044/8045

Concert of Waltzes Capitol H-2010 (10"); Capitol T588

Fabulous Hollywood Columbia CS 8172 [Also on CD]

Happiest Girl in the World Columbia CS 8429

Italian Romance—American Style ABC-Paramount ABC/ABCS 534

Modern Originals for Concert Orchestra (Compositions by De Vol) Capitol H198

More Old Sweet Waltzes Columbia CS 8656

More Radio's Great Old Themes Columbia 17788/8578

New Old Sweet Songs ABCS 563

Night with Rudolf Friml Columbia 1630/8430

Old Sweet Songs Columbia CS 8209 [Also on CD]

Old Sweet Waltzes Columbia CS 1856 [Also on CD]

Peyton Place US ABC/ABCS 513

Portraits Columbia CS 8010 [Also on CD]

Radio's Great Old Themes US Columbia 1613/8413

Symphonic Portrait of Jimmy McHugh Capitol L249

Theme from Peyton Place ABCS 513

Viennese Voices Capitol H98 (10")

Voices Columbia CS 8656

Waltzing on Air Capitol H 208 (10"); Capitol T 208

Compact Discs

Columbia **Album of Irving Berlin** W2K 75042 (2 discs)

Old Sweet Songs of Christmas Columbia 472019–2

More Old Sweet Songs Columbia (Australia) 47118

DEXTER, HARRY (1910–1973)

Harry Dexter was born in Sheffield, England. He obtained a bachelor of music degree at Durham University. He composed several choral and orchestral works and wrote a prize-winning symphony while serving as an army chaplain during World War II.

During the 1950s, his tuneful light orchestra pieces gained increasing acceptance in BBC broadcasts, one of them being the signature tune of the original *Maigret* series for television. He joined the staff of the London music publisher Francis, Day and Hunter, in charge of light orchestral and mood music output and became music critic for several important periodicals. In 1956, he founded the Light Music Society, with ERIC COATES as first president and served as its chairman for several years.

One of his best-known compositions was 'Siciliano', a dance in a quick, tripping rhythm. This has been recorded on the compact disc entitled *British Light Music* conducted by ERNEST TOMLINSON (Marco Polo 8.223522).

DOCKER, ROBERT (1919–1992)

Robert Docker was born in London and studied piano, viola and composition at the Royal Academy of Music, London from 1937 to 1941. After serving in the army during World War II, he became a freelance musician, playing the piano and arranging in broadcasting and recording sessions and appearing as soloist with guest orchestras. A regular assignment was with the BBC Scottish Variety Orchestra in Glasgow. For twelve years he had a successful piano duet partnership with Edward Rubach.

As an arranger, Docker did important work for film composers. He was also a brilliant improviser and performed in this capacity at music clubs. He wrote much music for the mood music libraries and numerous pieces in the light orchestral field. These often featured solo piano, as is evident in his popular piece 'Legend'. One of his most successful short pieces was 'Tabarinage', a humorous look at the French dance the cancan.

DOUGLAS, JOHNNY (b. 9 June 1920)

Johnny Douglas was born in London. He played the piano at an early age and by the time he was twelve, he was already arranging and writing music. He was educated at St. Olave's public school and became a clerk. He left this job to become a pianist in the West End of London in 1939. He was soon out of work and joined the Royal Air Force.

Johnny Douglas (used with permission)

In 1944, he won the Melody Maker Jazz Jamboree Award for the best arrangement/composition for dance band. An injury sustained during the war forced him to give up piano playing for a while and concentrate on composing and arranging. He became staff arranger for George Elrick and arranged many BBC programs. For a few years, he served as pianist-arranger for CYRIL STAPLETON and subsequently took on freelance work. He was in demand from artists such as BERT AMBROSE, Ted Heath, Edmundo Ros, Billy Cotton, Joe Loss, MANTOVANI, Jack Parnell and other British bands. To gain more experience, he joined a music publishing firm and was responsible for arrangements on a wide variety of instruments.

In 1953, he began scoring orchestral backings for Decca Record Company, working with artists such as Dickie Valentine, Joan Regan, David Whitfield and Lita Rosa. For the first time in 1958 he was invited to conduct a large orchestra, playing his own arrangements. From that year onward he scored and conducted over seventy LPs. The RCA album *Living Strings Play Music of the Sea* was the start of a long and successful initiative. His album *Feelings* won a gold disc. The LIVING STRINGS series became tremendously popular in the United States.

Douglas has scored some thirty-six feature films. The first movie for which Douglas composed music was a small B production called *The Traitors*, for which he won an award at the Cannes Film Festival. He subsequently worked on other film scores, including *Day of the Triffids, Crack in the World, Run like a Thief* and twenty-one films in the *Scales of Justice* series. He also scored the music for *The Railway Children* and *Dulcima.* For the latter film, Douglas conducted the Royal Philharmonic Orchestra. He was nominated for a British Oscar for the score of *The Railway Children.* In the 1980s he formed his own record company, Dulcima.

Select Discography

Note: All RCA Camden LPs were recorded with Living Strings.

Airport Love Theme RCA Camden CAS 2420

At a Sidewalk Cafe RCA Camden CAS 762

Broadway Waltzes London PS 185 (Reissued on Decca **Ace of Clubs** ACL 1013)

Darling Lili RCA Camden CAS 2421

Dr. Zhivago and Others RCA Camden CAS 2133

Ebb Tide and Other Favorites RCA Camden CAS 2291

Everybody Loves Somebody RCA Camden CAS 864

Feelings RCA Camden CAL/CAS 926; RCA APL1–2383 Stereo

Finian's Rainbow RCA Camden CAL/CAS 859

Gone with the Wind RCA Camden CAS 2161

Great Hits of Cole Porter RCA Camden CAS 2522

Handful of Stars London LL 1741

Holiday for Strings RCA Camden CAL/CAS 760

In the Still of the Night RCA Camden CAL/CAS 795

Living Voices on Broadway RCA Camden CAS 692

Make the World Go Away RCA Camden CAL/CAS 982

Man of La Mancha RCA Camden CAS 2606

Melody Lingers On RCA Camden CAS 847

Melody of Love RCA Camden CAS 830

Music for Young Lovers RCA Camden CAS 739

Music from the Broadway Hit 'Carnival' RCA Camden CAL/CAS 678

Music from Chaplin Movies RCA Camden CAS 2581

Music from Living Free RCA Camden CAS 2564

Music of the Sea RCA Camden CAL/CAS 682

Music to Help You Stop Smoking RCA Camden CAL/CAS 821

Music We All Love Best RCA Camden CAL/CAS 958

No, No, Nanette RCA LSP 4504

On a Sentimental Journey RCA Camden CAS 803

Plays Henry Mancini RCA Camden CAS 736

Songs Made Famous by Jim Reeves RCA Camden CAS 2216

Songs of Inspiration RCA Camden CAS 2103

Songs of Loretta Lynn RCA Camden CAS 2336

Songs of the Swinging 60s RCA Camden CAS 2397

Sound of Music RCA Camden CAL/CAS 869

Spirit of Christmas RCA Camden CAL/CAS 783

Sweetheart Tree RCA Camden CAL/CAS 926

Tennessee Waltz and Other Country Favorites RCA Camden CAL/CAS 716

Three O'Clock in the Morning RCA Camden CAL/CAS 915

Twilight Time RCA Camden CAL/CAS 930

Waltz Time RCA Camden CAL/CAS 855

Waltz You Saved For Me and Other Favorite Waltzes RCA Camden CAL/CAS 690

West Side Story RCA Camden CAS 2313

When Irish Eyes Are Smiling RCA Camden ARL 1–2383

Where Did the Night Go? RCA Camden CAS 738

White Christmas RCA Camden CAL/CAS 2258

Compact Discs

It's Magic Dulcima DLCD 115

On Screen Dulcima DLCD 110

On Stage Dulcima DLCD 109

DRAGON, CARMEN (28 July 1914–28 March 1984)

Carmen Dragon was born in Antioch, California. He learned to play many instruments. He studied at San Jose State College and California State University, San Jose. Initially he worked as a nightclub pianist in San Francisco. Thereafter he was employed by Meredith Willson, then NBC Radio's West Coast musical director. This post led to other important work in radio, records, motion pictures and television as well as appearances as guest conductor with symphony orchestras throughout the United States, South America and Europe.

He became tremendously popular for his light music concerts, particularly the evening concerts performed with the HOLLYWOOD BOWL ORCHESTRA. A Carmen Dragon appearance at the Hollywood Bowl in 1957 broke all attendance records to that date, with 18,740 admissions and thousands turned away.

Dragon worked for numerous radio shows and won wide popular recognition for his musical direction of the excellent program *Railroad Hour*, which also featured baritone Gordon MacRae. As conductor for twenty-five years of the Standard School Broadcasts, Dragon introduced the music of the great masters, folk and popular works to one and a half million youngsters in 60,000 classrooms. His long association with the Glendale Symphony Orchestra brought national respect and celebrity to that organization. His annual Christmas program with this orchestra earned him television's Emmy Award in 1964.

He worked in Hollywood as an arranger and won an Academy Award for his work with MORRIS STOLOFF on JEROME KERN's score for *Cover Girl* in 1944. This was one of more than thirty film scores that he provided. His recordings were produced by Capitol Recording Company, with Dragon often supplying notes for the sleeve covers.

Dragon's original compositions included the epic 'Sante Fe Suite'; the 'Suite Domestica', in which each movement represented one of his children, and the song 'I'm an American'. He also wrote the music for the *Invasion of the Body Snatchers* (1956).

In 1959, he made his first appearance in England and was invited to return in 1960 to conduct a series of concerts with the Royal Philharmonic and BBC orchestras. Dragon was a skillful performer in all areas of musical activity and acknowledged to be one of the most successful and best-known exponents of light classical music. He was a gifted arranger, conductor and composer. He died in Santa Monica, California.

Select Discography

Americana Capitol P 8523

La Belle France Capitol P 8427

Chopin by Starlight Capitol P 8371

Concert Gala Capitol P 8511

Concert Brilliants Capitol P 8559

La Danza Capitol P 8314

Evening with Cole Porter Capitol W/SW 1805 [Also on CD]

Evening with Sigmund Romberg Capitol W/SW 1804 (LP); EMI Angel CDM 769053.2 [CD]

Fiesta Capitol P 8335

L'Italia Capitol P 8351

Melody Capitol P 8476

Nocturne Capitol P 8363

Orchestra Sings Capitol P 8440

Over the Waves P 8547

Romantique Capitol P 8542

Serenade Capitol P 8413

Stephen Foster Melodies Capitol SP 8501

Tempo Espanol Pickwick/33 PC-4032, SPC-4032

World of Music Capitol P 8412, ZF-38

DUNCAN, TREVOR (**born Leonard Charles Trebilco**) (b. 27 February 1924)

Trevor Duncan was born in Camberwell, London. His musical skills were almost entirely self-taught. By the age of twelve he could play by ear and gained some knowledge of orchestration from private study. For a year he attended an external course at the Trinity College of Music on violin, harmony and counterpoint.

At the age of eighteen he joined the British Broadcasting Corporation as a technician. In 1943, he was conscripted into the Royal Air Force, where he became a wireless operator. In his spare time he played in RAF station dance bands.

In 1947, he returned to the BBC Radio as a sound and balance engineer working with light orchestras. His work allowed him to experiment with microphone placings, and he learned about the successful combinations of instruments. RAY MARTIN, the orchestra leader, encouraged him to develop his composing skills and performed Duncan's first work, 'Vision in Velvet', which he renamed 'Morning Star'. Martin also approved of Duncan's next composition, 'High Heels', and instructed him to approach Tom Elliott, the manager of Light Music Exploitation at Boosey and Hawkes, the Recorded Music Library. 'High Heels' enjoyed much success with numerous radio performances and a commercial recording by Sidney Torch for Parlophone. In the next few years, Duncan composed numerous works for Boosey and Hawkes. He was promoted to music producer at the BBC but had to leave in 1956, because of the BBC ruling that the compositions of its employees could not be scheduled in radio programs.

Duncan now concentrated fully on composing and his music received frequent radio airings. His works were accepted by other mood music libraries, including Inter-Art (Impress). Two of his most famous compositions were written in 1959, 'The Girl from Corsica' and the march from his 'Little Suite'. The latter became the signature tune for *Dr Finlay's Casebook*, a BBC television success of the 1960s. Other compositions were 'Sinfonia Tellurica', 'Panoramic Splendour', 'Schooner Bay', 'Broad Horizons', 'Passage to Windward', 'A Fog', 'Inhumanity' and 'Grand Vista'. In his early works he attempted to re-create the lush orchestral sound popular during the 1940s and 1950s. From his experience as a sound engineer, he knew exactly how to construct the correct sound. He was fond of using clear strings sustaining high notes, with background woodwinds, underscored by cellos and double basses. By the 1960s he was identified as a talented composer of symphonic stature in the English tradition.

DUNING, GEORGE (b. 25 February 1908)
George Duning was born in Richmond, Indiana, and completed his musical education at the Cincinnati Conservatory of Music. He began his career as a trumpet player and arranged for the Kay Kyser band during the 1940s. He also started to orchestrate films.

After war service in the navy, Duning was employed by Columbia Studios. He wrote over 250 scores and received Academy Award nominations for the films *Jolson Sings Again* (1949), *From Here to Eternity* (1953), and *Picnic* (1955). Other scores included *3.10 to Yuma* (1957), *Houseboat* (1958), *Bell, Book and Candle* (1958), *Toys in the Attic* (1963), *Any Wednesday* (1966), *Then Came Bronson* (1970) and *Beyond Witch Mountain* (1983). From the 1960s onward, Duning wrote scores for television series such as *Star Trek, The Partridge Family* and *The Big Valley.*

Select Discography

Bell, Book and Candle Citadel CT-6006

Picnic MCA MCAD31357

E

EASDALE, BRIAN (10 August 1909–30 October 1995)
Brian Easdale was born in Manchester and educated at the Westminster Abbey Choir School and Royal College of Music, London. After some success with opera and concert work, he joined the GPO Film Unit in 1936, working with Benjamin Britten and W. H. Auden. His scores include various documentaries. He also wrote a score for the Crown Film Unit production of *Ferry Pilot* in 1942. His most highly regarded work was for the film *The Red Shoes* (1948), which won an Academy Award. Other notable scores were for *Black Narcissus, The Small Back Room, Gone to Earth* (which received the Venice Film Festival Award in 1950), *The Battle of the River Plate* and *Peeping Tom*. In later years, he returned to the composition of serious music.

ELLINGTON, DUKE (EDWARD KENNEDY) (29 April 1899–24 May 1974)
Duke Ellington was born in Washington, DC. He was educated at the Wilberforce University, where he obtained an honorary doctorate in music, and Milton College. He gave up a career in art to play the piano with various groups. He joined Elmer Snowden and formed his first band, the Washingtonians, in 1923. Ellington was able to create a distinctive style and sound, which became well known after the band was engaged to play at the Cotton Club in Harlem in 1927. Under the guidance of Irving Mills, the band broadcast on radio, played for shows such as Ziegfield's *Show Girl* (1929) and appeared in the film *Check and Double Check* (1930).

Ellington began composing songs at an early age. In many cases, his compositions were played and recorded years before they were published. His first published song was probably 'Blues I Love to Sing' (1927), and the first song to achieve hit status was 'Ring Dem Bells' (1930) with lyrics by Irving Mills, for the film *Check and Double Check*. These compositions were followed by 'Mood Indigo' (1931), 'Creole Love Call' (1932) and 'Best Wishes' (1932).

Throughout Ellington's career of fifty years as a bandleader, his abilities as songwriter, as opposed to those as a composer for his orchestra, took second place. Nevertheless, he produced an impressive collection of song hits, which include the following titles: 'It Don't Mean a Thing' (1932); 'Sophisticated Lady' (1933); 'Drop Me Off at Harlem' (1933); 'Solitude' (1934); 'In a Sentimental Mood' (1935); 'Caravan' (1937); 'I Let a Song Go Out of My Heart' (1938); 'Do Nothin' Till You Hear from Me' (1943); 'I Didn't Know About You' (1944); 'Don't Get Around Much Anymore' (1942); 'I'm Beginning to See the Light' (1944); 'Just A-Sittin' and A-Rockin' ' (1945); 'Just Squeeze Me' (1946).

His main lyrical collaborators were Irving Mills, Billy Strayhorn, Mitchell Parish, Henry Nemo, Bob Russell, Paul Francis Webster, Eddie de Lange and Carl Sigman. Notable instrumental compositions were 'Rockin' in Rhythm', 'Saturday Night Function', 'Echoes of Harlem', 'Jack the Bear', 'Harlem Air Shaft', 'Mornin' Glory', 'Cotton Tail', 'Crescendo in Blue', 'Diminuendo in Blue', ' "C" Jam Blues', 'Come Sunday', and 'Satin Doll'.

His suites include *Black, Brown and Beige, New World A'Comin', Sepia Panorama, A Drum Is a Woman, Suite Thursday, Liberian Suite, Such Sweet Thunder, Far Eastern Suite, Perfume Suite* and *New Orleans Suite*. Ellington also wrote the scores for the shows *Jump for Joy* (1941) and *Beggar's Holiday* (1946) and the background music for the films *Anatomy of a Murder* (1959) and *Paris Blues* (1961).

Sophisticated Ladies, a tribute to Duke Ellington conceived by Donald McKayle and with an orchestra conducted by the composer's son, Mercer Ellington, was staged at the Lunt-Fontanne Theater, New York on 1 March 1981.

Additional Readings

Ewen, David. *American Songwriters*. New York: H. W. Wilson, 1987. pp. 147–52.

Select Discography

Kostelanetz, Andre. Music of Duke Ellington and Charlie Chaplin Columbia 34660

Montenegro, Hugo. Ellington Fantasy VIK LX 1106

101 Strings. Duke Ellington and Hoagy Carmichael Alshire S 5008

Valentino. Prelude to a Kiss. Symphonic Portrait of Duke Ellington W & G Records BPN 546 (New Zealand)

Young, Leon, String Chorale. Ellington for Strings Columbia 33SX1601

ELLIOTT, JACK

Jack Elliott was a pianist and arranger who traveled widely. He studied classical music at Tanglewood but turned later to jazz and formed his own group, which performed at The Embers in New York. He served as arranger and accompanist for the sophisticated night club singer, Jacqueline François and spent several years in Paris, where he made numerous recordings. He subsequently traveled throughout Europe, Asia and South America.

In 1960, he provided music for the American Exposition in Moscow. In the United States, he arranged and conducted for stars such as Patti Page, Jane Morgan and Barbara Carroll. His work in the theater included arranging dance sequences for the Broadway musicals *Fiorello* and *Tenderloin.* He also provided duo-piano accompaniment in the original cast album of the off-Broadway revue *Parade.*

Select Discography

Are You Lonesome Tonight? and Other Wonderful Melodies of the Sixties KAPP KS 3235

Dynamic Woodwinds KAPP ML 7505

Forever KAPP KL 1187

Great Movie Hits of the Forties KAPP ML 7531

ELLIS, RAY

Ray Ellis was born in Philadelphia and started studying the saxophone at the age of twelve. While still in his early teens, he taught himself to play all the reed instruments. He worked with many well-known bands shortly after turning sixteen. While in the army during World War II (1939–45), he wrote arrangements for the band at Fort Knox. After the war, Ellis worked in radio in Philadelphia and finally came to New York to write arrangements for The Four Lads recording sessions. He subsequently arranged for various popular music artists, including Mahalia Jackson, Guy Mitchell, Cathy Johnson and the DeJohn Sisters, and became an orchestra conductor and record producer of importance.

Select Discography

Ellis in Wonderland Columbia CL993

Gigi HS 11003

How to Succeed in Business RCA LSP 2493

I'm in the Mood for Strings MGM E/SE 3779

La Dolce Vita and Other Great Motion Picture Themes RCA LPM-2410

Let's Get Away from It All Columbia CS 8051

Our Man on Broadway RCA LPM/LSP 2615
Plays Top 20 RCA LSP 2400

ELLIS, VIVIAN (29 October 1904–20 June 1996)
Vivian Ellis was born in Hampstead, London into a musical family. His grandmother was a composer and pianist and his mother a fine violinist. He was educated at the Royal Academy of Music, where he studied piano and composition, one of his teachers being Dame Myra Hess.

He had a strong affinity for light rather than classical music. His first employment was with the London publisher Francis, Day and Hunter, where he served as reader and demonstrator of songs and piano pieces.

By his late teens, he was composing songs and musical numbers for the stage. He worked with artists such as Jack Hulbert, Francis Day and Sophie Tucker. At the age of twenty he was invited to write for the 1930 Revue of C. B. Cochrane, and this was the start of a long and successful collaboration. He produced a constant turnover of new revues and musical comedies, the most successful of which was *Mr Cinders* (1929), with its hit tune 'Spread a Little Happiness'. His many songs include 'Come and Dance the Charleston', 'The Wind in the Willows' and 'She's My Lovely'.

During World War II, Ellis served in the Royal Navy. After the war, he resumed his musical career, with three more C. B. Cochrane successes, *Big Ben, Tough at the Top* and *Bless the Bride.* The latter was written with the collaboration of author A. P. Herbert and contained the memorable songs 'This Is My Lovely Day' and 'Ma Belle Marguerite'.

Ellis also produced many fine pieces of light orchestral music, including the well-known 'Coronation Scot', written on a train journey between Paddington and Taunton in 1938. This piece was written for CHAPPELL'S Recorded Music Library and was used as the signature tune for the BBC radio program *Paul Temple.* Ellis was also responsible for another BBC signature tune, 'Alpine Pastures', used in the program *My Word.* Both of these compositions were orchestrated by SIDNEY TORCH. Among Ellis's other compositions for Chappells were 'Muse in Mayfair', 'The Jolly Juggler' and 'Flight 101'. His pieces for Boosey and Hawkes Recorded Music Library included 'Happy Weekend Suite', 'Holidays Abroad Suite', 'The Tune That Ran Away', 'Coach Tour', 'The Bingola', 'Interval Waltz', 'Air on a Shoestring', 'Holiday Camp' and 'New Town Suite'.

Ellis became a director of the Performing Arts Society in 1955 and its president in 1983. In 1985, the Vivian Ellis Prize was founded, financed by the Society to help promising young composers. Ellis was appointed a CBE in 1984 and died in London at the age of 91.

F

FAGAN, GIDEON (3 November 1904–20 March 1980)
Gideon Fagan was born in Somerset West, Cape Province, South Africa. His first musical instruction was from his brother, Johannes Jacobus Fagan, a composer. He then studied at the College of Music, Cape Town, until 1922 and the Royal College of Music, London, from 1923 to 1926. His major subjects were conducting under Adrian Boult and Malcolm Sargent and composition under Vaughan Williams.

He returned to South Africa after completing his studies but because of lack of opportunities in South Africa left for England a year later. He remained in England until 1949. His meeting with the theatrical personality Ernest Irving resulted in his entry into a career as arranger and orchestrator of music for the theater and for Ealing Studio productions, as assistant music director. He also arranged music for music publishers and for record companies.

He adapted a number of Afrikaans folk and picnic songs under the pseudonym of Albert Diggenhof for His Master's Voice. His film music included *David Livingstone* (1936), *Auld Lang Syne* (1937), *The Last Rose of Summer* (1937) and *The Captain's Table* (1937). His score for the film *David Livingstone* is based on an orchestral trilogy, 'Jungle Music-Pastoral-Lion Hunt'. In 1941, he composed the symphonic poem 'Ilala', based on motifs from the film music. He arranged the music for a series of films known as *The Music Masters*. He was also involved in two episodes of a film series entitled *Traveltalks*; he arranged the music for *Quaint Quebec* and composed the music for *Highlights of Cape Town*.

Some of his compositions that express mood and specific atmosphere are 'Five Orchestral Pieces and Mood Music' (1942), 'Heuwelkruin' (1954), various overtures, chamber music such as 'My Lewe' (1970), the suite 'Herinneringe aan Jojo se Besoek' (1973) and the 'Karoo-simfonie' (1976).

From 1939 to 1942, he served as conductor of the British Broadcasting Corporation's Northern Orchestra in Manchester. He subsequently conducted various symphony orchestras in Britain and did freelance work for the theater, film industry and London ballet performances.

In 1949, he returned to South Africa as assistant conductor of the newly formed Johannesburg City Orchestra, a position he held until 1953. He was then appointed music organizer for the Golden Jubilee of African Consolidated Theatres. In 1954, he became director of the South African Broadcasting Corporation's (SABC) music department in Johannesburg. He remained with the SABC until 1967, successively acting as music adviser, manager of music planning, acting head of music and finally head of music, from 1964 to 1966. He occasionally conducted the National Symphony Orchestra of the SABC and the city orchestras of Cape Town and Durban. He ensured that South African music received a hearing and during his term of office, the first South African radio opera was broadcast, 'The Coming of the Butterflies', by Stephen O'Reilly.

After his retirement from the SABC, Fagan taught conducting, orchestration and composition at the South African College of Music in Cape Town from 1967 to 1972. He then settled at Betty's Bay in the Cape to concentrate on his own compositions.

Additional Readings

Brook, Donald. *Conductors' Gallery: Biographical Sketches of Well-Known Orchestral Conductors*, 2nd ed. London: Rockliff, 1946, pp. 51–54.

FAHEY, BRIAN (b. 1919)

Brian Fahey was born in Margate, Kent. He learned piano and cello as a child and became interested in arranging, composition, big band music and jazz.

After demobilization from the army in 1946, he joined the band of Rudy Starita as pianist for an ENSA tour of Egypt and Palestine. He subsequently played in other bands and joined CHAPPELL Music Publisher, as an arranger (1949–54). He also worked for Cinephonic Music (1954–59). He specialized in arranging for bands such as AMBROSE, STANLEY BLACK, GERALDO, Ted Heath, Harry Roy, CYRIL STAPLETON, as well as various BBC bands and orchestras. He was responsible for many of the arrangements for the Starlight Symphony Orchestra, conducted by CYRIL ORNADEL.

After leaving the music publishers, Fahey worked on a freelance basis for record companies such as EMI and the BBC, with occasional ventures into theatre and film. He arranged and conducted many recording sessions for artists including Russ Conway, Gracie Fields, Connie Francis, Kathy Kay, Vera Lynn, Johnny Mathis, Shirley Bassey, Harry Secombe, and Andy Stewart. He toured the world with Shirley Bassey as her musical director.

From 1972 to 1981, Fahey was appointed musical director of the newly formed Scottish Radio Orchestra, based in Glasgow, which played exclusively for BBC radio and television shows. The orchestra accompanied many singers and artists including Moira Anderson, Sheila Buxton, Andy Cameron, Jimmy Logan, Lena Martell, Chic Murray, Julie Rogers, David Ward, Roger Whittaker and Lena Zavaroni.

After the disbandment of the Scottish Radio Orchestra, Fahey conducted many sessions of the BBC Radio Orchestra and the BBC Big Band. In 1981, he conducted an orchestra of seventy-five musicians for a concert with Ella Fitzgerald. He also conducted at the San Remo Song Festival, the Rio de Janeiro Song Festival and at Midem.

In retirement, he spent his time composing for a variety of combinations including orchestra, brass band, string orchestra, choir, big band and jazz ensembles. As an arranger, he attempted to combine the disciplines of orchestral and Big Band/jazz writing.

His best-known compositions include many theme tunes such as 'The Creep', which he wrote for the Ken Mackintosh Band; 'Fanfare Boogie' written for the Eric Winstone Band and which won an IVOR NOVELLO Award in 1955; 'At the Sign of the Swingin' Cymbal', which was adopted by Alan Freeman for his *Pick of the Pops* program. In 1991, Fahey was awarded the BASCA Gold Badge of Merit.

Select Discography

For the One I Love (The September Strings). Orchestrations and Musical Direction by Brian Fahey. Major Minor Records SMCP 5007 [Also on CD]

Stereo Explosion EMI Starline (U.K.) SRS 5072

FAITH, PERCY (7 April 1908–9 February 1976)

Percy Faith was born in Toronto. He began studying violin at the age of seven and changed his basic instrument to piano three years later. He pursued his piano studies at the Toronto Conservatory of Music and the Canadian Academy of Music. He made his debut as a concert pianist at the age of fifteen at Massey Hall, Toronto. He also varied his experience by playing in local movie houses and with dance bands.

When he was eighteen, his career as a concert pianist was disrupted by an accident to his hands. He turned to an intensive study of harmony and composition and within four years was scoring for orchestras and dance bands in the Toronto area and conducting on radio programs. During this period he developed the rich orchestral sound that became his trademark.

Percy Faith

His speciality was melody with various counterpoints, which was to later distinguish him as one of the best composers of background music for vocalists. Pop music critics noted that Faith had the ability to raise popular music to the level of symphonic playing.

By 1931, he was conducting a small string group on the air. This led to a position as staff conductor and arranger for the Canadian Broadcasting Company in 1934 as arranger and conductor. In 1937, the program *Music by Faith* was first aired and became popular throughout North America and Hawaii via the Canadian Network and the Mutual Broadcasting Company. He was also featured in a program called *Gaiety in Romance.*

In 1940, he migrated to the United States and took over the *Carnation Program*, broadcast from Chicago and subsequently the Coca-Cola program, *The Pause That Refreshes on the Air* in 1947. In 1950 he was appointed musical director of the Popular Division of Columbia Records. Along with Mitch Miller, he worked with stars such as Tony Bennett, Rosemary Clooney, Jerry Vale, Guy Mitchell and Johnny Mathis. His arrangements of 'Because of You', 'Cold, Cold Heart', and 'Rags to Riches', helped Tony Bennett win three gold records for sales topping the million mark. Faith's own song 'My Heart Cries for You', sung by Guy Mitchell, was another gold winner. In 1955, he took over *The Woolworth Hour* for CBS and produced two of the best-selling hits of all time, 'The Song from *Moulin Rouge*' and 'Theme from a Summer Place'. That same year, his first motion picture, MGM's *Love Me or Leave Me*, brought him an Academy Award nomination.

Faith has been among the pioneers of those who attempt to use the voice as an orchestral instrument. His 'Magic Voices' were used not to sing lyrics or carry the melody, but to add a new texture of sound.

With the advent of stereo, Faith won further awards; RIAA Gold Awards for the albums *Viva! (The Music of Mexico)*, *Bouquet* and *Themes for Young Lovers*. He traveled widely as a concert hall conductor in countries such as Japan, Italy, Monaco and England, where he performed with the BBC Orchestra.

His scores for motion pictures include *The Oscar, The Third Day, The Love Goddesses, I'd Rather Be Rich, Tammy, Tell Me True*, and *Love Me or Leave Me*. Among his television shows was the theme heard weekly on NBC's *The Virginian*.

In the mid-1990s there has been a renewed interest in Faith's work, particularly in Japan, where many of his albums have been reissued. New performances of his arrangements have been conducted by Nick Perito for a series of CDs.

The Percy Faith Society was established in January 1991 by Bill Halvorsen (chairman) and Reuben Musiker (secretary) in order to promote and revive interest in Percy Faith's music among the post-1976 generation of music lovers. During the four years of the society's existence (1991–95), Bill Halvorsen produced sixteen issues of a very informative newsletter, which focused on Faith and his music, some 250 pages in all. (This publication is available from the authors of this book). After the disbandment of the Percy Faith Society, the members joined forces with the Robert Farnon Society in their shared ideal of keeping popular orchestral music alive. The *Journal into Melody* continues to publish articles about Percy Faith and his music.

Musical Achievements

Faith's music is characterized by an amazing versatility. His arrangements range from lively Latin-American tunes and lilting continental music to sumptuous mood music and orchestral settings of the music from Broadway shows.

Tracing the development of Percy Faith's music, one is aware of a definite pattern. In the late 1950s and early 1960s, almost everything Faith recorded was vintage popular orchestral music of the highest caliber. Those were the days of unique Faith arrangements and a choice of repertoire free of commercialization and totally immune from the devastating influence of pop and rock sounds which were to come later. *Disco, Clair, New Thing, Angel of the Morning* and *Day by Day* were examples of the later period.

Faith had an intensely personal involvement in all his work. The record sleeves may credit a producer, but Faith himself watched over the selection of the tunes and wrote his own arrangements. Faith himself remarked toward the end of his career that he was afraid of running out of music with the market as it stood at that period. In twenty-five years of successful recording, with over eighty albums, he felt that it was rare still to be around. There were actually more recordings, if one included the very early LPs (Decca, RCA, Royale), the numerous LPs Faith shared with other orchestras (e.g., *Front Row Center, Late Night Music)* and the arrangements and backings Faith made for vocal artists such as Guy Mitchell, Tony Bennett, Rosemary Clooney and Johnny Mathis.

Select List of Musical Compositions

'Caribbean Night', 'Carmelita', 'Brazilian Sleigh Bells', 'Tropic Holiday'. Also responsible for the adaptation of 'The Song from *Moulin Rouge*' and 'Swedish Rhapsody'.

Select Discography (All Columbia, unless otherwise stated)

Academy Award Winner (Born Free) CL 2650/CS 9450

Academy Award Winner (Windmills of Your Mind) CS 9835

Adventure in the Sun CL 1010

American Serenade CL 1957/CS 8757

American Waltzes CL 6178

Amor, Amor, Amor CL 643

Angel of the Morning CS 9706

Beatles Album C 30097

Bim! Bam! Boom! CL 2529/CS 9329

Black Magic Woman CQ 30800/C 30800

Bon Voyage CL 1417/CS 8214

Bouquet! CL 1322/CS 8124

Bouquet of Love CL 1681/CS 8481

Broadway Bouquet CL 2356/CS 9156

Carefree CL 1560/CS 8360 [Also on CD]

Carefree Rhythms CL 6242

Carnival Rhythms CL 6214

Chinatown CQ 33224/KC 33244

Christmas Is . . . CL 2577/CS 9377

Clair CQ 32164/ KC 32164
Columbia Album of George Gershwin (2 LPs) C2L 1 [Also on CD]
Columbia Album of Victor Herbert (2 LPs) C2L 10/C2S 801 [Also on CD]
Continental Music CL 525
Corazon KC 32714
Country Bouquet KC 33142
Day by Day CQ 31627/KC 31627
Delicado CL 681
Disco Party KC 33549
Exotic Strings CL 1902/CS 8702
Fascinating Rhythms CL 6203
Fiesta Time DLP 5025 Decca
Football Songs CL 6148
For Those in Love CL 2810/CS 9610
Great Folk Themes CL 2108/CS 8908
Greatest Hits CL 1493/CS 8637
Hallelujah CL 1187/CS 8033
Hattori Melodies Soll30 (CBS-SONY)
Held Over! Great Movie Themes CS 1019
Hollywood's Great Themes CL 1783, CS 8583
It's So Peaceful in the Country CL 779 [Also on CD]
Jealousy CL 1501/CS 8292
Joanne Sings CL 6333
Joy CQ 31301/ C 31301
Jubilation CL 1188
Latin Themes for Young Lovers CL 2279/CS 9079
Leaving on a Jet Plane CS 9983
Look at Monaco CL 2019/CS 8819
Love Goddesses CL 2209/CS 9009
Love Story C 30502
Love Theme from Romeo and Juliet CS 9906
Malagueña CL 1267/CS 8081
More Themes for Young Lovers CL 2167/CS 8967
Mucho Gusto CL 1639/CS 8439
Music from The Most Happy Fella CL 905
Music for Her CL 705 [Also on CD]
Music from Camelot CL 1570/CS 8370

Music from Do I Hear a Waltz? CL 2317/CS 9117
Music from Hollywood CL 577 (12"), CL 6255 (10") [Also on CD]
Music from House of Flowers CL 640
Music from Jesus Christ, Superstar C 31042
Music from Kismet L6275
Music from Lil' Abner CL 955
Music from My Fair Lady CL 895 [Also on CD]
Music from Porgy and Bess CL 1298/CS 8105
Music from South Pacific CL 1105/ CS 8005
Music from Subways Are for Sleeping CL 1733/CS 8533
Music from The Most Happy Fella CL 905
Music from The Sound of Music CL 1418/CS 8215
Music of Brazil CL 1822/CS 8622
Music of Christmas (1954) CL 588
Music of Christmas CL 1381/CS 8176
Music Until Midnight CL 551
My Love CQ 32380/KC 32380
New Thing CQ 32803/KC 32803
Oscar OS 2950
Passport to Romance CL 880
Percy Faith in Concert SOPN 70 (CBS-Sony)
Program Decca DL 5439
Romantic Music CL 526
Shangri-La! CL 2024/CS 8824
Soft Lights and Sweet Music RCA LPM 1010
Summer Place '76 KC 33915
Swing Low in Hi-Fi CL 796
Tara's Theme from Gone With the Wind CL 1627/CS 8427
Themes for the 'In' Crowd CL 2441/CS 9241
Themes for Young Lovers CL 2033/CS 8823
Those Were the Days CS 9762
Today's Themes for Young Lovers CL 2704/CS 9504
Touchdown! CL 1182
Your Dance Date CL 6131
VIVA! CL 1075/CS 8038 442/CS 92451

Compact Discs

All-time Greatest Hits Sony 31588

Christmas Is Sony 9377

Columbia Album of George Gershwin Sony AK 47863. Also released as **George Gershwin** Sony AK 47863 2 CDs

Exotic Strings Columbia 471081–2

Fascination Sony 15898

Greatest Hits Sony CK 8637

Hello, Dolly JVC VICP-208

Instrumental Favorites Time-Life A 25065, R 986–02

Latin Hit Sounds Sony SMP 3189–2

Latin Rhythms RANWOOD 1013–2

Latin Themes for Young Lovers Columbia CK 9079

Malagueña JVC VICP-5472

Music from the Movies Columbia 475670.2 (Australia)

Music of Christmas SONY 38302

Orchestra by Candlelight Columbia 3641 (South Africa)

Orqestras Spectaculares CBS 464010 (Brazil)

Percy Faith Treasury Good Music Co. A2 25270/138727 (2 discs)

Plays Richard Rodgers Sony A 23232

16 Most Requested Songs Columbia CK 44398

Songs From Award-winning Movies RANWOOD 1016–2

16 Most Requested Songs SONY 44398

Theme from A Summer Place JVC VICP-5337

Theme from A Summer Place RANWOOD 1011–2

Themes For Young Lovers Sony 8823

Vintage Years Columbia 478036–2 (Australia)

Note: A comprehensive Percy Faith discography has been compiled by Alan Bunting (28 Pelstream Avenue, Stirling FKY OBE, Scotland, Great Britain) and is available from him. A discography of Percy Faith singles (45 and 78 rpm records) is available from the compiler, Robert Whitby, 421 Celeste Street, Everman, Texas 76140, U.S.A.

FARNON, ROBERT (b. 24 July 1917)

Farnon was born in Toronto, Ontario. At the age of eleven, he performed with the Toronto Juvenile Symphony Orchestra and could play several instruments by the age of fourteen.

In 1932, he joined the Canadian Broadcasting Corporation orchestra and did most of the choral arrangements for PERCY FAITH, who at that time

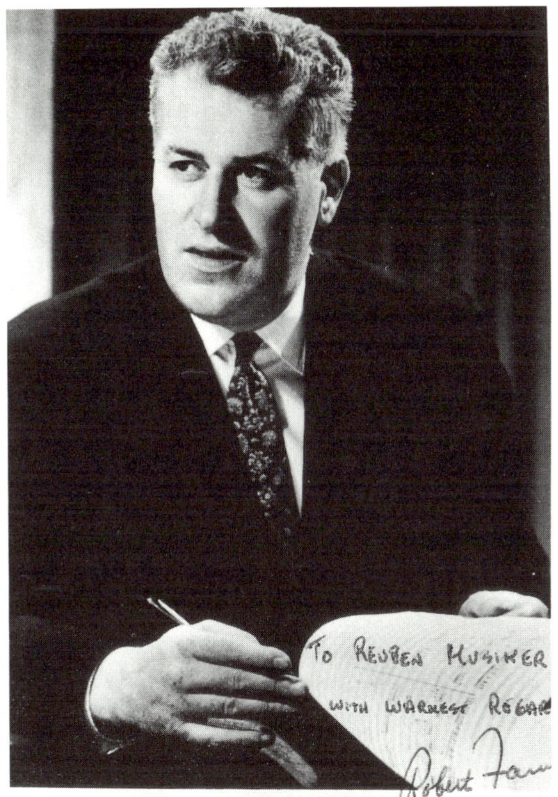
To Reuben Musiker
with warmest

Robert Farnon (used with permission)

was its director. In 1936, he worked on the *Happy Gang* radio show and wrote his *Symphony No. 1*, performed by Eugene Ormandy and the Philadelphia Orchestra. At the start of World War II, he enlisted in the Canadian army and was sent to Europe with the Canadian Band of the American Expeditionary Force. He stayed on in Britain after the war and worked as an arranger for band leaders, GERALDO and Ted Heath. He formed his own orchestra, which played regularly on the BBC, and he recorded for Decca. He wrote for CHAPPELL's Recorded Music Library and composed for films such as *I Live in Grosvenor Square* (1946), *Spring in Park Lane* (1948), *Maytime in Mayfair* (1949), *Lilacs in the Spring* (1949), *Elizabeth of Ladymead* (1950), *Paper Orchid* (1950), *Circle of Danger* (1951) and *Captain Horatio Hornblower RN* (1951).

In 1962, Farnon arranged and conducted for Frank Sinatra's *Great Songs from Britain*, the first album Sinatra recorded in the United Kingdom. In October 1971, he arranged and conducted Tony Bennett's Carnegie Hall concerts.

Farnon continued working in television, composing several television themes for top-rated programs such as *Panorama, Armchair Theatre, Colditz, The Secret Army* and *Kessler*. He made occasional radio broadcasts and assembled orchestras for special concerts and recording dates. By the end of the 1980s, he was living in semiretirement.

Farnon composed highly regarded light music, which included the following titles: 'Lake of the Woods', 'Canadian Caravan' (1944); 'Journey into Melody', 'Pictures in the Fire', 'A Star Is Born' (1947); 'How Beautiful Is Night', 'Jumping Bean' (1948); 'Portrait of a Flirt' (1949); 'Manhattan Playboy' (1950); 'Peanut Polka' (1951); 'Derby Day', 'White Heather' (1951); 'Hall of Fame' (1952); 'State Occasion' (1953); 'Melody Fair', 'Poodle Parade' (1954); 'A la Clair Fontaine' (1955); 'Westminster Waltz' (Ivor Novello Award, 1956); 'Piano Playtime' (1957); 'Little Miss Molly' (1959); 'On the Seashore' (1961); 'Portrait of Lorraine' (1965); 'Winter Jasmine' (1968) and 'Colditz March' (1972). The latter composition was used by the BBC in its television series called *Colditz* and won Farnon an IVOR NOVELLO Award.

His 'Three Impressions for Orchestra' were brought together by Chappell's library in 1952 and consist of 'High Street', 'In a Calm' and 'Manhattan Playboy'. 'Gateway to the West', included in a suite of tone poems in 1983, is a tribute to Winnipeg and was used as the introductory theme for CBC's shortwave transmissions from Canada.

His first and second symphonies and other serious compositions, several of them written for jazz musicians, gained him little recognition. Farnon is regarded primarily as one of the world's best light music arrangers, particularly in his use of strings and woodwinds.

Robert Farnon Society

The Robert Farnon Society was founded in 1956 and has been consistently active for forty years, continually growing in momentum, so that it is now one of the leading light music societies of its kind. The society has published 128 issues of its *Journal into Melody*. This publication is an excellent and effective source of articles (biographies, tributes, profiles, obituaries and discographies) about the world's leading musicians in the light classical, light, popular and jazz fields. The main emphasis of the journal is on the life and work of Robert Farnon, including his compositions, concerts, recording sessions and recorded music.

A notable feature of the Robert Farnon Society has been the fact that it has been a living society that did not depend entirely on the *Journal into Melody* for bonding its members. It also engaged in a variety of other activities such as musical and social meetings and the operation of a record and compact disc supply service. The membership of the society is drawn from all corners of the globe.

David Ades has been the society's anchor and its secretary/treasurer and magazine editor for many years. The society's address is Stone Gables, Upton Lane, Seavington St Michael, Ilminster, Somerset TA19OPZ, England.

Select Discography

Bennett-Sinatra 41048

By a Waterfall B 20006

Canadian Impressions London LL1267

Captain from Castile Philips 600–098 [Also on CD]

Cocktails for Two B 20005

Concert (10") LPB 126

Concert Music Reference 1992

Concert Works Reference 47

Dreaming Peerless DT007

Flirtation Walk London LL 1053 [Also on CD]

From the Emerald Isle LKM 4267

From the Highlands London LL 3007

Gateway to the West MGM E/SE 3804 (Also issued under the title: **Portrait of the West** Longines Symphonette LW 156 B)

Hits of Sinatra Philips 600–179

In a Dream World 15–10

Journey into Melody Decca

Melody Fair London LL 1280

Music of Vincent Youmans Decca [Also on CD]

My Fair Lady Philips 600–157

Pictures in the Fire London LL 1667

Porgy and Bess SPC 21013

Portrait of Farnon ECS 2107

Portrait of Johnny Mathis Philips 600–167

Portrait of the West SE 4107

Presenting Robert Farnon LL 812

Robert Farnon and Leroy Anderson Encores Philips

Robert Farnon Concert Decca

Schertzinger/Carmichael Suites LL 623 [Also on CD]

Sensuous Strings Philips 200–038

Shalako Philips 600–286

Showcase for Soloists Invicta INV 105

Something to Remember You By London LL 1231

Songs of Britain Decca

Stardust B 20002

Stephen Foster Melodies Decca

Sunny Side Up London LL 1435

Two Cigarettes in the Dark Eclipse ECS 2053, London LL 1052

Compact Discs

At the Movies Horatio Nelson Records CD SIV 6111

BBC Radio Classics (With BBC Northern Symphony Orchestra) BBCRD 9115

British Light Music Marco Polo 1992

Concert Works (With Royal Philharmonic Orchestra) Reference Recordings 47

Melody Fair TC PLE 526

Music of Robert Farnon Conifer 75605522692 [2 CDs]

More Famous Themes Chappell CHAP 2d

Porgy and Bess Suite (With London Festival Orchestra) Decca/London 425508-2

Note: A comprehensive discography of Robert Farnon has been published by the Robert Farnon Society.

FARRAN, MERRICK

Merrick Farran was of Irish-Italian descent and was a pupil of E. J. Muran, the well-known Irish composer. He was educated at Stonyhurst College and won a scholarship for composition and violin at Manchester Royal College of Music. He toured the United States with Sir Thomas Beecham and the Royal Philharmonic Orchestra. He wrote music for several British films and for the BBC. He conducted both classical and popular and light music.

Select Discography

The Last Time I Saw Paris: A Jerome Kern Concert (with the London Pops Orchestra) Regent MG 6059

FENNELL, FREDERICK (b. 2 July 1914)

Frederick Fennell was born into a musical family. He learned to play the drums at the age of six. He pursued a career as a percussionist until his graduation from high school in 1933. His ambition was to become a conductor, and he spent his high school vacations at National Music Camp in Interlochen, Michigan, where he studied conducting with Vladimir Bakalienekoff and Albert Austin Harding. Dr. Harding gave Fennell his first opportunity when he invited him to conduct the National High School Band at the 1933 World's Fair Exposition in Chicago.

After graduation from high school, Fennell was awarded a scholarship at the Eastman School of Music in Rochester, New York. In his first year at the school, he organized a marching band at the University of Rochester during the football season. He also organized the first symphonic band at the school, The Eastman School Symphony Band, which won popularity throughout America. In June 1937, Fennell received a bachelor of music degree from the Eastman School and in 1938 was awarded the International Fellowship in Conducting by the Institute of International Education. He completed a year of study in Salzburg under Herbert Albert. He returned to the school to complete his master's degree and became a member of the Eastman conducting faculty.

During the next few years, Fennell gave concerts for NBC and CBS broadcasts and served as guest conductor of the BOSTON POPS ORCHESTRA, the Houston Symphony, the Carnegie Hall Pops Orchestra and the Philadelphia Symphony Orchestra. He studied privately under Serge Koussevitzky at the Berkshire Music Center in 1942.

During World War II Fennell served as National USO Music Advisor, organizing orchestras and chamber music ensembles. After the war ended, Fennell was finally given the opportunity to create the Eastman Symphonic Wind Ensemble.

In 1962, he joined the Minneapolis Symphony Orchestra as associate conductor to Stanislaw Skrowaczewski. In 1965, he joined the University of Miami Symphony Orchestra as conductor and organized a companion group, the Symphonic Wind Ensemble. He became chairman of the Department of Applied Music at the University of Miami.

Select Discography

Broadway Marches Mercury SR 90390

Conducts Cole Porter Mercury PPS 6024/SRI 75110

Conducts Gershwin Mercury PPS 6006

Conducts Victor Herbert Mercury PPS 2007/6007

Hi-Fi à La Española and Popovers Polygram 34349

Malagueña and Other Favorites Mercury SRI 75097

Music of Eric Coates Mercury SR 90439

Music of Leroy Anderson (with Eastman-Rochester Pops Orchestra) Mercury SRI 75013

Music of Leroy Anderson Vol. 1 Mercury SR 90009

Music of Leroy Anderson Vol. 2 Mercury SR 90043

Popovers Mercury SR 90222

Sousa on Review Mercury ST 90284

Compact Discs

Conducts Carousel Waltz and Other Orchestral Favorites Polygram 34356

Conducts Leroy Anderson (With Eastman Rochester Pops Orchestra) Polygram 32013

Conducts Leroy Anderson and Eric Coates (With Eastman Rochester Pops Orchestra) Polygram 34376

Conducts Porter and Gershwin Polygram 3427

Country Gardens Polygram 34330

Fennell Favorites Reference Recordings 43

FENTON, GEORGE (b. 19 October 1950)

George Fenton was born in London and began his career as a guitarist; he turned to full-time composing after 1975. His main field of activity was in film, television and theater composition, although he wrote several concert works, including *Birthday*, a children's opera. His television credits include *Bergerac, Shoestring, The Monocled Mutineer*, *The History Man, Life in the Freezer*, and *Beyond the Clouds*. He also composed the signature tunes for the BBC's *Nine O'Clock News, The Money Programme, Newsnight* and *Telly Addicts*. The following film scores have received Academy Award nominations: *Gandhi* (1982), *Cry Freedom* (1987), *Dangerous Liaisons* (1988), *Memphis Belle* (1990), *Final Analysis* (1991) and *The Fisher King* (1991). His most recent scores were for *Shadowlands* (1993) and *The Madness of King George* (1994).

Select Discography

Company of Wolves (George Fenton conducting) TER CDTER1094

Madness of King George Epic 478477–2

Shadowlands EMI Angel CDQ5 55093–2

FIEDLER, ARTHUR (17 December 1894–10 July 1979)

Arthur Fiedler was born in Boston and studied at the Royal Academy of Music, Berlin. In 1915, he was appointed violinist of the Boston Symphony Orchestra. From 1929 onward, he served as conductor of the BOSTON POPS ORCHESTRA, a position he held for over thirty years. Fiedler sold around five million albums and ten million singles discs. One of his most famous recordings was the tango 'Jalousie' (Jealousy), composed by Jacob Gade and released by Victor in 1938.

Additional Readings

Dickson, Harry Ellis. *Arthur Fiedler and the Boston Pops: An Irreverent Memoir.* Boston: Houghton, 1981.

Select Discography

All the Things You Are RCA LSC 2906

Fiddle-Faddle RCA LSS 2638

Frank Loesser RCA LSC 2486

Getting Friendly With Music (2) RCA LM-1995
Greatest Hits of the 20's RCA ARL/ARS 1–0041
Greatest Hits of the 30's RCA ARL/ARS 1–0042
Greatest Hits of the 40's RCA ARL/ARS 1–0043
Greatest Hits of the 50's RCA ARL/ARS 1–0044
Greatest Hits of the 60's RCA ARL/ARS 1–0045
Greatest Hits of the 70's RCA ARL/ARS 1–0035
I Got Rhythm: Fiedler Conducts Gershwin RCA SPC 21185
Love Is a Many Splendored Thing RCA LSC 3223
More Music from Million Dollar Movies RCA LSC 2782
Music for a Summer Night LM-1910
Music from Million Dollar Movies RCA LSC-2380
Nutcracker Suite, Op. 71 RCA LSC-2052
Operetta Time-Life STLS 7020
Our Man in Boston RCA LM/LSC 2599
Pops Parade RCA LSC-3023
Pops Stoppers RCA LM-2270
Reverie RCA S 3248
Slaughter on 10th Avenue RCA LM-1726
Star Dust RCA LSC 2670
Tenderly RCA LSC 2798
Up, Up and Away RCA LCS 3041
Yesterday RCA LSC 3222

Compact Discs

American Salute BMG/RCA 6806–2-RG
Christmas at the Pops BMG/RCA 68266
Christmas Festival BMG/RCA 6428
Concert in the Park BMG/RCA 9359
Familiar Music for Family Fun BMG/RCA 5383
Fiedler Collection BMG/RCA 68011
Fiedler Favorites BMG/RCA 62698, Pro Arte Maxiplay 8012
Fiedler's Greatest Hits RCA Victor 3383
Fiedler on the Roof BMG/RCA 3201
Greatest Hits BMG/RCA 60835
Greatest Hits [of the] 50's BMG/RCA 508
Greatest Hits [of the] 60's BMG/RCA 45
Greatest U.S. Marches RCA 1334

Hi-Fi Fiedler BMG/RCA 61497

Irish Night at the Pops BMG/RCA 60746

Leroy Anderson's Greatest Hits BMG/RCA 61237

Lollypops BMG/RCA 4623

Lullaby BMG/RCA 60876

More Motion Picture Classics BMG/RCA 9541

Motion Picture Classics BMG/RCA 5690

Peace, Love and Pops: Greatest Hits Polygram 47891

Pops Christmas Party BMG 0902661685 2

Pops Around the World BMG/RCA 61544

Pops Caviar BMG/RCA 68132

Pops Concert BMG/RCA 6213

Pops Goes West BMG/RCA 5695

Pops Roundup BMG/RCA 61666

Popular Favorites Pair 1022

FOX, JOHN

John Fox is a British conductor and arranger. He studied at the Royal College of Music, where he won a composition scholarship and made his first broadcast in the 1950s. He was featured in the Radio Two network, arranging and conducting for the BBC Radio Orchestra, with emphasis on strings. These programs could be heard in Britain, Europe, the United States and Japan. He also produced many record albums and compact discs and appeared in live performances.

His first album commemorated the seventy-fifth birthday of GEORGE GERSHWIN and proved popular worldwide. The album *Here, There and Everywhere* was the second in the series on which producer John Fox and Chris Morgan of the BBC Radio 2 collaborated and was produced in 1974.

In the 1990s, he conducted concerts in Europe, using his own compositions and arrangements. The Cologne concert was particularly memorable.

He has written scores for films and television and has composed many large-scale works in different styles. He enjoys writing for voices. The John Fox Singers are used in some of his arrangements to add color to the orchestral texture. He is particularly fond of arranging his singers in a cappella style. His wife, the singer Joy Devon, produces albums with Fox and runs their music publishing company.

He is much involved in writing production (mood) music, where his compositions are used in television, films, radio and commercials. In 1994 he won a Stemra Music Award for the best film music in Holland. In 1993 he recorded in Budapest a vast amount of original symphonic music. The subjects were 'Seascapes' and 'Family Affairs', derived from American television film series. In 1994, Fox's 'Earth and Space' suite for orchestra and choir was performed at Huntingdon.

Select Discography

George Gershwin BBC Records REB 156 (Reissued under title: **Gershwin's Greatest Hits** BBC Records REC 32)

Here, There and Everywhere BBC Records REB 168

Compact Discs

Love Is A Many-splendored Thing. Starry Night Orchestra conducted by John Fox. Realm Records ICD 8205

All My Best John Sbarra

FRANKEL, BENJAMIN (1906–1973)
Benjamin Frankel was born in London and became a performer on piano and violin. In his late teens, he studied piano and composition at the Guildhall School of Music, London, and also played in night clubs as a jazz violinist. He began to orchestrate West End musical comedies and revues, including NOËL COWARD'S *Operette* and various C. B. Cochrane shows. From 1934 onward, he produced film scores, which included the *Curse of the Werewolf* and *The Importance of Being Earnest*. His music for the cinema is used with discretion and matches the mood and timing of the action so as not to be heard consciously. Occasionally certain episodes lend themselves to theme tunes, as in the 1950 film *So Long at the Fair*, from which Frankel produced the concert version of *Carriage and Pair*. In his mid-forties, he also produced numerous chamber and orchestral works, including eight symphonies.

FRIEDHOFER, HUGO (3 May 1902–17 May 1981)
Hugo Friedhofer was born in San Francisco, California. He began studying the cello at the age of thirteen, encouraged by his father, who was also a cellist. By 1925, he was playing the cello for silent movie theaters. He subsequently began studying and doing arrangements for the theater orchestra. In July 1929, he arrived in Hollywood to write the arrangements for *Sunny Side Up*. He worked for Fox for five years, arranging and orchestrating.

In 1936, he moved to Warner Brothers and orchestrated scores for the next eleven years, including the scores of MAX STEINER, ERICH WOLFGANG KORNGOLD and ALFRED NEWMAN. The only complete score he composed during this period was *The Adventures of Marco Polo* (1937).

In 1943, he accepted a contract from Alfred Newman to compose for Fox. His 1946 score for *The Best Years of Our Lives* was considered a landmark in the history of film music. He attributed much of his success to the influence of AARON COPLAND. Other scores include *Body and Soul* (1947), *A Song Is Born* (1948), *Joan of Arc* (1948), *Vera Cruz* (1954), *The Rains of Ranchipur* (1955), *Boy on a Dolphin* (1957), *The Young Lions* (1958), *One-eyed Jacks* (1960). He also composed the incidental music for several scenes in the film *An Affair to Remember* (1957). His last two scores were *Private Parts* (1972) and *Die, Sister, Die* in 1978.

Select Discography

Boy on a Dolphin (Conducted by Lionel Newman) MCA 7136

In Love and War (Conducted by Fritz Steiner) Entr'acte ERS 6506

Private Parts Delos DEL/F-25420

The Sun Also Rises (Conducted by Charles Gerhardt) RCA ARL1–0912

Compact Discs

An Affair to Remember (20th Century Fox Orchestra, Conductor Lionel Newman) Epic EK57568

Best Years of Our Lives (London Philharmonic Orchestra, Conductor Franco Collura) PRCD 1779

The Young Lions Varese Sarabande VSD2–5402/3

FRIML, RUDOLF (7 December 1879–12 November 1972)

Rudolf Friml was born in Prague, the son of a baker whose hobby was music. Friml showed great promise as a child and at the age of ten had a 'Barcarolle' for piano published. He was sent to the Prague Conservatory and at one time studied composition under Antonin Dvorak. Thereafter, he was engaged as an accompanist to the violin virtuoso, Jan Kubelik, touring the world for a decade with him. Friml emigrated to the United States in 1906 and from then onward proceeded to build up his career as a pianist and composer, playing his own piano concerts with the New York Symphony Orchestra.

Friml's debut as a composer for the musical theater came in 1912 when he wrote the score for the operetta *The Firefly*, which was acclaimed as one of the freshest and most charming scores to appear for some time. It was made into a film in 1937, when Friml added the song 'Donkey Serenade' to the score. The first jazz arrangement of 'Donkey Serenade' was played in a Paul Whiteman concert of 1924, which was notable in that it also featured the first performance of GEORGE GERSHWIN'S 'Rhapsody in Blue'.

Alongside other illustrious immigrants from Europe such as VICTOR HERBERT and SIGMUND ROMBERG, Friml helped establish a Viennese-style operetta and musical comedy, which were enormously popular in the United States and elsewhere. Friml's two greatest successes were *Rose-Marie* (1924) and *The Vagabond King* (1925). His last real stage success was *The*

Three Musketeers in 1928. He was never able to adapt to the new styles which started to dominate American musical theater after this period.

In the 1930s, he composed music for Hollywood films such as *Lottery Bride* (1930), *Music for Madame* (1937) and later still, *Northwest Outpost* (1947). He also wrote a considerable number of piano pieces in a light drawing-room style. However, even these became outmoded in the 1930s. In his most productive period, between 1913 and 1934, he composed the stage scores for no less than twenty musical shows. Friml died in Los Angeles at the age of 92.

Additional Readings

Traubner, Richard. *Operetta: a Theatrical History*. London: Victor Gollancz, 1984. pp. 378–384.

Ewen, David. *American Songwriters*. New York: H. W. Wilson, 1987. pp. 170–72.

Select Discography

Friml, Rudolf. **Friml Presents Friml.** Westminster WP 60609 [Reissued in stereo under the title: **Nostalgia** Westminster WCC 8157.]

Mantovani. **Music of Rudolf Friml (with music of Irving Berlin)** London PS 166 (USA)

Mantovani. **Music of Rudolf Friml** Decca LK 4096 (Britain)

Martinelli, Dino. **Treasury of Rudolf Friml** Harmony OK 5051

G

GERALDO **(born Gerald Bright)** (10 August 1904–4 May 1974)
Geraldo was a British bandleader who started his career at the Hotel Majestic at St. Anne's, Lancashire. He directed various orchestras in England and Europe before appearing at the Savoy Hotel in London, billed as Geraldo and his Gaucho Tango Orchestra. He eventually had two dance bands at the Savoy and became one of the most popular dance leaders of the 1930s. During World War II the band entertained the troops and after the war modernized its style, finally breaking up in the 1960s. Two well-known singers who appeared with Geraldo were Al Bowlly and Eve Boswell.

Certain of the LPs made by Geraldo appear in this discography, because of the lush string arrangements. This applies particularly to those made with the Living Strings.

Select Discography

Note: All RCA Camden LPs featured the Living Strings.

Alice's Restaurant RCA Camden CAS 2395

Marie and Other Songs Made Famous by Tommy Dorsey RCA Camden CAL/CAS 962

Plays Bert Kaempfert RCA Camden INTS 2059 (UK)

Popi and Other Cinema Gems RCA Camden CAS 2234

Songs of Charlie Pride RCA Camden CAS 2427

Sound of Music RCA Camden CXS 9017

Summer of '42 RCA Camden CXS 9022

Theme from Love Story RCA Camden CAS 2477

The World We Knew RCA Camden CAS 2190

GERSHENSON, JOSEPH (b. 1904)

Joseph Gershenson began his musical career as a violinist in a pit orchestra. He accompanied silent films in the 1920s. He conducted an orchestra for the first time in 1922, in a Broadway musical. After gaining experience leading the orchestra at the famous Palace on Broadway, he was appointed assistant musical director of the RKO Theatre Circuit, assuming responsibility for orchestras all over the United States and Canada.

Following a period of employment as independent producer and associate producer at Universal-International Studios, Gershenson joined that studio's music department, which he headed from 1950 onward.

A composer as well as a conductor, he arranged and directed music for some of the screen's greatest films such as *The Glenn Miller Story*, *Written on the Wind* and *Four Girls in Town*. He realized that using an established song title would help promote the popularity of his films. He therefore entered into contracts with music publishers, and hit song titles such as *She's Nobody's Sweetheart Now*, *Margie* and *Where'd You Get That Girl?* became film titles.

Select Discography

Four Girls in Town Brunswick LAT 8174

Glenn Miller Story Brunswick LA 8647

You and I and the Music Brunswick Records LAT 8196

GERSHWIN, GEORGE (26 September 1898–11 July 1937)

George Gershwin was born in Brooklyn, New York. He was a prolific composer for Broadway and Hollywood musicals, collaborating with his brother, Ira, who provided lyrics. He also composed a successful opera and concert works. His music in all genres was unusual for his time because of its sophisticated use of harmonic and rhythmic devices drawn from jazz and the blues.

He became interested in music at the age of ten and taught himself the elements of harmony, putting together tunes in imitation of the popular songs of the day. At the age of twelve he began formal piano lessons. One of his early tutors was Charles Hambitzer. He commenced his career as a pianist at entertainment resorts and later as a staff pianist and song plugger for the Tin Pan Alley publisher Jerome H. Remick. He was hired as a staff composer by the publishing house of T. B. Harms in 1918, in which year he composed his first song, 'The Real American Folk Song', with lyrics by his brother Ira. Gershwin's first complete Broadway score was for the show

La, La Lucille in 1919. His first real hit was 'Swanee', published in 1919 and popularized by the singer Al Jolson in 1920.

Other songs between 1920 and 1925 included 'I'll Build a Stairway to Paradise' (1922), 'Somebody Loves Me' (1924) and 'Do It Again'. He was only twenty-five years old when his most famous composition, 'Rhapsody in Blue', was performed at the Paul Whiteman concert given at the Aeolian Hall, New York, on 12 February 1924. In this same year, with Ira as lyricist, he composed the musical show *Lady Be Good*, which ran for 330 performances, with the title song and 'Fascinating Rhythm' as the highlights. Another song written at this time was 'The Man I Love', which became one of the most frequently recorded songs of all time.

Other Gershwin songs followed, including 'Looking for a Boy', 'That Certain Feeling' and 'Sweet and Low-Down', all from the musical *Tip-Toes* in 1925. In 1926, *Oh, Kay* was produced, in which Gertrude Lawrence introduced the Gershwin classic 'Someone to Watch over Me'. Other numbers from the show were 'Clap Yo' Hands', 'Do, Do, Do' and 'Maybe'.

Subsequent shows were *Funny Face* (1927, 'S Wonderful'); *Rosalie* (1927–28, 'How Long Has This Been Going On?'); *Treasure Girl* (1928, 'I've Got a Crush on You'); *Show Girl* (1929, 'Liza'); *Strike Up the Band; Girl Crazy* (1930, 'I Got Rhythm', 'But Not for Me', 'Embraceable You', 'Bidin' My Time') and *Of Thee I Sing* (1931, 'Who Cares', 'Love Is Sweeping the Country'). This latter show was the first musical to win the Pulitzer Prize in drama. Gershwin also composed the music for two Hollywood musical films, *Shall We Dance* (1937) and *A Damsel in Distress* (1937), both featuring Fred Astaire and Ginger Rogers.

Gershwin's concert music included *Rhapsody in Blue, Concerto in F* (1925), *Five Preludes for Solo Piano* (1926), *An American in Paris* (1928), *Second Rhapsody for Piano and Orchestra* (1932), *Cuban Overture* (1932) and *Variations on 'I Got Rhythm'* (1934). His final contribution was his folk opera *Porgy and Bess*, which opened in September 1935.

Additional Readings

Armitage, Merle (ed.). *George Gershwin.* New York: Da Capo Press, 1995. A reprint, with a new introduction by Edward Jablonski, of a book first published in 1938. Includes thirty-eight essays and tributes by Harold Arlen, Irving Berlin, Jerome Kern, Oscar Hammerstein II, Ira Gershwin and many other musical luminaries.

Armitage, Merle. *George Gershwin: Man and Legend.* New York: Arno Press, 1958. Reprinted 1970. Although similarly titled to the 1938 monograph, this book is not the same as the earlier work. It consists of essays on George Gershwin and his work, written by the author.

Ewen, David. *American Songwriters.* New York: H. W. Wilson, 1987. pp. 173–84.

Ewen, David. *George Gershwin: His Journey to Greatness* Westport, CT: Greenwood Press, 1977.

Ewen, David. *Great Men of American Popular Song.* Englewood Cliffs, NJ: Prentice-Hall, 1970, pp. 169–87.

George Gershwin Remembered. Interviews and Narration by Tony Thomas. FACET 8100 [CD]

Green, Benny. *Let's Face the Music.* London: Pavilion Books, 1989, pp. 9–24.

Hyland, William G. *The Song Is Ended.* New York: Oxford University Press, 1995, pp. 48–59, 77–88, 109–121, 136–145, 181–194, 221–234.

Hemming, Roy. *The Melody Lingers On.* New York: Newmarket Press, 1986, pp. 55–84.

Jablonski, Edward. *Gershwin: A Biography.* New York: Doubleday, 1987.

Jablonski, Edward. *Gershwin Remembered.* London: Faber & Faber, 1992.

Jablonski, Edward, and Lawrence Stewart. *The Gershwin Years.* New York: Doubleday, 1958. Revised edition: London: Robson Books, 1974.

Kendall, Alan. *George Gershwin: A Biography.* London: Harrap; New York: Universe Books, 1987.

Kimball, Robert, and Alfred Simon. *The Gershwins.* New York: Atheneum, 1973.

Peyser, Joan. *The Memory of All That: The Life of George Gershwin.* New York: Simon & Schuster, 1993.

Rosenberg, Deena. *Fascinating Rhythm: The Collaboration of George and Ira Gershwin.* New York: Dutton, 1991.

Schwartz, Charles. *Gershwin: His Life and Music.* Indianapolis: Bobbs-Merrill, 1973.

Wood, Ean. *George Gershwin: His Life and Music.* London: Sanctuary Publishing, 1996.

Select Discography

Chacksfield, Frank. Music of George Gershwin Decca LK 4113 [Also on CD]

Chacksfield, Frank. Glory That Was Gershwin

Faith, Percy. Columbia Album of George Gershwin Columbia C2-L1 [Also on CD]

Fennell, Frederick. Conducts Gershwin Mercury PPS 6006

Fiedler, Arthur. I Got Rhythm: Fiedler Conducts Gershwin (With Boston Pops) London SPC 21185

Fox, John. George Gershwin BBC Records REB 156, REC 320 (Reissue)

Kostelanetz, Andre. Music of George Gershwin Columbia CL770 [Also on CD]

Kostelanetz Plays Gershwin Columbia KG 32825

Luypaerts, Guy. Symphonic Portrait of George Gershwin Capitol P254 (12"); (Coupled with Symphonic Portrait of Jimmy McHugh by Frank de Vol) LC 6533 (10")

Ornadel, Cyril. Music of George Gershwin (Arrangements by Johnny Douglas) World Record Club

Poliakin, Raoul. Music of George Gershwin and Cole Porter Everest LPBR 5051

Pourcel, Franck. George Gershwin HMV CSDJ 3 (South Africa)

Rose, David. Love Walked In: Music of George Gershwin MGM E3123 [Also on CD]

Stott, Wally. Embraceable You: A Tribute to George Gershwin Philips B 10107 R
Thomas, Michael Tilson. Gershwin on Broadway: Overtures Columbia 34542

GIBBS, ARMSTRONG (1889–1960)

Armstrong Gibbs was born in Essex and studied history and music at Cambridge. He took up teaching at Copthorne School, East Grinstead and then at Brighton. In 1919, he asked the poet Walter de la Mare to write a play entitled *Crossings*, for the school, to which Gibbs added the music. On the strength of this performance, the conductor, Adrian Boult and de la Mare encouraged Gibbs to further his musical education. Gibbs took up his studies at the Royal College of Music (1920–21) under Boult, Charles Wood and Vaughan Williams. He then taught at the Royal College of Music, London, from 1921 to 1939.

Gibbs was commissioned to write incidental music for the theater. He also adjudicated at competitive music festivals. He wrote many large-scale choral works, three symphonies, nine string quartets, orchestral, chamber and piano music. Of his various light orchestral works the most popular was one movement of his *Fancy Dress Suite* of 1935, entitled 'Dusk', which was regularly performed by conductor Jay Wilbur with his string orchestra at the Savoy Hotel, London. Wilbur's arrangement of it for strings and harp was published in 1946 and became a standard favorite with many light orchestras of the period. A song version was published in 1949.

GLEASON, JACKIE (16 February 1916–24 June 1987)

Jackie Gleason was a most versatile celebrity. He was in his time an actor, comedian, musician, television producer, and master showman. Early on in his career, he made his mark in cabaret, carnivals, on radio and as an actor in films such as *The Life of Riley*, and he portrayed comic characters in his own *Jackie Gleason Show*, which ran for eighteen years, from 1952 to 1970.

Gleason was featured in fifteen motion pictures. He was nominated for an Oscar for his role in the film *The Hustler* (1961) and for his Chaplinesque portrayal of a mute janitor in *Gigot* (1963). He was elected to the TV Hall of Fame in 1985. He died in Fort Lauderdale, Florida.

Musical Achievements

Gleason's varied use of instrumentation resulted in some very unusual and fascinating selections from many of the LPs which show contrasting styles. Gleason's two Christmas LPs (*Tis the Season* and *Merry Christmas*) are without doubt among the best Yuletide albums in the light orchestral field. Both have been reissued on compact disc. Other LPs reissued on compact disc include *Nightwinds* and several compilation albums. Gleason used DUDLEY 'PETE' KING as arranger on his early LPs, but most of the later ones

Jackie Gleason

were arranged by George Williams. In the discography appended to this article the solo instruments are indicated.

The CD entitled *The Romantic Moods of Jackie Gleason* contains some interesting sleeve notes written by R. J. Smith, which provide an explanation of how Gleason, who never learned to read music, could record over forty albums with sales of more than 120 million copies and even compose some wonderful music himself.

The explanation is provided by Sydell Spear, daughter-in-law of Sammy Spear, long-time director of Gleason's orchestra. Sammy Spear related that Gleason would pick out a few notes on the piano, bang on his drums and somehow write the songs and conduct an orchestra. He frequently sat at the piano for hours, single-fingering melodies. Subsequently, a musical director would be commissioned to take down musical dictation. This was not always a simple process, due to Gleason's outbursts of frustration at not being clearly understood. Nevertheless, his output was considerable. One of his earliest tunes was 'Melancholy Serenade', which later became his well-known theme song.

Gleason's name always appeared on the LPs and on occasion he even painted the album covers, although Salvador Dali is credited with the cover of 'Lonesome Echo'. Capitol Records sold half-a-million copies of *Music for Lovers Only*, which was Gleason's 1952 debut album. He went on to become one of the first great album artists in the popular music field.

Additional Readings

Henry, William A., III. *The Great One: The Life and Legend of Jackie Gleason.* New York: Doubleday, 1992.

Weatherby, W. J. *Jackie Gleason: An Intimate Biography of the Great One.* New York: Pharos Books, 1992.

There is also an excellent article about Gleason in the 1955 issue of *Current Biography* and an obituary in the 1989 volume of the same publication.

Select Discography (All Capitol Records)

Aphrodisia: String Orchestra with Organ Solos by Wild Bill Davis. Capitol W 1250

Best of Jackie Gleason (2 volumes) SW 2796

Champagne, Candelight and Kisses. String and Brass Orchestras, Solo Instruments: Paired Trumpets, Paired Trombones, Clarinet and Alto Flute, Piano and Guitar SW 1830

Close-up (Compilation of reissues) SWBB 255 (2 LPs)

Doublin' in Brass: Brass Orchestra with Percussion and Solo Tenor Sax SW 2880

For Lovers Only/Misty W 475

Gentle Touch SW 1519

Gigot. Original music from the film, composed by Jackie Gleason, String Orchestra and Bal Musette Group.

How Sweet It Is For Lovers SW 2582

Irving Berlin's Music for Lovers (Compilation of reissues) SW 106

Jackie Gleason Deluxe Set (3 LPs).

Last Dance For Lovers Only SW 2144

Lazy Lively Love W/SW 1439

Lonesome Echo: Mandolins, Cellos, Domros. (Richer, Deeper Mandolins), Guitars and Marimba, Featured Solo Instrument: Oboe d'Amour (Romeo Penquie) W 627

Love Embers and Flame. Twin String Orchestras, Solo Instruments: Piano and Celeste, Trombones and Trumpets SW 1689

Love Hours W 816

Lovers' Portfolio (2 LPs) SWBO 1619

Lovers' Rhapsody 10"-H366

Lovers Only 10"-H352 SW 352

Lush Moods PAIR 2DL1069 (2 LPs)

Merry Christmas: String Orchestra with Keith Textor Singers. Solo Instrument: Electric Celeste (Hercules). W 758

Most Beautiful Girl in the World. (Compilation of reissues) Pickwick PC/SPC 3091

Movie Themes For Lovers Only SW 1877

Music Around the World: Twin String Orchestras. Featured Solo Instruments: Tenor Sax and Trumpet. SW 2471

Music for Lovers Only. String Orchestra. Solo Instrument: Trumpet (Bobby Hackett). (10" and 12"). LC 6588 (10") (S.A.)

Music, Martinis and Memories. String Orchestra, Solo Instrument: Trumpet (Bobby Hackett) SW 509

Music to Change Her Mind. DW 632

Music to Make You Misty. DW 455

Music to Remember Her . . . W 570

Night Winds: Massed Flutes DW 717

Now Sound for Today's Lovers: Twin String Orchestras with Exotic Instruments: Tavla (Sitar), African Finger Piano, Dhrama Bells, Javanese Aung Loung, Chinese Bell Tree, Kanjira. SW 2935

"OOOO!": Vocal Orchestra (Wordless Voices of Artie Malvin). W 905 Solo Instruments: Guitar (Tony Mottola), Piano (Bernie Leighton).

Opiate d'Amour: Twin String Orchestra and Brass Orchestra (24 Trumpets). Solo Instruments: Piano Flute, Trombone, Guitar, Oboe d'Amour SW 1315

Plays Pretty for the People (Compilation of reissues). Pickwick PC/SPC 3064

Rebound: String Orchestra. Solo Instrument: Piano (Bertie Leighton), Oboe d'Amour (Romeo Penique) SW 1075

Romantic Hits SW 2056

Romeo and Juliet: Twin String Orchestras with Oboe, English Horn, Vibes, Bells, Accordions. Solo Instrument: Trumpet. ST 398

Shangri La SPC 3218

Silk 'n' Brass SW 2409

Softly SL 6664

Taste of Brass SW 2684

Tawney H471 (10")

That Moment W 1147

'Tis The Season: Twin String Orchestras with Oboe, Accordion, English Horn, French Horn, Bells. Solo Instruments: Tenor Saxophone (Charlie Ventura), Trombone (Buddy Morrow), Trumpet (Pee Wee Erwin). ST 2791

Today's Romantic Hits for Lovers Only. (2 vols.): Twin String Orchestras, with Accordion, English Horn, Oboe. Solo Instruments: Tenor Saxophone and Trumpet SW 1978

Torch with the Blue Flame: Marimba Orchestra. (8 Marimbas with Strings), Guitar, Harp, Vibraphone, Piano, Bells. Solo Instruments: Trombone (Laurence Brown) SW 961

Velvet Brass: Brass Orchestra. Solo Instrument: Saxophone W/SW 859

Compact Discs

And Away We Go SCAMP 9706

Best of Jackie Gleason WEA/Atlantic/CURB DZ-77614

Body and Soul PAIR 1299

Champagne, Candlelight and Kisses Capitol

Entertainers: Jackie Gleason Sarabandas 390

How Sweet It Is/Velvet Brass Razor & Tie 2111

Jackie Gleason Entertainers CD 390

Lush Moods PAIR 1069

Merry Christmas Capitol CDP 748428

Movie Themes—For Lovers Only Capitol

Music, Martinis and Memories

Music to Make You Misty/ Night Winds Capitol 92088

Romantic Moods of Jackie Gleason. Capitol 72438 52541 2 3

Shangri-La PAIR 1176

'Tis The Season Capitol 89589

Note: Unless otherwise indicated, the LPs generally feature twin string orchestras with brass soloists.

GOLD, ERNEST (b. 13 July 1921)

Ernest Gold was born in Vienna, Austria. He studied first with his grandfather and subsequently at the Vienna State Academy. He emigrated to the United States in 1938, where he studied harmony with OTTO CESANA. In 1945, he moved to Hollywood and wrote his first film score for *Girl of the Limberlost*. His other film scores included *On the Beach* (1959), *Exodus* (1960), *Judgment at Nuremberg* (1961) *It's a Mad, Mad, Mad, Mad World* (1963) and *The Secret of Santa Vittoria* (1969). His score for *Exodus* won an Academy Award. He also wrote the musical *Solomon.*

Select Discography

Cross of Iron EMI EMA-782 OC

Exodus (Sinfonia of London; Ernest Gold conducting) RCA 1058–2R

GOLD, MARTY

Marty Gold was born in New York. He made his musical debut at the age of twelve. He arranged for Charlie Barnet and other big bands and worked as conductor for singers such as Sarah Vaughan and the Four Aces. For several years he was musical director for the Three Suns, Four Aces, Sarah Vaughan, Patti Page, Georgia Gibbs and Vaughn Monroe. His compositions include 'Sunshower', 'Wendy', 'Puppet on the String' and 'Rush Hour'.

Select Discography

Broadway Soundaroundus RCA LSP 3689

By the Waters of Minnetonka Kapp K1125 S

Classic Bossa Nova RCA LSP 3456

Doo Wacka Doo RCA LSP 2509

Easy Listening (With the Three Suns) RCA LPM 1316

For Sound's Sake RCA LSP 2787

Hank Williams RCA LSP 3516

High Fi and Wide (With the Three Suns) RCA LPM 1249

Higher than Fi Vik LX-1097

In a Young Mood RCA LSP 2942

It's Magic LSA 2290

More Wacky Doodlin's RCA LSP 2861

Organized for Hi-Fi (Marty Gold Organ Ensemble) VIK LX-1069

Rodgers and Hart RCA LSP 2535

Skin Tight RCA LSP 2230

Something Special RCA LSP 3342

Songs of College Days Kapp 1102 S

Soundaroundus RCA LSP 3599

Soundpower RCA LSP 2620

Sounds Unlimited RCA LSP 2714

Stereo Action Goes Hollywood LSA 2381

Sticks and Bones RCA LSP 2070

Sticks and Strings in Hi-Fi VIK LX 1082

Suddenly It's Springtime RCA LSP 2882

Swingin' West RCA LSP 2163

24 Pieces of Gold (2) RCA VPS 6012

Wired for Sound (Marty Gold and Organ Ensemble) VIK LX 1054

GOLDSMITH, JERRY (b. 10 February 1929)

Jerry Goldsmith was born in Los Angeles. He studied piano with Jakob Gimpel and composition with Mario Castelnuovo-Tedesco, before attending the Los Angeles City College and film music classes at the University of Southern California.

He began his musical career at CBS as a script typist. He frequented the music department and started scoring radio programs. In 1955, he was offered a contract to compose two or three hours of music a week for television. By 1957, he had scored his first film, *Black Patch*. His television credits include *Gunsmoke, The Twilight Zone* and *Thriller*.

From 1957 to 1993, he created an impressive body of distinguished work. His first film assignment was *Lonely Are the Brave*. His scores include suspense and action thrillers such as *The Blue Max, Planet of the Apes*, *Patton* (1970), *Omen* (1976), *Alien* (1979), *Poltergeist* (1982), *Rambo II* (1985) and the music for the *Star Trek* series. He also created scores for romantic sagas such as *Wind and the Lion* (1975), *Islands in the Stream* (1977) and *Forever Young* (1992), the whimsical *Dennis the Menace* (1993) and the heartwarming *Hoosiers* (1986), with its basketball theme. His television credits include *The Man from U.N.C.L.E* (1964 series) and *The Waltons* (1971).

Select Discography

Cassandra Crossing Citadel CT-6020

Chinatown ABC ABDP-848

Coma MGM MG-5403

Freud (Conducted by Joseph Gershenson) Citadel CT-6019

Last Run MGM ISE-30ST

Logan's Run MGM MG-1–5302

MacArthur MCA 2287

Omen (Conducted by Lionel Newman) Tattoo BJL1–1888

Papillon Capitol ST-11260

Patton 20th Century Fox S-4208

QB VIII (TV Score) ABC ABCD-822

Ransom Dart ARTS-65376

Wild Rovers (Conducted by Sydney Sax) MGM ISE-31ST

Wind and the Lion Artista AL 4048

Compact Discs

Alien Silva Screen FILMCD003

Bad Girls Milan 22054–2

Basic Instinct Varese Sarabande VSD5360

Blue Max Columbia JK57890

Hour of the Gun Intrada MAF7020D

Omen Varese Sarabande VSD5281

Planet of the Apes Intrada FMT8006D

Rambo III Intrada RVF6006D

Star Trek: The Motion Picture Carlton 983381–2

Star Trek V: The Final Frontier Epic EK45267

Total Recall Varese Sarabande VSD5267

Wind and the Lion Intrada MAF7005D

GOODMAN, AL (12 August 1890–10 January 1972)
Al Goodman was born in Nikopol, Russia. The family emigrated to the United States. Al Goodman received his first musical training from his father. At the age of five, he was singing in a choir, and he later played in the pit of a local movie house. He was educated at the Baltimore High School and won a scholarship for the Peabody Institute in Baltimore. He came to New York and began his musical career as a piano player in a music publishing house. He was discovered by Earl Carroll, who brought him to California in 1915 to arrange and conduct music for a new Carroll show. Their collaboration resulted in the hit show of the 1920s *So Long Letty*.

Goodman subsequently worked as conductor and arranger with Al Jolson and his arrangements appeared on the sound track of *The Jazz Singer 29*, the first talking picture. He was also director and composer for J. J. Schubert and Florenz Ziegfeld and was given a long-term contract as musical director of their productions, which included *Earl Carroll's Scandals* and the *Ziegfeld Follies*. He conducted for shows such as *The Student Prince, Blossom Time, The Band Wagon* and *Good News*.

He was associated with various radio shows as musical consultant and director in the 1930s and 1940s with orchestra and guest singers. His orchestral arrangements of pop songs and standards were always elegantly crafted. He produced many records over the years into the 1950s, many on little-known labels, which are all out of print.

His songs were effective in shows, but not hits outside the theater. The best-known is 'When Hearts Are Young', with SIGMUND ROMBERG.

Select Discography

Dinner Music RCA T 20065 (10")

Relax with Victor Herbert. RCA LPM 1023.

Salutes Irving Berlin. Promenade 2079

Speak Low RCA Camden CAL 317

Theme Music From Great Motion Pictures. RCA LPM 1008

Tribute to Jerome Kern Spinorama Records MK 3049

Ron Goodwin (used with permission)

GOODWIN, RON (b. 17 February 1925)
Goodwin was born in Plymouth, Devon, England, where his father was engaged in security work at the naval dockyard. He began piano lessons at the age of five. When he was nine, the family was transferred back to London and Goodwin learned to play the trumpet as a member of the school orchestra at Willesden County School. He continued his musical education at Pinner County School, where he formed his own dance band, The Woodchoppers. This band won the South London Championship of the Melodymaker Dance Band Championships.

He began his working life as a junior clerk with an insurance company. Eventually he became a music copier with a firm of music publishers, Campbell Connelly. He also studied trumpet and arranging privately with Siegfried de Chabot, professor at the Guildhall School of Music in London, and orchestrated for Harry Gold, who with NORRIE PARAMOR ran a company called Paramor Gold Orchestral Service. Goodwin occasionally played trumpet for Gold's Dixieland band, called Pieces of Eight.

The firm broke up when Paramor joined Columbia Records. Goodwin found work as a staff arranger with the publisher Edward Kastner, who later amalgamated with Sidney Bron to become Bron Associated Publishers. Goodwin became part of a large arranging department, which included GEOFF LOVE, Harry South, Berney Whibley, FRANK BARBER and JOHNNY GREGORY. Ron became friendly with the singer Dick James, who introduced him to George Martin at Parlophone Records. This introduction led to a career with Parlophone Records as chief arranger and musical director.

Goodwin wrote arrangements for broadcasting orchestras, including the orchestra of STANLEY BLACK, who ran the BBC Dance Orchestra. He arranged the vocal backings for the bands of Ted Heath and GERALDO and made several records, arranging and conducting the backing music for singers including Petula Clark. The BBC formed the BBC Showband, with CYRIL STAPLETON conducting, and engaged Goodwin and REG OWEN as staff arrangers.

He composed music in the classical form, including the 'Drake 400 Concert Suite' and 'New Zealand Suite', but made his greatest contribution as a writer for films. His first scores were for documentaries produced by the Film Producer's Guild, based at Merton Park Studios and controlled by Ken Lockhart-Smith.

Subsequently, he acted as composer and musical director for numerous feature films, commencing with *Whirlpool* in 1959, which was commissioned by Lawrence Bachmann. Goodwin's career in film scoring took off when Bachmann was appointed head of production for MGM in Europe. Other films followed including *The Witness*, *I'm All Right, Jack*; *In the Nick*; *Village of the Damned*; *The Trials of Oscar Wilde*; *The Man with the Green Carnation*; *The Man at the Carleton Tower*; *The Clue of the New Pin*; *Partners in Crime*; *Invasion Quartet*, a series of Miss Marple films starring Margaret Rutherford; *Day of the Triffids*; *Follow the Boys*; *Of Human Bondage*; *Children of the Damned*; *633 Squadron*; *A Home of Your Own*; *Those Magnificent Men in Their Flying Machines*; *Operation Crossbow*; *Alphabet Murders*; *That Riviera Touch*; *The Trap*; *Mrs. Brown, You've Got a Lovely Daughter*; *Where Eagles Dare*; *Battle of Britain*; *The Executioner*; *Frenzy*; *One of Our Dinosaurs Is Missing*; *Escape from the Dark*; *Ride a Wild Pony*; *Candleshoe*; *Force 10 from Navarone*; *The Spaceman and King Arthur*; *Clash of Loyalties* and *Valhalla*.

He has won several IVOR NOVELLO Awards, including the Entertainment Music Award in 1972 and a Life Achievement Award in 1993. In the 1970s, Goodwin toured the United Kingdom with an orchestra performing his film scores. He has continued to do radio broadcasts and to work in Canada. He also toured New Zealand in the 1990s.

Additional Readings

Blokker, Kees. *His Kind of Music.* Vorendaal, Holland: privately printed by the author, 1993. (An English translation of Elhaik, *Ron Goodwin.*)

Elhaik, Serge. *Ron Goodwin.* Evreux, France: Serge Elhaik, 1990. [Text in French].

Williams, John (ed). *The Magic of Ron Goodwin.* Dorset, England: Variations Publications, 1995.

Select Discography

Adventure Studio 2 TWO 142 (S)

Battle of Britain United Artists UAS 5201

Beatles Concerto Parlophone PAS 10014

Big Sounds of Ron Goodwin Studio 2 TWOX 1034

Burt Bacharach Studio 2 TWO 373

Christmas Wonderland Studio 2 TWO 189 (S)

Decline and Fall Stateside SSL 10259 (S) [Also on CD]

Drake 400 Chandos ABRD 1014

Elizabethan Serenade Regal (U.K. EMI) SRS 5018

Escape from the Dark EMI EMC 3148

Excitement Studio 2 TWO 318

Film Favourites Parlophone PMD 1014 (M)

First 25 Years Studio 2 TWOSP 108

Going Places Studio 2 TWOX 1074

Gypsy Fire Studio 2 TWO 178 (S)

Holiday in Beirut Parlophone PCS 3028 (S)

It Can't Be Wrong Capitol T10078 [Also on CD]

Jet Flight to Beirut Capitol International SP 10560

Legend of the Glass Mountain Studio 2 TWO 220 (S)

Love Album MFP 4157091

Monte Carlo or Bust Paramount SPFL 255

Music for an Arabian Night [U.K. title **Holiday in Beirut**], Parlophone PCS 3002 (S), Capitol ST 10251

Music in Orbit Capitol ST 10188

Music to Set You Dreaming Parlophone PMD 1038

New Zealand Symphony Orchestra Columbia EJ 2601721

Out of This World Parlophone PMC 1065 (M)

Out of This World (1960 stereo) Parlophone PCS 3006 (S)

Projections EMI EMS 1077691

Rhythm and Romance Studio 2 TWOX 1057

Ron Goodwin WRC SM 217

Ron Goodwin Collection 1 Studio 2 TWOX 1081

Ron Goodwin Collection 2 Studio 2 TWOX 1082

Ron Goodwin in Concert Studio 2 TWO 339

Ron Goodwin Plays Bacharach Studio 2 TWO 373

Serenade Parlophone PCS 3019 (S)

Selfish Giant EMI Oneup OU 2060

633 Squadron United Artists SULP 1071 (S)

Spellbound Studio 2 TWO 1007

Swinging Sweethearts Capitol T10177 [Also on CD]

This Is Ron Goodwin Studio 2 PMSS 2

Those Magnificent Men . . . Stateside SSL 10136 (S)

The Trap Polydor 582 004

Very Best of Ron Goodwin Studio 2 TWOX 1064

Warsaw Concerto MFP SPR 90027

Where Eagles Dare MGM CS 8012

Compact Discs

Adventure and Excitement E.M.I. Studio 2 UK CDP 7 46929 2

Battle of Britain and Other Films UA-EMI-UK CDMGM 21

British Light Music (With New Zealand Symphony Orchestra) MARCO POLO 8223518

Classic Love Songs MFP Premier UK CDPR 103

Drake 400 Chandos UK CHAN 8811 43.52

Fire and Romance E.M.I. Studio 2 UK CDP 7 91799 2

Golden Sounds EMI CD Sound (WB) 7 (South Africa)

Miss Marple Films Label X Europe LXE706

Mozart Magic MFP Premier UK CDM 7961192

My Kind of Music Chandos 797

633 Squadron Naxos/Marco Polo 8.223518

Ron Goodwin Collection E.M.I. New Zealand 4346492 2 CD set

Ron Goodwin Collection E.M.I. New Zealand 2505052 2 CD set

Ron Goodwin Conducting the New Zealand Symphony Orchestra Marco Polo 8223518

Ron Goodwin Conducts the Odense Symphony Orchestra Label "X" West German LXE 706

Where Eagles Dare/633 Squadron UA-EMI-UK CDMGM 13

GOULD, MORTON (10 December 1913–21 February 1996)
Gould was born in Richmond Hill, N.Y., of mixed Austrian and Russian

Morton Gould

parentage. At the age of four, Gould was able to play popular tunes of the day, note for note, by ear. Before long, he had progressed to the *William Tell Overture* and other classics. At the age of six, he played piano in a concert at the Brooklyn Academy of Music and during his first year at public school, he composed a waltz with the title 'Just Six', which was notated by a teacher and published. At the age of eight, he was awarded a scholarship at the New York Institute of Musical Art. He studied music at the Institute of Musical Art, New York University. He was forced to cut short his academic career because of the death of his father, and he earned a living playing for vaudeville acts. He also played in jazz bands and was staff pianist at Radio City Music Hall from 1931 to 1932.

From 1934 to 1942, he was director of the radio series 'Music for Today', broadcast over the Mutual Broadcasting System, and in 1943 became director of the Columbia Broadcasting System's 'Chrysler Hour'. Throughout most of the 1940s he headed the *Cresta Blanca* program on CBS Radio, which was a tremendous success.

Late in 1954, Gould began a long association with RCA Victor Records. For this company, he recorded much of the material he had done for Columbia. He has also recorded for other record companies, such as Everest,

Chalfont and Varese Sarabande. Gould and the London Symphony Orchestra made the very first digital recordings for Chalfont in 1978.

His compositions include 'Chorale and Fugue in Jazz' (1932) 'American Symphonette No. 1' (1933) 'Little Symphony' and 'Symphonette no. 2' (1936) and 'Piano Concerto' (1937) which bridged the worlds of classical and jazz music. He continued to make use of popular music in compositions such as 'Spirituals for Orchestra' (1937), 'Latin-American Symphonette' (1940), 'A Lincoln Legend' (1941), 'Cowboy Rhapsody' (1943), 'Fall River Legend' (1945), and 'American Ballads' (1976). For the theater he wrote *Million Dollar Baby* (1945), *Arms and the Girl* (1950) and various film scores, including *King of Steel* (1941), *Delightfully Dangerous* (1945), *San Francisco Conference* (1946), *Windjammer* (1948) and *Cinerama Holiday* (1955).

Between 1982 and 1986, Gould completed ten commissions of major works. These included the cello concerto commissioned by the Chamber Society of Lincoln Center and premiered in 1982; *I'm Old Fashioned* (Astaire Variations), based on the song by JEROME KERN, commissioned by the New York City Ballet and first performed in 1983; *American Sing*, commissioned by the Los Angeles Philharmonic with MICHAEL TILSON THOMAS conducting in 1984 and the flute concerto commissioned for the Chicago Symphony Orchestra, conducted by Sir Georg Solti in 1985. In 1986, Lorin Maazel conducted the Pittsburgh Symphony Orchestra in a work commissioned to celebrate the 200th anniversary of the Pittsburgh Post Gazette.

In January 1986, Gould was elected to the American Academy and Institute of Arts and Letters. In April of that year, he was elected president of the American Society of Composers, Authors and Publishers (ASCAP). In 1995, Gould won the Pulitzer prize in music.

Musical Achievements

Gould was one of America's most versatile musicians, equally at home in the popular and classical orchestral fields. He proved to be a first-rate composer of popular and classical music, arranged and conducted the world's best-loved and popular music and classical repertoire as well as being an excellent pianist in his own right and a leading figure in the American musical scene for well over half a century.

As a composer, Gould made serious music accessible to the man in the street by incorporating into his major compositions jazz, dance tunes and a wide range of folk music, such as cowboy ballads, spirituals, Christmas carols and war songs. Gould's best-known work, the 'Pavanne' from his *Second American Symphonette*, represents one of his more successful attempts to bring popular and classical work together. This piece has enjoyed wide popularity with symphony orchestras and dance bands alike and was recorded by Glenn Miller in 1939. The unmistakable American qualities present in a large number of Gould's compositions may help to explain why he is less well known in Great Britain.

In interpreting the music of other composers, Morton Gould has covered a vast amount of territory, ranging from GEORGE GERSHWIN's 'The Man I Love' to the traditional 'Yankee Doodle', one of numerous pieces he scored for concert band to Debussy's 'Clair de Lune'. Most reference works tend to dwell upon the more serious side of Gould's musical activities, saying little about the sympathy he had for lighter music. The sad state of today's popular music left Gould inactive in this field for approximately the last thirty years, but it was a far different story earlier in his career. As far back as the 1930s, he was treating radio listeners to sumptuous orchestral arrangements of popular songs and light classics. He helped to originate the genre of music that later came to be known as mood music, and the music between. He was aided in his efforts by ANDRE KOSTELANETZ, who shared Gould's belief that popular music is good music and that composers such as Gershwin, COLE PORTER, JEROME KERN and RICHARD RODGERS should be treated as seriously as Ludwig von Beethoven and Johannes Brahms. In both the radio studio and recording studio, these two conductors imparted to popular music in America a sophistication and polish it had never known before. Several albums of Gould's symphonic-styled popular tunes, which he recorded for Columbia during the 78 rpm years, attest to his pioneering efforts in this regard. These include *After Dark, Morton Gould Showcase, Rendezvous* and an almost legendary collection which he did for Decca, *Music for the Twilight Hour*, in which may be found the Gershwin melody, 'The Man I Love'.

Gould's operetta LPs are well up to the standard of his more popular discs. Topping this list is the LP *Famous Operettas*, with splendid renditions of RUDOLF FRIML, Franz Lehar, Kern, Emmerich Kálmán and Oscar Straus favorites. His LPs of semiclassical favorites never fall into the category of oversentimentality and include *Moon, Wind and Stars, Moonlight Sonata* and *Where's the Melody?* Gould has also explored the Latin American musical scene. Besides his own achievements as a composer in works such as 'Latin-American Symphonette', he has recaptured the authentic atmosphere and rhythms of Latin American popular music in such LPs as *Jungle Drums* and its sequel *More Jungle Drums*, *Latin, Lush and Lovely* and a recording of Ernesto Lecuona's music.

Gould's ability to create a period flavor in his arrangements is well illustrated by his LPs *Hits of the Golden Twenties* and *Memories*. His venture into Country and Western music resulted in a remarkably fine LP of its kind entitled *Wagon Wheels*. His arrangements of Christmas music have always been popular. *Christmas Music for Orchestra*, originally released on a 10" LP, reappeared in 1969 on a disc entitled *A Musical Christmas Tree* and more recently on a compact disc.

With his inventiveness, Gould was often able to inject new life into familiar tunes. This is evident in the orchestral suites which he arranged based on the music from *Oklahoma!* and *Carousel*. Gould's LPs in the context of dramatic world events are also masterpieces and include *World War I Music* and *Holocaust*, the latter composed for the American television series. He also excelled in his recordings of African-American spirituals. His *Spirituals for Strings* consists of arrangements of traditional spirituals for orchestra. Gould also produced *Spirituals for Orchestra*, which is an LP consisting of Gould's original composition in five movements. He attempted to experiment with the modern beat idiom in the LP *Makes the Scene* but subsequently withdrew from attempts to capture the music of the young generation. Unlike his illustrious contemporary, ANDRE KOSTELANETZ, who employed a fleet of arrangers, Gould always did his own arrangements.

Additional Readings

Peyser, Joan. 'Morton Gould'. In her *The Music of My Time*. White Plains, NY: Pro/Am Music Resources, 1995, pp. 127–34.

Select Discography

10" LP Records

Christmas Music for Orchestra Columbia ML 2065

Do You Remember? Columbia ML 2028

Grieg Program Columbia ML 2031

Hits of the Golden Twenties Columbia ML 2132

Legend (Docker); **Theme from 'Runnymede Rhapsody'** (King); **Mediterranean Concerto** (Semprini) (With the Boston Pops Orchestra) Columbia AL 36 [Also on CD]

Manhattan Moods Columbia ML 2144

Morton Gould at the Piano Decca CL 5067

Morton Gould Conducting the Columbia Concert Band Columbia AL 41

Morton Gould Program Columbia ML 2190

Morton Gould Symphonic Band Columbia ML 2029

Music at Midnight Columbia ML 2171

Music of Ketelby Columbia AL 47

Second Rhapsody for Piano and Orchestra; Variations on 'I Got Rhythm'; Three Preludes (Gershwin, with Oscar Levant at the piano) Columbia ML 2073

Soft Lights and Sweet Music Columbia ML 2021

South of the Border Columbia ML 2015 [Also on CD]

Tap Dance Concerto; Family Album (Gould) (With Danny Daniels, dance soloist, and the Rochester Pops Orchestra) Columbia ML 2215

12" LP Records

American in Paris; Porgy and Bess (Gershwin) RCA LM 2002

After Dark Columbia ML 4134

Ballet Music (Gould) RCA LM/LSC 2532

Band Plays On Columbia AL 57 (Reissued HL 7163)

Baton and Bows RCA LM/LSC 2217

Bewitched CB 3

Beyond the Blue Horizon RCA LM/LSC 2552 (Reissued as **Pure Gold** ANLI-2806) [Also on CD]

Billy the Kid—Ballet Suite; Rodeo—Ballet Suite (Copland) RCA LM/LSC 2195. Reissued on ARLI-4410 and AGLI-1335

Blues in the Night RCA LM/LSC 2104

Bolero (Ravel); **1812 Overture** (Tchaikovsky) RCA LM/LSC 2345

Brass and Percussion LM/LSC 2080 (U.S.A.); RCA RD 27009 (Britain)

Carmen for Orchestra (Bizet) RCA LM/LSC 2437

Clair de Lune Quintessence 7025

Coffee Time RCA LPM/LSP 1656 [Also on CD]

Curtain Time Columbia ML 4451 [Also on CD]

Derivations for Clarinet and Band (music by Gould; Benny Goodman, clarinet, with Morton Gould conducting the Columbia Jazz Combo) Columbia ML 6205/ MS 6805

Discovery (First Recordings of Music by George Gershwin, Cole Porter, Jerome Kern, Richard Rodgers, Morton Gould and Harold Arlen) RCA LM/LSC 2986

Doubling in Brass RCA LM/LSC 2308

English Music RCA LM/LSC 2719 (U.S.A.); RCA VICS 1530 (Britain)

Evening Serenade RCA LSC 3007

Famous Operettas Columbia CL 580 [Also on CD]

Film Music Varese Sarabande VCDM 1000.20

Finlandia—Music of Sibelius RCA LM/LSC 2666

Goodnight, Sweetheart RCA LM/LSC 2628 [Also on CD]

Grand Canyon Suite (Grofe); **Bolero** (Ravel) Quintessence 7043

Grand Canyon Suite (Grofe); **Wellington's Victory** (Beethoven) RCA LM/LSC 2433 (Reissued on AGLI-2700)

Hi-Fi Band Concert Columbia CL 954

Holocaust (Gould) (From the score of the TV movie) (With National Philharmonic Orchestra) RCA ARLI-2785

Jungle Drums LM/LSC 1994 (U.S.A.); RCA RD 27028 (Britain)

Kern and Porter Favorites RCA LM/LSC 2559

Latin-American Symphonette; Fall River Legend; Cotillion; Festive Music; Philhar-

monic Waltzes; Symphony of Marching Tunes; Quickstep (Gould) (With the London Symphony Orchestra) Varese Sarabande VCDM 1000.10

Latin, Lush and Lovely RCA LM/LSC 2752 [Also on CD]

Living Strings RCA LM/LSC 2317

Love Walked In RCA LM/LSC 2633 [Also on CD]

Memories Columbia ML 4796 [Also on CD]

Months Columbia ML/CML 4487

Moon, Wind and Stars RCA LM/LSC 2232

Moonlight Sonata RCA LM/LSC 2542

More Jungle Drums RCA LM/LSC 2768 [Also on CD]

Morton Gould Makes the Scene RCA LPM/LSP 3771

Morton Gould Showcase Columbia ML 4064

Movie Time Columbia ML 4595 [Also on CD]

Music for Summertime RCA Victor LM 2006 [Also on CD]

Music of Lecuona; Parade of the Wooden Soldiers; Dancing Tambourine; String Time (With the Robin Hood Dell Orchestra) Columbia ML 4361 [Also on CD]

Music of Bizet Quintessence 7024

Music of Morton Gould (With the Robin Hood Dell Orchestra of Philadelphia) Columbia ML 4218 [Also on CD]

Musical Christmas Tree RCA LSC 3110

Oklahoma Suite; Carousel Suite (Rodgers) RCA LM 1884 [Also on CD]

Orchestral Suite No. 2; Robert Browning Overture: Putnam's Camp (Ives) (With the Chicago Symphony Orchestra) RCA LM/LSC 2959

Piano Favorites Played by the Orchestra RCA LM/LSC 2579

Popular Classics VIC/VICS 1174

Popular Classics—Vol. 2 VIC/VICS 1381

Rendezvous Columbia ML 4070

Rhapsodies for Piano and Orchestra Columbia ML 4657 [Also on CD]

Sante Fe Saga; Battle Hymn of the Republic (arranged by Gould); **Formation; Revolutionary Prelude; Prologue** (With Knightsbridge Symphonic Band) Everest 3253

Scheherazade (Rimsky-Korsakov) RCA LM 1956 (Reissued on VICS 1444; Quintessence 7024)

Serious Gershwin (2-LP set) RCA LM 6033

Soundings; Columbia (Gould) (With the Louisville Orchestra) Louisville 716

Sousa Forever! RCA LM/LSC 2569

Spirituals for Orchestra (Gould); **Dance Symphony** (Copland) (With the Chicago Symphony Orchestra) RCA LM/LSC 2850 (Reissued on AGLI-4213)

Spirituals for Orchestra; Foster Gallery (Gould) (Direct-to-disc recording, with the London Philharmonic Orchestra) Crystal Clear CCS 7005 [Also on CD]

Spirituals for Strings RCA LM/LSC 2686 [Also on CD]

Starlight Serenade Columbia CL 664 [Also on CD]

Strike up the Band Columbia AL 41; Reissued CL 954

Symphonic Serenade Columbia CL 560

Symphony No. 1; Unanswered Question; Variations on 'America' (Ives) (With the Chicago Symphony Orchestra) RCA LM/LSC 2893

Symphony No. 2; Clarinet Concerto (Nielsen) (With the Chicago Symphony Orchestra) RCA LM/LSC 2920

Symphony No. 2 (Rimsky-Korsakov); **Symphony No. 21** (Miaskovsky) (With the Chicago Symphony Orchestra) RCA Victor LSC 3022

Symphony No. 2; Symphony No. 3 (Shostakovich) (With the Royal Philharmonic Orchestra)

Temptation LM 2128 (U.S.); RCA RD 27050 (Britain) [Also on CD]

Two Worlds of Kurt Weill RCA LC/LSC 2863

Wagon Wheels Columbia ML 4858 [Also on CD]

West Point Symphony; American Ballads; Cheers; Fanfare for Freedom (Gould) (With the University of Florida Symphony Band) Golden Crest ATH-5067

Where's the Melody? RCA LM/LSC 2224

Wonderful Waltzes of Tchaikovsky RCA LM/LSC 2890

Works for Harmonica and Orchestra (by Gershwin, Vaughan Williams, Malcolm Arnold, Arthur Benjamin and Darius Milhaud) (with Larry Adler and Royal Philharmonic Orchestra) RCA LSC 3078; RCA GL 42747 (Reissue)

World War I (Gould) RCA LM/LSC 2791

World's Best Loved Waltzes LM 2072 (U.S.); RCA RD 27015 (Britain)

Compact Discs

Blues in the Night BMG 68477

Brass and Percussion BMG 61255

Carmen for Orchestra BMG 68476

Fall River Legend BMG 1651

1812 Overture

Jungle Drums BMG 68173

Kern/Porter Favorites BMG 68478

Moon, Wind and Stars BMG 68479

Music of Morton Gould DEL 3166

Musical Christmas Tree BMG 7931–2

Scheherazade

Symphony of Spirituals CT VLA/HOUSE ALB 13 ALBANY

Tchaikovsky Waltzes

GRAINER, RON (11 August 1922–21 February 1981)
Ron Grainer, composer for film, radio and television, was born in Queensland, Australia, and came to Britain in 1952. He joined a variety act that toured Britain with Billy Eckstine, Frankie Laine and Al Martino, and he recorded with singers Charlie McGhee and Patrick O'Hagan from the late 1950s onward. He also accompanied songs by Shari and Jo Peters.

In the 1960s he became a pianist at BBC television rehearsals and began to write music for BBC plays. BBC Executive Producer Andrew Osborne commissioned Grainer to write episodes for the series *Maigret*. Later assignments were *Comedy Playhouse, Steptoe and Son, That Was the Week That Was* and *Panorama*. In addition, he composed various themes for *The Dales* for the light program of BBC Radio.

Grainer's best-known themes were for the TV series *Dr Who* and for the series *The Prisoner* (1967). Grainer's title music for ITV networks included *A Man in a Suitcase, The Prisoner, Tales of the Unexpected* and *Shelley*. He also composed the signature tunes for *Not So Much a Programme, More a Way of Life, Paul Temple, South Riding, For the Love of Ada* and *Edward and Mrs Simpson*.

Grainer won three IVOR NOVELLO awards. These were for his scores for the stage musical *Robert and Elizabeth*; for *Maigret* (1961); and for 'Old Ned', the theme for *Steptoe and Son* (1962).

His first film scores were written for two short documentaries, *Mozart* (1959) and *Terminus* (1961). His music for feature films included *A Kind of Loving, Some People* (1962), *Nothing but the Best* (1964), *To Sir with Love* (1967), *The Omega Man* (1971), *I Don't Want to Be Born* (1975) and *Mutiny on the Buses* (1972).

Some library music was recorded for CHAPPELL and for the Parry and Standard Mood Music Libraries. Versions of many of Grainer's themes were also played by The Eagles, a Bristol-based band discovered by Grainer.

GRAY, ALLAN (2 February 1902–10 September 1973)
Allan Gray, film composer, was born in Poland or Austria and worked in Berlin as music director for the Max Reinhardt theater company. In the early 1930s, he was employed by UFA in the film industry. His German films included *Berlin Alexanderplatz* and *Die Grafin von Monte Cristo* and two films with English versions, *Emil and the Detectives* and *F.P.I.* By 1936, he was resident in England where he worked on film scores and for radio and mood music publishers. He wrote music for the Shakespearean company at Stratford in the 1950s and composed a children's opera, *Wavelength ABC*.

His film scores include *Kate Plus Ten* (1938); *The Life and Death of Colonel Blimp* (1943); *A Canterbury Tale* (1944); *I Know Where I'm Going* (1945); assisted by Robert Farnon, *A Matter of Life and Death* (1946); *This Man Is Mine* (1946) and *The African Queen* (1952).

GREELEY, GEORGE (born Georgio Guariglia)

George Greeley, distinguished pianist, arranger and conductor, was the son of Italian emigrants who settled in Westerly, Rhode Island. He was taught the mandolin at the age of five, by his father, who had three music schools and a traveling orchestra.

He became an associate of PAUL WESTON when they were at Columbia University and frequently collaborated with him in arrangements for piano and orchestra. Greeley made several albums for Warner Brothers Records in the 1960s, for which he acted both as arranger, pianist and sometimes conductor. His classical background is evident in the use of the concerto form in arrangements. He also wrote and conducted for the CBS Sunday night series, *My Favorite Martian* (1963–64) and performed in concerts.

Select Discography

At the Piano Capitol LC 6614 (10")

Best Loved Christmas Piano Concertos (Reissued as **Christmas Rhapsody** Harmony H 30015)

Best of the Popular Piano Concertos (With Warner Bros. Orchestra) Warner X 1410

A Classic Affair: World's Most Beloved Popular Piano Concertos (With Warner Bros. Orchestra) Warner W/WS 1503

Gershwin Harmony H 511309

Greatest Motion Picture Piano Concertos (With Warner Bros. Orchestra) Warner W1319

Most Beautiful Music of Hawaii (With Warner Bros. Orchestra) Warner W/WS 1366

Piano Italiano Warner WS1402

Piano Rhapsodies of Love Reprise R 6092

Popular Piano Concertos from the Great Broadway Musicals (With Warner Bros. Orchestra) Warner W/WS 1415

Popular Piano Concertos of Famous Film Themes (With Warner Bros. Orchestra) Warner W/WS 1427

Popular Piano Concertos of the World's Great Love Themes (With Warner Bros. Orchestra) Warner W/WS 1387

World Renowned Popular Piano Concertos (With Warner Bros. Orchestra) Warner W/WS 1291

World's Ten Greatest Popular Piano Concertos (With Warner Bros. Orchestra) Warner W/WS 1249

GREEN, JOHN (10 October 1908–15 May 1989)
John Green was born in New York. He was educated at the Horace Mann School, New York and at New York Military Academy and graduated in economics from Harvard in 1928 to become a stockbroker. After six months he resigned and became piano accompanist for Gertrude Lawrence. He teamed up with Eddie Heyman to write songs, including 'Body and Soul' (1930), included in the Broadway revue *Three's A Crowd.* He also wrote 'I Cover the Waterfront' (1933) and 'Out of Nowhere' (1951).

In 1930 he began working for Paramount Studios. He arranged and orchestrated music for twelve films and conducted the Paramount Brooklyn Theater Orchestra. He left to work in broadcasting and theater. His 'Night Club Suite' was composed in 1932 on commission from Paul Whiteman. He visited London to compose the score for Jack Buchanan's *Mr Whittington.* One of his assignments was to work as musical director for the RICHARD RODGERS show *By Jupiter* (1942). He also conducted and arranged for the CBS series of concerts entitled *In the Modern Manner.*

In 1944 he was employed by Louis B. Mayer to arrange and conduct musicals for MGM. From 1950 to 1958, he served as head of the MGM music department. His credits include *Fiesta* (1947), *Easter Parade* (1948), *The Great Caruso* (1951), *An American in Paris* (1951), *Brigadoon* (1954), *High Society* (1956), *Raintree County* (1957), *West Side Story* (1961), *Bye, Bye, Birdie* (1963), *Oliver!* (1968) and *They Shoot Horses, Don't They?* (1969). In 1949, his score for Danny Kaye's *The Inspector General* was awarded the Foreign Correspondents' Golden Globe Award for the best motion picture of the year. He received Academy Awards for *Easter Parade, West Side Story* and *Oliver!*

Additional Readings

Ewen, David. *American Songwriters.* New York: H. W. Wilson, 1987. pp. 186–89.

Select Discography

Easter Parade Rhino 71960

Porgy and Bess: A Symphonic Picture (With Hollywood Bowl Pops Orchestra) Decca DL 4051

Sigmund Romberg Favorites (With Hollywood Bowl Pops Orchestra) Decca DL 9665

Stars and Stripes Forever and Other Sousa Marches (With Hollywood Bowl Pops Orchestra) Decca DL 4049

Compact Discs

Music From Hollywood (With Hollywood Bowl Pops Orchestra) Columbia CK 66691

Raintree County Entr'acte 2PRCD1781

GREEN, PHILIP (19 July 1911–6 October 1982)
Philip Green was born in London and began studying music at the age of seven, when he learned to play the piano. He won a scholarship to Trinity College, where he majored in orchestration, theory, harmony and composition. After college, he played in numerous orchestras and at nineteen became London's youngest conductor at the Prince of Wales Theatre in the West End. He conducted small bands and large orchestras in Great Britain and on the Continent. He subsequently became well known for his programs on Radio Luxembourg, which were broadcast in England.

During World War II, Green conducted many shows for the British Broadcasting Corporation that were designed for the armed forces. His many BBC programs included *Salute to Rhythm, Band Call, Cuban Caballeros* and *Music Society of Lower Basin Street.* He was also responsible for many original compositions and film scores. His orchestral compositions included 'Cuban Suite', 'White Orchids', 'Magic Bow', 'Shopping Centre', 'Horse Feathers', 'Follow Me Around' and 'Ecstasy' (as Jose Belmont).

Green made his first recording for the EMI Group, at the age of twenty-one and recorded consistently ever since that time. After the war, Green recorded for Capitol and MGM Records in America. His first important music for film was 'Romance' in *The Magic Bow* (1946), which became a great hit. His other films included *Saints and Sinners* (1948), *Ha'penny Breeze* (1950), *Isn't Life Wonderful?* (1952), *Inn for Trouble* (1953), *Conflict of Wings* (1954), *John and Julie* (1955), *The March Hare* (1956), *The Square Peg* (1958), *Operation Amsterdam* (1959), *The League of Gentlemen* (1960), *The Singer Not the Song* (1961) and *Victim* (1961).

Select Discography

Great Waltzes from Gilbert and Sullivan Riverside Records RLP 97530

Moods of London Capitol T 10059

Music of Irving Berlin: The Early Years International (Camden) INTS 1083

Music of Irving Berlin: The Golden Years International (Camden) Stereo INTS 1209

Music of Jerome Kern International (Camden) INTS 1082

Music of Rodgers and Hammerstein International (Camden) INTS 1081

Music of Rodgers and Hart: My Funny Valentine International (Camden) INTS 1207

Pan American Panorama Columbia 33SC 1121

Romantic Sound of the 40s State Records ETMP6

Serenade in the Night MGM E3119

Study in Green Coral CRL 57074

Tango Time MGM E175

Wings of Song Rank Records of America JAS 8002 [Also on CD]

GREENWOOD, JOHN (26 June 1889–15 April 1975)
John Greenwood, film composer, was born in London and educated at the Royal College of Music. He won the Grove scholarship and Arthur Sullivan composition award. He studied under C. V. Stanford and taught for a short period at Brighton and Hove Grammar School. During his early career he played piano, French horn and viola in various orchestras. He composed various classical works, songs and a ballet suite, many of which were played by the Queen's Hall Orchestra under Sir Henry Wood. A few were first played at the Proms in the early 1920s. During the 1920s he composed and edited scores for silent movies. In 1929 he wrote a new score for the part-talkie film *To What Red Hell?* Greenwood's increasing preoccupation with film work led to his cessation of all other forms of composing, but his music is of such quality that it can be performed in the concert hall, divorced from the movies it originally accompanied.

Some of his scores include *Man of Aran* (1934), *Elephant Boy* (1937), *Pimpernel Smith* (1941), *Hungry Hill* (1946) and *The Last Days of Dolwyn* (1949). The score of the latter film won the Venice Film Award.

GREGORY, JOHNNY (born John Gregori) (12 October 1928)
Johnny Gregory was a violinist, arranger and bandleader. He was the son of Frank Gregori, a bandleader at the London restaurant Quaglino's for ten years. He worked in his father's band at London Normandy Hotel, while he was still in his teens. He then became an arranger as well as a freelance performer in clubs. He became famous for his arrangements for recording artists such as Russ Hamilton, Connie Francis, Matt Munro, Cleo Laine, Anthony Newley and Nana Mouskouri. He conducted his own LPs using pseudonyms such as Nino Ricci. This led to his becoming well known for two very different types of music; the exciting big band jazz and Latin American sounds of his 'Chaquito' recordings and also as one of the most creative and talented writers for string orchestras. His string orchestra was called the New Cascading Strings and became famous in the 1960s, particularly in Japan.

He conducted frequently on BBC Radio 2, either with one of the two above-mentioned orchestras or with the BBC Radio Orchestra '84. He frequently played many of the arrangements he wrote especially for his records. He also conducted for films and for television music programs. Gregory was the principal arranger for the scintillating MOODS ORCHESTRAL Series.

Select Discography

Amazing Grace—The New Cascading Strings Philips 6308 082

Cascading Strings Philips 6308 016, Fontana SFL 13018

Cascading Strings Play Philips 6382 035

Chaquito Story (Double album) Philips 6641015

Chaquito Magic Philips 6308 050

Contrast—The New Cascading Strings Philips 6308 107

Golden Memories—The Cascading Strings Philips 846052

Great Chaquito Revolution Philips 6309013

Gregory Conducts . . . Philips 6499 308

Gregory Conducts the Sounds of Today Philips 6308 142

Hi-Fi Show Mood Music Allegro 1737

Hold Me . . . M.G.M. Records E 3479

Latin Colours Philips Cassette no. 7108 065

Melodies of Japan Fontana TL 5205

Sables and Sepia Fontana TFL 5009 (Reissued as I'll Be Around)

Serenade in Blue Contour 6870 604

Slaves of Love Rondo Record Corporation 111

Spies and Dolls—The Chaquito Big Band Philips 6308 111

TV Thrillers—Chaquito Philips 6308 087

See also **Moods Orchestral Series**

Compact Disc

Golden Memories Philips 84052–2

GRUSIN, DAVE (b. 26 June 1934)

Dave Grusin was born in Littleton, California. He began scoring films in 1967, with *Divorce American Style* and *The Graduate*. His musical style varies tremendously from extremely modern, as in *Tootsie* (1982) to lush, as in *On Golden Pond* (1981).

Other film scores include *The Heart Is a Lonely Hunter* (1968), *Murder by Death* (1976), *Heaven Can Wait* (1978), *The Champ* (1979), *Lucas* (1986), *The Milagro Beanfield War* (1988), *Clara's Heart* (1988), *The Fabulous Baker Boys* (1989), *Havana* (1990), *For the Boys* (1991) and *The Firm* (1993).

Grusin is co-owner of GRP Records and is a popular recording artist for his own independent jazz label.

Select Discography

Bobby Deerfield Casablanca NBLP 7071

3 Days of the Condor Capitol SW-11469

H

HALLETZ, ERWIN

Erwin Halletz was born in Vienna and began studying music at the age of six. His first instrument was the violin. At fourteen, he entered the Vienna Music School, where he specialized in theory, piano and clarinet. He began his musical career as a music teacher and cabaret musician. He subsequently conducted a radio dance orchestra, arranged for the Horst Winter orchestra and toured Europe with his own show orchestra. He has also composed, arranged and conducted the scores for numerous motion pictures.

Select Discography

Golden Award Songs: The Sound of Erwin Halletz and His Orchestra Polydor LPHM 46319

Music in Danube Blue Polydor LPHM 46077

Russian Themes (With Monte Carlo Symphony Orchestra) Polydor SLPHM 237634

HAYMAN, RICHARD (b. 1920)

Richard Hayman was born in Cambridge and brought up in Winthrop, Massachusetts. He taught himself to play the harmonica while still in high school. At the age of eighteen, he was invited to join Borrah Minnevitch's world-famous Harmonica Rascals. After three years, he left to form his own group and appeared in theatres around the country and as a soloist with many leading orchestras.

A tour with Horace Heidt's troupe brought Hayman to Hollywood, where he played small parts in several musical films and learned the art of arranging background music for films under the tutelage of George Stoll. Examples of his major credits were 'Meet Me in St. Louis' and 'State Fair'.

He worked with Vaughn Monroe for four years and then came to the attention of Mercury Records when a succession of his background scorings were instrumental in promoting the career of Bobby Wayne, a prominent recording artist for Mercury. It was decided to allow Hayman to arrange, conduct and in many cases write for his own recordings.

His first solo recording for Mercury was 'Ruby', which reached the top of the hit parade. Hayman's haunting virtuoso playing of the harmonica on that disc brought about the renewed popularity of that instrument. Mercury appointed Hayman artist and repertoire chief of its New York branch. Hayman later recorded with the Manhattan Pops Orchestra. More recently he recorded numerous compact discs for the Naxos label.

Examples of his compositions are 'Skipping Along', 'No Strings Attached', 'Huck Finn' and 'Carriage Trade'. ARTHUR FIEDLER and the BOSTON POPS ORCHESTRA have recorded some of Richard Hayman's arrangements.

Select Discography

Broadway Time Records S/2194

Cleopatra Time Records S/2080

Far Away Places Mercury MG 20129

Fiddlers on the Roof Time Records S/2186

Glory of Spain (With Manhattan Pops Orchestra) Stateside EMI Series 2000 Stereo SJSL 5016

Great Hits of the 40s Time Records S/2146

Great Motion Picture Themes of Victor Young Mercury SR-60012

Havana in Hi-Fi Mercury SR 60000

Melodies of Love (Manhattan Pops Orchestra) Time S/2191

Memories of You Mercury MG 25191

Motion Picture Themes Original Compositions (With Manhattan Pops Orchestra) Time Records S/2131

Music for a Quiet Evening Mercury MG 20018

Music from Great Motion Pictures (With Manhattan Pops Orchestra) Time S/2187

Paris-Soul of a People (With Manhattan Pops Orchestra) Time S/2184

Pride and Passion-Italy (With Manhattan Pops Orchestra) Time S/2185

Reminiscing Mercury MG 20113

Serenade for Love Mercury MG 20115

Tender Moments (Manhattan Pops Orchestra) Time S/2033

Time to Listen Mercury MG 20103

To My Love Mercury MG 20048

Two Tickets to Paris Mercury MG 20220

Two Tickets to Rome Mercury MG 20235

Voodoo SR 60147

Wonderful Girls Mercury Wing SRW 16285

Compact Discs on Naxos International

8 990000 Series

01 **Best of John Williams:** ET, Superman, Raiders of the Lost Ark

02 **Star Wars**

03 **Star Trek:** Star Trek I, II, III, IV, V

04 **Sound of Music:** South Pacific, Sound of Music, Carousel, Oklahoma

05 **Christmas Festival**

06 **Silent Night**

10 **World-Famous Marches**

11 **Music of Leroy Anderson**

13 **Joy to the World**

17 **Love's Themes**

18 **Irish Rhapsody**

19 **I Love You Truly:** Music for Weddings

20 **Great Love Songs**

21 **Melodies of Love**

22 **Love Is Blue**

23 **No Strings Attached:** Richard Hayman

24 **Great Hollywood Epics**

31 **Strike up the Band:** Music of George Gershwin

32 **When You Wish Upon a Star:** Salute to Walt Disney NAXOS 990032

33 **Phantom of the Opera:** Hit Shows by Andrew Lloyd Webber

34 **Classic Film Scores:** Wuthering Heights, For Whom the Bell Tolls, Taras Bulba

35 **An Evening in Paris**

36 **Viva España and Mexico**

37 **Julio Iglesias Song Book**

38 **Music of Henry Mancini**

39 **Music of Lerner and Loewe**

41 **Broadway Blockbusters**

42 Vintage Broadway
43 Romantic Broadway

Greatest Love of All NAXOS 8.990020
Harlem Nocturne KEM-DISC REM 1012
Romantic Broadway NAXOS 8.990043
Sound of Music NAXOS 8.990004

HEFTI, NEAL (b. 29 October 1922)
Neal Hefti was born in Hastings, Nebraska. He was a trumpet player and arranger, who first gained prominence in the early 1940s with the Charlie Barnet band. In succeeding years, he worked with Muggsy Spanier, Earl (Fatha) Hines, Charlie Spivak, Horace Heidt and Bobby Byrne. He subsequently arranged for Woody Herman from 1944 onward, producing numbers such as 'Apple Honey', 'Goosey Gander', 'Jones Beachhead' 'The Good Earth', 'Wildroot', 'Everywhere' and 'Northwest Passage'. He also updated the band's signature tune, 'Woodchopper's Ball', and changed the image of the group, who became known as Herman's Herd. He wrote for Charlie Ventura (1946), Harry James (1948) and arranged for Count Basie from 1950 to 1960.

He occasionally led his own bands and orchestras and acted as musical director for his wife, the singer Frances Wayne. He also recorded and scored the music for Hollywood and television films. From the mid-1970s onward, he undertook concert tours and lectures. His film scores include *Sex and the Single Girl* (1965); *Barefoot in the Park* (1966); *The Odd Couple* (1968). He also composed the television scores for *The Odd Couple* (theme and series) and *Batman* (theme and series)

Select Discography

Concert Miniatures RCA RD-27058

HENDERSON, SKITCH (b. 27 January 1918)
Skitch Henderson, bandleader, pianist and composer, was born in Birmingham, England but spent most of his boyhood in Halstad, Minnesota. He attended the University of California at Los Angeles. He studied theory and harmony with Arnold Schonberg and conducting with Albert Coates and Fritz Reiner. He also studied piano with Roger Aubert in Paris and subsequently changed to popular music. He played the piano in dance bands and theater orchestras. He accompanied Judy Garland on tour and was musical director of Bing Crosby's and Frank Sinatra's radio shows. From 1947 to 1949, he led his own dance band and recorded for Capitol Records.

From 1951 to 1966, he was a musical director of the National Broadcasting Company, during which time he directed the Steve Allen show (1955–56) and led the band on the television program *Tonight.*

From 1971 to 1972, he conducted the Tulsa Symphony Orchestra and acted as guest conductor for many other orchestras, including the New York Philharmonic and the Minneapolis Symphony. He was musical director for the New York City Opera revival of Kurt Weill's *Street Scene.*

Select Discography

Hollywood Award Winners Columbia Stereo CS 8826

Lush and Lovely Columbia CS 8623

Sketches by Skitch RCA Victor LPM-1401

Tribute to Cole Porter, Richard Rodgers, Jerome Kern SEECO CELP 405

Winter Holiday (New York Philharmonic) CBS BSF 9040

Compact Discs

From Berlin to Bernstein EMI CDC 7 542742

New York Pops Goes to the Movies ANGEL CDC 077775449921

HENDRICKS, BELFORD

Belford Hendricks, pianist, arranger, composer and conductor, was born in Evansville, Indiana. He was educated at Indiana State Teachers' College, where he majored in music. He worked his way through school by playing with various local bands.

His first professional job was as pianist with the Paul Stuart band in Indiana. He subsequently arranged the music and conducted the orchestra for recordings by singers such as Dinah Washington, Sarah Vaughan, Patti Page and Brook Benton. His compositions include 'Looking Back', 'Nothing in the World' (recorded by Nat 'King' Cole), 'Call Me' (recorded by Johnny Mathis) and 'It's Just a Matter of Time' (recorded by Brook Benton).

In 1962, Hendricks conducted the orchestra for the Nat 'King' Cole hit record 'Ramblin Rose' (music by Joe and Noel Sherman), which was sixteen weeks in the United States best-sellers, reaching No. 2.

Select Discography

Songs for Lovers Young and Old Mercury Wing SRW 16222

HERBERT, VICTOR (1 February 1859–26 May 1924)

Victor Herbert was born in Dublin. After the early death of his father, his mother moved to Stuttgart in 1867, where Herbert was educated. He became a professional cellist playing in various orchestras in Germany, France, Italy, Switzerland and Vienna. He eventually joined the Stuttgart

Court Orchestra and studied composition at the Conservatory. He married the soprano Therese Forster, who was engaged by the Metropolitan Opera, New York, in 1888. They became naturalized Americans, and Herbert began to identify himself with American music. He became principal conductor of the Pittsburgh Symphony Orchestra from 1898 to 1904 and was able to present many of his own orchestral works.

He composed many operettas, including *The Serenade* (1897); *The Fortune Teller* (1898); *Babes in Toyland* (1903, filmed 1934 and 1961); *It Happened in Nordland* (1904); *Mlle Modiste* (1905, filmed in 1931 as *Kiss Me Again*), *The Red Mill* (1906); *Naughty Marietta* (1910, filmed 1935); *Sweethearts* (1913, filmed 1938); *The Only Girl* (1914); *The Princess Pat* (1915); *Eileen* (1917); *Angel Face* (1919); *Ziegfeld Follies* (1921 and 1923); *Orange Blossoms* (1922) and *The Dream Girl* (1924).

In 1916, he composed the first musical score to accompany a silent film in America, *The Fall of a Nation*. Other scores were for *When Knighthood Was in Flower* (1922) and *Little Old New York* (1923). He composed for many other shows. One of his famous songs was 'Indian Summer' (1919), to which Al Dubin added words in 1939. In 1946, an operetta, *Gypsy Lady*, was staged in New York, with songs drawn from earlier operettas. At the time of his death in 1924, he was working on the next version of *Ziegfeld Follies*. A film of his life, *The Great Victor Herbert* was made in 1939, with Walter Connolly in the leading role.

Additional Readings

Ewen, David. *American Songwriters*. New York: H. W. Wilson, 1987. pp. 219–25.

Ewen, David. *Great Men of American Popular Song*. Englewood Cliffs, NJ: Prentice-Hall, 1970. pp. 70–86.

Waters, Edward N. *Victor Herbert: A Life in Music*. New York: Macmillan, 1955.

Select Discography

Faith, Percy. Columbia Album of Victor Herbert Columbia CZL10 [Also on CD]

Fennell, Frederick. Conducts Victor Herbert Mercury PPS 2007

Goodman, Al. Relax with Victor Herbert RCA LPM 1023

Gould, Morton. Victor Herbert Serenades Columbia AL50

Kostelanetz, Andre. Music of Victor Herbert Columbia CL765 [Also on CD]

Mantovani. Music of Victor Herbert London LL 746

Melachrino, George. Music of Victor Herbert RCA LAC/LSP 2129

Munro, Ronnie. Music of Victor Herbert Richmond B 20009

Stockholm String Orchestra (Conductor not named). **The Best of Victor Herbert** Somerset P400

Yorke, Peter. Melody Lingers On: The Music of Irving Berlin and Victor Herbert. Decca DL 8240

Yorke, Peter. Music for Sweethearts: Romantic Compositions of Victor Herbert Decca DL 8242

HERMAN, HARRY

Harry Herman was born in Brunn and brought up in Vienna and had an intensive classical background at the Vienna Academy. At the age of seventeen, he was playing with the Vienna Philharmonic Orchestra under the direction of Richard Strauss. In 1924, he became a member of the Guarneri Quartet, performing chamber music throughout Europe and North and South America. He gained recognition as conductor, composer, performer and arranger. He was equally interested in the range of serious music from the concert versions of great operas to the music of GEORGE GERSHWIN.

Select Discography

Harry Herman Plays Operetta Favourites Polydor LPHM 46824

Music for Cards, Conversation and Cuddling Decca DL 8563

Musik Zum Traumen Polydor LPHM 46823; Also issued as:

Sweet and Sentimental Polydor LPHM 46823

HERRMANN, BERNARD (30 June 1911–24 December 1975)

Bernard Herrmann was born in New York. He took violin lessons as a child and studied composition at New York University with Percy Grainger and Philip James. He became a fellowship student at the Juilliard School.

He became staff conductor for CBS Radio, New York City, in 1933. In 1938, he began working with Orson Welles and the Mercury Theater group at CBS, becoming musical director of the Mercury Theater radio shows. He commenced his first score for the Orson Welles film *Citizen Kane* in 1940. Herrmann subsequently worked with other directors. He won an Academy Award for *All That Money Can Buy* [aka *The Devil and Daniel Webster*] in 1941. In 1955, he scored his first Hitchcock film, *The Trouble with Harry*. Other Hitchcock films followed, notably *The Man Who Knew Too Much* (1956), *Vertigo* (1958), *North by Northwest* (1959), *Psycho* (1960), and *Marnie* (1964).

Other film scores included *The Kentuckian* (1955), *The Man in the Grey Flannel Suit* (1956), *Cape Fear* (1962), *Fahrenheit 451* (1966), *Sisters* (1973), *Obsession* (1976) and *Taxi Driver* (1976). For television, he scored episodes of *The Twilight Zone*.

Hermann died the night he finished recording his score for Martin Scorsese's *Taxi Driver*. He was said to be the most radical and innovative film composer of his era, who refused to recognize the distinction between writing for films and for the concert hall.

Select Discography

Battle of Neretva Entr'acte ERS 6501

Christmas Carol (TV Score) Unicorn RHS-850

Citizen Kane and the Classic Film Scores of Bernard Herrmann RCA ARL1-0707

Fantasy Film World of Bernard Herrmann London SP 44207

Ghost and Mrs. Muir (Conducted by Elmer Bernstein) Filmmusic Collection FMC-4

Kentuckian Suite (Conducted by Fred Steiner) Entr'acte ERS 6506

King of the Khyber Rifles (Conducted by Charles Gerhardt) RCA ARL-42005

Mysterious Film World of Bernard Herrmann London SPC 21137

Obsession London SPC 21160

Psycho Unicorn RHS-336

Sisters Entr'acte ERQ 7001ST

Taxi Driver (Conducted by Dave Blume) Arista AL4079

Torn Curtain (Conducted by Elmer Bernstein) Filmmusic Collection FMC-10

Vertigo (Conducted by Muir Mathieson) Mercury Golden Imports SRI-75117

Compact Discs

Citizen Kane (Australian Philharmonic Orchestra. Conductor Tony Bremner) Preamble PRCD1788

Day the Earth Stood Still (Conductors Bernard Herrman, Lionel and Alfred Newman) Arista 20th Century Fox 11010–2

Fahrenheit 451 (Seattle Symphony Orchestra, Conductor Joel McNeely) Varese Sarabande VSD5551

Ghost and Mrs. Muir (Royal Philharmonic Orchestra. Conductor Elmer Bernstein) Varese Sarabande VCD47254

Jane Eyre (Conductor Bernard Herrmann) Arista 20th Century Fox 11006–2

Magnificent Ambersons (Australian Philharmonic Orchestra. Conductor Tony Bremner) Preamble PRCD1783

Mysterious Island (London Symphony Orchestra. Conductor Bernard Herrmann) Cloud Nine ACN7017

North by Northwest (MGM Studio Orchestra. Conductor Bernard Herrmann) Rhino 72101

North by Northwest (London Studio Symphony Orchestra. Conductor Laurie Johnson) Unicorn-Kanchana UKCD2040; Varese Sarabande VCD47205

Psycho (National Philharmonic Orchestra. Conductor Bernard Herrmann) Unicorn-Kanchana UKCD2021

Taxi Driver (Original Score. Conductors Bernard Herrmann and Dave Blume) Varese Sarabande VSD5279

Torn Curtain. The Classic Film Music of Bernard Herrmann (City of Prague Philharmonic Orchestra. Conductor Paul Bateman) Silva Screen FILMCD162

HILL-BOWEN, WILLIAM

Hill-Bowen was a British conductor and arranger, who began his career in the early 1950s as a classical pianist. One of his first long-playing records was a recording of popular piano concertos performed with the GEORGE MELACHRINO Orchestra. Hill-Bowen went on to make his mark as an arranger and conductor. He arranged much of the recorded music of Melachrino in the late 1950s and early 1960s and also recorded under his own name as conductor. Many of his records were made for READER'S DIGEST. Some of them were marketed anonymously, under the name of the Singing Strings and occasionally, the Romantic Strings. (Not all of the Romantic Strings recordings can be attributed to Hill-Bowen.) The high point of his career as a light orchestral conductor was reached when he made numerous recordings with the LIVING STRINGS.

Select Discography

Beautiful Dreamer—Stephen Foster (Reader's Digest Album: **Magical Worlds of Melody**) RDM 2045/RDS 6045

Dancing in the Dark RCA RDS 2881

Dream Along RCA CSP 108

I Could Have Danced All Night RCA RAL 1001

I Married an Angel RCA RAL 1004

Instrumental Hits from Lerner and Loewe's Gigi. RCA Camden CAL 436

King and I RCA Camden CAS 502

Kiss Me, Kate RCA Camden CAS 482

Love on Broadway RCA RAL 1005

Music for Dreaming RCA RD 3241

Music Man RCA Camden CAS 428

My Fair Lady RCA Camden CAS 520/SND 5008

Oklahoma! RCA Camden CAS 499

Show Boat RCA Camden SND 5001

Slaughter on 10th Avenue/Victory at Sea Album: **Hits from the Shows** (Reader's Digest) RDM 2052

South Pacific RCA Camden SND 5003

Standards in Stereo RCA Camden CAS 461

Take Me Along RCA Camden CAL 580

Waltzes for Dancing (Reader's Digest Album: **Popular Music That Will Live Forever**) RDM 2008

Arrangements with Living Strings

'Charade' and Other Film Hits RCA Camden CAL/CAS 799

Music from 'Camelot' RCA Camden CAL/CAS 657

Music of George Gershwin RCA Camden CAL/CAS 675

Music of Hawaii RCA Camden CAL/CAS 661

Music for Romance RCA Camden CAL/CAS 637

Music to Help You Stop Smoking RCA Camden CAL/CAS 821

My Silent Love RCA Camden CAL/CAS 784

New From Broadway RCA Camden CAL/CAS 790

Shimmering Sounds RCA Camden CAL/CAS 761

Too Beautiful for Words RCA Camden CAL/CAS 791 [Also on CD]

HOLLYWOOD BOWL ORCHESTRA

The Hollywood Bowl is one of the largest natural amphitheaters in the world, with seating for 18,000 people. The first concert season was held in 1922 and since that time, some of the greatest performers have appeared in this venue, including such diverse artists as Jascha Heifetz, Otto Klemperer, LEONARD BERNSTEIN, Judy Garland, the Beatles and Sting.

The Hollywood Bowl Orchestra was founded by Leopold Stokowski in 1945 and gained immediate recognition for its distinctive sound and exciting programs. In the 1950's the orchestra was conducted by CARMEN DRAGON, who introduced the popular evening concerts. In 1991, JOHN MAUCERI took over the orchestra and greatly enhanced its proud tradition.

HOLMES, LEROY (b. 22 September 1913)

Leroy Holmes was born in Pittsburgh and studied music at Northwestern University, at Juilliard, New York and privately with composer Ernest Toch. He served as staff arranger for six years for Vincent Lopez and then became chief arranger to Harry James. He transferred from band work to studio arranging in Hollywood. After arranging a few tunes for Alf Lund's debut session on MGM, he came to the attention of the film-sponsored record company, which he joined as arranger-conductor. Holmes started recording material with his own orchestra and also composed and conducted scores for children's discs. In 1954, he scored a hit conducting his orchestra for the single number, 'The High and the Mighty', composed by DIMITRI TIOMKIN, with whistling soloist Fred Lowry.

Select Discography

All Time Latin Favorites United Artists UAL 3272

Alone Together: Songs By Howard Dietz and Arthur Schwartz MGM E 215 (10")

Candlelight and Wine MGM E 3288

50 Fabulous Waltz Favorites United Artists UAS 6395
Les Girls MGM E 3590
Los Violinos del Amour (2 LPs) United Artists LS 61024, 61047
Love Themes from Motion Pictures MGM E 3172
Lush Themes from Motion Pictures MGM E 3172
Music from the Broadway Musical All-American MGM E/SE 4034
Music from the Modern Screen MGM E 3753
Musical Portrait of Ray Charles MGM E 4059
Portrait of Bing MGM E 3569
Snuggled on Your Shoulder (With MGM Strings) MGM E246
Sophisticated Strings MGM E 3833
Spectacular Guitars and Strings MGM SF 2 MGM 4
Take Me in Your Arms MGM E 3378

I

INGLEZ, ROBERTO (born Robert Inglis)

Roberto Inglez was born in Elgin, Morayshire, and christened Robert Inglis. He learned to play the piano at the age of five and had passed many examinations by the age of twelve. He studied music at the Royal Academy of Music, London. His initial employment was in the field of jazz and dance music. He became interested in South American and Caribbean music and joined the Edmundo Ross rumba band at the end of World War II, as a pianist.

When he started up his own band, Inglis latinized his name to Roberto Inglez. From 1946 to 1954, his band played at the Savoy Hotel, London. In 1954 he left England to settle permanently in South America.

He began recording for Parlophone in 1946. His records and radio broadcasts with the Savoy Hotel dance unit, for the BBC and Radio Luxembourg were later augmented to orchestral proportions for records and broadcasts, by the addition of strings, woodwind and French horns. He frequently accompanied the orchestra with a soft, soothing one-finger piano presentation of the melody, usually in the bass clef, alternating with a dextrous South American exercise using all the fingers of both hands.

His style was a mixture of authenticity, commercial considerations and innate good taste and musicianship that became popular in Latin America itself. Two leading South American singers, Chilean-born Lucho Gatica and Dalva de Oliveira of Brazil, made a special journey to London to record with the Inglez orchestra. Inglez himself toured Brazil, with an orchestra composed of the best musicians, and played to packed concert halls.

Select Discography

The Melody Maker World Records EMI SH 206

IRVING, ERNEST (6 November 1878–24 October 1953)
Ernest Irving was born in Godalming, Surrey. He learned the piano, organ, harmony, composition and orchestration. His early career was spent as a traveling conductor and composer for pantomimes and variety shows. He worked with impresario George Edwardes as musical director on shows such as *The Dollar Princess*, *The Lilac Domino* and *Toto*. By 1914, he had become one of the most important conductors in London's West End. Later shows included *Miss Hook of Holland, Tom Jones, Kismet, The Dubarry, The Glass Slipper* and *Land of Smiles*.

In 1937, he joined Ealing Studios as musical director and remained with them for the rest of his career. He furthered the careers of film composers such as Tristan Cary and George Auric and scored numerous films himself. Notable contributions were *The Four Just Men* (1939), *The Proud Valley* (1940), *The Blue Lamp* (1949), *A Run for Your Money* (1949), *Whiskey Galore* (1949) and *I Believe in You* (1952). After his death, the musical direction of Ealing and Michael Bolton productions was taken over by Dock (John) Mathieson, brother of MUIR MATHIESON.

Select Discography

Famous Evergreens (With the Sinfonia of London) HMV CLP 1386

Philharmonic Pops (With the Sinfonia of London) HMV CLP 1225

J

JARRE, MAURICE (b. 13 September 1924)
Maurice Jarre, the film composer, was born in Lyons, France. His first important commission was for the score of *Lawrence of Arabia*, (1962), which began a close collaboration with David Lean, for whom he also scored *Doctor Zhivago* (1965) and *Ryan's Daughter* (1970). His scores were of an epic, lush-sounding nature, enhanced by the use of electronic music, as is evident in *The Year of Living Dangerously* (1983) and *Witness* (1985). All the electronic instruments were recorded simultaneously, with a small group of musicians. Other of his scores include *The Man Who Would Be King* (1975), *Mohammed, Messenger of God* (1977), *A Passage to India* (1984), *Mad Max Beyond Thunderdome* (1985), *No Way Out* (1987) and *Fatal Attraction* (1987).

Select Discography

Crossed Swords Warner BSK-3161

Doctor Zhivago Suite (Conducted by Stanley Black) London SP 44173

Island at the Top of the World Disneyland ST 3814

Life and Times of Judge Roy Bean Columbia S-31948

Man Who Would be King Capitol SW-11474

Mohammed Messenger of God EMI SLCW-1033

Ryan's Daughter MGM ISE-27ST

Compact Discs

Doctor Zhivago (Original Score. Conductor Maurice Jarre) Rhino 71957

Lawrence of Arabia (London Philharmonic Orchestra. Conductor Maurice Jarre) Varese Sarabande VSD5263

Maurice Jarre at Abbey Road (Royal Philharmonic Orchestra. Conductor Maurice Jarre) Milan 262 321

Walk in the Clouds (Original Score. Conductor Maurice Jarre) Milan 28666–2

JENKINS, GORDON (12 May 1910–24 April 1984)

Jenkins was born in Webster Groves, Missouri. He came from a musical family and as a child occasionally played the organ at the Chicago movie theater where his father was the regular organist. He learned to play six different instruments and took up a career as a professional musician after winning an amateur ukelele contest sponsored by Cliff Edwards in St. Louis.

During the Prohibition Era, he played piano in a St. Louis speakeasy. He then found work at St. Louis radio station KMOX, where he was required to make use of his multi-instrumental abilities. After a year or so of the radio station routine he joined up as a banjo player in a band headed by his brother, conductor Marshall Jenkins. In 1936, he became staff arranger for Isham Jones, who conducted a dance orchestra. He later composed and arranged for other conductors, including Woody Herman, Lennie Hayton, Vincent Lopez, Benny Goodman and ANDRE KOSTELANETZ.

He received his first Broadway job in 1936, arranging scores and conducting the orchestra for Beatrice Lillie's musical *The Show Is On*. In Hollywood he worked for a time for Paramount, scoring films and conducting. He then moved in 1939 to NBC as West Coast network musical director, where he remained for five years.

One of his first successful compositions was 'Goodbye', the closing theme for Benny Goodman. While working at NBC, he continued to produce memorable music for movies and nightclubs. He earned credits as author of popular hits such as 'Blue Prelude', 'P.S. I Love You', 'You Have Taken My Heart', 'When a Woman Loves a Man' (all with Johnny Mercer); 'Blue Evening', 'San Fernando Valley', 'I'm Homesick, That's All', 'How Old Am I?' and 'Tomorrow'.

In 1944, Jenkins left NBC to conduct a thirty-one-piece orchestra on the Dick Haymes radio show, where he collaborated with Tom Adair on the 'Capsule Operettas'. In 1945, he became staff conductor for Decca Records. In the same year, he wrote and recorded a long work entitled 'Manhattan Tower'. This piece for orchestra and singers was a song of praise to New York and has been performed by the Atlanta Symphony Orchestra in revues and on television.

In 1949, Jenkins appeared at the Paramount and Capitol theaters in New York. He also worked on the score for the Broadway show *Along Fifth Avenue*, moved to Paramount Studios in 1951 and then to Las Vegas, where he conducted at the Thunderbird and Riviera hotels for the next decade. At the same time, he composed shows for the Tropicana. In 1952, Jenkins composed the score for *Bwana Devil*, the first 3-D feature film. He returned to NBC as television producer from 1955 to 1957, which was when he conducted a show for Judy Garland in London.

Jenkins made records and albums with his own orchestra and with performers such as Louis Armstrong, Artie Shaw, Judy Garland, Peggy Lee, Martha Tilton, Ethel Merman, Nat 'King' Cole and Frank Sinatra. His work with Sinatra was much acclaimed, particularly the albums *Where Are You?* (1957) and *No One Cares* (1959). In 1965, he won a Grammy Award for his arrangement of Frank Sinatra's 'It Was a Very Good Year'. He served as arranger and conductor on the singer's 1973 comeback. His last major work was as composer of the 'Future' section of the *Sinatra Trilogy* three-record album for Reprise in 1981.

His scores for Nat 'King' Cole included the definitive arrangement of 'Stardust' for the album *Love Is the Thing* (1957). Jenkins was credited as promoting the popularity of the folk singing group, The Weavers. He arranged hit recordings for Pete Seeger, Ronnie Gilbert, Lee Hays and Fred Hellerman, which include 'Good Night Irene' and 'Tzena, Tzena, Tzena'. Other popular numbers arranged and conducted by Gordon Jenkins were 'I Don't See Me in Your Eyes Anymore', 'Again', 'Don't Cry, Joe', 'My Foolish Heart', 'Bewitched', 'I'm Forever Blowing Bubbles' and 'So Long (It's Been Good to Know You)'. Jenkins died in Malibu, California.

Musical Achievements

Jenkins is notable as an arranger/conductor and also as a recording artist in his own right. His orchestrations are characterized by an unusual richness, achieving sonority without sacrificing the essential line of melody.

Three 10" LPs which show up the quality of his orchestral arrangements to particularly good effect are *Music of Jerome Kern*, which includes a wonderful arrangement of 'Till The Clouds Roll By', *Musical Highlights from Me and Juliet* (Rodgers and Hammerstein) and *Can Can* (Porter), all of which were made for Decca.

Jenkins's subsequent recordings for Decca were highlighted by his 'Manhattan Tower', a combination of ingratiating melodies and symphonic scenario, and an LP of standards in the Latin idiom, entitled *In the Still of the Night*. One of his finest LPs in the light orchestral field appeared on the Capitol label under the title *Stolen Hours*. This is perhaps a lesser-known disc, but it ranks among the finest of Jenkins's instrumental albums. It displays a unique facility for using a choir of French horns to augment the string sound.

Time Records in the United States produced the LP *France*, which clearly demonstrates Jenkins's flair for orchestration. This album was marred by the irritating dialogue interpolated between the musical numbers, but a subsequent reissue on the same label, *Paris, I Wish You Love*, eliminated the irritation. Jenkins's original composition, the beautiful waltz 'Danse et Bougival', is included on both these discs.

When Jenkins turned to the songs commemorating particular ethnic groups, his arrangements for strings reached near perfection. This is evident in two examples, *Hawaiian Wedding Song and Other Sounds of Paradise*, which is one of the best orchestral portraits of Hawaii and *Soul of a People*, which is one of the finest anthologies of Jewish music on disc, scored with great sincerity and feeling.

For sheer nostalgia, one must listen to the twenty-six film themes of yesteryear included in *The Great Movie Themes of the 30's, 40's, 50's* or the truly wonderful arrangement of 'Love, Here Is My Heart' on the album *Heartbeats*. Although he achieved fame as an arranger for top vocalists and through his popular compositions, he ranks as a giant in his own right in the world of light orchestral music.

Additional Readings

Friedwald, Will. *Sinatra: The Song Is You: A Singer's Art*. New York: Scribner, 1995, pp. 317–361.

Select Discography

Almanac LXA X RCA 1026

Blue Prelude (Reissue of SDBD 1087) SUS 5149

Dream Dust Capitol T 1023

Dreamer's Holiday Vocalion VL 3615

France Time S/2061 (Reissued as **Paris, I Wish You Love** Time S/2130)

Great Movie Themes of the 30's, 40's, 50's Joy 102

Hawaiian Wedding Song and Other Sounds of Paradise Columbia CL 1764/CS 8564

Heartbeats Decca DL 8116

I Live Alone KS 3361

In a Tender Mood Columbia CS 8809

In the Still of the Night Decca DL 8077

Let's Duet WS 1464

Magic World Columbia CS 8682

Manhattan Tower (Jenkins) Decca DL 8011, DT 766

Music of Jerome Kern Decca DL 5276 (U.S.); Brunswick LA 8540 (U.K.)

Musical Highlights from Me and Juliet (Rodgers and Hammerstein)

Can Can (Porter) Decca DL 5469

My Heart Sings Decca DL 74714

Night Dreams Capitol T 781

Presents Marshall Royal Everest SDBR 1087

P.S. I Love You Decca DL 9109

Seven Dreams Decca DL 79011

Soft Soul DOT DLP 25752

Soul of a People Mainstream 56096/S6093, S/2050

Stolen Hours Capitol T 884

Tropicana Holiday Capitol ST 1048

Twenty-six Academy Award Winners CGS Zircon (Canada) 3002; Stereo Sounds SA 17 (US)

Way Back Now Capitol ST 2035

Yours Pickwick SPC 3005

JOBIM, ANTONIO CARLOS (1927–8 December 1995)

Jobim, the Brazilian composer, author, pianist, guitarist and singer, is noted for his interest in Brazilian music. This interest became internationally famous when he and Luis Bonfa wrote the score for the film *Orfeu Negro* (*Black Orpheus*, 1959). His songs helped popularize the bossa nova style of music in the 1960s. Jobim gave concerts and made many recordings in the United States.

Jobim's works have a haunting, evocative quality with great musical sophistication and subtle rhythms. They have proved durable beyond the initial bossa nova craze, and include: 'Samba de uma nota só' ('One-note samba' 1961), 'Desafinado' (1962), 'Chega de saudade' ('No more blues', 1962) 'Agua de beber' ('Drinking water', 1962), 'Meditação' ('Meditation', 1963), 'Corcovado' ('Quiet Night of Quiet Stars', 1963/64), 'Garota de Ipanema' ('The Girl From Ipanema 1963/64), 'Insensatez' ('How Insensitive', 1963/64), 'So todos fossem iguais a você' ('Someone to light up my life', 1965), 'Por causa de você' ('Don't ever go away', 1966), 'Bonita' (1967), 'Wave' (1969), 'Triste' (1970) as well as numerous instrumental and orchestral works. He also wrote the soundtrack for the film *Copacabana Palace* (1963).

Select Discography

Antonio Carlos Jobim: The Composer of Desafinado, Plays. (Arrangements by Claus Ogerman) Verve V6–8547 [Also on CD. Verve 823011]

The Composer Plays Verve 823011 [CD]

JOHNSON, LAURIE (b.1927)

Laurie Johnson was born in Hampstead, London. He published several light orchestral works while still in his teens. He studied at the Royal College of Music, London, where he later taught. From 1945 to 1948, he was a member of the Band of the Coldstream Guards.

His professional career commenced in the 1950s, when he arranged music for band leaders such as AMBROSE, Ted Heath and GERALDO. He subsequently concentrated on film and television scoring, commencing with *The Good Companions* in 1956 and *The Moonraker* in 1958. This was followed by *Tiger Bay* (1959), *Dr. Strangelove* (1963), *First Men in the Moon* (1964), *Her Millions* (1968) and *Belstone Fox* (1973). His television work included *No Hiding Place* (1959), *Riviera Police* (1964), *The Avengers* (1965), *Jason King* (1971), *The New Avengers* (1976) and *The Professionals* (1978). His most recent television scores were for a 1991 Barbara Cartland series, including 'A Hazard of Hearts', 'The Lady and the Highwayman', 'A Duel of Hearts' and 'The Ghost in Monte Carlo'.

Johnson's music for the theater include *Lock Up Your Daughters* (1960), with lyrics by Lionel Bart, which won an IVOR NOVELLO Award. In 1967, another of his musicals, *The Four Musketeers*, was first staged at Drury Lane. A revue entitled *Pieces of Eight*, with lyrics and sketches by Peter Cook, first appeared at the Apollo Theatre in 1959.

Recordings in Johnson's own name were produced in the mid-1950s on Polygon and His Master's Voice. Between 1958 and 1967, he was contracted to record with Pye Records. He also made many recordings for the Keith Prowse Music Library (KPM), and these were frequently used to accompany television shows in the sixties. Examples of these are *This Is Your Life*, *Animal Magic*, *Bachelor Life* and *Whicker's World*.

In 1979, he released an album of music entitled *It's Alive* 2, on which he reorchestrated and conducted BERNARD HERRMANN's original music for *It's Alive*. In the early 1980s he recorded themes from his television shows under the Unicorn-Kanchana label. These included *The Avengers*, *The New Avengers* and *The Professionals*. Further albums were Bernard Herrmann's score from *North by Northwest*, *The Western World of Dimitri Tiomkin* and a selection of music from his own films *Dr. Strangelove, Captain Kronos, Hedda* and *First Men in the Moon*. His most recently released compact disc is *The Rose and the Gun*, which features his most popular themes from film and television, originally released in 1969 under the title *Themes And . . .* (M.G.M). He also developed business interests in film production companies in partnership with Albert Fennell and Brian Clemens.

Select Discography

Belston Fox Ronco RR 2006

Big New Sound Strikes Again PYE NPL 18103

Dr. Strangelove and Other Great Movie Themes COLPIX CP 464 (M), COLPIX SCP 464 (S)

Hedda Unicorn DPK 9001 (UK), Starlog SV 95002-D (US)

New Big Sound of the Laurie Johnson Orchestra PYE NPL 18088

It's Alive II Starlog SR 1002 (US)

Music from First Men in the Moon Unicorn DKP 9001 (UK), Starlog SV-95002D (US)

Music from The Avengers, The New Avengers, The Professionals Unicorn KPM 7009 (UK), Starlog/Varese ASV 95003 (US)

North by Northwest (Music composed by Bernard Herrmann) Unicorn DKP 9000(UK), STARLOG SV 95001 (US)

Themes And . . . CS 8104

Top Secret PYE Golden Guinea GGL 0108

Western Film World of Dimitri Tiomkin Unicorn DKP 9002(UK)

Compact Discs

The Avengers Varese Sarabande VSD5501

Hedda Varese VCD 47270

First Men in the Moon Cloud Nine ACN7015

The Rose and the Gun. The Music of Laurie Johnson Fly FLYCD103

Western Film World of Dimitri Tiomkin Unicorn UKCD 2011

K

KAEMPFERT, BERT (16 October 1923–21 June 1980)
German composer, conductor, arranger and musician Bert Kaempfert was born in Hamburg and studied at the Hamburg Conservatory of Music. He played four instruments, piano, clarinet, saxophone and accordion and became composer, arranger, producer and conductor for Polydor Records, Germany.

He first worked in the band of Hans Busch in Danzig and made many broadcasts. During World War II, he was in the German Army music corps and later formed a band in a prisoner-of-war camp. In 1947, he formed his own band and was director of North German Radio from 1949. At first he provided accompaniments for vocal records, including 'Die Gittare und das Meer' for Freddy and 'Morgen' for Ivo Robic.

He subsequently began to write songs and instrumentals for his own orchestra, many of which became famous. These included 'Spanish Eyes' (1959), 'Wooden Heart' (1960), 'Now and Forever' (1961), 'Swinging Safari' (1962), 'Sweet Dreams' (1963), 'Blue Midnight' (1965) and 'Strangers in the Night' (1966) from the film *A Man Could Get Killed.* This latter song was made into a hit by Frank Sinatra. In 1965 he also made an outstanding revival of the 1948 song 'Red Roses for a Blue Lady' (Decca, USA), composed by Sid Tepper and Roy Brodsky. It was included in one of Kaempfert's best-selling albums, *Blue Midnight.*

In 1960 he scored a hit with the Polydor single *Wonderland by Night,* a tribute to Manhattan, composed by Klauss-Gunter Neuman, words by Lincoln Chase, and was the first European to be honored as the Up-and-

Coming Orchestra of the Year in a United States disc jockey poll. Kaempfert then composed the background music for the film *90 Minutes to Midnight*, which he also conducted.

The Kaempfert orchestral style varied from full orchestrations to novelty numbers. In the 1970s the orchestra became commercialized and specialized in easy listening, with the use of electric bass and solo trumpet against sustained strings.

Kaempfert spent part of his time in New York and Miami Beach, his permanent home being in Hamburg. He died while on holiday in Spain.

Select Discography

Blue Midnight Decca DL 4569, DL 74569 (S)

Bye Bye Blues Decca DL 74847

Greatest Hits Decca DL 4810, DL 74810 (S)

Lights Out, Sweet Dreams Decca DL 4265. DL 74265 (S)

Strangers in the Night Decca DL 4795, DL 74795 (S)

Compact Discs

Bert Kaempfert's Greatest Hits Decca 74810

Best of Bert Kaempfert Mobile Fidelity 795

KAPER, BRONISLAU (5 February 1902–25 April 1983)

Bronislau Kaper was born in Warsaw, Poland, and began his career as a songwriter. Louis B. Mayer of MGM discovered him in Paris and offered him a contract. Kaper stayed in Hollywood from 1936 to 1966. At first he wrote hit songs such as the title song from *San Francisco* (1936), 'All God's Chillun Got Rhythm' and 'Cosi, Cosa' for the Marx Brothers film *A Night at the Opera.*

His first scoring assignment was in 1941, with an adaptation of *The Chocolate Soldier.* One of his most important themes was for *Green Dolphin Street* (1947), which was immortalized by Miles Davis. *Invitation* (1952) also contained a theme that was played worldwide.

Other scores include *Bataan* (1943), *Gaslight* (1944), *Bewitched* (1945), *Our Vines Have Tender Grapes* (1945), *The Red Badge of Courage* (1951), *Lili* (1953), *Auntie Mame* (1958), *Butterfield 8* (1960), *Mutiny on the Bounty* (1962), *Lord Jim* (1965) and *Counterpoint: A Flea in Her Ear* (1968).

Select Discography

Film Music of Bronislau Kaper Delos DEL/F-25421

KELLY, MONTY **(born Montgomery Jerome Kelly)** (8 June 1910–15 March 1971)

Monty Kelly was born in Oakland, California. He learned the trumpet and became a professional musician. He played the trumpet in various orchestras, including Buddy Marino's, and also worked for CBS in San Francisco. In the early 1940s, he became first trumpeter and arranger for Paul Whiteman. He also acted as arranger and assistant musical director for the *Bob Hope Show* orchestra. He scored many film music arrangements. He arranged and conducted for a number of leading vocalists in the United States, such as Al Martino's hit song of the early fifties, 'Here in My Heart'.

In 1953, his orchestra was voted by the *Cash Box* magazine as the most promising in the United States. From 1954 to 1959, he made some recordings with his own orchestra for the Essex label, including *Monte Kelly I Love* and *Stereorchestration of Porgy and Bess*. His most famous arrangements and compositions were recorded by the 101 STRINGS. These included albums such as *Soul of Spain*, *Soul of Mexico* and *Soul of Israel*. He also did very interesting arrangements for two 101 Strings albums with guitar solos; *101 Strings Plus Guitars Galore*, Volumes 1 and 2. For these albums, 130 musicians were employed with four guitarists. In 1960, he composed some fine scores for a choir of guitars on Guy Mitchell's LP for U.S. Columbia, *Sunshine Guitar*.

Select Discography

Far Away Places Monty Kelly and his Orchestra. Essex ESLP-108 London HAF 2002 (U.K.)

Guitars Galore Vol. 1 101 Strings US 33 Alshire (S) 5065, FR 33 MODE CMD 9528 (S)

Guitars Galore Vol. 2 101 Strings US 33 Alshire (S) 5141

Million Seller Hits of 1967 101 Strings US 33 Alshire (S) 5070

Monty Kelly I Love Monty Kelly and his Orchestra US Essex 111. ESEXP 111

Passport to Romance Monty Kelly and his Orchestra, Bob Hunter, Organ. Marble Arch. Alshire MAL 624

Pops Concert Extravaganza Monty Kelly Orchestra and Buddy Cole (Organ) US 33 Audio Spectrum 601 (S)

Porgy and Bess Stereorchestrations Monty Kelly and his Orchestra. Carlton LP12/111

Songs of Love 101 Strings US 33 Alshire (S) 5072

Soul of Israel 101 Strings US 33 Alshire (S) 5044

Soul of Mexico 101 Strings US 33 Somerset SF17000, Alshire 5032 (S), PYE GGL 0164 (U.K.)

Soul of Spain Vol. 1 101 Strings US 33 Somerset SOM 6600, Alshire S-5018

Soul of Spain Vol. 2 101 Strings US 33 Alshire S-5052

Spanish Eyes 101 Strings US 33 Alshire (S) 5051

SRO Broadway Hits 101 Strings US 33 Alshire (S) 5061, Fr 33 MODE CMD 9526 (S)

Stereorchestrations by Monty Kelly and His Orchestra STLP 12/111

Sunshine Guitar CL1552 (M), CS 8352 (S)

Compact Discs of 101 Strings

Arrangements or Compositions by Monty Kelly

Best of Latin US CD Alshire ALCD 4

101 Strings Plus Guitars US CD Alshire ALCD 33

Plus, Plus, Plus US CD Alshire ALCD 18

Romantic Songs of the Sea US CD Alshire ALCD 20

Soul of Israel US CD Alshire ALCD 38

Soul of Spain US CD Alshire ALCD 5

KERN, JEROME (27 January 1885–11 November 1945)

Jerome Kern was born in New York City. His mother, Fanny Kern was an excellent pianist who gave Jerome his first piano lessons at the age of five. He was educated at the Newark High School and New York College of Music, where he studied piano with Alexander Lambert and Paolo Gallico and harmony with Austin Pierce and Albert von Doenhoff.

His first published composition appeared in 1902, when he was seventeen. In 1903, he commenced work in New York as a song plugger, sheet music salesman and arranger. His first visit to London was in 1902. He returned in 1903 and 1905, where he collaborated with P. G. Wodehouse. He continued to shuttle back and forth between New York and London. In 1915, he began working with Guy Bolton, and this was a turning point in his career.

Between 1920 and 1924 he composed the music for fourteen Broadway musicals. In 1927, he began a long collaboration with Oscar Hammerstein II as lyricist, starting with *Show Boat* (1927), which produced evergreen songs such as 'Make Believe', 'Can't Help Lovin' That Man of Mine', 'Why Do I Love You?' and 'Old Man River'.

In the 1930s, he wrote the music for many shows such as *Cat and the Fiddle* (1931), *Music in the Air* (1932), *Roberta* (1933) and *Very Warm for May* (1939). During the 1930s, he also tried his hand at music for the talking films, particularly those starring Fred Astaire and Ginger Rogers. *Roberta* was filmed in 1935, with the addition of an extra song, 'Lovely to Look At'. This was followed by *Swing Time* (1936) and *High, Wide and Handsome* (1937). The film version of GERSHWIN's *Lady, Be Good* had a single Kern number, 'The Last Time I Saw Paris'. He won Oscars for 'The Way You Look Tonight' in 1936 and 'The Last Time I Saw Paris' in 1940.

Other great songs include 'They Didn't Believe Me' (from *The Girl from Utah*, 1914); 'Till the Clouds Roll By' (from *Oh Boy*, 1917) and 'Wild

Rose', 'Look for the Silver Lining' and 'Whip-Poor Will' (from *Sally*, 1920). The show *Roberta* also contained famous melodies including 'Yesterdays' and 'Smoke Gets in Your Eyes'. Kern died in 1945, just before commencing the score for *Annie Get Your Gun*, which was then taken up by IRVING BERLIN.

Additional Readings

Bordman, Gerald. *Jerome Kern: His Life and Music.* New York: Oxford University Press, 1980.

Paperback edition, with new preface and some new material, published in 1990.

Ewen, David. *American Songwriters.* New York: H. W. Wilson, 1987. pp. 240–48.

Ewen, David. *Great Men of American Popular Song.* Englewood Cliffs, NJ: Prentice-Hall, 1970. pp. 123–143.

Ewen, David. *The World of Jerome Kern: A Biography.* New York: Holt, Rinehart and Winston, 1960.

Freedland, Michael. *Jerome Kern.* New York: Stein and Day, 1981.

Green, Benny. *Let's Face the Music.* London: Pavilion Books, 1989. pp. 25–50.

Hemming, Roy. *The Melody Lingers On.* New York: Newmarket Press, 1986. pp. 55–84.

Hyland, William G. *The Song Is Ended.* New York: Oxford University Press, 1995. pp. 64–76, 235–249, 275–291.

Select Discography

Black, Stanley. Music of Jerome Kern (With Kingsway Promenade Orchestra) (Arrangements by Wally Stott) London LL 579 [Also on CD]

Farran, Merrick. Last Time I Saw Paris: A Jerome Kern Concert (With London Pops Orchestra) Regent MG 6059

Goodman, Al. Tribute to Jerome Kern Spinorama MK 3049

Gould, Morton. Baton and Bows: Music of Jerome Kern and Fritz Kreisler RCA LM 2217

Gould, Morton. Kern and Porter Favorites RCA LSC 2559 (LP) BMG D9026-684782 (CD)

Jenkins, Gordon. Music of Jerome Kern Decca DL 5276 (10")

Kostelanetz, Andre. Music of Jerome Kern Columbia CL776 [Also on CD]

Melachrino, George. Music of Jerome Kern RCA LPM 2283

Ornadel, Cyril. Dearly Beloved: Music of Jerome Kern (Arranger not named) Rama RLP 5005 [Also on CD]

Ornadel, Cyril. Musical World of Jerome Kern (Arranged by Brian Fahey) MGM E/SE 3906

(*Note*: The two Jerome Kern LPs by Ornadel are entirely different in their arrangements.)

Rose, David. The Song Is You. Melodies by Jerome Kern MGM E 3555

Stott, Wally. The Song Is You: Tribute to Jerome Kern Philips B10108R

Stride, Fred. Showboat and other Jerome Kern Classics CBC MVCD 1099 (Canada)

Weston, Paul. Columbia Album of Jerome Kern Columbia CZL

KIESSLING, HEINZ (pseudonym Christian Mondstein) (b. 1926)

Heinz Kiessling was born in Nuremberg, where he studied piano and conducting at the music conservatory from 1946 to 1949. He became a concert pianist and traveled extensively. His interest shifted to jazz, dance and light music, and he began composing in these fields in 1950. He became one of the leading composers of light music and was active in radio broadcasts, recording and later television and film scoring, as composer, arranger and orchestra director.

Kiessling began to collaborate with WERNER TAUTZ in 1960, composing instrumental light music. In 1964 they founded their own record label Brillant-Musik whose first album, *Coloured Strings*, with arrangements by Kiessling, became internationally famous.

Among his most popular radio compositions are 'Spanische Impressionen' (1953), 'Pariser Bilderbogen' (1957), 'For Strings Only', (1968) and 'San Francisco Suite' (1970). In the 1960s, he supervised more than 140 German television shows, which included performers such as Caterina Valente and Peter Alexander. He also produced scores for television and feature films including *Casino de Paris* (1957), *Das Madchen un der Staatsanwalt* (1962) and *Romeo und Julia '70'* (1969). In 1969, he recorded his song 'In the Shadows of the Moon' with Frank Sinatra, in Hollywood. In the 1990s, Kiessling worked mainly for German television. He alternated between Germany and Florida.

Select Discography

Coloured Strings Elite SO30015

Happy Rallye STEREO 7 S7.016

Compact Discs

Sunny Times Heinz Kiessling and various German Radio Orchestras. Bliss Records BRA 10006

KILBY, REGINALD

Reginald Kilby began his musical career as a cellist and later changed to orchestra conducting. His orchestra, known as the Strings by Starlight Orchestra was formed in 1963 for the performance of light and semipopular music, orchestrated by English arrangers such as Jack Byfield and led by Reginald Leopold.

Select Discography

Nights of Gladness Columbia Studio TWO 334

Sound of Strings World Record Club ST 974

String Serenade E.M.I. Studio 2 TWO 151

Strings by Starlight CLP 1761 CSD 1552

World's Most Glorious Melodies, Volume 1 EMI STUDIO TWO 181

World's Most Glorious Melodies, Volume 2 EMI STUDIO TWO 276

KING, C. DUDLEY (PETE)

Pete King specialized in mood music, conducting and arranging for vocalists such as Bing Crosby, Eddie Fisher, Dean Martin, Julie London and Kay Starr. He arranged the original mood music albums for JACKIE GLEASON and the film scores for *April Love, An Affair to Remember, Mardi Gras, Bernadine* and *South Pacific.*

Select Discography

Donnybrook! KS 3242

50 Velvet Brass Liberty LSS 14029

Hit Songs from Oliver KS 3315

Ice Follies of 1967 DOT DLP 25757

Intermezzo DOT DLP 3810/DLP 2580

Jewish Rhapsodies Bravo B 35502

Last of the Secret Agents: A Paramount Picture Music from the Score by Pete King DOT DLP 3714

Mind if I Make Love to You? Warner Bros W 1294

Moon River KAPP ML 7533

More Hits KS 3291

Music for the Girl You Love Liberty LRP 3042/LST 7003

Music from New Shipstad & Johnson Ice Follies DOT DLP 3757

Percussion Concert KL 1256

Pocketful of Hits MS 7535

KNIGHTSBRIDGE STRINGS

This orchestra, which was formed in the 1950s, combined the top talents of the English recording industry. The best of musicians were employed and two very fine British conductors, REG OWEN and Malcolm Lockyer, were responsible for the arrangements. The string section consisted of thirty-two violins, six violas, six cellos and two string bass. There were also three clarinets, two oboes, four trumpets and three trombones.

Select Discography

Big Beat Riverside RLP 97533

Cinema Monument MAM 3002/MAS 13002

España Monument MAS 13000

Go Pop Monument MAS 13003

More Swinging Strings Top Rank RS 629

Movie Music Top Rank RX 3017

Spanish Mood Universal Record Club (Australia) U 814

Strings on the March Riverside RLP 7518/97518

Strings Sing Top Rank RM 303

Theatre Showcase Top Rank 35/036

¾ Time Monument MAM 3002/MAS/13001

Waltzes Top Rank BUY 010

KORNGOLD, ERICH WOLFGANG (29 May 1897–29 November 1957) Erich Wolfgang Korngold was named after Wolfgang Amadeus Mozart and like his namesake was a child prodigy pianist-composer. He was born in Czechoslovakia and wrote his first ballet at the age of eleven. In 1934, he arrived in Hollywood to work for Warner Brothers and from 1935 to 1947, he scored nineteen films, becoming the highest-paid composer at that time. In 1947, following a heart attack, he retired from film scoring, except for *Magic Fire* in 1956. He returned to Vienna to continue his concerts and operatic composing.

Korngold had a lasting effect on film music history, because of his symphonic style for romantic dramas, which established a definitive approach for this type of score. He was extremely selective about his choice of scores and insisted on more time than usual for completion. His music was usually orchestrated by HUGO FRIEDHOFER. Tribute was paid to his genius by later film composers such as ANDRÉ PREVIN.

His scores include *A Midsummer Night's Dream* (1935 adaptation), *Captain Blood* (1935), *Give Us This Night* (1936), *The Green Pastures* (1936), *Anthony Adverse* (1936), *The Prince and the Pauper* (1937), *Another Dawn* (1937), *The Adventures of Robin Hood* (1938), *The Private Lives of Elizabeth and Essex* (1939), *The Sea Hawk* (1940), *The Sea Wolf* (1941), *King's Row* (1942), *The Constant Nymph* (1943), *Between Two Worlds* (1944), *Devotion* (1946), *Of Human Bondage* (1946), *Deception* (1946), *Escape Me Never* (1947).

Select Discography

Adventures of Robin Hood Delos DEL/F-25409

Captain Blood, the Classic Film Scores of Errol Flynn RCA ARL1–0912

Elizabeth and Essex and The Classic Film Scores of Erich Wolfgang Korngold RCA ARL1–0185

The Sea Hawk and the Classic Film RCA LSC-3330

Compact Discs

Adventures of Robin Hood (Utah Symphony Orchestra. Conductor Varujan Kojian) TER CDTER 1066; Varese Sarabande VCD47202

King's Row (National Philharmonic Orchestra. Conductor Charles Gerhardt). Varese Sarabande VCD47203

Private Lives of Elizabeth and Essex (Munich Symphony Orchestra. Conductor Carl Davis) Milan 873 122

Sea Hawk (Utah Symphony Orchestra and Chorus. Conductor Varujan Kojian) TER CDTER 1164; Varese Sarabande VCD47304

KOSTELANETZ, ANDRE (23 December 1901–13 January 1980)
Andre Kostelanetz was born in Russia. He made his debut as a pianist in a private recital at the age of five. He was only twenty when he was appointed an assistant conductor at the Imperial Opera in Petrograd. The hardships of postrevolutionary life led to his emigration to the United States in 1922. He spent his early American years as a voice coach and served as an accompanist to well-known opera singers. His skill as an arranger led to a number of radio engagements. He made his debut as a conductor in 1924 in early broadcasts from New York. A few years later he was appointed permanent staff conductor to the Columbia Broadcasting System, for which he supervised both straight and swing programs.

Kostelanetz made a great success of his radio programs, which he meticulously planned and supervised. Often a thousand work hours were invested in half an hour of actual broadcast time. The unique Kostelanetz sound was attributed largely to his skill as an arranger, but other devices were employed, such as microphone adaptation, use of a special floor for the violinists and the positioning of the trumpets on a carpet to absorb enough sound to prevent the violins from being drowned out.

Kostelanetz's receptiveness to electronic innovations resulted in interesting symphonic variations. His music took on sounds and sonorities previously unknown.

In the 1940s, Kostelanetz conducted *Tune Up Time* every Monday evening between 8:00 and 8:30 P.M., on the Columbia network. This program was rebroadcast to the Pacific Coast at midnight and was enthusiastically received by a wide audience.

In 1950, Columbia Records celebrated Kostelanetz's tenth anniversary with them by confirming him as their best-selling Masterworks artist. In August of that year, Columbia revealed that the American public had bought more than twenty million Kostelanetz records in the preceding decade. Between 1940 and 1952, some thirty million Kostelanetz records were sold.

Kostelanetz travelled widely in the cause of music interests and activities. He was associated with all the major American orchestras, including the

Andre Kostelanetz

New York and Los Angeles philharmonics and the Boston, Chicago, San Francisco, New Orleans and Minneapolis symphonies. Abroad, he worked as guest conductor with the Royal Philharmonic, Philharmonia Orchestra, London Symphony, Paris Conservatoire Orchestra, Berlin Philharmonic, Israel Philharmonic and Orchestre de la Suisse Royale as well as orchestras in Rome, Stockholm, Tokyo and South America. His wife, the famous singer Lily Pons, was often featured as the soloist in the concerts he conducted. In 1963, he conceived the Lincoln Center Promenade Concerts with the New York Philharmonic Orchestra; these were a great success.

Musical Achievements

Kostelanetz had a profound influence in the popularization of light classical music and light orchestral music. He believed that there was no fundamental difference between classical and popular music and that the only valid classifications were 'good' and 'bad.' He drew attention to the fact that some classical music had originally seen the light of day as popular music. He maintained that one of the great achievements of popular music was to pave the way for audiences to appreciate the works of the great classical masters. He was aware that mood music and show music were something of stepchildren in the eyes of many in the classical field, but he firmly believed that there should be no barriers between the different modes of musical expression.

This outlook is evident when his recording repertoire is examined. His prolific output ranged from classical composers such as P. I. Tchaikovsky, Dmitry Shostakovich and Sergey Rachmaninoff, through operatic masterpieces by Giuseppe Verdi and Giacomo Puccini, to the composers of show music, including JEROME KERN, COLE PORTER, RICHARD RODGERS, VINCENT YOUMANS, IRVING BERLIN and GEORGE GERSHWIN. His recordings also featured popular and light classical music drawn from Spain, France, Hawaii, the Pacific and elsewhere.

Kostelanetz conducted an extensive correspondence with America's leading composers of popular and show music, with whom he shared his musical inspiration, including Porter, Rodgers and Berlin. He is considered to be without equal in the orchestral interpretation of popular music, lending deeper meaning to the lyrics.

The discography of Kostelanetz, with specific reference to his LPs in the mood music category, can be grouped into two phases. In the years up to 1950, Kostelanetz produced some remarkably fine discs highlighting the work of American popular composers. His anthologies of the melodies of HAROLD ARLEN, Kern, Youmans, Porter, ARTHUR SCHWARTZ, Rodgers and Gershwin are examples of definitive albums that have not been bettered to this day. The quality of his orchestrations is such that they never sound dated.

In this phase, Kostelanetz employed a variety of excellent arrangers including David Terry, Carroll Huxley, Van Cleave and possibly RAOUL POLIAKIN and George Bassman. According to Kostelanetz himself, writing in his memoirs, it was Carroll Huxley who arranged the original Cole Porter album and many others at that time.

The second phase of his popular music recording career covered the period from the 1960s to 1979 and featured a new series labeled *Wonderland of Sound*, obviously intended to keep abreast of current trends in popular music. In order to ensure a marketable commodity, the superb quality and standard of the earlier style of Kostelanetz disc were not maintained. These discs are certainly unrecognizable; they do not bear the hallmarks of the Kostelanetz sound of old. There is hardly a recording artist who escaped this commercialization syndrome in the 1960s and 1970s, but it was sad that the master himself succumbed to this trend.

Additional Readings

Kostelanetz, Andre. *Echoes: Memoirs of Andre Kostelanetz.* New York: Harcourt Brace Jovanovich, 1981.

Select Discography (All Columbia Recordings)

[Berlin] **Music of Irving Berlin** Columbia CL 768 [Also on CD]

[Bizet] **Carmen Highlights/Offenbach: Gaîté Parisienne** ML 5429/MS 6106

Black Magic ML 4741; CL 712

Bolero CL 833

Bravo CL 758

Broadway Spectacular CL 865

Broadway Theatre Party Harmony HL 7371/11171

Broadway's PC 34864

Broadway's Greatest Hits (Wonderland of Sound) CL 1827/CS 8627

Cafe Continental CL 863

Calendar Girl CL 811

Carnival Tropicana ML 4082

[Chaplin] **Music of Charlie Chaplin and Duke Ellington** PC 34660

Chicago C 31002

[Chopin] **Music of Chopin** 10"—ML 2056; 12"—CL 862

Chorus Line/Chicago Treemonisha KC/CA 33954

Clair de Lune and Other Popular Favorites ML 4692; CL 798

Concert in the Park CL 2688; CS 9488

Concerto Themes ML 5876; MS 6476

Dance with Me PC 34352

Debussy, Ravel, R. Strauss, etc. CL 798

Eight All-time Hits ML 2106

Ellington, Duke. *See* **Music of Charlie Chaplin and Duke Ellington**

Encore! C 1135/CS 8008

Everything Is Beautiful C 30037

Exotic Nights CS 9381

Extravaganza MS 7427

Favorite Romantic Concertos (Ivan Davis, Piano) Ml 6226; MS 6826

Fire and Jealousy (Wonderland of Sound) CL 1898/CS 8698

For All We Know C 30672

For the Young at Heart CS 9691

[Foster] **Beautiful Dreamer: Music of Stephen Foster/Kern: Mark Twain/Grofé: Mississippi Suite** CL 864

[Foster] **Music of Stephen Foster** ML 2007

[Gershwin] American in Paris/Rhapsody in Blue (With Alec Templeton) CL 795 Reissue: HS 11359

[Gershwin] Concerto in F (With Oscar Levant) CL 700

[Gershwin] Cuban Overture, Mine, Highlights from Porgy and Bess, Love Walked In CL 783

[Gershwin] George Gershwin PG/PGA 32825

[Gershwin] Gershwin Wonderland CS 8933

[Gershwin] Music of George Gershwin ML 2026; ML 4819; CL 770 [Also on CD]

[Gershwin] Porgy and Bess/Tchaikovsky: Queen of Spades CL 721

[Gershwin] Rhapsody in Blue/Concerto in F (With André Previn) CS 8286

God Created Great Whales M 30390

Golden Encores CS 8878

Grand Tour CL 981

Great Hits of Today KC 32415

Great Movie Themes CL 2467; CS 9267

Great Romantic Ballets MS 7018

Great Waltzes CL 1321

Greatest Hits CS 9740

Greatest Hits of Broadway and Hollywood KH 31414

Greatest Hits of the Sixties CS 9973

[Grofé] Grand Canyon Suite CL 716

[Grofé] Hudson River Suite/Norodom; Cambodian Suite/ De Falla: Spanish Dance/ White: Mosquito Dance/ Tucci: La Bamba de Vera Cruz/Kruz: Saturday Night CL 763

[Grofé] Mississippi Suite ML 2046

Gypsy Passion CL 1431; CS 8228

[Herbert] Music of Victor Herbert ML 4430; CL 765 [Also on CD]

Hits from Funny Girl, Finian's Rainbow and Star CS 9724

I Wish You Love CL 2185; CS 8985

I'll Never Fall in Love CS 9998

I'm Easy KC 34157

Images in Flight CSP 105128

Invitation to the Dance ML 4957

Invitation to the Waltz ML 2069

Joy to the World H 7432; HS 11232

Just for Listening: Kern: A Portrait in Music/Gershwin: Prelude II in C Sharp Minor; Bess, Oh Where's My Bess?/Grofé: On the Trail, Mississippi Suite ML 5607; MS 6133

[Kern] Music of Jerome Kern ML 4063; CL776 [Also on CD]

[Ketelby] **Music of Ketelby** AL 47

Kostelanetz Conducts (UK title: **Manhattan Serenade**) Columbia 33 SX 1040

Kostelanetz Favorites ML 4065; CL 791

Kostelanetz Festival ML 5607; MS 6207

Kostelanetz Program L 4150; CL 792

Kostelanetz Sound of Today CS 9409

Kostelanetz Strings ML 2100

[Kreisler] **Music of Fritz Kreisler/Music of Sigmund Romberg** ML 4253; CL 771

Last Tango in Paris KG 32187

[Legrand] **Michel Legrand's Latest Hits** KG 32580

Lincoln Portrait ML 5347

Love Story C 30501

Love Theme from 'The Godfather' KH 31500

Lure of France CL 1054/CS 8111

Lure of Paradise CL 1335/CS 8144

Lure of Spain CL 943

Lure of the Tropics ML 4882; CL 780

Magic of Music Harmony HS 805

Meet Andre Kostelanetz KZ 1

Mood for Love CL 704

Moon River C 32243

Motion Picture Favorites ML 2022

Murder on the Orient Express PC 33437

Music for Strings M30075

Music from Spain MG 32455

Musical Comedy Favorites ML 4241; CL 775 [Also on CD]

Musical Evenings MS 7319

Musical Reflections KC 33061

Never Can Say Goodbye KC/CA 3350

New Orleans Wonderland of Sound CL 2250; CS 9050

New York Wonderland CL 2138/CS 8938

[Offenbach] **Gaîté Parisienne/Bizet: Carmen Highlights** ML 5429/MS 6106

[Porter] **Andre Kostelanetz Plays Cole Porter** KG 31491

[Porter] **Music of Cole Porter** ML 4682; CL 729 [Also on CD]

[Prokofiev] **Peter and the Wolf/Saint Saëns: Carnival of the Animals** CL 720

Promenade Favorites ML 6206; MS 6806

Promenades MG 31415

[Puccini] La Boheme for Orchestra CL 797

[Puccini] Madame Butterfly (Opera Wonderland of Sound) CL 17878/CS 8587

Quad Pop Concert CQ 32856

[Ravel] Bolero/William Tell ML 2009

Repeat Performance ML 4087

[Rodgers] Columbia Album of Richard Rodgers C2L3; CSP EN 2–13725

[Rodgers] Music from Flower Drum Song CL 1280/CS 8095

[Rodgers] Music of Richard Rodgers ML 4130; CL 784 [Also on CD]

[Rodgers] Oklahoma! Medley/Roumanian Fantasy AL 4

[Rodgers] Richard Rodgers (vol. 1 KH31579; vol. 2 KH 31711

Romantic Arias for Orchestra CL 1263

Romantic Strings ML 6111; MS 6711

[Romberg] Music of Fritz Kreisler/Music of Sigmund Romberg ML 4253; CL 771

Saint-Saëns: Carnival of the Animals/Prokofiev: Peter and the Wolf CL 720

Scarborough Fair and Other Great Movie Hits CS 9623

Seasons M 31077

Shadow of Your Smile and Other Great Movie Themes CL 2467/CS 9267

[Shostakovich] Light Music of Shostakovich MS 6867

Show Boat, South Pacific, Slaughter on Tenth Avenue CL 806

Showstoppers ML 6129/MS 6729

Sound of Today CL 2609/CS 9409

Sounds of Love GP 10

[Sousa] The Thunderer: Sousa Marches CL 2359; CS 9159

Spirit of 76 MG 33728

Star-spangled Marches (Wonderland of Sound) CL 1718/CS 8518

Stardust ML 4597; CL 781 [Also on CD]

[Strauss] Blue Danube and Other Strauss Waltzes CL 805

Strauss Waltzes ML 2011

Strike Up the Band KH 32170

Superman and Other Pop Hits JC 35788

[Tchaikovsky] Music of Tchaikovsky C2L11/CS 8112

[Tchaikovsky] Music of Tchaikovsky CL 730

[Tchaikovsky] Nutcracker Suite CL 730

[Tchaikovsky] Nutcracker Suite/Between Birthdays (Spoken by Peter Ustinov) ML 5664/MS 6264

[Tchaikovsky] Queen of Spades/Gershwin: Porgy and Bess CL 721

[Tchaikovsky] Romantic Waltzes by Tchaikovsky MS 6824

[Tchaikovsky] Romeo and Juliet Overture CL 747
[Tchaikovsky] Sleeping Beauty Ballet CL 804
[Tchaikovsky] Swan Lake CL Tender Is the Night CL 886
That's Entertainment PG/PGA 33065
Theater Party CL 1199/CS 8026
Today's Golden Hits CL 2534/CS 9334
Today's Great Hits (Wonderland of Sound) CS 8457
Today's Greatest Movie Hits L 2756/CS 9556
Traces CS 9823
Unsinkable Molly Brown CL 1576; CS 8376
[Verdi] Aida for Orchestra CL 755
[Verdi] Rigoletto for Orchestra CL 970
[Verdi] La Traviata for Orchestra CL 799
Very Thought of You CL 843
Vienna, City of My Dreams MS 7087
Vienna Nights CL 769
[Villa Lobos] Music of Villa Lobos M 32821
Way We Were C 32578
Wishing You a Merry Christmas ML 6179; MS 6779
Wonderland by Moonlight D 229
Wonderland of Christmas CL 2068; CS 8868
Wonderland of Golden Hits CL 2039; CS 8839
Wonderland of Hits CSPEN-13088
Wonderland of Opera CL 1995; CS 8795
Wonderland of Sound CL 1657/CS 8457
World Wide Wonderland AKS 1/AK 1
World's Greatest Waltzes (Wonderland of Sound) CL 1938; CS 8738
World's Greatest Love Songs KG 32002
You and the Night and the Music CL 772; H 7368; H 11168
You Light Up JC 35328
[Youmans] Music of Vincent Youmans ML 4382; CL 734 [Also on CD]

Compact Discs

Broadway's Greatest Hits Columbia 471161–2
Columbia Album of Richard Rodgers Sony A2K-47867/8
Greatest Hits of Broadway CBS MLK-45735
I Wish You Love Good Music A2–26624 [2 CDs]
Moon River Sony A15897

16 Most Requested Songs Columbia CGK 40218

Stereo Wonderland of Golden Hits Columbia CK 08839

Strauss Waltzes Columbia CK 08162

KUNZEL, ERICH

Erich Kunzel is a classically trained conductor who has also worked in the jazz and pop fields. He has collaborated with Dave Brubeck, DUKE ELLINGTON, Ella Fitzgerald and others. In 1977, he founded the Cincinnati Pops Orchestra and has made many recordings of popular music with them. He has also conducted the Rochester Pops, Indianapolis Pops, Toronto Symphony Promenades and the Winnipeg Symphony Pops. Kunzel also appears regularly with the Chicago Symphony, Los Angeles Philharmonic, National Symphony, Philadelphia Orchestra and Cleveland Orchestra. He has appeared as guest conductor of the BOSTON POPS annually since his first appearance there on 10 June 1970, and has done over seventy performances in Symphony Hall and on tour in the United States and England.

Compact Discs

American as Apple Pie (Cincinnati Pops Orchestra) VOX 3035

American Jubilee (Cincinnati Pops Orchestra) Telarc 80144

Best of Broadway Pro Arte 252

Bond and Beyond (Cincinnati Pops Orchestra) Telarc 30251

Chiller (Cincinnati Pops Orchestra) Telarc 80189

Christmas at the Pops Pro Arte 220

Classic Broadway Scores (Winnipeg Pops Orchestra) Imperial 6600022

Classics of the Silver Screen (Cincinnati Pops Orchestra) Telarc 80221

Dance (Cincinnati Pops Orchestra) VOX 5130

Disney Spectacular (Cincinnati Pops Orchestra) Telarc 80196

Down on the Farm (Cincinnati Pops Orchestra) Telarc 80263

Ellington and Gershwin Greatest (Rochester Pops Orchestra) Pro Arte 8020

Fantastic Journey (Cincinnati Pops Orchestra) Telarc 80231

Fiesta (Cincinnati Pops Orchestra) Telarc 80235CD7

Great Fantasy Adventure Album (Cincinnati Pops Orchestra) Telarc 80342

Greatest Hits of Henry Mancini (Cincinnati Pops Orchestra) Telarc 80183

Hollywood's Greatest Hits (Cincinnati Pops Orchestra) Telarc 80168

Hollywood's Greatest Hits, Vol. 2 (Cincinnati Pops Orchestra) Telarc 80139

International Salute (Cincinnati Pops Orchestra) VOX 5132

Kunzel on Broadway Fanfare 9017

Kunzel Plays Gershwin Pro Arte 408

Lerner and Loewe Songbook for Orchestra (Cincinnati Pops Orchestra) Telarc 80375

Mancini's Greatest Hits (Cincinnati Pops Orchestra) Telarc 80183

Magical Music of Disney (Cincinnati Pops Orchestra) Telarc 80381

Meredith Willson's Music Man Telarc 80276

Movie Love Themes (Cincinnati Pops Orchestra) Telarc 80243

Music of Richard Rodgers Pro Arte CDD 275

My Fair Lady and More of the Magic of Broadway (With Winnipeg Symphony Orchestra) Pro Arte CDD 382

Night at the Pops Pro Arte 359

Opening Night Pro Arte 528

Puttin' on the Ritz (Cincinnati Pops Orchestra) Telarc 80366

Rodgers and Hammerstein Songbook for Orchestra (With Cincinnati Pops Orchestra) Telarc 80278

Round-Up: Favorite Western Tunes (Cincinnati Pops Orchestra) Telarc 80141

Sailing (Cincinnati Pops Orchestra) Telarc 80292

Star Tracks (Cincinnati Pops Orchestra) Telarc 80146, Telarc 80094

Syncopated Clock and Other Favorites by Leroy Anderson Proarte 264

Ties and Tails: Music of Duke Ellington and George Gershwin (Rochester Pops Orchestra) Proarte CDD 276

Time Warp (Cincinnati Pops Orchestra) Telarc 8010

Top 20: Very Best of Erich Kunzel (Cincinnati Pops Orchestra) Telarc 80401

Vive La France! (Cincinnati Pops Orchestra) VOX 5131

Young at Heart Telarc 80245

L

LEFEVRE, RAYMOND

Raymond Lefevre was a member of a well-known musical family in France and rivaled FRANCK POURCEL and PAUL MAURIAT as orchestral conductor in the late 1950s and 1960s. In 1958, he had a hit with his string arrangement of 'The Day the Rains Came' (La Jour ou la Pluie Viendra). Lefevre recorded successfully under the Barclay label and scored another bestseller with 'Soul Coaxing' from *Raymond Lefevre, Volume 2* (1968). He made many transcontinental concert tours and regularly released albums of theme music in stereo. These consisted mainly of light classics, film material, tributes to artists, standards, French songs and easy-listening versions of current hits. In later years he moved away from lush string arrangements and attempted to appeal to changing tastes with albums such as *Sheep in Wolves' Clothing*, attributed to Raymond Lefevre and The Broken Hearts (1985).

Select Discography

Jingle Bells Riviera 80007

La La La Four Star FCS 4250

Merry Christmas RCA INTS 1360

Moulin Rouge KAPP 1121

Paris in Stereo KT 41009

Romantica ED 8044

Michel Legrand

LEGRAND, MICHEL (b. 24 February 1932)
Legrand was born in Paris, the son of the orchestra leader and film composer Raymond Legrand. He studied at the Paris Conservatoire and became a pianist and arranger. In the late 1940s, he made contact with jazz, when he was invited to score strings for a Dizzy Gillespie album that was being recorded in Paris. In the 1950s he was invited to go to America by CBS and record an album entitled *I Love Paris*, which stemmed from an NBC special starring Maurice Chevalier that he had worked on. This album proved popular, and Columbia Records assigned Nat Shapiro to work with Legrand on further recordings. These included an album of COLE PORTER compositions and an album of 'Legrand Jazz', featuring twenty-two of the best of American jazz players.

After his move to New York, Legrand arranged music for artists such as Miles Davis and John Coltrane, led his own bands and wrote compositions that were performed by artists such as Stan Getz and Phil Woods. He occasionally played with jazz artists such as Shelly Manne.

In 1953, he had begun to compose music for French films and in the 1960s, his scores for films included *Bonjour Tristesse* (1958), *Terrain Vague* (1959), *Le Coeur Battant* (1960), *Lola* (1961), *Eve* (1962) and *All This and Money Too* (1963), which produced the U.S. title song, 'Love Is a Ball'.

In 1964, he received an Academy Award nomination for *The Umbrellas of Cherbourg* (original French title *Les Parapluies de Cherbourg)*, which contained 'I Will Wait for You' and 'Watch What Happens' (English lyrics by Norman Gimbel). His second Oscar was for his work on *The Young Ladies of Rochefort* (1968).

In the late 1960s, he began to compose for American and British films. The earliest of these included *How to Save a Marriage and Ruin Your Life* and *Ice Station Zebra*, both in 1968. His score for *The Thomas Crown Affair* included the song 'The Windmills of Your Mind' (lyrics by Alan and Marilyn Bergman), which was popularized by Noel Harrison and Dusty Springfield and won an Academy Award in 1968. Legrand collaborated with the same lyricists to produce 'What Are You Doing the Rest of Your Life?' from *The Happy Ending* (1969). He continued to write scores for films throughout the 1970s, including such titles as *Picasso Summer, The Go-Between, Summer of '42* (another Oscar), *Pieces of Dreams, A Time for Loving, Wuthering Heights, Lady Sings the Blues, One Is a Lonely Number* and *The Three Musketeers.*

Legrand also contributed the musical score for Barbra Streisand's film *Yentl* (1983), with the Bergmans as lyricists. Once more, the complete score won an Academy Award. His other film music included *Never Say Never Again, Secret Places* (title song written with Alan Jay Lerner), *Switching Channels* (theme written with Neil Diamond), *Fate, The Burning Shore, Dingo* (written with Miles Davis, 1991) and *Prêt-à-porter* (1994).

Legrand also wrote music for television, including *Brian's Song, The Adventures of Don Quixote, It's Good to Be Alive, Cage Without a Key, A Woman Called Golda, The Jesse Owens Story, Promises to Keep, Sins, Crossings, Casanova* and *Not a Penny More, Not a Penny Less.*

Musical Achievements

Legrand demonstrated a superb command of orchestration as early as the 1950s, when he made his first orchestral recordings. In the late 1950s, he attempted to combine straight orchestral techniques with jazz phrasing and modern voicing; at times these pieces seemed somewhat overbalanced, but they were an effective contrast to the bland music in vogue at that period. This tendency proved eminently suitable for film music. His visit to Hollywood in the early 1960s brought him into contact with American jazz musicians, and he worked regularly there as well as in Britain and France. He produced some of the most imaginative film themes of the 1960s and 1970s.

Examples of his jazz output are *Legrand Jazz* and *Le Jazz Grand.* Besides the jazz aspect of his work, Legrand also demonstrates that he is equally at home in the lush symphonic treatment of music. This is evident in his LPs *Rendezvous in Paris, Holiday in Rome, Castles in Spain,* and *Vienna Holiday.*

Legrand also displayed a masterful interpretation of show and film music, which is evident in the albums *Broadway Is My Beat* and *Cinema Legrand. Strings on Fire* demonstrates his artistry with string instruments.

Select Discography

Bonjour Paris Columbia CL 947

Broadway Is My Beat Philips BBL 7546, Philips PHM 200–000, 600–000 Stereo

Castles in Spain Columbia CL 888

Cinema Legrand MGM E/SE 4491 [Also on CD]

Cole Porter (2 Records) C2L-4

Concert Legrand RCA RS 1087

Holiday in Rome Columbia CL 647

I Love Movies Columbia CL 1178

I Love Paris Columbia CL 555, CL 1640/CS 8440

Images RCA SF8457

Legrand in Rio Columbia CL 1139

Legrand Jazz Philips BBE 12342

Legrand Piano Columbia CL 1441

Le Jazz Grand Gryphon 623951 AT

Matter of Innocence Decca DL 79160

Music from the Films Columbia WL 107

New I Love Paris Columbia CS 8440

Paris à la Hi Fi Columbia CL 2599 (10")

Plays for Dancers Philips 600–155

Rendezvous in Paris Philips 200045/600045 [Also on CD]

Scarlet Ribbons Columbia CL 1338/CS 8146

Special Magic of Legrand MGM Select 2353–130

Strings on Fire Columbia CL 1725/CS 8525, Philips SBBL 666

Symphonic Suite From 'The Umbrellas of Cherbourg' and Theme and Variations For Two Pianos and Orchestra From 'The Go-Between' [Michel Legrand conducting the London Symphony Orchestra] CBS 73886 (Britain) Columbia M35175 (USA)

Theater Music with the French Touch Columbia CB 15

Themes and Variations Bell 213

Thomas Crown Affair (Soundtrack) Sunset SLS 50300

Twenty Songs of the Century Bell 4200

Vienna Holiday Columbia CL 706

Violent Violins Mercury SML 30020

Young Girls of Rochefort United Artists UAS 6662

Compact Discs

Cole Porter Sony AK 47860

Columbia Album of Cole Porter Sony AK 47860

I Love Paris Sony 64367

Legrand Piano Columbia/Sony CK 10129

Musique & Cinema/Music and Cinema Auvidis Travelling K1020

Michel Plays Legrand Laserlight 12306

Paris Was Made for Lovers BBC PREC 5001

Strings on Fire Columbia (Australia) 471102

Umbrellas of Cherbourg Travelling 1020

Violent Violins Mercury MWY 222021

LEVY, LOUIS (b. 1893)

Louis Levy, a notable British film composer and musical director, was born in London and started his career in 1910, arranging and performing music for silent pictures. In 1916, he became musical director at the New Gallery Cinema in London. In 1921, he went to the Shepherd's Bush Pavilion as music chief and is credited with being the first to develop the theme song in movies, in the silent film days. At the beginning of talkies, he joined the Gaumont British Studios at Shepherd's Bush, where he became the head of the music department for all Gainsborough productions from 1933 onward.

Select Discography

Porter and Gershwin Suites London LL9.

LEYDEN, NORMAN

Musical director, conductor and arranger of Broadway shows in the 1950s.

Select Discography

Broadway Spectacular RCA Camden CAS-467

LITER, MONIA (b. 1906)

Monia Liter was born in Odessa, South Russia, and spent his youth in the Malay States. He became a naturalized British subject and studied music in Singapore. For seven years, he led a dance band at the Raffles Hotel there that included the singer Al Bowlly. Liter traveled to Britain with Bowlly in 1929.

He began playing with well-known bands, including Lew Stone's orchestra and Harry Roy. He also wrote scores for films and revues. In the 1940s, he formed the 20th Century Serenaders, that established him as a creator and interpreter of light music. He toured both in Britain and overseas and also broadcast. He subsequently became conductor of the KNIGHTSBRIDGE STRINGS.

Select Discography

Lovers in Paris Decca LK 4183

Mississippi Melody (With Knightsbridge Orchestra) CUB 8007

LIVING STRINGS

The Living Strings Orchestra was created exclusively in the 1950s for RCA Camden records. It was composed of some of the world's finest string virtuosi, mainly drawn from Europe. The Living Strings performed with a unity and closeness of musical spirit equivalent in every respect to that of long-established orchestral groups.

The extensive series of recordings that they produced featured leading conductors and arrangers. These records are listed in this book's discographies under the conductors including JOHNNY DOUGLAS, WILLIAM HILL-BOWEN, BOB SHARPLES, Chucho Zarzosa, GERALDO and Mario Ruiz Armengol.

Select Discography

For Lovers Only (2 records. Conductors unnamed) CXS 9030

In a Mellow Mood (Conductor Al Nevins) CAS 709

Nostalgia (Conductors Douglas/D'Artega/Geraldo/Hill-Bowen) CAS 2505

Richard Rodgers (Conductors Addeo/Gold/Douglas/Phil Bodner) CAS 2458

Windmills of Your Mind (Conductors Johnny Douglas/Bob Armstrong/Anita Kerr) CAS 2319

LOESSER, FRANK (29 June 1910–28 March 1969)

Frank Loesser, the son of German émigrés, was born in New York and educated at Townsend Harris Hall and the College of the City of New York. His father was a piano teacher, and Frank showed an interest in popular music from an early age.

His first published lyrics were for a song by William Schuman entitled 'In Love with the Memory of You' (1931). This was followed by 'I Wish I Were Twins' (1934), with music by Eddie de Lange. It was featured in one of Lew Leslie's *Blackbirds* series of revues. During these years, Frank earned a living from playing piano and singing in night clubs.

In 1936, Loesser became lyricist for Universal Pictures. He soon transferred to Paramount, where he had his first success with 'Moon of Manakoora', with music by ALFRED NEWMAN, which was featured in the film *The Hurricane* (1937). As a lyric writer he had hits with songs such as 'Small Fry' and 'Two Sleepy People' (music by HOAGY CARMICHAEL), 'The Boys in the Back Room' (music by Frederick Hollander), and 'I Don't Want to Walk Without You, Baby' (music by Jule Stein). He also wrote the lyrics for composers such as JIMMY MCHUGH, VICTOR YOUNG, Manning Sherwin and ARTHUR SCHWARTZ.

Loesser's first successful independent composition was 'Praise the Lord and Pass the Ammunition', which became a million-seller in 1942. Subsequently he wrote several songs for films including 'Spring will Be a Little Late This Year' (*Christmas Holiday*, 1943), 'Tallahassee' (*Variety Girl*, 1947) and 'Baby, It's Cold Outside' (*Neptune's Daughter*, 1949). In 1948, he achieved a Broadway success for the score of *Where's Charley?*. In the same year, he had a simultaneous success with the popular song 'On a Slow Boat to China'.

In 1950 he made his greatest contribution as composer and lyricist with the Broadway production of *Guys and Dolls*, which was filmed in 1955. This was followed by his score for the Danny Kaye movie *Hans Christian Andersen* (1952) and the stage musicals *The Most Happy Fella* (1956), *Greenwillow* (1960) and *How to Succeed in Business Without Really Trying* (1961).

Additional Readings

Ewen, David. *American Songwriters*. New York: H. W. Wilson, 1987. pp. 260–65.

Ewen, David. *Great Men of American Popular Song*. Englewood Cliffs, NJ: Prentice-Hall, 1970. pp. 259–71.

Green, Benny. *Let's Face the Music*. London: Pavilion Books, 1989. pp. 135–52.

Loesser, Susan. *A Most Remarkable Fella: Frank Loesser and the Guys and Dolls in His Life*. New York: Donald I. Fine, 1993.

Select Discography

Ornadel, Cyril. Music by Moonlight. Presenting Frank Loesser World Record Club (UK) Showcase LM23 (UK)

LOEWE, FREDERICK (10 June 1901–14 February 1988)

Frederick Loewe was born in Vienna. His father, Edward, had sung in operetta, and his mother was an actress. He was educated at Stern's Conservatory in Berlin, where he studied piano and composition. His song 'Katrina' (1919) achieved modest success in Europe. He emigrated to the United States in 1924 but had little success as a composer until he began his association with Alan Jay Lerner (1918–86), lyricist and librettist. Their first show was *Life of the Party*, staged in Detroit in 1942. This was followed by *What's Up* (1943) and *The Day Before Spring* (1945). Their major successes were *Brigadoon* (1947), *Paint Your Wagon* (1951) and *My Fair Lady* (1956). The shows *Camelot* (1960) and *Gigi* (1958, filmed in 1973) also enjoyed a great deal of popularity. Tributes to the partnership were celebrated in the television show *Salute to Lerner and Loewe* in 1961. *The Lerner and Loewe Songbook* was published in 1962.

Additional Readings

Ewen, David. *American Songwriters*. New York: H. W. Wilson, 1987. pp. 265–71.

Ewen, David. *Great Men of American Popular Song*. Englewood Cliffs, NJ: Prentice-Hall, 1970. pp. 299–309.

Green, Benny. *Let's Face the Music*. London: Pavilion Books, 1989. pp. 113–34.

Lees, Gene. *Inventing Champagne: The Worlds of Lerner and Loewe*. New York: St. Martin's Press, 1990.

Select Discography

Ornadel, Cyril. **Musical World of Lerner and Loewe** (With Starlight Symphony Orchestra) MGM E/SE 3781 [Also on CD]

Compact Discs

Kunzel, Erich. **Lerner and Loewe Songbook for Orchestra** (with Cincinnati Pops Orchestra) Telarc 80375

LONGINES SYMPHONETTE

This was a major record project of the mid–1960s. A number of prominent conductors and arrangers were involved in this venture, which resulted in the release of numerous boxed albums and individual records as well.

Among the conductors and arrangers who were featured were WALLY STOTT (who was responsible for most of the arrangements), Ronnie Hazelhurst, Peter Knight and Ken Thorne. These conductors and arrangers were never named on the records themselves. The recordings were initially made at the CTS Studios in Westbourne Grove, England, and thereafter at a new studio in Wembley.

Select Discography

Blues in the Night

Christmas at the Fireside

Dearly Beloved

Greatest Broadway

Love Letters

Memory Years

No Business like Show Business

Geoff Love

Port of Call—Romance

Sentimental Journey

Those Wonderful Years

LOVE, GEOFF/MANUEL AND HIS MUSIC OF THE MOUNTAINS
(4 September 1917–8 July 1991)

Geoff Love was born in Todmorton, Yorkshire. He was the son of Kid Love, a black American dancer and grandson of a Cherokee Indian. At an early age, he became interested in a local brass band, where he learned to play the trombone under the instruction of Doctor Maver.

On leaving school, he became a motor mechanic. After winning a Charleston competition at the age of seventeen, he entered show business as a singer and tap dancer. He made his first broadcast as a trombonist in 1937 on Radio Normandy. He played with violinist Jan Ralfini's Dance Band in London and with the Alan Green Band in Hastings. During World

War II (1939–45), he served with the King's Royal Rifle Corps and learned the art of orchestration with the unit's band.

After the war, Love worked from 1946 to 1949 with Harry Gold and his Pieces of Eight. In 1952, he branched out on his own, making records, arranging in London's Tin Pan Alley and appearing on radio and television. In 1955, Love formed his own band for the television show *On the Town*. He started recording for EMI/Columbia with his orchestra and concert orchestra.

His career flourished after he began recording under the name of Manuel and His Music of the Mountains in 1959. Under this pseudonym, he recorded mainly South American music for EMI's Studio Two stereo series. Love also provided the accompaniment and arrangements for artists such as Connie Francis, Russ Conway, Paul Robeson, Judy Garland, Frankie Vaughan, Johnny Mathis, Des O'Connor, Ken Dodd, Marlene Dietrich and Gracie Fields.

Apart from his performances in Radio Luxembourg shows and his television programs with Russ Conway, Love was also responsible for the theme tune for the *This Is Your Life* program. His most successful television appearances were with Max Bygraves and his pianist Bob Dickson in the comic series *Singalongamax*.

In the 1970s, he formed yet another group known as Billy's Banjo Band, later Geoff Love's Banjo Band and also produced several volumes of 'Geoff Love's Big Disco Sound' to take advantage of the dance fads of the period. At the same time, he retained his more conservative image by producing albums such as *Big War Themes, Big Western Movie Themes* and *Big Love Movie Themes*.

Love's compositions range in character from the Latin-styled 'La Rosa Negra' to the theme for the hit television comedy *Bless This House*. His vast output of albums included mostly film or television themes.

Select Discography

As Geoff Love

All-time Orchestral Hits Columbia TWOX 1029

Big Love Movie Themes Music for Pleasure MFP 5221

Christmas with Love Music for Pleasure MFP 50037

Dreaming with Love Music for Pleasure MFP 50244

Love with Love Music for Pleasure MFP 5246

Showbusiness Columbia TWOX 1008

Thanks for the Memories Capitol ST 10207

Top TV Themes Music for Pleasure MFP 5272

Compact Discs

Big War Themes EMI CC 211 CDB 7 52037 2

Going Latin with Geoff Love EMI CC 270. CDB 7962752

Great Western Themes EMI CD CC 204. CDB 7 52031 2, CC211
In the Mood for Love EMI CC 245. CDB 7.92194–2
In the Mood for Waltzing EMI CC 261. CDB 7 94227 2

As Manuel

Blue Waters Columbia TWO 131
Carnival Columbia TWO 337
Cascade Columbia TWO 336 KLP 1141
Exotica Columbia TWO 103 TAW 15001
Mountain Fiesta REG 30108
Music of Movies Columbia TWO 303 Starday-King KLP 1140
Music of the Mountains Capitol T 6156
Spanish Harlem MGM SE 4299
Sunrise, Sunset Columbia TWO 162

Compact Discs

Big Suspense Movie Themes Music for Pleasure MFP 50035
Golden Sounds CD SOUMWB 8 (South Africa)
Latin Hits EMI CDP 790765
Latin Romance EMI CDP 796277
Magic of Manuel EMI CDP 797527
Mountain Fiesta EMI CC 253. CDB 7 94109 2
With Love EMI CC 289. 07778044727
Y Viva Espana EMI CDP 79502

LUBBOCK, MARK (1898–1986)

Mark Lubbock was educated at Eton and Vienna, where he developed an affinity for operetta. He joined the BBC as light music conductor from 1933 to 1944 and also conducted in broadcasts and for the theater. He conducted West End shows, such as *Night in Venice* and compiled a reference book, *The Complete Book of Light Opera*. Besides composing incidental music, he wrote a number of light orchestral pieces, including the well-known *Polka Dots*.

LUPAR, GUY. *See* LUYPAERTS, GUY

LUYPAERTS, GUY (born c. 1917)

Guy Luypaerts was born in Paris of Belgian parents. His father played in a Brussels brass band and became Guy's copyist of scores. Guy was raised in an artistic and musical environment and showed early talent as a pianist.

He won a fine reputation as a musician in Paris nightclubs. He subsequently became conductor of the French orchestra known as the Nouvelle Association Symphonique de Paris and broadcast over the Paris radio station. He conducted frequently in many other European cities as guest conductor of radio stations in Luxembourg, Brussels, Hamburg and Stockholm and composed and arranged light music.

Select Discography

Hits from 'Pipe Dream' RCA Camden CAL 319

Music of the Danube RCA LPM-1416

Music of the Volga RCA LPM-1417

One Night in Monte Carlo RCA LPM 1304

Reveries d'Europe Capitol T 10024

Symphonic Portrait of Cole Porter Capitol LC 6501

Symphonic Portrait of George Gershwin Capitol P 254, LC 6533

Symphonic Portrait of Irving Berlin Capitol LC 6538

Symphonic Portrait of Richard Rodgers Capitol LC 6539

Y a d'la Joie. There Is Joy: The Music of Charles Trenet MGM E 3595

Your Musical Holiday in the South Brunswick LAT 8126 [Also on CD]

M

MANCINI, HENRY (ENRICO) (16 April 1924–14 June 1994)
Mancini was born in Cleveland, Ohio. His parents moved to Aliquippa, Pennsylvania. At the age of eight, Mancini was introduced to the flute by his father, who played the instrument himself. When he was twelve, Mancini took up the piano and within a few years became interested in arranging. He was instructed in this aspect by Max Adkins, who was conductor and arranger for the house orchestra at the Stanley Theatre in Pittsburgh.

After graduating from the Aliquippa High School in 1942, Mancini enrolled at the Juilliard School of Music. His studies were interrupted by a period of war service in the Air Force and Infantry. In 1945, Mancini joined the Glenn Miller–Tex Beneke Orchestra as a pianist and arranger. He also studied privately with composers Ernst Krenek, Mario Castelnuovo-Tedesco and Dr. Alfred Sendry.

In 1952, Mancini joined the music department of Universal-International Studios, where, over a period of six years, he contributed to over 100 films. The most notable of these was *The Glenn Miller Story* (1954), for which he received an Academy Award nomination. For this film, he modernized all the original Miller arrangements and added a few more numbers, including 'Love Theme'. He completed work for *The Benny Goodman Story* (1956), *High Time* (Bing Crosby), *Rock Pretty Baby* and *Touch of Evil* (1958). He also composed material for the nightclub acts of Dinah Shore, Polly Bergen, Billy Eckstine and Betty Hutton.

After leaving Universal-International, Mancini was engaged by producer

Blake Edwards of Spartan Productions to create the score for the NBC-TV series *Peter Gunn*, which had famous musicians playing original jazz music during the action of the filmed show. For this work, Mancini was nominated for an Emmy Award by the Academy of Television Arts and Sciences. The album *The Music from Peter Gunn*, released by RCA Victor in 1958, earned him a Gold Record. The album was voted two Grammys by the members of the National Academy of Recording Arts and Sciences.

In 1959, Mancini scored another success with another collaboration with Blake Edwards, entitled *Mr. Lucky*. The album *Music from Mr. Lucky* was also awarded two Grammys. His album *The Blues and the Beat* was awarded a Grammy that same year.

Between 1960 and 1978, Mancini produced notable movie scores, which included the following titles: *High Time, The Great Imposter, Mr. Hobbs Takes a Vacation, Bachelor in Paradise, Breakfast at Tiffany's, Hatari, Experiment in Terror, Days of Wine and Roses, Charade, The Pink Panther, Soldier in the Rain, Dear Heart, Shot in the Dark, The Great Race, Moment to Moment, Arabesque, What Did You Do in the War, Daddy?, Two for the Road, Wait Until Dark, Gunn, The Party, Me, Natalie, Gaily, Gaily, The Molly Maguires, Sunflower, Darling Lili, Sunflower, The Hawaiians, The Night Visitor, Sometimes a Great Notion, The Thief Who Came to Dinner, The White Dawn, Once Is Not Enough, Oklahoma Crude, W. C. Fields and Me, House Calls, The Revenge of the Pink Panther, Who Is Killing the Great Chefs of Europe?* and *Visions of Eight*. The latter was the official film of the 1978 Olympics.

Scores for more recent films include *Nightwing, Prisoner of Zenda, 10, Little Miss Marker, Back Roads, Mommie Dearest, Victor, Victoria* (1982 Academy Award), *Lifeforce, The Glass Menagerie, Without a Clue, Switch, Tom and Jerry: The Movie.*

In 1962, he was awarded two Oscars; one for best original score for *Breakfast at Tiffany's* and another for best song, 'Moon River' (lyrics Johnny Mercer). He was also nominated for an Oscar for the song 'Bachelor in Paradise' (lyrics Mack David). Mancini was also awarded five Grammys for his recorded versions of the same movie and score. In 1963, Mancini was again awarded an Oscar for 'Days of Wine and Roses' (lyricist Johnny Mercer).

By the late 1970s, Mancini had received a record twenty Grammys. His gold records totaled six: *The Music from Peter Gunn, Breakfast at Tiffany's, The Pink Panther, The Best of Mancini, Love Theme from Romeo and Juliet* and *A Warm Shade of Ivory.*

Mancini was given a thirteenth Oscar nomination for the song 'All His Children' (lyricists Alan and Marilyn Bergman), which was featured in the Paul Newman film *Sometimes a Great Notion*. This song, performed by Charlie Pride, reached top spot on the country music charts.

In 1969, Mancini composed the music and conducted the Philadelphia Orchestra Pops in its first album for RCA. Mancini included in the repertoire a suite in three movements entitled 'Beaver Valley-'37', written especially for the orchestra. In the same year, he performed at the White House at a dinner honoring the Apollo 10 astronauts.

Mancini became a familiar television personality. He hosted his own TV music series, *Mancini Generation* as well as several hour-long specials, featuring his own and other orchestras. He also composed the theme music for series such as *What's Happening; The Thorn Birds*, the 1983 miniseries and the *NBC Nightly News*. He also toured extensively in the United States and abroad. Among the symphony orchestras he conducted were the Philadelphia, the BOSTON POPS, the Cleveland, the Pittsburgh, the Los Angeles Philharmonic, the Israel Philharmonic, the London Symphony and the Royal Philharmonic of London.

In 1976, Duquesne University in Pittsburgh, Pennsylvania, conferred upon him the title of honorary doctor of music. He donated scholarships and fellowships to the Juilliard School, New York, UCLA and USC on the West Coast and the American Federation of Music's Congress of Strings.

Mancini has written a book for budding musicians entitled *Sounds and Scores: A Practical Guide to Professional Orchestration*. He also completed an autobiography entitled *Did They Mention the Music?* (written with Gene Lees).

Musical Achievements

Mancini made use of the jazz idiom, applied dramatically to the story in scores for the *Peter Gunn* series and also for the *Pink Panther* films. He often presented his music with a contemporary pop twist. The Blake Edwards–Henry Mancini collaboration produced notable scores, including the *Pink Panther* series, *10* and *Victor/Victoria.*

In the song 'Moon River' from *Breakfast at Tiffany's*, Mancini revealed his ability to create exquisite melodies and creative orchestrations. He used a plaintive harmonica to first express the tune, repeated by strings, hummed and sung by a chorus and finally resolved with the harmonica.

The 'Love Theme from Romeo and Juliet' (1969) was another instance in which Mancini created a beautiful arrangement that became a top instrumental single recording in the United States. The theme was based on NINO ROTA's score for the film. A vocal version entitled 'A Time for Us' was written by Eddie Snyder and Larry Kuisk.

In general, Mancini emphasized his pop-oriented material on his many sound track albums, to the exclusion of his dramatic scoring. However, he was capable of composing heavier dramatic scores, as is evident in his outstanding music for *Wait Until Dark, The White Dawn* and *Lifeforce.*

Additional Readings

Ewen, David. *American Songwriters*. New York: H. W. Wilson, 1987. pp. 272–75.

Ewen, David. *Great Men of American Popular Song*. Englewood Cliffs, NJ: Prentice-Hall, 1970. pp. 340–46.

Mancini, Henry, and Lees, Gene. *Did They Mention the Music?* New York: Contemporary Books, 1989.

Select Discography

Academy Award Songs (2) RCA LSP 6013

Best of RCA LSP 2693

Blues and the Beat RCA LSP 2147

Brass on Ivory 38–393

Breakfast at Tiffany's RCA LSP-2362

Concert Sound RCA LPM-2897

Gems Forever London/Decca (U.K.)

Latin Sound RCA LSP 3356

Love Songs (With Mancini Pops Orchestra) RCA RD 60974

Love Story and Other Themes RCA LSP 4466

Love Theme from 'Romeo and Juliet' Victor (U.S.)

Mancini and Other Composers RCA Camden CAS 2158

Mancini Touch RCA LSP 2101

Mr. Lucky Goes Latin RCA LSP 2360

More Music from Peter Gunn RCA LSP 2040

Music from Mr. Lucky RCA LSP 2198

Music from Peter Gunn RCA LSP 1956

Our Man in Hollywood RCA LSP 2604

The Party RCA LSP 3997

Pink Panther RCA LSP 2795

Terribly Sophisticated Songs BS 1210

Theme from 'Z' RCA LSP 4350

The Versatile Liberty LT 7121

Warm Shade of Ivory RCA LSP 4140

Compact Discs

Academy Award Collection PAIR 1213

All-time Greatest Hits BMG/RCA 8321

American Melodies MCS 105 024 2

As Time Goes By BMG/RCA 60974

Best of Mancini BMG/RCA 53822

Cinema Italiano BMG/RCA 60706

Classic Movie Scores BMG/RCA 55938

Days of Wine and Roses (3 CDs) RCA 07863.66603.2

Godfather and Other Movie Themes BMG/RCA 61478

In Surround BMG/RCA 60471

Legendary Performer BMG/RCA 51843

Love Story PAIR 1296

Mancini Collection PAIR 1092

Mancini Country BMG/RCA 53668

Mancini in Hollywood BMG/RCA 61517

Mancini in Surround. Mostly Monsters, Murders and Mysteries RCA Victor RD60471

Mancini Rocks the Pops Denon 73078

Mancini Touch RCA 74321 357 442

Mancini's Greatest Hits Telarc CD80183

Merry Mancini Christmas BMG/RCA 362

Moon River BMG/RCA 61513

Moon River and Other Hits BMG/RCA 2077

Mr. Lucky—TV Soundtrack RCA 2198

Music from 'Peter Gunn' RCA 1956

Pure Gold BMG/RCA 3667

Second Time Around RCA Camden 928

Top Hat: Music from the Films of Astaire and Rogers (With Mancini Pops Orchestra) RCA 09026 60795 2

MANDEL, JOHNNY (JOHN ALFRED) (b. 23 November 1925)

American composer, arranger, conductor, trumpeter and trombonist Johnny Mandel was born in New York. He first became interested in composing at the age of twelve, when he was influenced by the music of DUKE ELLINGTON, Count Basie and Benny Goodman.

He learned to play the piano but later changed to trumpet playing. He was educated at the Manhattan School of Music and Juilliard. He joined the band of Joe Venuti in 1943 and subsequently worked with trumpeter Billie Rogers.

At this stage, Mandel first took up the trombone. He changed to trombone playing completely when he joined Henry Jerome's band. His subsequent engagements were with Boyd Raeburn, Jimmy Dorsey, Buddy Rich, Georgie Auld, Alvino Rey and Count Basie. He was staff composer for television shows and films. His scores included *You're Never Too Young* (1957); *I Want to Live* (1958); *The Third Voice* (1959); *The Americanization of Emily* (1964); *The Sandpiper* (1965), which won a Grammy Award for 'The Shadow of Your Smile'; *Harper* (1966); *The Russians Are Coming* (1966); *An American Dream* (1966); *Point Blank* (1967); *M*A*S*H* (1970); *The Last Detail* (1973); *Freaky Friday* (1976); *Agatha*

Mantovani and His Orchestra

(1979); *Being There* (1979); *The Baltimore Bullet* (1980); *Deathtrap* (1982) and *The Verdict* (1982).

MANTOVANI, ANNUNZIO PAOLO (15 November 1905–30 March 1980)
Mantovani was born in Venice. His father was principal violinist at La Scala in Milan, under Arturo Toscanini, Pietro Mascagni, Hans Richter and Camille Saint-Saëns and subsequently led the Covent Garden Orchestra. Mantovani learned to play the piano and violin. His father discouraged him from taking up a musical career. After the family moved to England, however, he studied at Trinity College of Music, London, and made his professional debut at the age of sixteen, playing the Bruch *Violin Concerto*.

At the age of twenty, he was conducting his own orchestra at the Hotel Metropole in London and began his broadcasting career. In the early 1930s, he formed the Tipica Orchestra and began lunch-hour broadcasts from the Monseigneur Restaurant in Piccadilly. He also started recording for Regal Zonophone. His hits of the 1935 to 1936 period include 'Red Sails in the Sunset' and 'Serenade in the Night'. Samples of his work of this time are on *The Young Mantovani, 1935–1939*.

In the 1940s, Mantovani acted as musical director for various London West End shows, including *Lady Behave, Twenty to One, Meet Me Victoria, And So To Bed, Bob's Your Uncle* and *La-Di-Da-Di-Da*. He also took part in NOËL COWARD's *Pacific 1860* and *Sigh No More* and the show *Ace of Clubs*. One of his last shows was *And So To Bed* in 1951. His records for UK Decca included 'The Green Cockatoo', 'Hear My Song, Violetta' and 'Tell Me, Marianne'. He conducted for artists such as Lupino Lane, Pat Kirkwood, Mary Martin, Sally Gray and Leslie Henson.

After World War II, there was a growing demand for his records in the United States, and Mantovani was anxious to develop something different. The final choice was an orchestra of forty-five that included thirty-two string players. RONALD BINGE is credited with having developed the famous sound of the 'cascading strings' that became Mantovani's trademark and was first used to great effect in 1951, with Mantovani's recording of 'Charmaine'. This was the first of several million-selling singles for his orchestra, which included 'Wyoming', 'Greensleeves', 'Song from the Moulin Rouge', 'Swedish Rhapsody' and 'Lonely Ballerina'.

Mantovani's own compositions include 'A Poem to the Moon', 'Royal Blue Waltz', 'Dance of the Eighth Veil', 'Toy Shop Ballet' (Ivor Novello award 1957), 'Red Petticoats', 'Brass Buttons', 'Serenata d'amore', 'Tango in the Night' and 'Cara Mia', written with Bunny Lewis. This latter composition, recorded by David Whitfield with Mantovani's orchestra in 1954, sold over a million copies. Mantovani also issued an instrumental version of the song, featuring himself on the piano.

Mantovani excelled as an album artist and is said to have been the first to sell over a million stereo records, which were produced with superb sound quality by Decca. Between 1955 and 1966 twenty-eight of his albums were in the U.S. top twenty. He toured many parts of the world, including Europe, South Africa, Canada and Japan, but his popularity was always greatest in the United States, which he first visited in 1955. He was awarded a special Ivor Novello award in 1956 for services to popular music and a diamond-studded baton in 1966 for his twenty-five years of service with Decca.

He continued to perform throughout the 1960s and 1970s. By 1971, he had achieved fifty million LP sales in the United States alone, with eighteen gold discs among them. After his death at Tunbridge Wells, Kent, various other conductors continued to conduct the Mantovani Orchestra.

Select Discography

Album of Favorite Melodies Decca LK 4065

Album of Favorite Melodies Vol. 2 Decca LK 4079

Album of Favorite Melodies Vol. 3 Decca LK 4122

Album of Favorite Waltzes Decca LK 4051

All-time Romantic Hits London 2BP 910/911

American Scene LPM 70018

American Waltzes PS 248, London LL 3260

Big Hits from Broadway and Hollywood London PS 419
Candlelight Decca LK 4150, London LL 1502
Carnival London LL 3250
Christmas Magic (Mantovani Orchestra conducted by Roland Shaw) EXCL 3
Classical Encores London LL 3269
Concert Encores London PS 133
Continental Encores London LL 3095, London PS 147
Enchanted Evening London LL 766
Favorite Melodies from the Operas Decca LK 4127
Favorite Waltzes London LL 570
Film Encores London LL-1700
Film Encores Vol. 1 London PS 124
Film Encores Vol. 2 London LL 3117, PS 164
Film Encores Vol. 3 London LL 3117
Flamingo (Mantovani Orchestra conducted by Stanley Black) Bainbridge BT 6239
From Monty with Love XS 585/6 (2)
Gems Forever London LL 3032, LPM 70001
Great Theme Music London PS 224
Herbert and Romberg London PS 165
In Concert London PS 578
In Vienna (Double album) DLPL 479/80
Incomparable Mantovani and his Orchestra Decca PFS 34043, London PS 392
Italia Mia London PS 232
Latin Rendezvous Decca LK 4528, LL 3295
Love Themes (Double album) SIV 101
Manhattan London PS 328
Mantovani Hollywood London PS 516
Mantovani Magic London PS 448
Mantovani Memories London PS 542
Mantovani Scene Stereo London PS 548
Mantovani Sound London PS 419
Mantovani Today London PS 572
Mantovani Touch London PS 526
Mantovani's Golden Hits SKL 4818
Memories Decca 820181
Moon River London PS 249
More Film Encores Decca 820469

More Golden Hits Polygram 20037

Mr Music London PS 474

Music from the Films (With Rawiez and Landauer, duo pianists) London PS 112 (U.S.); Decca LK 4254 (U.K.)

Music of Irving Berlin and Rudolf Friml London PS 166

Music of Sigmund Romberg London LL 1031; Decca LK 4082

Music of Rudolf Friml Decca LK 4096

Music of Victor Herbert London LL 746

Operetta Memories London LL 3181, SKL 4093

Romantic Melodies London LL 979

Sentimental Strings S 5050/5 (6)

Showcase MS 5

Song Hits from Theatreland Decca LK 4112, London PS 125

Songs to Remember London PS 193

Stop the World/Oliver London PS 270

Themes from Broadway London PS 242

To Lovers Everywhere London XPS 598

Waltz Encores London PS 119

Waltz Time Decca LK 4105

Waltzes of Irving Berlin London LL 1452

World of Mantovani London PS 565

World's Favourite Love Songs Decca LK 4215

World's Favourite Melodies Reader's Digest GCAND-A-9–204

Compact Discs

And I Love You So ECLIPSE 844 185 2

At the Movies Memoir 506

At the Theatre Horatio Nelson SIV 6108

Besame Mucho Laserlight 12399

Bravo Madacay 5430

Broadway Encores Decca 82047

Christmas Favorites Polygram 20540

Christmas Classics Chicago Music Co. 105

Concert Encores Polygram 33209

Deep Purple MCPS GAL 069

Elisabeth Serenade TREND 156.481 (Germany)

Film Themes Horatio Nelson SIV 6105

Gems Forever Decca 840477

Golden Hits Bainbridge 6288

Golden Hits Madacy 2353

Golden Hits Masters 1101

Golden Hits Polygram 85

(The four Golden Hits CDs do not constitute a uniform series, and the contents of each are different.)

Golden Instrumentals Laserlight 15134

Great Songs of Christmas Bainbridge 6238, Point 2641352

Hello Columbus Bainbridge 8006

In a Classic Mood Madacy 4938

In a Classical Mood Bainbridge 6296

In a Latin Mood Madacy 4905

In the Mood for Romance Madacy 4952

Incomparable Mantovani Polygram Laserlight 55505

Instrumental Favorites Time Life R986–05

Italia Bainbridge 6277

Italia Bella Madacy 2350

Latin Dreams Success 16213

Latino Connection Laserlight 12307

Love Songs PAIR 1288

Lovely Way to Spend an Evening Bainbridge 6294

Maestro PAIR 1170

Magic of the Mantovani Orchestra Bainbridge BCD 8001

Magical Moods of Mantovani Special Music Company 4969

Manhattan London 820475–2, Decca 820037

Mantovani at His Very Best TWINS TTCDO75 (2 discs)

Mantovani at the Movies CDMOIR 506 AAD

Mantovani Collection Double Play GRFO40

Many Moods of Mantovani Madacy 5652

Masterworks Telstar TCD 2335

Music by Candlelight 4 vols. ELAP FK 510, EVER. 47652CD to 47655CD

Night in Vienna OBJECT ORO 152

Operetta Memories London 436568–2

Pure and Luscious Public Music 9004

Romantic Sounds Special Music Company

16 Greatest Magic Melodies PRIME 5821

Strictly Latin Bainbridge 6299

Vaya Con Dios Laserlight 12400

Vintage Mantovani Pearl Flapper 9724

World Hits Laserlight 15095

MANUEL. *See* LOVE, GEOFF

MARTIN, RAY (11 October 1918–7 February 1988)
Ray Martin was born in Vienna. He came to England in 1938 and served in the Intelligence Corps during World War II. In 1947, he came to prominence with a series of BBC radio broadcasts featuring his Melody from the Sky Orchestra. He became conductor of the BBC Variety Orchestra and conductor, arranger and producer of EMI Records. He accompanied various EMI artists and had recorded successes with his own songs and orchestral compositions.

In 1957, he went to work in New York and Hollywood, where he wrote for films and television and recorded for RCA and Polydor. He returned to Britain in 1972, to resume recording his own and other works. He moved from his luscious mood music of the 1950s to more experimental idioms in the 1970s.

His compositions include 'Melody from the Sky' (1946), 'Once upon a Wintertime (1948), 'Blue Violins' (1951), 'Any Old Time' (1952), 'Waltzing Bugle Boy' (1953), 'Airborne' (1953), 'Ballet of the Bells' (1954), 'You Are My First Love' (1955), 'Tango of the Bells' (1956), 'Big Ben Blues' (1956), 'Never Too Young' (1965), 'Sounds Out of Sight' (1966), 'If' (1973).

Select Discography

Favorite TV Themes SPA 333

Global Hop Capitol T 10101

High Barbaree Capitol T 10067

I Love ESLP-105 (10")

Latin Nights (With Norrie Paramor) Columbia 33JS 1078

Memories Are Made of Music Decca PFS 4275

Mexican Shuffle—Living Brass RCA Camden CAS 907

Million Dollar Melodies Columbia (Britain) SCX 3255

My London Capitol T 10056

Rainy Night in London Capitol T 10017

Sound of Sight Decca PFS 4043

Tijuana Sounds—Living Brass CDS 1104

What Now My Love—Living Brass CDS 1065

MATHIESON, MUIR (24 January 1911–28 June 1975)
Muir Mathieson was born in Stirling, Scotland. At the Royal College of Music, he studied piano under ARTHUR BENJAMIN and conducting under Malcolm Sargent. In early 1932, he was employed by Kurt Schroder,

musical director for Alexander Korda, as assistant on several films, including *The Private Life of Henry VIII*. After Schroder's departure for Germany, Mathieson took over as musical director of London Films. Throughout the 1930s he acted as freelance musical director and commissioned and conducted many major productions, such as *Things to Come* (1935, score by ARTHUR BLISS), *Knight Without Armour* (1936, MIKLOS ROZSA), *Sixty Glorious Years* (1938, ANTHONY COLLINS) and *South Riding* (RICHARD ADDINSELL).

From 1940 to 1945, he was appointed musical director for the Ministry of Information, supervising and often conducting scores for army, navy and Royal Air Force film production units. After the war, Mathieson became music director for the J. Arthur Rank organization. One of the productions directed by him was *Instruments of the Orchestra* (1946), scored by Benjamin Britten. Over twenty years later, he produced a series of short films with a similar objective, entitled *We Make Music*. Estimates of the total number of film scores produced under his directorship vary from 600 to 1,000.

Mathieson was on the board of governors of the British Film Institute for twenty-five years. He took part in many concerts for children and students, made several appearances at the Philharmonic Concerts of the 1970s and was awarded the OBE for services to music.

MAUCERI, JOHN (b. 12 September 1945)

John Mauceri was born in New York and studied at Yale University and Tanglewood. Mauceri was a protégé of LEONARD BERNSTEIN and has had a highly successful conducting career on both sides of the Atlantic. He is equally at home in the opera house or on Broadway, conducting shows.

John Mauceri has conducted productions at various opera houses including La Scala, the Royal Opera, Covent Gardens, the San Francisco Opera and New York's Metropolitan Opera. His many contributions to the American musical theater include the Broadway productions of *On Your Toes, Candide* and *Song and Dance*.

He is particularly fond of Bernstein's music and conducted the European premiere of *Mass* at the Vienna Konzerhaus in 1973, the performance recorded for television. He conducted Bernstein's opera, *A Quiet Place*, at La Scala in 1984. He also played a crucial role in restoring much of the original music to *Candide* and has performed this and other Bernstein compositions in Europe, Israel and the United States.

Mauceri is currently conductor of the HOLLYWOOD BOWL ORCHESTRA, appointed in 1991. He is one of a few conductors attempting to restore full scores of vintage musical shows, presented in new studio recordings with classically trained singers.

Select Discography/Compact Discs

(*Note*: All CDs with Hollywood Bowl Orchestra)

Always and Forever: Movies Greatest Love Songs Philips 446 681.2

Gershwins in Hollywood Philips 434 274 2

Great Waltz Philips 438 685–2

Hollywood Bowl on Broadway Philips 446 402–2

Hollywood Dreams Philips/Polygram 432.109.2

Hollywood Nightmares Philips/Polygram 442.4252

Journey to the Stars Philips/Polygram 446403

Opening Night: Rodgers and Hammerstein Overtures Philips 434 932 2

Salute to Hollywood Philips

Songs of the Earth Philips/Polygram 438.8672

Sound of Hollywood Philips 446499.2

MAURIAT, PAUL (b. 1925)

Mauriat was born in France and studied music from the age of four. His father was a musician descended from generations of classical musicians. When Paul was ten, the family moved to Paris where he studied at the Conservatoire de Musique. His first ambition was to be a classical pianist, but he became attracted to lighter music and jazz. By the time he was seventeen, Mauriat had formed his own orchestra, playing in cabarets and concert halls throughout France and the rest of Europe. After several years of touring, he returned to Paris, where a producer arranged a recording session. This launched him on his career, arranging and conducting for artists such as Charles Aznavour and joining the select group of famous band leaders and arrangers including CARAVELLI, RAYMOND LEFEVRE and FRANCK POURCEL. Mauriat led the way in popularizing light instrumental music in France.

He made his debut on United States television in February 1968, with an album entitled *Blooming Hits*. This contained the tune 'Love Is Blue' (L'amour est bleu), which was composed by André Popp (lyrics Pierre Cour) in 1967 and became a hit in the United States, earning a Gold Disc award in March of that year.

Mauriat later made regular appearances in Japan and Latin America, in addition to tours of the United States. He is joint author of the book *I Will Follow Him*, which he wrote with Franck Pourcel.

Select Discography

Blooming Hits Philips 600–248

From Paris with Love Fontana Philips (Australia) 6 444 001

Listen Too! Philips 600–197

Paris by Night Fan Fantasy (San Francisco) 8380

Soul Of . . . Philips 600–299

Compact Discs

Best of France Philips 834370

Love Is Blue Mercury 830769

MAXIN, ERNEST

Ernest Maxin began his career as an all-round entertainer, singer, dancer, pianist and violinist. He subsequently became a television and film producer, working with artists such as Jack Benny, Victor Borge, Buddy Greco, Sarah Vaughan, Tom Jones, Engelbert Humperdinck, Robert Mitchum, Eddie Fisher and Tommy Steele. His flair for comedy created hit series for Dick Emery and Charlie Drake, with whom he shared the Golden Rose of Montreux TV award for 1968. Maxin had his own television spectacular series which featured many international stars and his own Television Orchestra consisting of fifty-five musicians.

Select Discography

F# . . . Where There Is Music Top Rank RM 307

Getting Sentimental: Ernest Maxin and His Television Orchestra Fontana SFL 13160, 859 098 FZY

Great Themes from Great Movies Riverside RLP 97519

Nearness of You Major Minor Records SMLP 12

With My Love Top Rank RM 321

Compact Disc

As Time Goes By Spectrum U4068

McHUGH, JIMMY (10 July 1894–23 May 1969)

Jimmy McHugh was born in Boston and first received professional piano and music tuition from his mother. He was educated at St. John's Preparatory School and Holy Cross Convent, where he received an Honors Degree in Music. His first job was that of rehearsal pianist at the Boston Opera House. He was subsequently employed as music plugger with the Boston office of Irving Berlin Music.

In 1921, he went to New York and had his first hit song success with 'When My Baby Walks Down the Street' in 1924. This was followed by 'I Can't Believe That You're in Love with Me' (1926). At this time, he began writing the music for the *Cotton Club Revues*, which he did for seven years. He also became professional manager of Mills Music, the publishing company of Irving Mills. In partnership with lyricist Dorothy Fields he wrote the music for *Blackbirds of 1928*, which proved to be his first big break.

This partnership lasted almost to the end of the 1930s and resulted in Broadway shows, such as *Hello Daddy* (1928) and *The International Revue* (1930). Their collaboration also was evident in Hollywood films, including *The Cuban Love Song* (1930), *Dancing Lady* (1933), *Dinner at Eight* (1933), *Every Night at Eight* (1935, *Hooray for Love* (1933) and *Roberta* (1935) in which McHugh collaborated with JEROME KERN.

Other lyricists with whom McHugh collaborated were Al Dubin, Harold Adamson, Ted Koehler and FRANK LOESSER. McHugh was still writing songs up to 1959, when he produced 'Let's Have an Old-fashioned Christmas'. He was awarded a Presidential Certificate of Merit during World War II. He founded the Jimmy McHugh Polio Foundation and had his own publishing company.

Some of his finest songs include 'Exactly like You', 'On the Sunny Side of the Street' (both 1930), 'Cuban Love Song' (1931), 'Don't Blame Me' (1933), 'I Feel a Song Coming On' (1935), 'South American Way' (sung by Carmen Miranda, 1939), 'A Lovely Way to Spend an Evening' (1943), 'I Can't Give You Anything but Love,' (1944) and 'I'm in the Mood for Love' (1944), which sold millions of copies. In 1943, his patriotic wartime song 'Coming In on a Wing and a Prayer' became a hit. In 1948 he wrote 'It's a Most Unusual Day' which also became a standard.

Additional Readings

Ewen, David. *American Songwriters.* New York: H. W. Wilson. 1987. pp. 275–79.

Hemming, Roy. *The Melody Lingers On.* New York: Newmarket Press, 1986. pp. 123–150.

Select Discography

Chacksfield, Frank. Lovely Lady: The Music of Jimmy McHugh Decca LK 4172

De Vol, Frank. Symphonic Portrait of Jimmy McHugh Capitol P254 (12") LC 6528 (10")

MELACHRINO, GEORGE (1 May 1909–18 June 1965).

George Melachrino was born in London. His stepfather was a violist and George was given considerable encouragement from childhood onward to become a musician. He first played a miniature violin at the age of three and composed his first composition at four. At thirteen, he made his first public appearance as a violin soloist in a Sunday concert at a London music hall. It was at Trinity College of Music, London, that Melachrino formed a jazz band and learned to play different instruments.

Melachrino was a versatile musician. He played the viola, oboe, clarinet, saxophone and the piano. In 1926 he became a member of Geoffrey Kettner's Five, where he doubled reeds and flute. From 1927 onward he made frequent appearances on the BBC programs at Savoy Hill and by 1938 was enjoying star billing. During this early period he also recorded with Harry

George Melachrino

Hudson's Melody Men. In 1932, Melachrino began playing in the Savoy Orpheans. In 1939, Melachrino became deputy leader at the Cafe de Paris.

Melachrino saw service in the Second World War, initially as a military policeman. By 1943, he had attained the rank of sergeant and was regularly conducting All-Services Orchestra programs on the air. Toward the end of the war, he was promoted to regimental sergeant major and formed and led the British Band of the Allied Expeditionary Force (AEF). This band was a miniature symphony orchestra, with a dance band reed and rhythm. Incidentally, Melachrino appeared with the Glenn Miller band as a vocalist and sang with ROBERT FARNON's band in a Farewell AEF Program on 28 June 1945.

Shortly after the end of World War II the Melachrino Music Organisation was set up. It consisted of the British Band of the Blue Rockets, the Masqueraders, Jack Coles' Music Masters and Ronnie Selby. Concerts, broadcasts, films and recordings all flowed from this organization.

In June 1965, Melachrino succumbed to domestic and work pressures. He went to sleep in his bath and was found drowned. Some years after his death, several LPs were made, with Robert Mandell conducting the Melachrino Strings and Orchestra.

Select List of Compositions

Incidental Film Music

Appointment with Crime (1945)

Dark Secret (1949)

Eight O'Clock Walk (1953)

Forbidden (1949)

Gamma People

House of Darkness (c. 1946) (Includes the First Rhapsody theme)

Lady Craved Excitement (1950)

No Orchids for Miss Blandish (1948)

Odango (1956)

Old Mother Riley, Headmistress (1950)

Old Mother Riley's New Venture (1949)

Shop at Sly Corner (U.S. title: Code of Scotland Yard).

Story of Shirley York (1949) (Including Portrait of a Lady theme)

Woman to Woman (1947)

Select List of Other Compositions

Up the Mountains (Written at age four)

Vision d'Amour

Winter Sunshine

Woodland Revel

Amoureuse

Concerto for Carroll

Waltz in Water Colours

Music for the Revue 'Starlight Roof'

Select Discography

Melachrino's recorded output was so voluminous that it is not possible to list all of it. Some eighty-six recordings with the British Band of the AEF are known to exist. There were at least 95 78 rpm discs, (eighty-five on HMV, four on Decca and six on Parlophone), covering a wide variety of light orchestral and popular music. Many of these recordings later found their way onto LPs. The majority were arranged by Melachrino himself. There were also at least twenty-one 45 rpm E.P. recordings as well.

Note: RCA unless otherwise indicated.

April in Paris LPM/LSP 2739
Ballads of Irving Berlin LPM/LSP 2817 [Also on CD]
Bells are Ringing, Music from [The Show] RD/27182/SF5070; LPM/LSP 2279
Best of George Melachrino RCA ANL 1–1093
Christmas in High Fidelity RCA LPM 1045
Christmas Joy RD27136/SF5049
Cool Water and Other Songs of the West CAL/CAS 2204
Famous Themes for Piano and Orchestra (10") DLP 1167
Gershwin and Kern Gala (Conducted by Robert Mandell) Pressit LC 775
Great Show Tunes CLP 1229
Greenwillow, Music from LPM/LSP 2279
I'll Walk Beside You LPM 1329
Immortal Ladies [Also on CD]
Immortal Melodies of Victor Herbert and Sigmund Romberg Decca DPA 3007/8
Light Classics in Hi-Fi ABC Paramount 255/S255
Lisbon at Twilight RD 27124/SF 5034; LPM/LSP 1762
Magic of Melachrino Strings ENC 133
Magic Strings ABC Paramount 249/S249
Melachrino Concert LPM 1003
Melachrino Magic Strings DLP 1014 (10")
Melachrino on Broadway LPM 1307
Melachrino Orchestra LPM 3077 (10")
Melachrino's Magic Strings ABC Paramount 249
Melachrino Magic Strings, Vol. 2 CLP 1134
Melodies for Romance RCA Camden CSP 6702
Midnight on Park Avenue DLP 1101 (10")
Moonlight Concerto CLP 1197/ CSD 1276
More Music for Dining LPM/LSP 2412
More Music for Relaxation RD 27219/SF 5101; LPM/LSP 2278
Most Happy Fella, Music from RD 27219/SF 5059
Music for Courage and Confidence LPM 1005
Music for Daydreaming LPM 1028
Music for Dining RD 27081; LPM/LSP 1000
Music for Faith and Inner Calm LPM 1004
Music for Reading LPM/LSP 1002
Music for Relaxation RD 27108, LPM/LSP 1001
Music for Romance LPM/LSP 2979
Music for the Nostalgic Traveller CLP 1068/LPM 1053

Music for Two People Alone LPM 1027

Music of Irving Berlin RCA Camden 2220/S2220

Music of Jerome Kern LPM/LSP 2283 [Also on CD]

Music of Rodgers and Hammerstein RD/SF 7517, LPM/LSP 2513

Music of Sigmund Romberg RD27174/SF 5063; LPM/LSP 2106

Music of Victor Herbert RD 27200/SF 5086; LPM/LSP 2106

Music to Help You Sleep LPM 1006

Music to Work or Study By LPM 1029

My Fair Lady DLP 1090 (10")

New Sound of Broadway LPM/LSP 3323

Now Melachrino Strings Pickwick SPC 3234

Oliver, Music from LPM/LSP 2660

Our Man in London RD/SF 7548; LPM/LSP 2608

Paris: The Sounds, the Sights LPM 1261; [with 12 page illustrated booklet]

Rendezvous in Rome RD 27150SF/5049; LPM/LSP 1955

Reverie DLP 1083 (10")

Romantic Serenade (Conducted by Robert Mandell). Pressit LC 776

Serenade in the Night DLP 1127 (10")

Serenade My Lady MFP 1173 [Also on CD]

Show Tunes LPM 1008

Soft Lights and Sweet Music DLP 1046 (10")

Something to Remember You By LPM/LSP 3398

Stardust MFP 1020

Stardust (Conducted by Robert Mandell) Pressit. LC 773

Strauss Waltzes RD 27113/SF 5025; LPM/LSP 1757; Eclipse ECS 2127

This Is Melachrino: Memorial Album (2 LPs) RCA VPS 6083

Under Western Skies RD 27094; LPM/LSP 1676

Waltzes of Irving Berlin LPM/LSP 2561 [Also on CD]

World of Melachrino Decca PA/SPA 48

World of Melachrino, Volume 2 Decca SPA 247

World's Greatest Melodies CLP 1496/CSD 1391

You and the Night and the Music RCA LPM/LSP 2866

Compact Discs

Historic Recordings EMI 077780132

Fantastic Strings Vol. 1 [A reissue of the LP **Stardust**. Melachrino's name is not given on the CD] Laserlight 15176

MONTENEGRO, HUGO (b. 1925)

Hugo Montenegro was born in New York City. During World War II, he spent two years in the United States Navy, where his musical arrangements for service bands provided the experience for later successes. While conducting the band at the Naval Training Station in Newport, Rhode Island, he had a meeting with ANDRE KOSTELANETZ, who complimented and encouraged him.

In the postwar years, he attended the Manhattan School of Music. He was subsequently engaged by John Gart, conductor on the Paul Winchell TV show, to do the musical arrangements for the ventriloquist and his guests. Other TV scoring work included *Big Town, Chance of a Lifetime* and *Arthur Godfrey Time*. He also wrote background material for nightclub acts.

He moved to California and wrote and conducted the scores for Otto Preminger's *Hurry Sundown* and *The Ambushers*. From 1955 onward Montenegro was engaged by Herman Diaz, Jr., RCA Victor's director of artists and repertoire. His first album for RCA Victor was *Music from The Man From U.N.C.L.E.* In 1968, he scored a hit with the disc *The Good, The Bad and the Ugly*, in which he made use of unusual instruments such as an electric violin, the piccola trumpet, an electronic harmonica and the ocarina. Hugo also served as staff arranger for Kostelanetz and arranger-conductor for Harry Belafonte.

Select Discography

Arriba TIME S/2030

Best of Hugo Montenegro RCA 38–224

Broadway Melodies Everest CBR 1003

Ellington Fantasy Vik LX-1106

Great Hits of the 50s Time 52147

Great Songs from Motion Pictures, 3 volumes Time S/2044, 2045, 2046

Hugo Montenegro and His Orchestra Time Records Process 70 52062

Loves of My Life Vik LX-1089 [Also on CD]

Montenegro in Italy Time S/2051

Overture: American Musical Theatre [1924–1960], 4 volumes Time S/2035, 2036, 2037, 2038

Scenes and Themes RCA APD 1–0025

Sound of the Hugo Montenegro Strings Movietone 71023 (M), S 72023(S)

MOODS ORCHESTRAL

The Moods Orchestral Series was originally conceived and designed by Philips in 1967, primarily for motorists. It was first issued on audiocassettes and subsequently on long-playing records. There are eighteen discs in the series. The conductors were Johnny Arthey, JOHNNY GREGORY (who was also responsible for most of the arrangements), Peter Knight, Ivor Raymonde, Les Reed, Ken Thorne, Reg Tilsley and Dennis Wilson.

The 216 songs included in the series are all standards. The arrangements are excellent and the series as a whole outstanding in every respect, a landmark in the field of popular orchestral music.

Select Discography (All Philips Recordings)

Around the World SBL 7801

Broadway Melody SBL 7802

Dancing in the Dark SBL 7811

Falling in Love with Love SBL 7809

Fascinating Rhythm SBL 7795

Hello, Young Lovers SBL 7808

Hit the Road to Dreamland SBL 7797

Isn't This a Lovely Day? SBL 7805

It's Magic SBL 7800

Language of Love SBL 7807

Let's Face the Music and Dance SBL 7806

Mister Wonderful SBL 7810

The Party's Over SBL 7803

Small World SBL 7794

Thank Heaven for Little Girls SBL 7804

Thanks for the Memory SBL 7796

There's No Business like Show Business SBL 7793

You Are My Lucky Star SBL 7798

MOONEY, HAL

Hal Mooney was born in Brooklyn and first intended to make law his career. He subsequently changed to songwriting. The best known of his compositions was 'Swamp Fire'. He later changed to arranging, first for Hal Kemp and later for Jimmy Dorsey.

He served in World War II and afterward settled in California, where he arranged for vocalists such as Dick Haymes, Helen Forrest, Kay Starr, Judy Garland and Dinah Washington. He also conducted for Mercury recording company, assembling an orchestra of twenty-eight musicians.

Select Discography

Dreamland U.S.A. Mercury MG 20180/ SR 60047

Flutes and Percussion. Time-Oriole OT2515

Jerome Kern: Flutes and Percussion. Time-Oriole OT2501.

Passion of Paris TIME 52005

MORGAN, RUSS (29 April 1904–8 August 1969)
Russ Morgan was born in Scranton, Pennsylvania. He was a bandleader, trombonist, singer, songwriter and arranger. He began life as a coal miner and then switched to cinema pianist and player in small groups. He bought his first trombone from money saved from these occasional jobs and moved to New York City in the early 1920s, where he arranged for VICTOR HERBERT and John Philip Sousa. He worked for Jean Goldkette in Detroit in 1926.

Morgan became musical director on Detroit Radio and arranged music for Fletcher Henderson, Chick Webb, Louis Armstrong, the Dorsey Brothers and the Boswell Sisters. He conducted orchestras on Broadway, wrote for Cotton Club Revues and became musical director for Brunswick. Morgan composed 'Phantom Phantasie' (on Bluebird record label) and possibly collaborated on 'Tidal Wave' (Bluebird and Decca).

He played with Freddy Martin's band in 1934 and formed his own band in 1936, for which he both played the trombone and sang. His radio program was entitled *Music in the Morgan Manner*. He cowrote the songs 'Somebody Else Is Taking My Place' (1937), 'Sweet Eloise', (1942), 'You're Nobody Till Somebody Loves You' (1944) and 'So Tired' (1948). He had many hits in the period 1942 to 1951, including 'Forever and Ever', 'Sunflower' and 'Cruising Down the River'. His two brothers and sons were members of his band.

His films include *Disc Jockey* (1951) and television shows in the mid-1950s. From 1965 onward he resided in Las Vegas for most of the year. His compilations include *Golden Favorites* (Decca), *There Goes That Song Again* (Pickwick), *One Night Stand 1944–46* (Joyce).

Select Discography

Does Your Heart Beat for Me? Decca DL 8332

Everybody Dance Decca DL 8337

Songs of Jimmy McHugh Decca DL 8423

Tap Pleasure for Dancing Decca DL 8336

Velvet Violins Decca DL 8642

MORLEY, ANGELA. *See* STOTT, WALLY/ANGELA MORLEY

MOROSS, JEROME (1 August 1913–25 July 1983)
Jerome Moross was born in Brooklyn and was a contemporary and friend of BERNARD HERRMANN. He studied music at the Juilliard School, New York. Throughout the 1930s, he wrote theater music and played the piano in pit orchestras. He arrived in Hollywood in 1940 and worked as an orchestrator. Moross established himself as a film composer in 1958 with his score for *The Big Country*. Other film scores included *The Adventures of Huckleberry Finn* (1960) and *The Cardinal* (1963).

Select Discography/Compact Discs

The Big Country (Philharmonic Orchestra. Conductor Tony Bremner) Silva Screen FILMCD030

The Valley of Gwangi. The Classic Film Music of Jerome Moross (City of Prague Philharmonic Orchestra. Conductor Paul Bateman) Silva Screen FILMCD161

The War Lord (Original Score. Conductor Joseph Gershenson) Varese Sarabande VSD5536

MORRICONE, ENNIO (b. 10 November 1928)
Ennio Morricone was born in Rome and studied trumpet and composition at the Conservatorio di Santo Cecilia. His early film scores were for light comedies and costume dramas. He went on to work under the director Sergio Leone, who created the spaghetti Westerns that began with *A Fistful of Dollars* in 1964. Morricone achieved international recognition for these scores, particularly for *Once upon a Time in the West* (1969) and *Once upon a Time in America* (1984). Other outstanding scores included *The Good, The Bad and the Ugly* (1966), *The Exorcist II* (1977), *The Heretic* (1977), The Thing (1982), *The Mission* (1986), *The Untouchables (1987), Casualties of War* (1989), *Cinema Paradiso* (1989), *City of Joy* (1992) and *In the Line of Fire* (1993).

Select Discography

Exorcist II Warner BS-3068

Novecento RCA TBL1–1221

Once upon a Time in the West RCA LSP-4736

Moses the Lawgiver (TV Score) RCA TBL1–1106

Red Tent (Conducted by Bruno Nicolai) Paramount PAS 6019

Sacco and Vanzetti RCA Italiana OLS-4

Two Mules for Sister Sarah Kapp 5512

Compact Discs

Cinema Paradiso DRG CDSBL12598

Ennio Morricone Anthology DRG DRGCD32908

Ennio Morricone with Love DRG DRGCD32913

Legendary Italian Westerns RCA 9974

The Mission (London Philharmonic Orchestra. Conductor Ennio Morricone) Virgin CDV2042

Once upon a Time in America (Original Score. Conductor Ennio Morricone) Mercury 822 334–2

Once upon a Time in the West RCA 4736–2

The Thing Varese Sarabande VSD5278

The Untouchables A&M 393 909–2

MULLER, WERNER (b. 2 August 1920)

Werner Muller was born in Berlin. He studied violin and trombone. In 1946, he joined Kutte Widmann as trombonist. He was appointed leader of the RIAS Tanzorchester in 1948 and made numerous recordings, including 'How High the Moon' (1951 Polydor.48557). He became a well-known conductor and arranger, noted for his perfectionism. In the United States, his skill was recognized after he arranged and recorded 'Malagueña' with Caterina Valente in the early 1950s. Muller toured Japan in 1958 and became the leader of the Cologne WDR Tanzorchester in 1967.

His best jazz records date from the period 1950 to 1957. Thereafter his recordings became more light orchestral in character, and he acquired an excellent string section. A great variety and number of such albums followed in the late 1950s, 1960s and 1970s. These are included in the discography appended to this article. Several of these recordings, such as the *Musical Holiday* series, were made in Europe, under the pseudonym of Ricardo Santos, although the same albums were issued in the United States under the conductor's real name.

The LP recording entitled *Sentimental Journey*, on the American London label, is essentially a tribute to Glenn Miller and is the second of Muller's discs to bear this title. It represents a high point in his light orchestral recording career, as the arrangements are outstanding.

Select Discography

Cascading Strings Polydor LPHM 46028

Evergreen Memories CONTOUR 2870105

Fireworks in Strings Polydor LPHM 46062

Germany PFS 4073

Golden Award Songs Decca DL 8887/Polydor SLPHM 237518

Gypsy! SP 44086

Hawaiian Swing Decca PFS 34022

Italian Festival London SP 44132

Latin Splendour London SP 44139

Leroy Anderson SP 44057
Million Strings Polydor LPHM 46012
Music for Lovers Telefunken TP 2516
On Broadway London SP 44047
On the Move London SP 44026
Percussion in the Sky London SP 44008
Primavera! Polydor 237659
Sentimental Journey Decca PFS 4383/London SP 44267 [Also on CD]
Sentimental Journey Decca DL 8803
(The two Sentimental Journey LPs are totally different in content and arrangement.)
Silvery Strings Polydor LPHM 46050
So Easy to Love Telefunken TPS 12517
Sumptuous Strings London SP 44187
Tango London SP 44098
Tropical Nights Telefunken TP 2521
Two Million Strings (with Helmut Zacharias) Polydor LPHM 46091
Wild Strings PS 302
Your Musical Holiday in Italy Decca DL 8162/Polydor 46010
Your Musical Holiday in Paris Decca DL 8161/Polydor 46009
Your Musical Holiday in New York Decca DL 8263/Polydor LPHM 46007

N

NASH, TED

Ted Nash was born in Somerville, Massachusetts, and started his professional career at seventeen, playing with dance orchestras, including Les Brown's and Jerry Gray's. He subsequently settled in California, where he became a recording-studio and motion-picture musician, able to perform equally well on the tenor saxophone, alto saxophone, flute and alto flute. He also played in small Hollywood instrumental groups, specializing in West Coast jazz.

Orchestra and band leaders for whom he worked included PAUL WESTON, Spencer-Hagan, Billy May and Frank Comstock. When he recorded with his own orchestra, many of his above-mentioned associates did the musical arrangements, while Nash performed some solo items on alto saxophone and alto flute.

Select Discography

Star Eyes Columbia CL 989

NEVINS, AL

Al Nevins was born in New York and originally studied architecture. He subsequently concentrated on the study of the violin and viola. He began his musical career in Washington in classical music and eventually was able to play virtually any string instrument. In the 1940s he teamed up with Morty Nevins and Artie Dunn to form a group known as the Three Suns, the first guitar-organ-accordion combination. They scored a hit with the number 'Twilight Time' (Victor USA, 1950), originally written in 1944 and first recorded on Majestic Label in 1946. In the 1950s he recorded with his own orchestra for RCA Victor.

Al Nevins formed Aldon Music in the late 1950s with Don Kirschner. This firm, just one part of the Nevins-Kirschner organization of leading New York publishers, record producers and managers, became one of the most profitable music concerns in the United States, employing over thirty of America's top writers. In April 1963, the organization became affiliated with Columbia Pictures–Screen Gems Music.

Select Discography

Bon Voyage RCA LPM-1337

Dancing with the Blues RCA LPM-1654

Escapade in Sound RCA LPM-1166

Lights and Shadows RCA LPM/LSP-1475 [Also on CD]

Living Strings RCA Camden CAS 709

Night Themes RCA Camden CAS 755

With the Three Suns

Dancing on a Cloud RCA 31,433 LPM 2307

Easy Listening RCA LPM-1316

High Fi and Wide RCA LPM-1249

Let's Dance with the Three Suns RCA31,136

Love in the Afternoon RCA LPM-1669

NEWMAN, ALFRED (17 March 1901–17 February 1970)
Newman was an important figure in the history of film music as composer, conductor, arranger and musical director. He was born in New Haven, Connecticut, and as a child prodigy on the piano studied piano and harmony in New York before he was ten years old. At the age of thirteen he was playing in vaudeville and also performing as soloist with various classical orchestras. At seventeen he was conducting Broadway shows. While still in his teens he conducted the New York Philharmonic Orchestra, an experience that inspired in him an ambition to be a conductor. He worked with Al Jolson and Fred and Adele Astaire; he conducted GEORGE GERSHWIN and RICHARD RODGERS and Lorenz Hart shows in the 1920s.

In 1930, Newman was brought to Hollywood by IRVING BERLIN for three months of work on *Reaching for the Moon.* He never returned to New York and was given the position of musical director of United Artists. In 1931, he conducted *City Lights* for CHARLIE CHAPLIN. He also worked on films such as *The Devil to Pay, Indiscreet, The Unholy Garden, Arrow-*

smith and *Street Scene*. In 1934, Newman became general music director for Sam Goldwyn and Darryl Zanuck at Twentieth Century Films. He was appointed to the same position at Twentieth Century–Fox in 1939.

Newman won Oscars for his work on *Alexander's Ragtime Band* (1938), *Tin Pan Alley* (1940), *Mother Wore Tights* (1947), *With a Song in My Heart* (1952), *Call Me Madam* (1953), *The King and I* (1956 with cowriter Ken Darby), *Camelot* (1967, again with Darby) and *Hello Dolly!* (1969, with Lennie Hayton). He gained additional Academy Awards for his complete background music to *The Song of Bernadette* (1943) and *Love Is a Many-Splendored Thing* (1955).

Many pieces of his film music became popular apart from the sound tracks. These included the title song from *The Best of Everything* (1959, lyrics by Sammy Cahn), sung by Johnny Mathis; 'Moon of Manakoora' (lyrics by FRANK LOESSER) from *The Hurricane*; 'Through a Long and Sleepless Night' (lyrics by Mack Gordon) from *Come to the Stable* and the title songs from *How Green Was My Valley, Anastasia* and *The Best of Everything*. In the 1960s Newman's scores for *How the West Was Won* and *The Greatest Story Ever Told* produced best-selling albums. His last work for the big screen was the music for *Airport* (1970). In 1960, Newman resigned as Fox music director and continued to work on a freelance basis until his death in 1970.

Extremely popular throughout his career and generally acknowledged to be the finest conductor in Hollywood, Newman helped many young artists in their careers, including DAVID RAKSIN and JERRY GOLDSMITH. His close-knit family has been musically active in Hollywood, including brothers Lionel and Emil, sons David and Thomas and nephew Randy.

Select Discography

Fiorello/Sound of Music Capitol ST 1343

Hit Musical Favorites MG 25094 (10")

Hollywood Pops! Decca SP 8639

Magic Islands Decca DL 79048

Hollywood Pops Decca SP 8639

Love Dreams Decca DL 8299

Magic Islands Decca DL 79048

Ports of Paradise Capitol Premium STAO 1447

Serenade to the Stars of Hollywood Decca DL 8123

Star Eyes Columbia CL 989

Themes Capitol ST 1652

Film Music

Airport Decca DL 79173

Captain from Castile: A Symphonic Suite Delos DEL/F-25411

Captain from Castile and the Classic Film Scores of Alfred Newman RCA ARL1–0814

Diary of Anne Frank 20th Century Fox GXH-6049

Down to the Sea in Ships. Suite (Conducted by Fritz Steiner) Entr'acte ERS 6506

Greatest Story Ever Told United Artists LA277-G

Hollywood Maestro: Themes . . . Citadel CT-6003

Prisoner of Zenda (Conducted by Leroy Holmes) United Artists LA374-G

Wuthering Heights (Conducted by Elmer Bernstein) Filmmusic Collection FMC-6

Compact Discs

Airport Varese Sarabande VSD5436

Anastasia Varese Sarabande VSD5422

Captain from Castile. The Classic Film Scores of Alfred Newman RCA GD80184

How Green Was My Valley Arista 20th Century Fox 11008–2

The Robe Arista 20th Century Fox 11011–2

NORTH, ALEX (4 December 1910–8 September 1991)

Alex North was born in Chester, Pennsylvania, of Russian parents. He obtained a scholarship to study at the Curtis Institute of Music and at Juilliard. From 1934 to 1936, he studied at a Russian conservatory.

In 1936, he returned to New York, where he composed for ballet and theater. North's breakthrough into incidental music occurred in 1951, for Elia Kazan's production of *Death of a Salesman.* In the same year, Kazan filmed *A Streetcar Named Desire* and recommended that North should write the music. North's emphasis on New Orleans jazz indigenous to the story was a unique concept at that time, which gained him instant recognition. He received Oscar nominations for both *Streetcar* and *Salesman*, also released in 1951. One of his best-known scores was for *Spartacus* in 1960. North enjoyed researching the music of the period for which he wrote and attempted to recreate historic atmosphere in a contemporary setting.

Other of his scores included *Viva Zapata!* (1952), *Unchained Melody* (1955), *The Rose Tattoo* (1955), *I'll Cry Tomorrow* (1956), *The Rainmaker* (1956), *The Misfits* (1961), *Cleopatra* (1964), *The Agony and the Ecstasy* (1965), *Who's Afraid of Virginia Woolf?* (1966), *The Shoes of the Fisherman* (1968), *2001: A Space Odyssey* (1968), *Dragonslayer* (1981), *Under the Volcano* (1984), *Prizzi's Honor* (1985), *Good Morning, Vietnam* (1987) and *Rich Man, Poor Man* for television in 1976.

Select Discography

Film Music Citadel CT-6023

Rich Man, Poor Man (TV Score) MCA 2095

Spartacus MCA 2068

Streetcar Named Desire Angel S-36068

Viva Zapata! and Death of a Salesman Filmmusic Collection FMC-9

Compact Discs

Cinerama South Seas Adventure Label X LXCD2

Spartacus MCA MCAD10256

A Streetcar Named Desire (National Philharmonic Orchestra. Conductor Jeremy Goldsmith) Varese Sarabande VSD5500

2001: A Space Odyssey (National Philharmonic Orchestra. Conductor Jeremy Goldsmith) Varese Sarabande VSD5400

NOVELLO, IVOR (born David Ivor Davies) (15 January 1893–6 March 1951)

Ivor Novello was born in Cardiff, Wales, the son of Madame Novello Davies, a singing teacher, and David Davies, an accountant and enthusiastic amateur musician. As a child Novello played the piano and had a fine soprano voice. He started to compose songs at the age of fifteen and had some published the following year. In 1914 he wrote one of his most famous songs, 'Keep the Home Fires Burning', introduced at the Alhambra Theatre by the Welsh singer Sybil Vane.

Novello spent World War I as a clerk in the Naval Air Service. In 1919, he appeared in his first film, *The Call of the Blood*, and subsequently appeared in many movies, from silent to sound. He also performed on the stage and became a symbol of high romance in the 1920s. He contributed to the revue *A to Z* in 1921. He spent much of his later years writing for the theater and achieved success in this field in the 1930s. His musical plays included *Glamorous Night* (1935), *Careless Rapture* (1936), *Crest of the Wave* (1937), *The Dancing Years* (1939), *Arc de Triomphe* (1943), *Perchance to Dream* (1945) and *King's Rhapsody* (1949). Most of his songs had lyrics by Christopher Hassall (1912–1963). His final musical was *Gay's the Word*, a parody of his own theatrical style.

Additional Readings

Harding, James. *Ivor Novello*. London: W. H. Allen, 1987.

Macqueen, Pope W. *Ivor: The Story of an Achievement*. London: W. H. Allen, 1952.

Noble, Peter. *Ivor Novello: Man of the Theatre*. London: Falcon Press, 1951.

Wilson, Sandy. *Ivor*. London: Michael Joseph, 1975.

Select Discography

Trent, Ronnie. **The Magical Melodies of Ivor Novello** (With the Palace Players) Parlophone PMEM 6012 (New Zealand)

Paramor, Norrie. **The Magnificence of Ivor Novello** Polydor 2383 149

O

OGERMAN, CLAUS

Claus Ogerman is a German-born composer, arranger, writer and conductor who first rose to prominence in the early 1960s, when he worked with Quincy Jones on a number of projects, including many of Lesley Gore's hits. Ogerman was keenly interested in jazz and worked with ANTONIO CARLOS JOBIM on his *Wave* album. He also was responsible for arranging for Bill Evans and his orchestra and for Barbra Streisand's top-selling release *The Classical Album.* He established a firm working relationship with producer Tommy LiPuma and jazz guitarist/vocalist George Benson that resulted in the string arrangements for *Breezin', In Flight* and *Livin' Inside Your Love.* The Ogerman/LiPuma collaboration was also evident in Michael Franks' album *The Sleeping Gypsy.*

In 1976, Ogerman was commissioned to write a ballet for the prestigious American Ballet Company entitled *Some Times.* On the suggestion of LiPuma, Ogerman took highlights from the ballet and wove them into an album-length song suite. The result, played by the Claus Ogerman Orchestra and featuring artists such as George Benson, Joe Sample, David Sanborn and Michael Brecker, was entitled *Gate of Dreams.*

Select Discography

Golden Waltzes of Broadway (With Broadway Strings Orchestra) United Artists UAL 3253

Music from the Motion Picture Fiddler on the Roof RCA LSP4583

Compact Discs

Cityscape Warner 23698

Gate of Dreams Warner Brothers 3006–2

OLIVIERI, DINO

Dino Olivieri was an Italian composer, arranger and conductor in both the classical and popular fields. One of his most popular compositions was the song 'J'attendrai', which he originally titled 'Tornerai'. He worked as artists' director for the Voce del Padrone Record Company in Milan and Rome.

Select Discography

Dino Olivieri Odeon Qelp 8071

Romance in Rome Capitol T10029

Two in a Gondola Capitol T10026

Viaggio Musicale HMV Q ELP6040 (Italian 10")

101 STRINGS

This orchestra was formed in the 1950s and its output has been prolific, both on LP records and on compact discs, with over 200 recordings. The conductors are generally unnamed, with few exceptions. MONTY KELLY did the arrangements for *The Soul of Spain* and *The Soul of Mexico* LP records, and NELSON RIDDLE conducted several LPs and CDs. The quality of the arrangements fluctuated considerably; some of the earlier recordings were in many respects superior to the later ones.

Select Discography

American Waltzes Alshire S 5022

Award-winning Songs from the Silver Screen Alshire S 5041

Camelot Alshire S 5058

Cole Porter Alshire S 5007

Doctor Zhivago Alshire S 5068

Down Memory Lane PYE GGL 0061

Fire and Romance of South America Alshire S 5040

For Dining and Dreaming Alshire S 5034

George Gershwin Alshire S 5006

Hawaiian Paradise Alshire S 5028

Henry Mancini Alshire S 5015

Hits of the Thirties Alshire S 5035

Hits of the Forties Alshire S 5036

Hits of the Fifties Alshire S 5037

Hits of the Sixties Alshire S 5038

Hoagy Carmichael and Duke Ellington Alshire S 5008

Irving Berlin Alshire S 5005, Compact Disc ALCD 14

Italia Con Amore Alshire S 5030

Jerome Kern and Vincent Youmans Alshire S 5004

John Philip Sousa and George M. Cohan Alshire S 5002

Lerner and Loewe Alshire S 5014

Million Sellers of the 60s Alshire S 5038

Mood Vienna Alshire S 5023

Music to Relax By Alshire S 5073

My Fair Lady Alshire S 5039

Paris Avec Amour Alshire S 5029

Quiet Hours Alshire S 5026

Rhapsody Alshire S 5042

Richard Rodgers and Lorenz Hart Alshire S 5009

Richard Rodgers and Oscar Hammerstein Alshire S 5010

Sigmund Romberg and Rudolf Friml Alshire S 5003

Songs for Inspiration and Meditation Alshire S 5031

The Soul of Greece Alshire S 5047

The Soul of Israel Alshire S 5044

The Soul of Mexico Alshire S 5032

The Soul of Spain (2 vols.) Alshire S 5018, S 5052

The Soul of the Gypsies Alshire S 5024

Spanish Eyes Alshire S 5051

Stephen Foster Alshire S 5000

Victor Herbert Alshire S 5001

Victor Young and Leroy Anderson Alshire S 5012

World's Greatest Standards Alshire S 5020

Compact Discs

Best of the Great American Composers Alshire ALCD 46

Cole Porter Alshire ALCD 30

Great Love Songs Alshire RTBCD 2015

Irving Berlin Alshire ALCD 14

Moonlight Serenades Alshire RTBCD 2016

Music of Rodgers, Hammerstein & Hart Emporio 007

Music for Lovers Alshire RTBCD 2017

Music from Mexico

World's Greatest Standards Alshire CD 23

ORMANDY, EUGENE (1899–1985)

Eugene Ormandy was born in Budapest and was head of master classes at the Budapest Conservatory of Music until 1919. In 1921, he emigrated to the United States and became an American citizen in 1927. In 1924, he was appointed conductor of the orchestra at Capitol Cinema in New York. He conducted the Minneapolis Symphony Orchestra from 1931 to 1936 and from 1938 to 1980 was musical director of the Philadelphia Orchestra. He was made an honorary Knight of the British Empire in 1976.

Select Discography

Love Story: Love Themes of Today and Yesterday RCA LSC 3210

ORNADEL, CYRIL (b. 2 December 1924)

Ornadel was born in London. He studied piano, double bass and composition at the Royal College of Music. He was with ENSA and later toured Europe with the singer Dorothy Carless. He led the all-girls' band at Murray's Club in London and worked as a concert party pianist. Ornadel provided musical and vocal arrangements of the Players' Theatre and was appointed musical director of the touring show *Hello, Beautiful.* This led to his first London employment as pantomime conductor at the People's Palace in the Mile End Road.

In 1950, he became conductor of the musical revue *Take It from Us* at the Adelphi Theatre. During the 1950s he conducted the London productions of various American musicals including *Kiss Me, Kate, Call Me Madam, Paint Your Wagon, Pal Joey, Wish You Were Here, Wonderful Town, Kismet, Plain and Fancy* and *My Fair Lady.* He also conducted for revivals of *The King and I* and *The Sound of Music.*

Ornadel collaborated with David Croft on the scores of productions of *Star Maker, The Pied Piper* and the 1956 London Palladium pantomime *The Wonderful Lamp.* In the 1950s he was also resident musical director at the London Palladium, where he was responsible for the television program *Sunday Night at the London Palladium* and for three Royal Variety Performances. In 1960, he and lyricist Norman Newell won IVOR NOVELLO awards for the ballad 'Portrait of My Love'. He also won Ivors for 'If I Ruled the World' (1963, lyricist Leslie Bricusse) from the musical *Pickwick* and for the scores for the musicals *Treasure Island* (1973) and *Great Expectations* (1975), both with Hal Shaper. Ornadel and Shaper rewrote the score for *Great Expectations*, and the revised version was presented at the Liverpool Playhouse (1989) and in Sydney (1991). Other recent productions include *Winnie, Camelot* at the Liverpool Playhouse, *Sherlock Holmes, The Musical* at the Cambridge Theatre and *Overture for Beginners* at the Buxton Festival.

Ornadel's other stage musicals have included *Ann Veronica* (1969 with Croft), *Once More, Darling* (1978 with Newell), *Winnie* (1988, additional songs with Arnold Sundgaard), *Cyrano, The Musical* (with Shaper) and *The Last Flower on Earth* (1991, with Kelvin Reynolds).

His work for radio, films and television included *Some May Live, Subterfuge, The Waitors, I Can't, I Can't, Wedding Night, Man of Violence, Europa Express, Cool It, Carol, Die Screaming, Marianne, Yesterday, The Flesh and the Blood Show, Strauss Family* (series), *Edward VII* (series), *Christina, Brief Encounter* (1974 remake), *Tom Keating on Painters* series and *Changing Faces* series. Ornadel acted as musical director for the *Strauss Family* series; and his record of the music, featuring the London Symphony Orchestra, won the first gold disc for classical music.

He has specialized in recording work, was active in World Records and became partner in the FCM recording and promotion company.

His albums have proved particularly popular, especially those featuring his Starlight Symphony Orchestra. He also created the Stereoaction Orchestra for RCA Records. He has composed songs and incidental music for the *Beatrix Potter Stories*; background music for the *Living Bible* series, featuring Laurence Olivier and the *Living Shakespeare* series. His songs have been recorded by international artists such as Shirley Bassey, Tony Bennett, Matt Munro, Sammy Davis, Jr., Bing Crosby, Des O'Connor and Sir Harry Secombe and was presented with the prestigious Gold Badge of Merit by the British Academy of Song Writers, Composers and Authors for his services to British music.

Select Discography

With the Starlight Symphony Orchestra (Arrangements by Brian Fahey)

Best of the British on Broadway MGM E/SE 4338

Carnival: Music from the David Merrick Production MGM E/SE 3945

Forever Young MGM E/SE 34432 [Also on CD]

Great Jewish Melodies MGM E/SE 4237

Hollywood Sound Stage MGM E/SE 4033

Music from Lerner and Loewe's Camelot MGM E/SE 3916

Music from the Motion Picture Gone with the Wind Metro M/MS 613

Musical World of Cole Porter MGM E/SE 3843; reissued as **The Cole Porter Songbook** Polydor 2482 353 [Also on CD]

Musical World of Jerome Kern MGM E/SE 3906; reissued as **The Jerome Kern Songbook** Polydor 2482 352 [Also on CD]

Musical World of Lerner and Loewe MGM E/SE 3781 [Also on CD]

Musical World of Rodgers and Hammerstein MGM E/SE 3817 [Also on CD]

Opening Night: Broadway Overtures MGM E/SE 3816

Plays Music from Billy Rose's Jumbo and Other Richard Rodgers and Lorenz Hart Songs MGM E/SE 4097; reissued as **The Rodgers and Hart Songbook** Polydor 2482356 [Also on CD]

With the Westminster Orchestra of London

An Enchanted Evening: Music of Rodgers and Hammerstein RAMA RLP 5002

Bewitched and Other Songs by Rodgers and Hart RAMA RLP 5006

Dearly Beloved: Music of Jerome Kern. RAMA RLP 5005

My Fair Lady (Orchestral Suite) World Record Club (U.K.) TP 219

So Nice To Come Home To: Music of Cole Porter RAMA RLP 5003

Others

Always: The Music of Irving Berlin (Arrangements by Bruce Campbell) World Record Treasures SC18

Carnivalito Philips

El Cid MGM

I've Got The World on A String: Music of Harold Arlen World Record Club

King of Kings MGM

Maurice Chevalier MGM

Music by Moonlight: Presenting Frank Loesser Conquest/Showcase LM 23

Our Love Is Here to Stay: Music of George Gershwin World Record Club

Over the Rainbow (Arrangements by Johnny Gregory) World Record Treasures SC 10

Portrait of My Love MGM

Some Enchanted Evening: Music of Richard Rodgers World Record Club

Song Without End MGM

Will You Remember? The Music of Sigmund Romberg LRP 3030 World Record Club

With a Song in My Heart: The Music of Rodgers and Hart World Record Club

OSBORNE, TONY

Osborne was born in Cambridge, England, and won prizes for his accordion-playing when he was only twelve. He played many different instruments with the Royal Air Force Command Orchestra during World War II. He took up the trumpet in the postwar years, playing in the Carroll Gibbons and AMBROSE bands. After playing with the CYRIL STAPLETON Orchestra, Osborne found that the demands of his services as an arranger and conductor were so great that he had to give up active playing and concentrate on making long-playing records with his own orchestra, playing his own arrangements. Osborne then joined the E.M.I. Record Organization and provided the musical arrangements for singers such as Dennis Lotis, Gracie Fields, Connie Francis, Dick Francis, Millicent Martin and more recently Shirley Bassey.

Osborne also excelled as a composer. His compositions include 'Streets of Sorrento', 'Lights of Lisbon' (the signature tune of the weekly television show *Close Up*), 'Windows of Paris' (the signature tune of the British Broadcasting Corporation's program *Roundabout*), 'Follies Bergere', 'South Sea Bubble', 'Turkish Coffee' and 'Secrets of the Seine'. Osborne became well known for his many appearances on the British Broadcasting Corporation's *Six Five Special* and *Juke Box Jury*. He has also written the scores for the films *The Secret Door* and *Every Day's a Holiday*. Distinctive arrangements on his own LPs include 'Hands Across the Table' and 'A Trip to Romance'.

Select Discography

Brass in the Night SML 704

Great TV Themes Philips 6382 069

Hands Across the Table RCA RAL 1002

Incidentally AFSD 6225

Kind of Hush AFSD 6185

Lennon & McCartney Go Latin Rediffusion ZS 59

Moods for Romance Rediffusion ZS 108

Music from the Movies Rediffusion ZS 66

Nights to Remember HMV JCLP 1734 (South Africa)

Passing Strangers Fontana SFL 13141

Romantic Mr Osborne Rediffusion ZS 135

That's Paris Regal SREG 2005

Trip to Romance RCA RAL 1011

Where in the World Nixa NSPL 83000

OSSER, GLENN (b. 28 August 1914)

Glenn Osser was born in Munising, Michigan, the son of Russian emigrants. He began to study the violin as a child and in addition was eventually able to play the piano, clarinet and saxophone. He graduated from the University of Michigan with a degree in music theory in 1935 and began his career as a player and arranger for New York big band leaders such as Bob Crosby, Charlie Barnet, Bunny Berigan and Les Brown. He was also staff arranger at NBC.

From 1944 to 1957, Osser worked as arranger and assistant conductor for Paul Whiteman, musical director of the ABC Network. They did many radio and television shows and Osser usually conducted for the singers. After Whiteman's retirement in 1957, Osser continued as staff conductor until 1970. In the 1950s and 1960s, as a freelance arranger and conductor, he worked for various recording companies including Mercury, Kapp, MGM, Columbia and RCA. Many of his recordings were with singers such as Georgia Gibbs, Vic Damone and Vivian Blaine. He also arranged numbers for the BOSTON POPS ORCHESTRA, on their album *Swing, Swing, Swing*.

Osser and his wife, Edna, were involved in the Miss America beauty pageants for television. From 1968 to 1972, they wrote five original songs as production numbers. Subsequently, they composed the opening original song. His arrangements 'Miss America, You're Beautiful' and 'Look at Her' were used each year in the production. In 1987, Osser was music director and arranger for the entire pageant. He composed many pieces for concert bands that were performed by high school and college bands throughout the United States. In 1981, the Musique Band of the French Air Force recorded Osser's composition entitled 'Holiday for Winds'.

After 1972, with the decline of light music, Osser did very little recording. In the 1980s, he was responsible for a series of television shows for public television, featuring all the great singers of the light music and big band era.

Select Discography

All-time Favorite Song Hits Mercury MG 25050 (10")

But Beautiful Kapp KL 1022 (1955); reissued as **Love Songs From The Hollywood Screen** Kapp KL 1078 (1958) [Also on CD]

Marching Along, Sing Along United Artists UAL 3073

OWEN, REG (b. February 1928)

Owen was born in England. He was a British bandleader who became popular in 1959 in both the United States and United Kingdom with his version of the song 'Manhattan Spiritual', written by Billy Maxted. The song was issued on the Palette label in the United States and on Pye International in England. Owen placed one other single on the English chart 'Obsession' in 1960.

Owen became one of Britain's leading arrangers and also conducted his own orchestra, producing many albums for RCA Victor. An interesting series, entitled 'Holiday Abroad', was produced in the late 1950s.

Together with Malcolm Lockyer, Owen formed the KNIGHTSBRIDGE STRINGS in the late 1950s, an orchestra which varied in size from time to time, depending on the needs of the arrangers. The Knightsbridge Strings recorded on the Top Rank International label. Owen died in the early 1970s (exact date could not be found).

Select Discography

With Own Orchestra

Best of Irving Berlin RCA LPM 1542

British Isles RCA LPM-1675 [Also on CD]

Coffee Break RCA LSP 1582

Cuddle Up a Little Closer RCA LSP 1914

Dreaming RCA LPM 1580

Dream-time Waltzes (Reg Owen conducts Vienna State Opera Orchestra) RCA CSP 102

Get Happy SPZ 37004

Girls Were Made to Take Care of Boys RCA LSP 1908

Holiday Abroad in Dublin RCA LPM-1597

Holiday Abroad in Lisbon (Augusto Alguero conducting; arrangements by Reg Owen) RCA LPM-1596

Holiday Abroad in London RCA LPM-1599

Holiday Abroad in Paris (Pierre Sommers conducting; arrangements by Reg Owen) RCA LPM-1600

Holiday Abroad in Rome (Carlo Savina conducting; arrangements by Reg Owen) RCA LSP-1595

Holiday Abroad in Vienna (Muller-Lampertz conducting; arrangements by Reg Owen) RCA LPM-1598

I'll Sing You a Thousand Love Songs RCA LPM/LSP-1906 [Also on CD]

Under Paris Skies Decca DL 78859

You Don't Know Paree RCA LPM-1915

With Knightsbridge Strings

Cinema Monument Artistry Series MAM 3002, MAS 13002

Knightsbridge Strings Play Movie Music Top Rank RX 3017

Spanish Mood Universal Record Club, Australia U-814

Strings Sing Top Rank RM 303

Theatre Showcase Top Rank 35/036

¾ Time Monument Artistry Series MAM 3001, MAS 13001

P

PARAMOR, NORRIE (1913–9 September 1979)
Norrie Paramor was a British conductor, composer, arranger and producer. He was born in London and studied piano. He left school at the age of fifteen to become an office boy. He was talented musically and found work as an accompanist to the singer Gracie Fields. He subsequently worked in leading London dance bands, such as that of Maurice Winnick. He acted as musical director for the Ralph Reader Gang Shows during his time in the RAF in the war years and entertained servicemen in the company of SIDNEY TORCH and Max Wall. He also scored music for NOËL COWARD, MANTOVANI and Jack Buchanan.

After the war, he worked with Harry Gold and his Pieces of Eight as featured pianist and toured with Bing Crosby. In the 1950s, he made recordings under his own name and with the Big Ben Banjo Band and Big Ben Hawaiian Band. He cut some sides for the Oriole label with Marie Benson, an Australian singer. In 1952, he became a record producer with EMI, a Columbia subsidiary and worked with Eddie Calvert, Ruby Murray, Michael Holliday and the Mudlarks, Cliff Richard, Frank Ifield, the Shadows, Helen Shapiro and others until 1968.

He wrote and cowrote many successful songs, several of which were featured as the scores of films. These included *Expresso Bongo* ('A Voice in the Wilderness', Cliff Richard); *The Young Ones* ('The Savage'); *The Frightened City* (title song); *Play It Cool* ('Once Upon a Dream'); *It's Trad, Dad* ('Let's Talk About Love') and *Band of Thieves* ('Lonely'). He also com-

Norrie Paramor

posed several complete movie scores and TV themes such as those of *A Summer Place* and *Z Cars*.

Paramor composed some light orchestral works under titles such as 'The Zodiac' and 'Emotions', which he recorded with his concert orchestra. He released several mood music albums in the United States which became very popular. These included *London After Dark*; *Amor, Amor!*; *Autumn*; *In London; In Love* and its sequel *In London, In Love Again*. In 1960, Paramor became musical director for Judy Garland and arranged and conducted for her British recording sessions and her appearances at the London Palladium and in Europe. He was musical director of the BBC Midland Radio Orchestra from 1972 to 1978, but he continued to work in independent production for the Excaliburs and for Cliff Richard.

Select Discography

Amor, Amor! Capitol ST 10238

Autumn Capitol ST 10212

BBC Top Tunes BBC Records REB 171

BBC Top Tunes, Vol. 2 BBC Records REB 202

Classic Film Themes 2489 024

Classical Rhythm

Dreams and Desires Columbia 33SX 1059

Emotions

Glenn Miller Symphony (With Luxembourg Pop Orchestra) Polydor 2310006 [Also on CD]

Great Waltzes 2489 023

I Love 10" Essex ESLP-102

In London, In Love Capitol T 10025. Reissue of **The Very Thought of You** Columbia S1084 UK 10"

In London, In Love Again Capitol ST 2071

In Tokyo, In Love Capitol ST 2526

Jet Flight Capitol ST 10190

Just We Two Capitol T 10111

Latin Nights (with Ray Martin) 33JS 1078 (10")

Law Beat 2870 369

London After Dark Capitol T 10052

Love at First Sight Polydor 543.123

Lovers in Latin Columbia 33 SX 1162

Magnificence of Ivor Novello Polydor 2383 149

Magnificence of Noel Coward Polydor 2310 279

Moods Capitol T 10130

My Fair Lady Capitol T 10100

New York Impressions Capitol T 10063. Reissue of **Holiday in New York** Columbia 33 S 1098 (UK) 10" LP

Norrie Paramor Plays the Hits of Cliff Richard Capitol ST 15041

Paramor in Paris

Radio Two Top Tunes, Vol. 1

Radio Two Top Tunes, Vols. 2 and 3

Satin Latin Polydor 184 351

Shadows in Latin Columbia TWO 107

Silver Serenade

Soul Coaxing Columbia TWO 207

Staged for Stereo—Strings EMI SCX 3399 (Mono)

Strings! Staged for Sound Capitol T 1639 (Stereo)

Note: Staged for Stereo and Strings! Staged for Sound are identical in content.

Temptation

Warm and Willing Capitol ST 2357

Wonderful Waltz Capitol ST 10173

The Zodiac Suite Capitol ST10073

PARKER, CLIFTON (5 February 1905–2 September 1989)
Clifton Parker was born in London and spent his early years as organist with the Folkestone Municipal Orchestra, during which time he composed light popular items. He married ballet dancer Yoma Sasburg, for whom he wrote the ballet/pantomime *The Glass Slipper*. The overture became a popular orchestral work.

Parker was noticed by MUIR MATHIESON, who launched him into a distinguished film career. He scored over sixty films, including *Western Approaches* (1944), *The Man Within* (1947), *The Wooden Horse* (1950), *Treasure Island* (for Walt Disney, in 1950), *The Gift Horse* (1952), *The Story of Robin Hood and His Merry Men* (Disney, 1952), *The Sword and the Rose* (1953), *Campbell's Kingdom* (1957), *Sink the Bismarck* (1960), *H.M.S. Defiant* (1962) and *The Informers*. Parker's 'Seascapes' from *Western Approaches* is regarded by many as one of the finest scores ever written for the cinema.

PERKINS, FRANK (b. 21 April 1908)
Frank Perkins was born in Salem, Massachusetts. His family was musical, and his mother was a performer. He was educated at the Moses Brown School and Brown University in Providence. In 1929 he obtained a doctorate in economics. Perkins then started studying music seriously, taking private lessons in piano, organ, trombone, saxophone and percussion as well as composition. His tutors included Tibor Serly, the noted music educator.

In college he had conducted his own successful dance band and, after traveling in Europe, he returned to the United States to become a songwriter. He joined Mills Music in 1929 as arranger and composer. In 1934, he became an arranger for Fred Waring and the Pennsylvanians and remained with them until 1938, when he went to work for Warner Brothers as conductor and composer. After 1946, he devoted more time to his own compositions, achieving many screen credits for his motion picture work.

Perkins's compositions include 'Cabin in the Cotton', 'Emaline', 'Scat Song', 'Sentimental Gentleman from Georgia' and 'Stars Fell on Alabama'. The songs were written between 1932 and 1934, in collaboration with lyricist Mitchell Parish. In 1952, Perkins composed 'Fandango' as a piano piece. It was turned into a song with words by Johnny Bradford.

In Hollywood he wrote music for television series such as *Hawaiian Eye*, *The Dakotas* and *77 Sunset Strip* and did background scores for films *Mary, Mary* (1963) and *The Incredible Mr. Limper* (1964). He was nominated for an Academy Award for his musical direction of the film of *Gypsy*.

Select Discography

Music for My Lady Decca DL 8395

Pictures in Music Decca 8467

Premiere Decca DL 7551

Compact Disc

Fiesta! Dallas Wind Symphony (Conducted by Howard Dunn, contains a recording of 'Fandango' by Frank Perkins) RR-38 CD

PHILLIPS, DONALD (1914–11 March 1994)

Donald Phillips was a British popular song composer and arranger. He was born in Dalston, East London, and had little formal musical education. At the age of fourteen, he was talent-spotted by the musical writer and publisher, Lawrence Wright, who later published his sheet music.

He joined the Musician's Union in 1936 and remained a member for nearly sixty years. During World War II, he served in the Royal Air Force and was part of a forces entertainment team. After the war, he became musical director and accompanist for many entertainment stars, including the Marx Brothers, Beverley Sisters, Dickie Valentine, Shirley Bassey, Donald Peers, Alan Jones, Dick Emery, Anne Shelton, Yana, Jill Day, Joan Regan, Anita Harris, Susan Maughan and Ted Rodgers.

Among his compositions were 'Old Piano Rag', 'A Live Show Is the Best Show', 'Broken Date', 'To Him We're All the Same', 'Concerto in Jazz' and 'Skyscraper Fantasy'. His music was played and sung by artists such as Winifred Attwell, Russ Conway, Lalo Schifrin, Liberace, Billy Cotton, Sid Phillips and SIDNEY TORCH.

He took part in the 1954 royal command performance at the London Palladium and in 1958 won the IVOR NOVELLO Award for his contribution to British popular music with 'Melody of the Sea'. In the early 1960s he composed entries for Ronnie Carroll and Matt Monroe in the British Eurovision song contest. He won an international music competition organized by Radio Prague (1963). In 1977, he wrote the musical *The Barrier*, which was performed in Holland and recorded by Elaine Paige.

PLEIS, JACK

Jack Pleis was born in Philadelphia, studied classical piano at the age of four, gave his first concert three years later and was featured on children's radio programs at the age of eleven.

When he entered college, he became interested in popular and jazz music and played piano with local bands to help further his medical career. He abandoned medicine for music and went to New York, where he attained success as a pianist, arranger, conductor and composer. He played with artists such as Bing Crosby, Sammy Davis, Jr., Benny Goodman, Earl Grant, Brenda Lee, Louis Armstrong, The Four Aces, Harry Belafonte and Joe Williams. He made recordings for Decca and Columbia Records in the 1960s.

Select Discography

Broadway Goes Hollywood Brunswick LAT 8083; Decca DL 8167
Fifty Memorable Melodies in Hi Fi Decca DL 8706
Music for Two Sleepy People Decca DL 8763
Music from Disneyland Decca DL 8105
Serenades to Remember Decca DL 8586
Stage Left, Stage Right Columbia CL 1662
Strings and Things Decca DL 8422
Valentino Tangos (With the Castilians) Decca DL 8952

POLIAKIN, RAOUL

Raoul Poliakin was born in Cairo and received his musical education in Paris, where he studied violin with René Benedetti and conducted with Pierre Monteux. He toured extensively as a concert violinist.

In 1941, he emigrated to the United States, where he became a member of several major symphony orchestras, playing under Leopold Stokowski, Sir Thomas Beecham, Fritz Reiner, Monteux and Ernst Ansermet. He served as assistant conductor to ANDRE KOSTELANETZ for over five years. Subsequently, he joined Everest Records, where his function was to act as overall musical director, planning the classical repertoire with Bert White and supervising the actual recording sessions. In addition, he conducted his own fifty-four-piece orchestra and twenty-voice chorale and played arrangements of the masters of light orchestral music in a rhapsodic manner that emphasized the melodic line. He considered the chorus an organic section of the orchestra, which he often used in wordless lines and counterlines to add a new dimension to performances.

Select Discography

Fly with Me Everest LPBR 9003
I'll Remember April Everest SDBR 1001
I Want to Be Happy: The Music of Vincent Youmans Everest SDBR 1062

Irving Berlin, Great Man of American Music: A New Interpretation Everest 6058/3058

The Music of George Gershwin and Cole Porter Everest LPBR 5051

The Music of Richard Rodgers and Harold Arlen. Everest LPBR 5066, LPBR 1066

Waltz Masterpieces Everest LPBR 3025

PORTER, COLE (9 June 1891–15 October 1964)

Cole Porter was born in Peru, Indiana, the grandson of a millionaire and son of a prosperous fruit farmer. He was educated at Yale University and began studying law at Harvard. He eventually switched his studies to the Harvard School of Music. While at Yale he wrote college songs, music for college shows and a musical comedy entitled *See America First*, which enjoyed a short run in 1916. During a stay in France he produced his first hit, 'An Old-fashioned Garden', which was used with other Porter compositions in the Raymond Hitchcock Revue, *Hitchy-Koo of 1919*.

He continued to contribute to revues such as *A Night Out* (1920), *Mayfair and Montmartre* (1922), *Kitchy-Koo of 1922* and *Greenwich Follies of 1924*. His collaboration with E. Ray Goetz on the show *Paris* (1928) brought him his first great success, with songs such as 'Let's Do It'. It was followed by other successful shows, for which Porter wrote both lyrics and music. These included *Fifty Million Frenchmen* ('You Do Something to Me', 1929); *Wake Up and Dream* ('What Is This Thing Called Love?' 1929); *The New Yorkers* ('Love for Sale', 1930); *Gay Divorcee* ('Night and Day', 1932); *Nymph Errant* ('Experiment', 'The Physician', 1933); *Hi-Diddle-Diddle* (1934); *Anything Goes* ('I Get a Kick Out of You', 'You're the Top', 'Blow, Gabriel, Blow', 1934); *Jubilee* (1935); *Red, Hot and Blue* (1936); *Leave It to Me!* ('My Heart Belongs to Daddy', 1938); *Dubarry Was a Lady* (1939); *Around the World in Eighty Days* (1956); *Kiss Me, Kate* ('Wunderbar', 'So in Love', 1948); *Can-Can* ('I Love Paris,' 1953) and *Silk Stockings* ('All of You', 1955).

Porter had a sophisticated style of song writing, both in his lyrics and music. He was at his best in the consciously clever and witty songs such as 'Let's Do It' and 'You're the Top'. His film scores were equally brilliant and included *Anything Goes* (1936); *Born to Dance* (1936); *Rosalie* (1937); *Broadway Melody of 1940; Night and Day* (a film biography, 1946); *The Pirate* (1948); *Stage Fright* (1950); *Kiss Me, Kate* (1953); *Anything Goes* (1956); *High Society* (1956); *Silk Stockings* (1957); *Les Girls* (1957); *Can-Can* (1960) and *At Long Last Love* (1975), which revived many of his older songs.

In 1937, he had a serious riding accident, which culminated in the amputation of his leg in 1956. Many of his later songs were composed in conditions of great pain. After the death of his wife in 1956, he became a sad recluse and so remained for the rest of his life.

Cole Porter

Additional Readings

Eells, George. *The Life That Late He Led.* New York: Putnam, 1967.

Ewen, David. *American Songwriters.* New York: H. W. Wilson, 1987. pp. 293–301.

Ewen, David. *Great Men of American Popular Song.* Englewood Cliffs, NJ: Prentice-Hall, 1970. pp. 208–227.

Gill, Brendan. *Cole.* New York: Holt, Rinehart & Winston, 1971. Reprinted: New York: Dell Publishing, 1992. Paperback.

Grafton, David. *Red, Hot and Rich: An Oral History of Cole Porter.* New York: Stein and Day, 1987.

Green, Benny. *Let's Face the Music.* London: Pavilion Books, 1989. pp. 51–72.

Hemming, Roy. *The Melody Lingers On.* New York: Newmarket Press, 1986. pp. 151–186.

Hubler, Richard G. *The Cole Porter Story.* New York: World Publishing Co., 1965.

Hyland, William G. *The Song is Ended.* New York: Oxford University Press, 1995. pp. 160–76, 250–59.

Schwartz, Charles. *Cole Porter.* New York: Dial Press, 1977.

Select Discography

Black, Stanley. Symphonic Suite of the Music of Cole Porter London LL 565

Chacksfield, Frank. Music of Cole Porter London SP44185

Dragon, Carmen. An Evening With Cole Porter (With Hollywood Bowl Pops Orchestra) Capitol W/SW 1805 [Also on CD]

Fennell, Frederick. Music of Cole Porter Mercury SRI 75110

Joseph, Irving. And Then I Wrote Cole Porter Time S2114

Kostelanetz, Andre. Music of Cole Porter Columbia CL 729 [Also on CD]

Kostelanetz Plays Cole Porter Columbia KG 31491 [This is a double LP record which features the voice of Douglas Fairbanks, Jr. on six of the tracks.]

Legrand, Michel. Columbia Album of Cole Porter Columbia C2L4

Luypaerts, Guy. Symphonic Portrait of Cole Porter Capitol LC 6501

Ornadel, Cyril. Musical World of Cole Porter (With Starlight Symphony Orchestra) MGM E/SE 3843 [Also on CD]

Poliakin, Raoul. Music of Cole Porter and George Gershwin Everest LPBR 505

Rose, David. Cole Porter Review RCA LPM 32 (10")

POSFORD, GEORGE **(born Benjamin George Ashwell)** (23 March 1906–24 April 1976)

George Posford, the British composer and conductor, was born in Folkestone, England, and educated at Downside and Christ's College, Cambridge, where he studied law. Subsequently he studied composition and orchestration at the Royal Academy of Music and became a professional composer in 1930, specializing at first in radio work for the BBC and then moving into theater. He wrote many wartime revues for Jack Hulbert and Cecily Courtneidge. During World War II, he was in the London Fire Service and the Royal Corps of Signals. Later he worked for the Overseas Recorded Broadcasting Service.

His first operetta, written in collaboration with Eric Maschwitz, was *Goodnight, Vienna* (1931). It was originally broadcast and later became the first British musical to be filmed. Posford also composed the score for J. B. Priestley's *The Good Companions* (1933). Other scores included *Balalaika* (1936), *Magyar Melody* (1939), *Full Swing* (1942) and *Zip Goes a Million* (1952). He also composed symphonic poems, one of the most famous being *Transatlantic Rhapsody* (1942), commissioned by the BBC to commemorate the maiden voyage of the *Queen Mary.*

Select Discography

Barber, Frank. Room Five-Hundred-and-Four: The Music of George Posford Columbia 33 SX 1233

POURCEL, FRANCK (b. 1913)

Franck Pourcel was born in Marseilles. His father, who was a member of the orchestra of the French navy, gave him his first musical education. At the age of seven he was sent to study the violin at the Marseilles Conservatoire and completed his musical education at the Paris Conservatoire. He won many awards and in 1931 was engaged as a violinist at the Marseilles Opera, after spending a short time as conductor of the operetta theater Les Varietes Casino. He turned increasingly to light music and the music hall, where he accompanied a new rising singer, Yves Montand. Pourcel was becoming interested in jazz and made a study of percussion instruments that helped in the formulation of 'new sound' orchestrations. He spent several years with his own ensemble at the Côte d'Azur, where he played until 1939.

After the liberation of France, he accompanied the famous singer Lucienne Boyer on her tour of Europe and South America, and spent two years in the United States. In 1950, he returned to Paris, where he achieved his ambition of forming a string orchestra of fifty musicians, in which the strings were supplemented by brass, winds and rhythm instruments. He specialized in portraying the music of France, as well as songs of the rest of the world.

His first successful single was 'Blue Tango' in 1952. In 1959, the single 'Only You' was released by Pathé-Marconi, France. This song was an original version of the 1955 song written by BUCK RAM and André Rand. Pourcel sold fifteen million discs by 1979. 'Only You' was released by Capitol in the United States and sold over two million. Since then he has won many musical awards and conducted in New York, Los Angeles, Denver, Hollywood and San Francisco. He was a great admirer of Stephane Grappelli and Eddie South and for a while attempted to play like Grappelli.

Select Discography

Aquarius Atco 33 299

Boulevards of Paris EMI DLP 1150

Concert Promenade Capitol 8593

La Femme (Arranged by Les Baxter) Capitol DT 10015 [Also on CD]

Franck joué pour les amoureux No 4 Pathé Marconi GSDF 251 [Also on CD]

French Sax Capitol T 10126

French Touch Capitol T 10103

French Wine-drinking Music (S) T 10229

George Gershwin EMI CSDJ 3

Girls Columbia Studio Two 381

Honeymoon in Paris Capitol T 10040

Italia Romantica Pathé Marconi GSDF 314, FELP 314

James Bond Paramount PAS 6064

Latino Americana Columbia Studio 2 114J

Made in France Pathé Marconi C 048–50747

Magical Melodies EMI JCLP 1368

Magnifique EMI Studio 2 149

Midnight Cowboy Paramount PAS 5015

Music from Great French Motion Pictures Capitol SP 8603

My Paris EMI DLP 1156

1925–1930 EMI CSDQ 8180

1930–1935 EMI CSDQ 8187

Our Paris Capitol T-10002

Paris Pathé Marconi, EMI 2 C 066–15572

Pourcel of Paris Capitol T 10174

Pourcel Pastels Capitol T 10260

Pourcel Portraits Capitol ST 1855

Rainy Night in Paris Capitol T 10151

Sound of Magic Columbia Studio 2 158

Treasured Moments of Melody Capitol P 8592

Viennese Waltzes Capitol T 10214

World Is a Circle Paramount PAS 6047

PREVIN, ANDRÉ (b. 6 April 1929)

André Previn was born in Berlin and musically educated in Berlin and Paris. He came to Los Angeles in 1939, when his father emigrated. His musical talents were evident when he was a teenager, and he was engaged as an arranger at the age of sixteen by MGM. After three years as an arranger, he was given his first score, *The Sun Comes Up*. Besides producing scores such as *Elmer Gantry* and *The Four Horsemen of the Apocalypse*, he was also performing professionally as a pianist, both jazz and classical. He later left the film world to continue his profession as a conductor. His first success came in the mid-1950s with a series of jazz albums with Shelly Manne, the first of which featured music from *My Fair Lady*. In the 1960s, Previn continued to divide his time between jazz and studio work, but he gradually became more interested in classical music.

By the 1970s, Previn was acknowledged as one of the world's leading classical conductors. He served as conductor of the London Symphony Orchestra until 1976, when he took up the baton successively with the Pittsburgh Symphony Orchestra, the London Philharmonic and the Los Angeles Philharmonic. He continued to involve himself with many varying facets of music throughout the 1980s and 1990s.

Select Discography

The Four Horsemen of the Apocalypse Polydor MGM-Select 2353.125

Like Blue (With David Rose Orchestra) MGM E/SE 3811

Like Love Columbia CL 1437

Like Young (With David Rose Orchestra) MGM E/SE 3716

Previn Plays Gershwin EMI ASD 2754

Touch of Elegance: The Music of Duke Ellington Columbia CL 1649

Compact Discs

Gigi Sony 45395

Subterraneans CBS 47486

R

RAKSIN, DAVID (b. 4 August 1912)
David Raksin was born in Philadelphia, where his father conducted the orchestra for silent movies at the Metropolitan Opera House. As a teenager, David worked part-time in his father's music shop, played in the school orchestra and taught himself to play the organ. He was also able to play saxophone and clarinet and had a gift for improvisation. He studied under Harl McDonald at the University of Pennsylvania and became interested in jazz. He moved to New York and found employment with music publisher, Harms, Inc., working under ROBERT RUSSELL BENNETT. He arrived in Hollywood in 1935 to work with CHARLIE CHAPLIN on Chaplin's music for *Modern Times*. He was fired by Chaplin for being too argumentative but rehired at the urging of ALFRED NEWMAN.

From 1936 to 1944, Raksin arranged, orchestrated and composed for numerous projects. In 1940, he was put under contract to Fox Studios. His score for the 1944 film *Laura* was a turning point. With words by Johnny Mercer, the title song became a hit. Raksin's score for *The Bad and the Beautiful* (1952) was another classic. He left Fox in 1946, preferring to freelance. He continued to compose and also taught film scoring at the University of Southern California and UCLA.

Other scores included *Forever Amber* (1947), *The Secret Life of Walter Mitty* (1947), *Force of Evil* (1948), *Carrie* (1952), *Pat and Mike* (1952), *Separate Tables* (1958), *Al Capone* (1959), *Two Weeks in Another Town* (1962), *Invitation to a Gunfighter* (1964), *The Redeemer* (1966), *Will Penny* (1968).

Select Discography

Conducts Great Film Scores RCA ARL 1–1490

Laura; The Bad and the Beautiful, Scenarios: Forever Amber, Suite RCA ARL 1–1490

Compact Discs

Laura. Forever Amber. The Bad and the Beautiful RCA GD81490

RAM, BUCK (born Samuel Ram, 21 November 1907)

Buck Ram was born in Chicago and graduated from law school, though never practiced the law. He worked for Mills Music as an arranger, toured with bands, wrote songs and managed groups such as the Three Suns, who were formed in 1939.

Ram formed a talent agency in Los Angeles in 1954 and became manager of the singing group known as the Penguins, who were then active. He went on to become vocal coach of The Platters, who recorded Ram's songs 'Only You', 'The Great Pretender', 'I'm Sorry' and 'Remember When'. The group became the first African-American act of the era to reach number one on the pop chart. Another of The Platters' songs with which Ram was associated was 'Twilight Time', for which he wrote the words and which was originally performed by the Three Suns in 1942. Buck Ram made an album of recordings of his own compositions, with his own orchestra, for the Compagnie Phonographique Française in Paris, which was issued under the Mercury label.

Select Discography

The Magic Touch of Buck Ram and His Orchestra Mercury MG 20392

READER'S DIGEST

Reader's Digest has issued numerous albums of light and popular orchestral music throughout the second half of the twentieth century. Each of the boxed albums has several long-playing records. Many of the albums feature great conductors and arrangers. Occasionally there is partial duplication between the albums. The following selective discography is limited to those albums that are principally popular orchestral in scope.

Select Discography

All-Time Broadway Hit Parade

All-Time Operetta Favorites [Also on CD]

Background Moods

Candlelight Classics (Includes both light classical and popular music).

Castaway's Choice

Concert in the Park

Great Music from the Movies. UK edition: 5 records; U.S. edition: 4 records. The American edition has a ten-page pamphlet entitled *The Fascinating Story of Film Music* by Charles Gerhardt (1968).

In a Quiet Mood

Hits from the Shows. The first edition [195–?] is entirely different from a subsequent edition, issued some years later.

Magical World of Melody

Mood Music for Every Moment

Mood Music for Listening and Relaxation

Most Beautiful Melodies of the Century [Also on CD] (The British and South African editions of this set have entirely different contents.)

Most Beautiful Songs of the Century [CDs]

Orchestral Magic

Popular Music That Will Live Forever

Quiet Music for Quiet Listening

Romantic Magic [CDs]

Romantic Strings Play Your Favorite Light Classics (The title is a misnomer. The album consists of popular music, mostly standards, and is not the same as **Romantic Strings Play Classics of Popular Music**, another Reader's Digest album, also mostly of standards).

Serenade for Lovers

Soft Lights and Sweet Music

Some Enchanted Evening

Wonderful World of Melody

World's Favorite Music

REED, LES

Les Reed trained in Great Britain as a classical musician and spent two years in an army band. He became interested in jazz and in 1959 formed part of the group known as the John Barry Seven. After three years he left to establish himself professionally as a composer, arranger and musical director. He composed singles for many artists, including Tom Jones, Dave Clark, Steve Lawrence, Mark Murphy and Herman's Hermits. One of his greatest hits, cowritten with Gordon Mills, was 'It's Not Unusual' (1964), which was sung by Tom Jones and won an IVOR NOVELLO Award. It reached the top of the charts in the United Kingdom in 1965.

Select Discography

Fly Me to the Sun Deram Records SML 1008

Noel Coward Favorites Fontana STL 5255

REHBEIN, HERBERT

Herbert Rehbein was an associate of the German musician and composer BERT KAEMPFERT, with whom he collaborated in musical arrangements. Rehbein was also musical director of Swiss radio. His recordings for Decca Records include many compositions with Kaempfert.

Select Discography

And So to Bed Decca DL 5107/75107

Love After Midnight Decca DL 4847/74847

Love Music of Bert Kaempfert . . . And So to Bed Decca DL 75107

Music to Soothe That Tiger Decca DL 4584/74584

RENÉ, HENRI (b. 1906)

René was born in New York City of a father of German and a mother of French descent. He was taken to Berlin as a boy and enrolled at the Royal Academy of Music in Berlin, where he spent seven years training in the German classical tradition.

He returned to the United States and started playing popular music on the piano, banjo and guitar in various dance orchestras. In 1926, he returned to Europe and toured with his own orchestra. Eventually he settled in Berlin as chief arranger for the Electrola Company, then the RCA German affiliate. A few years later, he became musical director for Electrola, as well as for UFA, a German motion picture company. He wrote for radio stations, film studios and bands.

In 1936, he returned to the United States, where RCA Victor offered him the post of musical director for its international division. He made German import records unobtainable from Europe and also Swedish, Polish, Jewish, Italian and Spanish records. At the same time, René formed a musette orchestra that played music with a Continental sound.

During World War II, he was an instructor for soldier shows in Special Services. After René left the service in 1945, RCA offered him his position back as head of the international division. He was so successful that he was appointed musical director for the RCA popular record department. He arranged background music for singers and also arranged and conducted his own orchestra. He accompanied many singers on records, including Perry Como, Maurice Chevalier, Mindy Carson, Dinah Shore, Tony Martin, Howard Keel, Eartha Kitt and Gogi Grant.

At the end of 1957, René left RCA Victor and moved back to New York. He concentrated on writing, orchestrating and composing his own pieces and also worked for READER'S DIGEST and LONGINES SYMPHONETTE musical album projects. He was commissioned to make quite a number of recordings in Germany. One of his most popular instrumental recordings was 'Pink Champagne'.

Select Discography

By the Time I Get to Phoenix and Other Country Favorites (With Living Strings) RCA Camden CAS 2285

Compulsion to Swing RCA LSP 1947

Dynamic Dimensions RCA LSA 2396

In Love Again RCA Camden CAL 312

Intermezzo RCA LPM 1245

Listen To RCA LPM 3076 (10")

Man of La Mancha KAPP KS 3521

Melodic Magic RCA Camden CAL 353

Melodies of Love in Hi-Fi RCA Camden CAL 353

Music for Bachelors RCA LPM 1046

Music for the Weaker Sex RCA LPM 1583

Paris Loves Lovers Decca DL 74269

Passion in Paint RCA LPM 1033

Riot in Rhythm RCA LSP 2002

Serenade to Love RCA LPM 3076; T3102 (S.A.)

Swinging '59 LP 12040

They're Playing Our Song Decca DL 74574

Waltzes RCA LPM 1066

White Heat LP 3521

RICHARDSON, CLIVE (b. 23 June 1909)
Clive Richardson was born in Paris and raised in England. He studied various instruments, orchestration and conducting at the Royal Academy of Music. His first employment was arranging popular songs and dance music for Walford Hayden's Cafe Colette Orchestra. He also toured with Harold Ramsey's Rhythm Symphony Orchestra. Richardson was musical director for several Andre Charlot revues, including *Please* (1933), composed by VIVIAN ELLIS, and Herbert Farjeon's *Spread It Abroad* (1936). During the 1930s, he toured with the singer Hildegarde as accompanist and musical director.

In 1936, Richardson joined Gaumont British Film Company as arranger and assistant musical director to LOUIS LEVY. Working with CHARLES WILLIAMS, Richardson wrote most of the music for Gainsborough Films, including *Oh! Mr Porter* and scored several others, including *French Without Tears* (1939), officially credited to NICHOLAS BRODSKY.

During World War II, he served in the Royal Artillery Regiment. In 1944, he became famous for the many arrangements he made for the radio show *ITMA*. He also composed the *London Fantasia*, based on his experiences of an antiaircraft battery during bombing raids. This composition was recorded by MANTOVANI.

After the war, Richardson teamed up with Tony Lowry in a piano duet known as *Four Hands in Harmony*. This act was noted for its inventiveness and harmonious arrangements.

Richardson wrote many light orchestral compositions for the numerous mood music libraries that sprang up after the war. These pieces included *Holiday Spirit* (used as a children's TV newsreel theme), *Girl on the Calendar, Melody on the Move, Running off the Rails* and *Beachcomber*. In 1988, he received the BASCA Gold Award for lifetime services to the music industry.

RIDDLE, NELSON (1 June 1921– 6 October 1985)
Nelson Riddle was born in Oradell, New Jersey. He studied piano but changed to the trombone at the age of fourteen. In the late 1930s, he played in big bands including those of Jerry Wald, Charlie Spivak, Tommy Dorsey and Bob Crosby.

With Dorsey he was drafted into the army in 1945 and played with an army band. After discharge he found employment with Bob Crosby and accompanied him to the West Coast, where Riddle studied arranging with Mario Castelnuovo-Tedesco in California. He took up employment with NBC Radio West Coast staff as an arranger and conducted with Victor Bay. In 1950, while freelancing, he was commissioned to arrange the songs 'Mona Lisa' and 'Too Young' for Nat 'King' Cole. He obtained a contract with Capitol Records as an arranger-conductor and became famous with the release of the first Sinatra-Riddle collaborations, which included *Songs for Young Lovers, Swing Easy, Songs for Swingin' Lovers* and *In the Wee Small Hours*. His most famous album with Sinatra was *I've Got You Under My Skin* in 1956. In 1966, he made *Moonlight Sinatra* and in 1968 did the *Frank Sinatra Family Christmas Album*. He provided the music for *The Frank Sinatra Show* from 1950 to 1952 on CBS and from 1957 to 1958 on ABC.

Riddle also worked with Ella Fitzgerald, Judy Garland, Rosemary Clooney, Sammy Davis, Jr., Eddie Fisher, Jack Jones, Peggy Lee, Dean Martin, Johnny Mathis, ANTONIO CARLOS JOBIM, Shirley Bassey and Dinah Shore. He was featured on nonvocal albums containing his own orchestra, the first of which was *The Tender Touch*. The music on these albums varied from lush arrangements to the exuberance of *Hey . . . Let Yourself Go* and *C'mon, Get Happy*. His 1958 album *Cross Country Suite* won a Grammy.

In 1954, Riddle had some success with his version of 'Brother John', adapted from the French song 'Frere Jacques'. In 1956, his instrumental version of 'Lisbon Antigua' became a million seller.

From the mid-1950s, Riddle was active in television and feature films.

His television themes included the series *Route 66, The Untouchables* and *Naked City*. He worked with his orchestra on the *Smothers Brothers Comedy Hour* (CBS, 1967–75), *Rowan and Martin's Laugh-in* (NBC, 1968–73), *Leslie Uggams Show* (CBS, 1969), *Tim Conway Show* (1970), *Julie Andrews Hour* (ABC, 1972) and *Helen Reddy Show* on NBC in 1973. Besides being musical director for the *Frank Sinatra Show*, mentioned earlier, he was also involved in the *Nat King Cole Show* and received a television Academy Award nomination for his musical contribution to *Our Town*.

Riddle also provided the background scores for movies such as *Li'l Abner*, *Can-Can*, *Robin and the Seven Hoods*, *Lolita*, *Come Blow Your Horn* and *Paint Your Wagon*. He was nominated for five Oscars and won an Academy Award in 1974 for his music for *The Great Gatsby*. Other film credits include *The Pajama Game, St. Louis Blues, Merry Andrew* and Sinatra movies such as *The Joker Is Wild* and *Pal Joey*.

Riddle made a comeback in the 1980s when he recorded three albums with Linda Ronstadt: *What's New, Lush Life* and *For Sentimental Reasons*. He made his last album, *Blue Skies*, featuring standards of popular composers, with Kiri Te Kanawa; it appeared in 1985. He was the author of a book entitled *Arranged by Nelson Riddle* which appeared in June 1985, a few months before his death in New Jersey in October 1985.

Additional Readings

Friedwald, Will. *Sinatra: The Song Is You: A Singer's Art*. New York: Scribner, 1995. pp. 203–73.

Wright, Alan. *Nelson Riddle: A Musical History*. 1994. Supplemented by *Newsletters. No. 1, August 1994–*. (Compiled and distributed by Alan Wright, 1 Ash Grove, Stoke Poges, Bucks SL2 4AG, England).

Select Discography

Best of Nelson Riddle DT 1990

Bright and the Beautiful LST 7508

Can-Can Capitol ST 1365

Changing Colors MB BASF 20887

C'Mon, Get Happy Capitol T 893

Come Blow Your Horn R9 6071

Communications MB BASF 20888

Contemporary Sound UAS 6670

Gay Life Capitol ST 1670

The Great Gatsby Paramount PAS 2–3001

Great Music Reprise RS 6138

Hey, Let Yourself Go T 814

Joy of Living Capitol ST 1148

Let's Face the Music Pickwick SPC 3036

Love Is a Game of Poker Capitol ST 1817

Love Tide Capitol ST 1571 [Also on CD]

More Hit TV Themes Capitol ST 1869

Nat RS 6162

Oklahoma! Capitol T 596

Paint Your Wagon STF 1016

Paris When It Sizzles Reprise RS 6113

Riddle of Today LST 7532

Riddle Touch SUS 5233

The Rogues RCA LSP 2976

Route 66 Capitol 1771

Sea of Dreams Capitol ST 915 [Also on CD]

Sing a Song Capitol Premium STAO 1259

Swinging Brass Cl 1011

Tender Touch Capitol T 753

Tenderloin Capitol ST 1536

Vive Legrand DR 2015

What a Way to Go 20th Century Fox TFS 4143

White on White Reprise RS 6120

With 101 Strings Alshire S 5203

Witchcraft Pickwick SPC 3007

Wives and Lovers Solid State (United Artists) SS 18013

Compact Discs

Batman TV Soundtrack Polygram 834908

Best of Nelson Riddle Capitol 1990

Best of the Capitol Years EMI 78189

Route 66 and Other Great TV Themes CEMA 9452

RODGERS, RICHARD (28 June 1902–30 December 1979)
Richard Rodgers was born on Long Island, New York, the younger of two sons of a physician, William Rodgers, and Mamie (Levy) Rodgers. His father enjoyed books, theater and music and was an amateur baritone, while his mother was a trained musician. At the age of four, Richard was already showing an interest in the piano. By the time he was six, he was receiving musical tuition. In 1918, a family friend introduced him to the gifted lyricist Lorenz Hart, who was destined to work with Rodgers for more than two decades.

Richard Rodgers

In the early 1920s, Rodgers curtailed his studies at Columbia University and took up studies in harmony, ear training and music history at the Institute of Musical Art in New York City. The musicals he wrote with Hart, included the following: *Dearest Enemy* (1925); *The Girl Friend* ('The Blue Room', 1926); *Garrick Gaieties I*, ('Mountain Greenery', 1925); *Garrick Gaieties 2* (1926), *Betsy* (1926), *A Connecticut Yankee* ('My Heart Stood Still', 'Thou Swell' 1927, revised 1943); *Spring Is Here* ('With a Song in My Heart', 1929, filmed 1930); *Heads Up* (1929, filmed 1930); *Jumbo* ('The Most Beautiful Girl in the World', 'Little Girl Blue', 1935, filmed 1962); *On Your Toes* ('There's a Small Hotel', 1936, filmed 1939); *Babes in Arms* ('My Funny Valentine', 'The Lady Is a Tramp', 'Where or When', 1937); *I'd Rather Be Right* (1938); *Too Many Girls* (1939); *Pal Joey* ('Bewitched', 'I Could Write a Book', 1940, filmed 1957) and *By Jupiter* ('Wait Till You See Her', 1942).

Rodgers and Hart also wrote for films, including *The Hot Heiress* (1931); *Love Me Tonight* ('Isn't It Romantic?', 1932); *The Phantom President*

(1932); *Hallelujah, I'm a Bum* ('You Are Too Beautiful', 1933); *Hollywood Party* (1934); *Manhattan Melodrama* (1934) and *Mississippi* (1935).

The Rodgers and Hart partnership ended in 1942. In 1943, Rodgers found a new collaborator in Oscar Hammerstein II, who for almost two decades was his lyricist. Their musicals were *Oklahoma!* (1943, filmed 1955); *Carousel* (1945, filmed 1956); *Allegro* (1947), *South Pacific* (1949, filmed 1958); *The King and I* (1951, filmed 1956), *Me and Juliet* (1955), *Pipe Dream* (1955), *Flower Drum Song* (1958, filmed 1965) and *The Sound of Music* (1959, filmed 1965).

Hammerstein died on 23 August 1960. Rodgers subsequently wrote his own lyrics for *No Strings* (1962) and worked with several other collaborators, including Alan Jay Lerner, Samuel Taylor and Stephen Sondheim. With Sondheim he wrote *Do I Hear a Waltz?* in 1965, *Two by Two* with Martin Charnin (1970) and *Rex* with Sheldon Harnick in 1976.

Other Rodgers works included the sound track music for the television production *Victory at Sea* (1952) and *Winston Churchill: The Valiant Years* (1960). Some of his best orchestral writing was for 'Slaughter on Tenth Avenue', the ballet scene incorporated into *On Your Toes* that has since been recorded separately on various occasions.

Rodgers's career as composer for the musical theater spanned six decades and included forty-three stage musicals, ten film musicals and four television productions. His achievements were recognized by two Pulitzer prizes, the Donaldson and Tony Awards (four times each), the New York Drama Critics' Circle Award, two Emmys, an Oscar and a Grammy. Nine of his albums were awarded gold records.

Additional Readings

Ewen, David. *American Songwriters.* New York: H. W. Wilson, 1987. pp. 313–29.

Ewen, David. *Great Men of American Popular Song.* Englewood Cliffs, NJ: Prentice-Hall, 1970. pp. 188–207, 272–98.

Ewen, David. *Richard Rodgers.* New York: Holt, 1957.

Green, Benny. *Let's Face the Music: The Golden Age of American Popular Music.* London: Pavilion Books, 1989. pp. 183–208.

Green, Stanley. *Rodgers and Hammerstein Fact Book.* Milwaukee: Lynn Farnol Group/Hal Leonard Publishers, 1986.

Green, Stanley. *The Rodgers and Hammerstein Story.* New York: John Day, 1963.

Hemming, Roy. *The Melody Lingers On: The Great Songwriters and Their Movie Musicals.* New York: Newmarket Press, 1986. pp. 211–52.

Hyland, William G. *The Song Is Ended: Songwriters and American Music, 1900–1950.* New York: Oxford University Press, 1995. pp. 64–76, 235–49, 275–91.

Morden, Ethan. *Rodgers and Hammerstein.* New York: Harry N. Abrams, 1992.

Nolan, Frederick. *The Sound of Their Music: The Story of Rodgers and Hammerstein.* New York: Walker, 1978.

Rodgers and Hammerstein in Conversation With Arnold Michaelis. MGM 2E4 RP [2 LPs]

Rodgers and Hammerstein Interviews with Tony Thomas. FACET F/CD 8108 [CD]

Rodgers, Richard. *Musical Stages.* New York: Random House, 1976.

Taylor, Deems. *Some Enchanted Evenings: The Story of Rodgers and Hammerstein.* New York: Harper, 1953.

Select Discography

Black, Stanley. Music of Richard Rodgers London LL1209

Gold, Marty. Music of Rodgers and Hart RCA LSP 2535

Kostelanetz, Andre. Columbia Album of Richard Rodgers Columbia C2L3 [Also on CD]

Kostelanetz, Andre. Music of Richard Rodgers Columbia ML 4130 [Also on CD]

Luypaerts, Guy. Symphonic Portrait of Richard Rodgers Capitol LC 6539 (10")

Melachrino, George. Music of Rodgers and Hammerstein RCA LPM/LSP 2513

Ornadel, Cyril. Musical World of Rodgers and Hammerstein (With Starlight Symphony Orchestra) MGM E/SE 3817 (Reissued as The Rodgers and Hammerstein Songbook. Polydon. 2482 355) [Also on CD]

Ornadel, Cyril. Some Enchanted Evenings (With Westminster Orchestra of London) RAMA RLP 5002

Poliakin, Raoul. Music of Richard Rodgers and Harold Arlen Everest LPBR 5066

Rodgers, Richard (With Philharmonic Symphony Orchestra of New York) Columbia ALD 6004 (South Africa)

Siravo, George. Rodgers and Hart: Percussion and Strings Time S 2015

ROGER, ROGER (5 August 1911–12 June 1995)

Roger Roger was born in Rouen, the son of Edmond Roger, a well-known French opera conductor and contemporary of Claude Debussy. Roger Roger's music education began at an early age with the study of piano, harmony, counterpoint and the fugue. At the age of eighteen, he made his debut conducting a five-man orchestra in a French music hall.

He subsequently worked as conductor and composer for radio and films, devoting much time to recording. Roger composed the scores for over 500 film productions. In the mid-1970s, he had composed works for more that fifty radio programs in France via the networks of Radio-diffusion–Television Française and the radio services of Radio-Tele-Luxembourg and Radio-Monte Carlo. He also composed the scores for over 500 film productions and concentrated on television shows. His composition 'Versailles', specially written for a TV appearance of René Coty, became the president's theme on every television appearance thereafter.

Since the early 1950s, his music has been used to accompany BBC Trade Test Transmissions. Among the first pieces of music from the Roger Roger

Orchestra to be used by the British Broadcasting Corporation in 1955 were 'Laissez-Faire' and 'Bolero', the latter one of his own compositions. From 1961 onward, a wealth of Roger's music was broadcast. It was characterized by a typically French flavor and included accordions. Examples of this music are 'Mademoiselle de Paris', 'Reine de Musette', 'Some of These Days', 'La Java' and 'Les Triolets'. In 1976, he released an LP in the United Kingdom that featured fourteen of his own compositions, played by him on three types of synthesizer. These included 'Chattanooga Chew Chew', 'Double Yellow Line' (also called 'Double Yellow Doris') and 'Pullman Special' (also known as 'Marylin's Munch Hour'). Other of his compositions included 'Mambo for Strings' and 'Danse Roumaine'.

Select Discography

Beyond the Sea: The Music of Charles Trenet MGM E3395

Grand Prix (with Valjean) CL-1919

Heart of Paris Decca DL 8599

Invitation to Paris SDBR 1093

Musique Pour Rever Disques Vega V 30 725 [Also on CD]

Thrilling MGM E3201

Tourbillon de Paris Golden Guinea (PYE U.K.) GGL 0310

ROMBERG, SIGMUND (29 July 1887–9 November 1951)
Sigmund Romberg was born in Nagy Kaniza, Hungary, educated at the Polytechnische Hochshule and studied music in Vienna. He emigrated to the United States in 1909, becoming an American citizen in 1912.

He began his musical career in New York as a pianist in cafes before forming his own orchestra in 1912. He became staff composer for the Shubert Brothers who commissioned him to write the music for *The Whirl of the World* in 1914. This led to his involvement in forty other productions for the Shuberts. These included the shows *Maytime* (1917), *Sinbad* (1918), *Blossom Time* (1921), *The Student Prince* (1924), *The Desert Song* (1926) and *New Moon* (1928). Many of his Broadway successes were made into film musicals. He wrote a number of scores for Hollywood, including *Viennese Nights* (1930), *Children of Dreams* (1931), *The Night Is Young* (1935), *The Girl of the Golden West* (1938), *Broadway Serenade* (1939) and *Up in Central Park* (1945). He also toured many American cities with his orchestra, which was featured on the radio program *An Evening with Romberg*. He had one show produced posthumously in 1954, *The Girl in Pink Tights* (lyrics by Leo Robin).

Lyricists who worked with Romberg included Otto Harbach, Oscar Hammerstein, Dorothy Fields, Gus Kahn and Leo Robin. His music was unique in that he was able to fuse the tradition of Viennese operetta with popular American song.

Some of his outstanding songs were 'Deep in My Heart' and 'Serenade' from *The Student Prince* (1924); 'One Alone' and 'Desert Song', from *The Desert Song* (1926); 'Lover Come Back to Me' and 'Stout Hearted Men' from *New Moon* (1928); 'When I Grow Too Old to Dream' from the film *The Night Is Young* (1935) and 'Who Are We to Say' from the film *Girl of the Golden West* (1938).

Additional Readings

Arnold, Elliot. *Deep in My Heart: A Story Based on the Life of Sigmund Romberg.* New York: Duell, Sloan and Pearce, 1949.

Ewen, David. *American Songwriters.* New York: H. W. Wilson, 1987. pp. 330–35.

Select Discography

Dragon, Carmen. An Evening with Sigmund Romberg (With Hollywood Bowl Pops Orchestra) Capitol W 1840 [LP] Angel CDM 7690532 [CD]

Green, Johnny. Sigmund Romberg Favorites (With Hollywood Bowl Pops Orchestra) Decca DL 9665

Hunsberger, Donald. Sigmund Romberg: When I Grow Too Old to Dream (With Eastman Dryden Orchestra) Arabesque 26540 [CD]

Kostelanetz, Andre. Music of Sigmund Romberg Columbia CL771

Mantovani. Music of Sigmund Romberg London LL 1031

Melachrino, George. Music of Sigmund Romberg RCA LPM/LSP 2106

Ornadel, Cyril. Will You Remember? The Music of Sigmund Romberg (Arrangements by John Gregory) Conquest CL 1004

Weston, Paul. Columbia Album of Sigmund Romberg Columbia C2L14 [Also on CD]

ROSE, DAVID (15 June 1910– 23 August 1990)

David Rose was born in London and emigrated as a child to America with his parents. The family settled in Chicago, where he studied at the Chicago Musical College. He began his musical career as a member of Ted Fio Rito's Orchestra. In his early days, he wrote arrangements for dance bands such as those of Bud Freeman and Benny Goodman. Later, he became a radio pianist and arranger first for NBC Radio in Chicago and later for Mutual in Hollywood. An example of his work during the period of the late 1930s and early 1940s is the program *California Melodies.*

During World War II he served in the U.S. Air Force. In the late 1940s, he joined MGM Studios and composed, arranged and conducted for numerous films, including *The Unfinished Dance, Everything I Have Is Yours, Rich, Young and Pretty, Operation Petticoat, Please Don't Eat the Daisies, Quick Before It Melts, Never Too Late* and *Hombre.*

Much of Rose's music was composed for the screen, and some compositions have become popular music classics: 'Our Waltz', 'Holiday for Strings', 'Dance of the Spanish Onion' and 'The Stripper'. He became musical director for comedian Red Skelton's radio program in the late 1940s

David Rose

and remained with Skelton when he moved over to TV. He also scored for NBC-TV spectaculars.

Over the years, Rose wrote well over a thousand compositions. Much of this work is stored in the libraries of two transcription companies, the World Broadcasting System and Standard Transcriptions. World and Standard became the property of radio and TV producer Frederick Ziv. Rose's transcription music could be heard on numerous radio stations in the United States until the mid-1950s. For this music, he used a smaller string section than he used for commercial recordings.

David Rose received an Emmy Award for the music he contributed to Fred Astaire's TV show in 1959. He also provided music for TV programs such as *The Bob Hope Show, The Tony Martin Show, Shower of Stars, The Ford Program, Little House on the Prairie*, and selected episodes of *Bonanza*. He also composed for *Father Murphy*, another TV show.

Rose composed the music for a patriotic stage show, directed by Moss

Hart, called *This Is the Army*, which ran for 212 performances at the 44th Street Theater in New York. In 1950, he wrote much of the music for *Red, White and Blue*, a touring musical, produced for the purpose of raising funds for the rehabilitation of ex-servicemen and for child welfare.

In 1968, he established the David Rose Foundation, which set up music scholarships at two universities. He toured extensively with his orchestra and produced a vast output of recorded music. He became conductor of the Pasadena Pops Concerts for several years and conducted the David Rose Concerts at Hollywood Bowl.

Musical Achievements

Rose's music often contained elements of the novel and unexpected. He was one of the first to employ the echo chamber, then a new trend in popular music presentation. He adapted this innovation to his 1942 recording of 'Holiday for Strings'. This brilliant original work was called the most unusual musical composition in years by its publisher, created a sensation in the United States and has become one of the all-time hits of the music world.

A touch of humor is also evident in Rose's compositions 'Dance of the Gremlins' and 'The Stripper'. Many of his compositions were written late at night and contain a nostalgic flavor associated with the night. Examples are 'Under the Stars', 'Waltz of the Night', 'Shadows', and his rare album 'David Rose Serenades'. He specialized in arrangements for the string section of the orchestra. An example of his ingenuity is evident in his composition 'Busy Afternoon' in which an invigorating pizzicato introduction is used to excellent effect.

'Holiday for Strings' made Rose famous. It first appeared in 1942 and became a million seller by 1958. The second of his million-selling discs was 'Calypso Melody', composed in 1957 by Larry Clinton. The disc reached number 42 and was twelve weeks on the United States best-seller list. His third million seller was his own composition, 'The Stripper', top seller in the United States charts in 1962 and seventeen weeks on the best-sellers.

As a conductor, Rose was supremely efficient, making use of a minimum of rehearsals and ably meeting frequent deadlines. An example of this is the 1946 radio series *Holiday for Music*, for which he produced a new composition each week.

Select List of Compositions

'A La Bien Aimée'; 'A Nous'; 'After Midnight' (later retitled 'Under the Stars'); 'Ancient Arabian Cake Walk'; 'Angela'; 'As Kreutzer Spins'; 'Autumn Mist' (originally 'Indian Sunset'); 'Big Ben'; 'Butterfly and Alligator'; 'Christmas Tree'; 'Conversation Mood'; 'Das Easta'; 'Dance of the Spanish Onion'; 'Dreams Do Come True'; 'Esenada Escapade'; 'Flying Horse'; 'Happy Music'; 'Hollywood Bowl Suite'; 'In the Dawn'; 'Indian Sunset'; 'March of the Pretzels'; 'Mask Waltz'; 'My Dog

Has Fleas'; 'My Dream Book of Memories'; 'No Rest for the Weary'; 'Nursery Without Rhyme'; 'On a Little Country Road in Switzerland'; 'Once Upon a Lullaby'; 'Orpheus Takes a Holiday'; 'Parade of the Clowns'; 'Plantation Moods'; 'Poor Whippoorwill'; 'Rose Waltz'; 'Saxophone City'; 'Serenades to a Dream'; 'Shadows'; 'So-o-o in Love'; 'Stringopation'; 'Strip of Sunset'; 'Under the Stars'; 'Valse de Nuit'; 'Violin'; 'Waltz'; 'Waltz of the Stars'; 'Waukegan Concerto' (dedicated to the comedian Jack Benny'); 'Winged Victory'; 'Won't You Be Mine?'; 'You're so Sweet to Remember'.

Select Discography

10" LPs

Cole Porter Review RCA Victor LPM 32

David Rose Hits and Other Standards Royale 1827

Holiday for Strings MGM E 506 (U.S.), D 106 (U.K.)

Magic Music Box MGM E 196

Music of George Gershwin MGM E 85

Sentimental Journey MGM E 352

Serenades MGM E 515

Wonderland of Music MGM D 149

12" LPs

Autumn Leaves MGM E/SE 3592

Beautiful Music to Love By MGM E 3067

Bonanza MGM E/SE 3960

Box Office Blockbusters MGM E/SE 3894 (Reissued as **Great Orchestras of the World** Polydor 2482367)

Cimarron and Other Great Themes MGM E 3953

Concert with a Beat MGM SE 3852 (U.S.), C847 (U.K.)

David Rose Plays David Rose MGM E 3748, SE 3811

Enchanted Strings Spinorama M 103

Fiddlin' For Fun MGM E 3108

Gigi MGM E/SE 3640 (U.S.), C775 (U.K.)

Great Waltzes of the Fabulous Century KAPP S3100

Hi Fiddles MGM E 3481

Holiday for Strings Columbia Studio Two 216 (U.K.); Capitol ST 2717 (U.S.); MGM D 106 (10"); MGM E 506; RCA 31231 (SA) (Contents of these five LPs are all different, despite the similar record titles.)

In a Mellow Mood Masterseal (no number), Musirama Remington LP (no number). Rereleased in Stereo as **Memories Are Made of This** PALACE PST 614

In the Still of the Night Polydor 2482297 (Reissue of the album **Portrait**)

Let's Fall in Love (Music of Harold Arlen) MGM E 3101 (U.S.), C 754 (U.K.)

Like Blue MGM E/SE 3811 (U.S.), C 828, CS 6003 (U.K.)

Love Walked In (Music of George Gershwin) MGM E 3123 [Also on CD]

Lovers' Serenade MGM E 3289

Magic Melodies of David Rose Lion 70109 (U.S.), C 788 (U.K.)

Magic Music Box MGM E 196

Melody Fair Polydor 2383459

Merry Christmas to You MGM E 3469

Music for Pleasure MFP 1261

Music from Jamaica MGM E 3612

Music from Motion Pictures MGM E 3397

Music of the 1930s MCA 2–4276

Nostalgia E 3134

Of Human Bondage MGM E/SE 4261

Reflections in the Water MGM E 3603

San Francisco, My Enchanted City SEAL LS 1530

Secret Songs for Young Lovers (With André Previn) Also issued as **Like Young** MGM E/SE E3716

Sentimental Journey MGM E 532

Serenades MGM E 515

The Song Is You (Music of Jerome Kern) MGM E 3555

Songs of the Fabulous Thirties KAPP 1205 S, 1206 S; KAPP 3205 S, 3206 S (Stereo)

Spectacular Strings MGM E/SE 3895

Special Magic of David Rose MGM SELECT 2353102

The Stripper MGM CESS 34

Themes from the Great Screen Epics Capitol ST 2627

The Very Thought of You Memoir Noir 102 (Reissue of 1974 Polydor album)

Whoop Up! MGM E/SE 3746

Compact Discs

The Stripper and other Favorites Emporio 501

Very Best of David Rose Taragon Records TARCD-1015

ROTA, NINO (3 December 1911–10 April 1979)

Nino Rota was born in Milan and studied at the Milan Conservatory and Accademia de Santa Cecilia. He received instruction on conducting from Fritz Reiner in Philadelphia. His first success was the score for the British film *The Glass Mountain* (1949). From 1952 to 1978, he collaborated with director Federico Fellini to produce scores for films such as *La Dolce Vita* (1960), *8½*, (1963), *Juliet of the Spirits* (1965), *Fellini Satyricon* (1970) and *Fellini's Roma* (1972). Credits with other producers included *War and Peace* (1956), *Il Gattopardo (The Leopard)* (1963), *Romeo and Juliet* (1968), *The Godfather* (1972), *The Godfather Part II* (1974) and *Death on the Nile* (1978). His themes for *Romeo and Juliet* and *The Godfather* became top-selling records.

Select Discography

The Clowns Paramount PAS 1003

Fellini's Roma United Artists LA052-g

Film Music: Themes . . . (Conducted by Carlo Savina) Cam SAG 9054

Rota and Fellini Cam SAG 9053

War and Peace (Conducted by Franco Ferrara) Columbia ACL 930

Compact Discs

The Godfather Suite (Milan Philharmonic Orchestra. Conductor Carmine Coppola) Silva Screen FILMCD077

Symphonic Fellini/Rota (Czech Symphony Orchestra. Conductor Derek Wadsworth) Silva Screen FILMCD129

ROZSA, MIKLOS (18 April 1907–27 July 1995)

Miklos Rozsa was born in Budapest. He learned piano and violin and started composing at the age of seven. He spent much of his childhood collecting Magyar folk songs. He studied at the Leipzig University. In 1928, he signed a contract with music publishers Breitkopf and Hartel for his symphonic and chamber music. He moved to Paris in 1931 to continue his music career and there met the Korda Brothers. Jacques Feyder heard his 'Ballet Hungaria' and commissioned him to write the music for the Marlene Dietrich film *Knight Without Armour* (1937), produced by Sir Alexander Korda. Rozsa moved to London with the Korda Brothers, working at the Denham Studios. In 1939, he joined the Kordas in Hollywood, where he scored the music for films such as *The Four Feathers* (1939), and *The Thief of Baghdad* (1940). In 1942, excerpts from *The Jungle Book* were released as a 78 rpm album on RCA Victor, the first of its kind in the United States.

Rozsa subsequently moved to Paramount Studios and worked with Billy Wilder on movies such as *Double Indemnity* (1944) and *The Lost Weekend* (1945). At the end of the war, Rozsa wrote one of his most famous scores for Hitchcock's *Spellbound* (1945) in which he used a theremin to suggest the world of psychosis. He also included a love theme in the film, for which he won his first Oscar. Other Academy Awards were for *A Double Life* (1947) and *Ben-Hur* (1959). From 1945 to 1965, he served as professor of film music at the University of Southern California.

From 1949 to 1962, Rozsa worked for MGM Studios, where he was responsible for the scores of productions such as *Quo Vadis* (1951), *Ivan-*

hoe (1952), *Lust for Life* (1956) and *El Cid* (1961). In the 1960s Rozsa turned from film scoring to concert work but scored only four films from 1962 to 1970. His violin concerto, commissioned by Jascha Heifetz, was used by Billy Wilder in *The Private Life of Sherlock Holmes* (1970). Rosza wrote the scores for three more films toward the end of his career, *Providence* (1977), *Time after Time* (1979) and *Dead Men Don't Wear Plaid* (1982).

Rozsa's film scores are characterized by a blend of intellect and emotion. His 'psychological' music for *Lost Weekend* and *Spellbound* provide insight into the minds of the screen characters. After *The Red House* (1947), he decided not to use the theremin again, for fear of becoming typecast. His scores have been well represented on commercial recordings. The CHARLES WILLIAMS 12" 78 recording of *The Spellbound Concerto* (DX1264, reissued on EMI CDHMV6) was a big seller on Columbia. With the advent of long-playing records, a wide range of Rozsa's music became available.

Select Discography

Miklos Rozsa Conducts His Great Film Music Polydor 2383.327

Miklos Rozsa Conducts the Royal Philharmonic Orchestra Polydor 2383.384

Rozsa Conducts Rozsa Polydor 2383.440

Spellbound and the Classic Film Scores of Miklos Rozsa RCA ARL1–0911

Compact Discs

All the Brothers Were Valiant PCD131

Dead Men Don't Wear Plaid Prometheus PCD126

Ivanhoe Intrada Excalibur Collection MAF7055

Julius Caesar Intrada Excalibur Collection MAF7056D

Lust for Life. Background to Violence Suite Varese Sarabande VSD5405

Thief of Baghdad. Jungle Book Colosseum CST348044

Time After Time Southern Cross SCCD1014

Young Bess Prometheus mono PCD133

S

SAVINA, CARLO

Carlo Savina studied music at the Giuseppe Verdi Conservatoire in Turin. He specialized in violin, piano, composition, conducting and choral music. He received his diploma in music at the Accademia Chigiana. While studying there, he composed the opera *Il Vecchio Gelosa*, which won him first prize in a competition. The opera was presented at the Rozzi in Siena and also broadcast by Radio Italiana. His *Cinq Canzoni* for string quartet won first prize in the National Composers' Review.

In 1945, he began arranging music for radio broadcasts. He was soon given his own orchestra and rapidly rose to fame. Recording contracts followed, and he joined Durium Records as arranger and conductor.

Select Discography

Amarcord [Music of Nino Rota] RCA ARL1-0907

Carlo Savina and His Orchestra Durium DLU 96050

The Girl Is You, the Boy Is Me RCA LPM 1913

The Godfather [Music of Nino Rota] Paramount PAS 1003

Holiday Abroad in Rome RCA LSP 1595 [Also on CD]

My Darling RCA LPM 1912

Stavisky [Music of Stephen Sondheim] RCA ARL1-0952

SAVINO, DOMENICO (b. 1881)

Domenico Savino was born in Taranto, Italy, and studied piano and composition at the Royal Conservatory of Naples. He emigrated to the United

States in the early 1920s, where he composed under the name of D. Onivas, producing songs such as 'Indianola' and 'Burning Sands'.

He became musical director for Pathé Phonograph, where he acted as conductor and supervisor of recording sessions. He worked with such famous singers as Claudio Muzio, Tito Schipa and Lina Cavalieri. He composed many orchestral background music scores for silent films for MGM and Twentieth Century–Fox, including the film *The Patriot*, starring Emil Jannings.

For a while, he was chief editor and stockholder of the music publishing house Robbins Music Corporation, for whom he compiled a catalogue of motion picture music. This company was later taken over by MGM. He also worked on radio programs such as the *Paramount Hour*, the *La Palina Cigar Program* and the *American Telephone and Telegraph Hour*. He was also musical director of one of the major radio networks.

His considerable fortune enabled him to retire from the field of light music and devote himself to classical music compositions, which were produced by the Radio Symphony Orchestra of Rome under Savino's direction. With over 900 compositions to his credit, he was able to rely on a steady income from his membership in the American Society of Composers, Authors and Publishers (ASCAP). He also took up the art of painting.

Select Discography

All I Do Is Dream of You RCA Camden RAL 1009

Hits from My Fair Lady RCA Camden CAL 319

Music for a Perfect Day RCA Camden CAL-357

Rome at Midnight Brunswick LAT 8188

South American Moods RCA Camden CAL-429

Strings in Hi-Fi RCA Camden CAL-487

SCHWARTZ, ARTHUR (25 November 1900–3 September 1984)
Arthur Schwartz was born in New York and educated at New York University and Columbia University. He passed his legal examinations in 1924, taught English and practiced law before becoming a composer. He gave up his law practice in 1929 and collaborated with lyricist Howard Dietz to contribute to the shows *Dear Sir* (1924) and *Grand Street Follies* (1926). In 1929, he had a hit with the song 'I Guess I'll Have to Change My Plan', from *The Little Show*. He contributed to the London productions, including *The Co-Optimists* in 1930, and wrote the score of *Here Comes the Bride* in the same year.

From 1930 to 1935, Schwartz composed for Broadway shows including *The Second Little Show* (1930); *Princess Charming* (1930); *Three's a*

Crowd (1930); *The Band Wagon* ('Dancing in the Dark', 'I Love Louisa', 1931, filmed 1953); *Flying Colors* ('Louisiana Hayride', 1932); *Revenge with Music* ('You and the Night and the Music', 1934); *At Home Abroad* ('Paree', 1935); *Between the Devil* ('I See Your Face Before Me', 1937); *Stars in Your Eyes* (1939); *American Jubilee* (1940); *Park Avenue* (with Ira Gershwin, 1946); *A Tree Grows in Brooklyn* ('Look Who's Dancing', 1951); *By the Beautiful Sea* (1954); *The Gay Life* (1961) and *Jennie* (1963).

He produced theme songs for radio and television, including *High Tor* (1956) and *A Bell for Adano* (1957) and also wrote for films such as *Follow the Leader* (1930); *She Loves Me Not* (1934); *That Girl from Paris* (1936); *Navy Blues* (1941); *Cairo* (1942); *Thank Your Lucky Stars* (1943); *The Time, the Place and the Girl* (1946); *Dancing in the Dark* (1949); *Dangerous When Wet* (1953) and *You're Never Too Young* (1955). He produced JEROME KERN'S *Cover Girl* (1944) and the film biography of COLE PORTER, *Night and Day* (1946).

Additional Readings

Dietz, Howard. *Dancing in the Dark*. New York: Quadrangle Books, 1974.

Ewen, David. *American Songwriters*. New York: H. W. Wilson, 1987. pp. 347–54.

Ewen, David. *Great Men of American Popular Song*. Englewood Cliffs, NJ: Prentice-Hall, 1970. pp. 228–36.

Select Discography

Farnon, Robert. Something to Remember You By: Music of Schwartz and Dietz. London LL 1231

Holmes, Leroy. Alone Together: Songs by Howard Dietz and Arthur Schwartz MGM E215 (10")

SCOTT, RAYMOND (born Harry Warnow, 10 September 1910)

Raymond Scott was a pianist, arranger, composer and band leader. He was born in New York City, studied at Juilliard and played the piano in his brother Mark's band.

From 1937 to 1940, Scott led a quintet that performed on radio, recordings and in the movies. He also wrote music that often consisted of clever novelty arrangements, requiring skillful playing. From 1941 to 1944, he was musical director of CBS Radio. During this time he assembled a talented jazz group known as the Million Dollar Band, although Scott himself was not a jazz musician. His musicians included Ben Webster, Trummy Young, Charlie Shavers, bassists Billy Taylor, John Simmons and Sid Catlett.

In the mid-1940s, he wrote the songs for the musical *Lute Song*, starring Mary Martin. From 1946 to 1949, Scott toured with a dance band and then with a new version of his quintet. From 1949 to 1957, he took over the Hit Parade Orchestra, following the death of his brother, Mark Warnow. He also accompanied his wife, singer Dorothy Collins.

In the 1950s, he completed the film scores *Never Love a Stranger* and *The Pusher* and the musical *Hat in Hand*. Scott had his own Audiovox label and was musical director for Everest Records. He later manufactured electronic instruments.

Select Discography

Amor (With the Swinging Strings) Everest LPBR 5080

SCOTT, ROLLO (2 September 1925–1 October 1995)
Rollo Scott, the South African conductor, composer and arranger was born in Queenstown, Eastern Cape, and educated at Queen's College, Queenstown and Rhodes University, Grahamstown, where he obtained a bachelor of music degree. He studied composition with Hubert du Plessis, a leading South African composer.

Scott taught music for a few years in East London. In 1951, he wrote and produced a successful musical *One Touch of Midas*. In 1952, he left for London in order to gain further study and experience. He played for six years in London's West End night spots while studying with top arrangers including Jack Rourke and BOB SHARPLES. He also completed a course with the London School of Contemporary Arrangers. His first string arrangement was broadcast on the BBC by the Jack Salisbury orchestra in 1956.

Scott returned to South Africa in 1959. He opened a music department and taught at Selbourne College, East London. In 1962, he joined the light music department of the South African Broadcasting Corporation (SABC) in Johannesburg. In 1966, he became organizer of light music for the SABC. He devised and presented many radio musical programs, including *Songs from the Shows*, *Making Music*, *Voices in Harmony*, *On Wings of Strings*, *South African Serenade*, *Over the Rainbow*, *Nelson Riddle: A Man for All Sessions*. For eight years he compiled the South African music contribution to South African Airways in-flight music programs on the international services.

In 1970, he promoted the South African entry at the Greek Olympiad of Song in Athens. In 1971, he visited Brussels as guest conductor with the Brussels Radio and Television Orchestra, recording forty South African compositions. He also attended the Light Music Forum of European Broadcasting Union in Munich and visited recording studios in various European centers.

Scott organized the SABC Song Writing Competition. His own compositions include 'Jacaranda Time', 'The Things I Like About You', 'My Heart Is Yours', 'Last Spring', 'Liefling Kom Wals Saam Met My' (recorded for

Decca by Kenneth McKellar in London), 'Liefde Regdeur Die Jaar' and 'The Pitter Patter Song'.

His television credits included musical director and arranger for the original eight part series *Mimi* (with Mimi Coetzer, soprano); *Musikale Seisoene; Musiek Vir Almal; Liefdeslag and Liefdeslied; Rudi Neitz; Ateljee 4* and two *Big Band Shows*. He arranged and recorded with Andrea Catzel, SABC Cape Town's contribution to *No Jacket Required*, a television special, and a centennial birthday tribute to IRVING BERLIN.

In October 1985, Scott retired from his position with the SABC and went to live in Fish Hoek, Western Cape. He continued to produce his popular Saturday evening radio program *Over the Rainbow*, presented from the Sea Point studios of the SABC, until shortly before his death.

Select Discography

Amanda Music for Pleasure MFP 54596

Music After Six Music for Pleasure MFP 5781

Over the Rainbow EMI CEY 330

Over the Rainbow 2 Teal Trutone MMTL 1470

Place in the Sun Music for Pleasure MFP 54527

SHAINDLIN, JACK

Jack Shaindlin was born in Yalta but moved to America after the Russian Revolution. Shortly after landing in America, he won first prize in a newspaper-sponsored piano contest. He studied at the Glenn Dillard Gunn Conservatory in Chicago. He began his professional career by playing piano in small clubs and landed his first movie job at the age of sixteen, playing an organ at a theater. At the age of eighteen he joined a large orchestra and became a conductor. He subsequently performed at the Palace Theatre playing the piano, writing and acting in skits.

At the age of twenty-two, he started working for Universal Pictures and thereafter for RKO, Columbia and Louis DeRochemont as well as a twelve-year association with OWI films as musical director. In 1947 and 1948, he received critical acclaim for his conducting of pops symphony concerts at Carnegie Hall. He also lectured on movie music and was associated with the Ford Foundation's television series. He was credited with the music of films such as *Lost Boundaries*, *Teresa* and *Cinerama Holiday*.

Select Discography

Academy Award Favorites Mercury MG 20061

Hollywood's Greatest Forum (Roulette) FCS 9080

Musical Themes Hollywood U.S.A. Forum SF 9008

SHARPLES, BOB (born Robert Frederick Standish)
Bob Sharples was born in Bury, Lancashire. As a child, he learned to play the piano and organ. At sixteen, he was deputy suborganist at Manchester Cathedral. He studied composition, orchestration and conducting under Sir Hamilton Harty. After the death of his father, he chose a career in the field of lighter music and moved to London.

During the late 1930s, Sharples played with and arranged music for West End bands, including those of AMBROSE, Roy Fox and Harry Roy. In 1938, he met Thomas 'Fats' Waller and the pianist George Shearing.

During World War II, he joined the Royal Army Service Corps as a driver in 1940. He was commissioned in 1942 and reached the rank of lieutenant-colonel in 1945. After his release in 1946, he commenced arranging for music publishers and the BBC. From 1947 to 1952, he arranged exclusively for GERALDO and from 1952 onward for CYRIL STAPLETON and the BBC Show Band. He joined Decca in 1954.

Select Discography

Contrasts in Hi-Fi Decca LK 4213

Hoagy Carmichael's Ballads for Dancing Coral CRL 57034

Music in the Night (With Living Strings) RCA Camden CAL/CAS 638

Music To Help You Stop Smoking (With Living Strings) RCA Camden CAL/CAS 821

SILVESTER, VICTOR MARLBOROUGH (25 February 1900–14 August 1978)
Victor Silvester was a well-known British bandleader and composer who gave up a military career after winning a World Ballroom Championship in 1922. He operated a successful dancing school on Bond Street, London, from 1927 onward and wrote *Modern Ballroom Dancing* in 1928. He found most records unsuitable for his style of dancing and produced sides by pianist Gerry Moore in 1934. In 1935, he formed his own orchestra, which included strings for dancing orchestra as well as conventional dance band music. He had a radio series known as *BBC Dancing Club '41*. In 1948, his radio show was transferred to television.

Select Discography

Recordings With Silver Strings

Bewitched: Music of Richard Rodgers EMI SCX 3254

Getting to Know You: Great Show Tunes EMI 33SX1339

Great Film Music EMI SCX 3452

I Only Have Eyes for You: Music of Harry Warren EMI 33SX 1554

In France EMI 33SX 1495

Love Is a Many-Splendored Thing EMI TP 616

More Great Show Tunes EMI SCX 3564

Music to Watch Films By EMI SCX 6156

A Pretty Girl Is Like a Melody: Music of Irving Berlin EMI 33SX 1109

Stay as Sweet as You Are: Music of Harry Revel and Mack Gordon EMI 33SX 1414

Strings in Tempo EMI SAEG 1015

Valentino EMI OU 2190

You Do Something to Me (Music of Cole Porter) EMI SCX 3273

You Were Never Lovelier (Music of Jerome Kern) EMI 33 SX1061

Compact Discs

Sound of Musicals EMI SCX 6156

SLATKIN, FELIX

Felix Slatkin started his professional career at the age of ten as a concert violinist in the United States. He later turned to conducting, composing and arranging and appeared with the HOLLYWOOD BOWL ORCHESTRA and the Concert Arts Orchestra. He was associated with the motion picture industry as head of the music divisions of Warner Brothers and Twentieth Century–Fox and was one of the producers of Liberty Records.

Select Discography

Love Strings Liberty SUM-1106 (M), SUS-5106 (S)

Many-Splendored Themes Liberty LMM 13011

Magnificent XII Liberty LMM-13004 (M), LSS-14004 (S)

Our Winter Love Liberty LRP 3287

Paradise Found Liberty LSS 1401

Porgy and Bess Suite Pickwick SPC 4044

Street Scene Liberty SPLY 509

Tender Strings Liberty SUM-1170 (M), SUS-5170 (S)

SLATKIN, LEONARD (EDWARD) (b. 1 September 1944)

Leonard Slatkin, the American conductor and pianist, was born in Los Angeles. He first studied conducting with his father, FELIX SLATKIN and continued with Walter Susskind at Aspen and Jean Morel at the Juilliard School. He made his debut with the Youth Symphony Orchestra of New York in 1966. He became assistant conductor to Susskind of the St. Louis Symphony Orchestra in 1968, associate conductor in 1971 and principal guest conductor in 1975. From 1977 to 1978, he served as musical director of the New Orleans Philharmonic Orchestra, the St. Louis Symphony Orchestra from 1979 to 1995 and the National Symphony Orchestra of

Washington from 1996 onward. During this time he appeared frequently as guest conductor with various famous orchestras within the United States and abroad. He has also conducted opera at the Metropolitan, in Chicago, Vienna, Stuttgart and Hamburg.

Select Discography

Copland: Music for Films (St. Louis Symphony Orchestra) 09026–61699–2

The Typewriter: Leroy Anderson Favorites (St. Louis Orchestra) RCA 09026-68048–2

SPOLIANSKY, MISCHA (28 December 1898–28 June 1985)
Mischa Spoliansky, film composer, was born in Bialystock, Russia, and received his musical education in Germany. With Freidrich Hollander, Spoliansky dominated the German cabaret scene in the late 1920s. He wrote songs for Marlene Dietrich and worked in the German film industry. He came to England to escape the threat of Nazism and was employed by Alexander Korda. He worked on the scores for the films *The Private Life of Don Juan* (1934) and *Sanders of the River* (1935). His first full score was *The Ghost Goes West* (1936).

Spoliansky is credited with over fifty British and American film scores, including *Wanted for Murder* (1946); *The Happiest Days of Your Life* (1950); *Melba* (1953); *Saint Joan* (1957); *Northwest Frontier* (1959) and *Hitler—The Last Ten Days* (1973).

STAPLETON, CYRIL (31 December 1914–25 February 1974)
Stapleton was born in Nottingham, England. He played the violin as a child and made his first broadcast at the age of twelve, playing as solo violinist on the old 5NG radio station at Nottingham. He broadcast regularly from the BBC Birmingham between 1928 and 1932. At the age of eighteen, he went to Czechoslovakia to study briefly under Ottokar Sevĕik, the famous violin teacher. On his return to England, he gained a scholarship to the Trinity College of Music in London. He played with pit orchestras for silent movies and was leading his own band in the provinces at the age of twenty.

In the early 1930s, he joined the Henry Hall BBC Dance Orchestra as a violinist and moved on to working under Billy Ternent, through the good offices of Jack Payne, with whom he had toured South Africa in 1935. In 1937, he formed his own small orchestra, which played regularly at a West End restaurant. His first broadcast with his own band took place in March 1939. He married impressionist Beryl Orde.

During World War II he served in the Royal Air Force, later conducting the RAF Symphony Orchestra at the Potsdam Summit Conference. After the war, he formed a band to play at Fisher's Restaurant on New Bond Street, London. The band was featured on BBC programs *Hit Parade* and

Golden Slipper in the late 1940s. In the 1950s, he became leader of the all-star BBC Show Band, which first appeared on the Light Program on 2 October 1952 and was broadcast three nights a week thereafter. He became known as Mr. Music and led the band for five years. Guest artists such as Frank Sinatra, IRVING BERLIN and Nat 'King' Cole appeared on the show, as well as residents Janie Marlow and the Stargazers group. He gave radio and TV breaks to 'Born Free' singer Matt Munro.

From 1955 to 1957, he recorded with his own band for Decca and produced United Kingdom chart hits such as 'Elephant Tango', 'Blue Star' (theme from the U.S. television series *The Medics*), 'The Italian Theme', 'The Happy Whistler' and 'Forgotten Dreams'. Stapleton also made a hit on both sides of the Atlantic with 'The Children's Marching Song' theme of the movie *The Inn of the Sixth Happiness* (1959). This song was written by Cecil J. Sharp, with lyrics by S. Baring Gould.

He joined Pye Records in January 1966 with his band and became artists and repertory (AR) controller and independent producer. He was responsible for the production of the multimillion-selling *Singalong* series of albums by Max Bygraves. In the last few years of his life, Stapleton began a tour with a big band, attempting to recreate the music of his heyday.

Select Discography

Big Hits from Broadway Ace of Clubs ACL 1003

Broadway Richmond Stereo S 30042

Congress Dances Decca LK4321

Crown Jewels Imperial LP 9165

Dancing in the Dark London LL 1539 [Also on CD]

Dim Lights and Blue Music MGM E3351 (U.K. title: **New York After Dark**)

Golden Hits of '67 Pye NPL 18189

Great Film and Television Hit Themes PYE QUC 1003

Hits from the Classics Richmond 20025

I Wish You Love Lion (MGM) L70056

Italy After Dark Decca LK 4144 (U.K.); MGM E3302 (U.S.)

Just For You Decca SKL 4015

Movie Hits Vol. 1 Richmond Stereo S 30061

Movie Hits Vol. 2 Richmond Stereo S 30062

Music for a Starry Night Decca LK 4162; London LL 1526

Music for Dancing in the Dark London LL 1539 [Also on CD]

Music for Dream Dancing Richmond B 20026

Paris After Dark Decca LK 4143

Song of the Golden West London LL 1723

Songs You Won't Easily Forget Decca SKL 4511

Strings on Parade London LL 1487

Women in Love Pye NSPL 18330

STEINER, MAX (10 May 1888–28 December 1971)
Max Steiner was born in Vienna, Austria. He studied at the Imperial Academy of Music and composed his first operetta, *The Beautiful Greek Girl*, at the age of fifteen. He conducted operettas throughout Europe and England until the outbreak of World War I, in 1914. He moved to the United States, where he arranged and conducted Broadway shows, including those of GEORGE GERSHWIN, VICTOR HERBERT and JEROME KERN. In December 1929, he arrived in Hollywood, first as an orchestrator and subsequently as a composer of scores. His first scores were for *Symphony of Six Million* (1932) and *King Kong* (1933).

After working for RKO, Steiner moved to Warner Brothers in 1936 and composed an average of eight film scores over the next ten years. One of his most notable successes was the music for *Gone with the Wind* (1939). By 1965, the year of his retirement, he had completed over 200 scores. As one of the pioneers of music for talking films, his scores set a precedent that is still evident in Hollywood today. He had a flair for characterization and for exotic local color. He used a direct emotional approach and established the style of scoring dramatic films by accenting the action and emphasizing major dramatic points in the unfolding story of the film. He established the practice of a theme or motif for each character and situation.

Other scores included *Of Human Bondage* (1934), *The Gay Divorcee* (1934), various RKO musicals from 1934 to 1937, *The Informer* (1935), *The Charge of the Light Brigade* (1936), *The Life of Emile Zola* (1937), *Jezebel* (1938), *Dark Victory* (1939), *Now Voyager* (1942), *Casablanca* (1943), *Since You Went Away* (1944), *Rhapsody in Blue* (adaptation, 1945), *Night and Day* (adaptation, 1946), *Johnny Belinda* (1948), *The Flame and the Arrow* (1950), *The Miracle of Our Lady of Fatima* (1952), *The Caine Mutiny* (1954), *A Summer Place* (1959) and *Rome Adventure* (1962).

Select Discography

Gone with the Wind (Conducted by Charles Gerhardt) RCA ARL1–0452

King Kong (Conducted by Fred Steiner) Entr'acte ERS 6504

King Kong (Conducted by Leroy Holmes) United Artists LA373-G

Now Voyager and The Classic Film Scores of Max Steiner RCA ARL1–0136

Since You Went Away, Now Voyager and The Informer Angel S-36068

A Star Is Born (Conducted by Leroy Holmes) United Artists LA375-G

A Summer Place and Helen of Troy (Conducted by Elmer Bernstein) Filmmusic Collection FMC-1

Compact Discs

Classic Max Steiner Silva Screen FILMCD144

Gone with The Wind (National Philharmonic Orchestra. Conductor Charles Gerhardt) RCA Victor GD80452

King Kong (National Philharmonic Orchestra. Conductor Fred Steiner) Label X LXCD10

Now Voyager: The Classic Film Scores of Max Steiner (National Philharmonic Orchestra. Conductor Charles Gerhardt) RCA Victor GD80136

STOLOFF, MORRIS (b. 1 August 1898)

Morris Stoloff was born in Philadelphia and studied the violin. His musical education was financed by W. A. Clark, Jr., backer of the Los Angeles Philharmonic Orchestra. Stoloff was a pupil of Leopold Auer and studied harmony and theory with Brookhoven. He went on a United States concert tour at the age of sixteen and joined the Los Angeles Philharmonic Orchestra in 1918 as its youngest member. Years later he became its guest conductor. From 1928 to 1936, he was associated with Paramount Pictures as concertmaster and subsequently was appointed musical director of Columbia Pictures. Stoloff received Academy Awards for best scoring for the movie *Cover Girl* in 1944, *The Jolson Story* in 1946 and *Song Without Words* in 1960. The film *Picnic* received three Academy Awards and the theme and song 'Moonglow' from the film, recorded by Decca, became a best-selling disc in 1956.

Select Discography

Love Sequence: Themes and Counter-Themes Decca DL 8407

Picnic: Music from the Sound Track of the Columbia Picture Decca DL 8320

STORDAHL, AXEL (8 August 1913–30 August 1963)

Stordahl was born in New York City. He first played trumpet with the Bert Block Band and joined Tommy Dorsey in 1936, where he acted as arranger. Stordahl was able to write swinging music for big bands but preferred sensitive interpretations of ballads. In this capacity he was able to arrange for Frank Sinatra, during his period of employment with Dorsey and later, during his work with record companies.

After leaving Dorsey, Stordahl arranged for and led studio bands on radio and television. He was also employed by record companies. In collaboration with PAUL WESTON, Stordahl wrote the music for 'Day by Day' (lyrics by Sammy Cahn). He died in Encino, California.

Additional Readings

Friedwald, Will. *Sinatra: The Song Is You: A Singer's Art.* New York: Scribner, 1995. pp. 121–61.

Select Discography

Christmas in Scandinavia Decca DL 8933

Dreamtime Capitol H 445 (10")

Guitars Around the World Decca DL 74337

Jasmine and Jade DOT DLP 3282

Lure of the Blue Mediterranean Decca DL 79073

Magic Islands Revisited Decca DL 79096

STOTT, WALLY/ANGELA MORLEY (b. 10 March 1924)
Wally Stott was born in Leeds. He learned the piano at the age of eight but was forced to give up lessons on the death of his father. The family moved to live with his mother's parents, near Rotherham. Stott took up playing the piano accordion and won a competition for juveniles. In the 1930s he learned to play the saxophone and was engaged by Mexborough military band. He left school at the age of fifteen to become a professional woodwind player and found work with Archie Robinson, who ran a touring juvenile band. He also found temporary employment as an assistant projectionist in 1939.

In 1940, he left the employment of Archie Robinson and worked with various dance bands, including those of Tommy Smith, Billy Merrin, Bram Martin and Oscar Rabin, making his first BBC broadcasts. He stayed with the latter until 1943 and for the first time tried his hand at arranging music.

In 1944, Stott joined the GERALDO Orchestra as second alto player and continued to write arrangements. He came into contact with ROBERT FARNON at this period, from whom he learned much about arranging scores.

In 1946, he went back to studying music under the tuition of Matyas Seiber and later with Hugh Wood. He also studied conducting in classes given by Walter Goehr. This period of study ended in 1950.

Stott finally left Geraldo in 1948 but continued to arrange for him. He wrote for the BBC's radio bands and sometimes for Ted Heath, who had been a fellow member of Geraldo's band. He also did work for SIDNEY TORCH and STANLEY BLACK in the early 1950s.

Stanley Black at this period was employed in film composing, concert conducting and extensive recording for Decca. Black asked Stott to ghostwrite some film scores. He was also hosting the *Goon Show*, which he handed over to Stott each week. After a while, Black stepped down from this show, and Stott took over completely. He also became involved in the musical production aspect of *Hancock's Half Hour*, which was just starting at this period.

Stott wrote the scores for several films in the 1950s, including *Will Any Gentleman?* (1953), *For Better or Worse* (1954), *It's Never Too Late*

(1955) and a musical with Vera-Ellen and Tony Martin entitled *Let's Be Happy*.

In 1953, Philips started their own label in England, and Stott was appointed musical director. He made his first recordings as conductor/arranger under his own name. From 1954 to 1959 he continued to do radio shows. He wrote extensively for the CHAPPELL 'Mood' Label at the invitation of Robert Farnon. One of the singers Wally introduced to Philips was Frankie Vaughan. Stott also scored Vaughan's first two films, *The Lady Is a Square* (1957) and *The Heart of a Man* (1958). He gave up film work in 1960 to concentrate on recording.

American material for the Philips's label came mainly from Columbia Records in the United States. Norman Newell was in charge and commissioned Stott to arrange several 10" LPs of the well-known composers GEORGE GERSHWIN, IRVING BERLIN, RICHARD RODGERS and JEROME KERN. Newell was succeeded by Johnny Franz. One of his first visitors from the United States was the producer Nat Shapiro, who was anxious to obtain material in the same style as MICHEL LEGRAND's *I Love Paris* album. Stott was assigned to write *London Pride.* Other albums followed, including *Spellbound, Venezuela, A Kid for Two Farthings* and *A Girl Called Linda.* Stott also did backings for various singers, including Anne Shelton, Shirley Bassey, Harry Secombe, Rosemary Squires, Dusty Springfield and Susan Maughan.

He was chosen to score an album of Marlene Dietrich's German cabaret songs during her visit to London to perform at the Café de Paris. He derived great pleasure from his recordings of Mel Tormé on a 10" LP entitled *Mel Tormé Meets the British.* A subsequent album was completed in partnership with GEOFF LOVE and TONY OSBORNE. This album, released in 1962, was entitled *My Kind of Music.* Stott also made an album with NOËL COWARD during this period.

In 1959, Stott was given a short contract with Pye Records. He made a Christmas album entitled *Christmas by the Fireside.* In 1960 the influence of rock and roll caused a change in the record business. This new trend did not appeal to Stott, and he turned his attention to projects away from the English market.

In January 1961, he began a series of albums in collaboration with his close friend, Norman Luboff, the American choral director. The first album was called *A Choral Spectacular.* The second album, issued in 1962, was entitled *Grand Tour.* This was followed in the same year by *Inspiration*, which also featured the conductor Leopold Stokowski. Luboff and Stott also did two albums for READER'S DIGEST under the pseudonym, John Norman. Stott arranged or conducted on at least six other Reader's Digest sets.

In 1964, he returned to film scoring when he did the music for documentaries on Florentine art *The World of Florentine Sculpture* (1962) and *The World of Florentine Painting* (1963). He collaborated on Michael

Lewis's score for *The Mad Woman of Chaillot* and wrote the music in 1969 for *The Looking Glass War, Captain Nemo* and *The Underwater City*. The last film Stott scored before his gender change was Alistair Maclean's *When Eight Bells Toll* (1970). He also arranged for the Benny Goodman Band recording for Philips in 1969.

In 1970, Wally became Angela Morley and spent eighteen months studying clarinet chamber music at Watford School of Music. Her return to film scoring began in 1972, with her contributions to *The Little Prince* and *Jesus Christ Superstar*. She received an Academy Award nomination for *The Little Prince* in 1974. Between 1974 and 1976, she worked on the music for *The Slipper and the Rose*, which also received an Academy Award nomination in 1977. A year later she contributed most of the score for *Watership Down*, which opened in autumn of 1978 and received the IVOR NOVELLO Award nomination for best score. She then moved to California, where she worked on other film scores, including *Star Wars*, *The Empire Strikes Back*, *Superman*, *E.T.*, *Equus*, *Carney*, *Death Trap*, *The Verdict*, *Fire and Ice*, *Dead Men Don't Wear Plaid*, *The Day After*, *Max Duggan Returns*, *The Buddy System*, *Cuba*, *The Right Stuff*, *Karate Kid*, *Sudden Impact*, *Dirty Harry*, *Home Alone*, *Hook*, *Home Alone II* and *Schindler's List*.

In 1990, Morley made a suite of ALEX NORTH's music from the film *A Streetcar Named Desire*. From 1979 onward she worked on television films such as *Friendships, Secrets and Lies* (Warner Bros. 1979); *Madame X* (Universal, 1981); *Summer Girl* (Finnegan's Associates, 1983) and *Threesome* (CBS, 1984). Scores for television episodes included *Wonderwoman*, *McClain's Law*, *Emerald Point*, *Two Marriages*, *Dynasty*, *The Colbys*, *Falcon Crest*, *Blue Skies*, *Cagney and Lacey*, *Hotel*, *Island Sun* and *Dallas*.

Angela Morley has written arrangements and in several cases conducted for Leopold Stokowski, Frederica von Stade, Barbara Hendricks, the London Symphony Orchestra, the London Philharmonic Orchestra, and Sergio Franchi. She also arranged and orchestrated for famous Hollywood composers and for Mel Tormé, Julie Andrews, Benny Goodman Band, Rosemary Clooney, Cincinnati Pops Orchestra and the BOSTON POPS ORCHESTRA. On summer visits to the United Kingdom she conducted the BBC Radio Orchestra from 1974 until its disbandment in 1991. She has conducted recordings in London, Los Angeles, Stockholm, Paris, Milan, Luxembourg and Vienna.

She has been awarded three Emmy Awards, received eleven Emmy nominations, two Academy Award nominations, an Ivor Novello Award nomination and a British BAFTA [British Academy of Film and Television Arts] nomination.

She has given an annual lecture at the University of Southern California to students studying film and television composing and has served on the executive committee of the music branch of the Academy of Arts and Sciences from 1980 to 1990. She was a founding governor of the Society of Composers and Lyricists, Inc.

From 1980 to 1994, Morley was a resident of Los Angeles. In 1994, she moved to Scottsdale, Arizona. She no longer scores for television but writes occasional arrangements for JOHN WILLIAMS's films or CDs.

Compositions

Orchestra

Chappell LPs LPC 501–506 'Crosstalk', 'Italian Street Music', 'Austrian Tyrol', 'Tradewind', 'Swissair', 'Gypsy Theme', 'Neapolitan Love Song', 'Norwegian Pastoral Dance', 'Norwegian Spring Dance', 'Zoo Cues'; LPC 1038 'Dancing Jack'; LPC 1027 'Bright Eyes', 'Picadilly', 'Plastic Jam', 'Jay Walker', 'Monique'; LPC 1033 'Show the Flag'; LPC 1037 'Quickies 1–11; C 155020 'Light Atmosphere, Vol. 3', 'Holiday Highway', 'Rotten Row', 'Fun in the Sun'.

In the United States a package of four records, 'Overseas Interludes', was produced in 1958 containing the following compositions: 'Travelling Along' CH102 (CH88584); 'A Canadian in Mayfair', 'Quizz' CH103 (CH88587); 'Lap of Luxury/Starlight' (CH88588); 'Miss Universe' CH104; CH88585 'Adrift in a Dream/Dreamy Mood'. Other compositions include 'Kehaar's Theme' (From *Watership Down*) Alto Sax and Orchestra, 'When Eight Bells Toll' (From film of same name), 'The Looking Glass War' (From film of same name) and 'White Wing' (From episode of *Hotel*).

Chamber Music

Four Characters for Clarinet and Piano 1983 (Novello)

Select Discography

Best of Gershwin and Berlin U.K. WING WL 1031

Christmas by the Fireside U.K. NPL 18038; condensed reissue MAL 689. American title **Happy Holiday Christmas in Hi Fi/Stereo** Warner Brothers W/WS 1341

Choral Spectacular (Arranger with RCA Victor Symphony Orchestra) RCA LPM/LSP 2522

Chorale in Concert Great Britain LPS 16000

Embraceable You: Tribute to George Gershwin U.K. BBR 8004; U.S. EPIC 1009 LG

Great American Show Tunes (Kern/Gershwin/Berlin) U.S. EPIC LG 3085

Little Prince (sound track) U.S. Dunhill Abdp 854

London Pride U.K. BBL 7255 (SBBL 501); reissue London Souvenir AL 3432/SAL 3432; revised issue 6460/103; U.S. Columbia CL 1170 [Also on CD]

Slipper and the Rose U.S. EM 3116 (OCO62/97419

The Song Is You: Tribute to Jerome Kern U.K. BBR 8082; U.S. EPIC LG 1012

There's No Business Like Show Business: Tribute to Irving Berlin U.K. BBR 8053; U.S. EPIC LG 1007

Two in the Balcony U.S. Epic 10011

Watership Down (sound track) U.S. Columbia 35707; U.K. CBS 70161

Note: Numerous Wally Stott recordings were also released in a variety of Reader's Digest albums, such as:

Background Moods RDS 6107

Fabulous Fifties RD 9431–9440

Great Music from Great Movies RDS 6315

Hits From the Shows

Magical World of Melody RDS 6040

Stardust Melodies RD 9401–9408

Orchestrations

Choral Spectacular. Norman Luboff Choir and the RCA Victor Symphony Orchestra U.S. RCA Victor LPM/LSP 2522 1962

Grand Tour. Norman Luboff Choir U.S. RCA Victor LPM/LSP 2821 1962

Living Strings. Geraldo Orchestra U.K. Camden CAL/CAS 835

Music of Jerome Kern. Stanley Black and Kingsway Promenade Orchestra U.S. London LL579 1954; Reissue Richmond B Z0011/S 30011; Great Britain Decca Reissue Ace of Clubs ACL 1031 [Also on CD]

T

TAUTZ, WERNER (b. 1922)
Werner Tautz was born in Leipzig. He began his career as a pianist for dance and light orchestras, after the end of World War II (1946). He also began to compose at this time, producing about 500 pieces ranging from jazz music to symphonic concert waltzes. He started collaborating with HEINZ KIESSLING in 1960 in the composition of instrumental light music for various record labels. The two founded their own label, Brillant-Musik, in 1964. Their first album, *Coloured Strings* was issued in Berlin and became internationally famous, mainly due to Kiessling's arrangements.

During this period, Tautz wrote his most successful composition, 'Dream Concert', which was frequently performed on the radio. In the 1980s, his son, Joachim, founded the CD label Bliss Records, which reproduced many of the titles popular in the 1960s and 1970s.

TERRY, DAVID
David Terry served as chief arranger for ANDRE KOSTELANETZ and worked closely with other important conductors, including PERCY FAITH. He also served for many years as chief arranger at National Broadcasting Corporation, supervising musical scores, and was musical director of several Broadway shows in the 1950s and 1960s.

Select Discography

Bernstein's Broadway: The Great Show Music of Leonard Bernstein. Warner WS 1325

Waltzing in Hi-Fi Warner W/WS 1302

THOMAS, MICHAEL TILSON (b. 1944)
Michael Tilson Thomas, the American pianist and conductor, was born in Hollywood, California. He served as assistant conductor to Pierre Boulez at the Ojai Festival in 1967, assistant conductor to the Boston Symphony Orchestra in 1969 and associate conductor in 1970. He became musical director of the Buffalo Philharmonic Orchestra from 1971 to 1979.

He has traveled extensively and acted as guest conductor in various cities throughout the world. He was principal conductor of the London Symphony Orchestra from 1988 to 1995, after making his debut in 1970 and has performed and recorded in England, the Continent, and worldwide. In 1991, he conducted the orchestra with LEONARD BERNSTEIN and shared in the Pacific Musical Festival in Japan.

Tilson Thomas has strong ties with the American music scene. He conducted the Boston Symphony Orchestra and the Chicago Symphony Orchestra and has been the principal conductor of the San Francisco Orchestra since 1995. He has an affinity for American composers such as Charles Ives. His 1975–76 season featured the orchestral works of Carl Ruggles, a contemporary of Charles Ives, as part of the celebration of the American Bicentennial. In 1981, he conducted a new production of Janacek's *The Cunning Little Vixen* at the New York City Opera. In 1987, he founded the New World Music Festival in Miami and conducted the orchestra between 1987 and 1991.

Select Discography

George Gershwin (Columbia Jazz Band) CBS 76509

Gershwin on Broadway: Overtures (Buffalo Philharmonic Orchestra) Columbia 34542 [Reissued on compact disc]

TIOMKIN, DIMITRI (10 May 1894–11 November 1979)
Dimitri Tiomkin was born in St. Petersburg, Russia, and studied piano and composition at the St. Petersburg Conservatory. He then moved to Berlin, where he studied under Ferruccio Busoni. He worked with Michael Kariton as a duo-piano team and visited the United States in 1925. In 1928, Tiomkin performed the European premiere of GERSHWIN's *Concerto in F*, in Paris.

In 1929, he moved to America, where his wife, the choreographer Albertina Rasch, found employment in Hollywood, devising ballet sequences for musical films. In 1930, Tiomkin composed some short ballets for MGM musicals. His first original score was for *Resurrection* (1931). His major breakthrough was the score for *Lost Horizon* (1937), directed by Frank Capra. He developed an exceptional skill in composing scores for Western films, such as *The Westerner* (1940), *Duel in the Sun* (1946), *The Big Sky* and *High Noon* (both 1952), *Giant* (1956) and *Gunfight at the O.K. Corral* (1957). He won an Academy Award for the score and ballad 'Do Not

Forsake Me', which, as sung by Tex Ritter, was featured in *High Noon* (1955).

Later film scores included *The Guns of Navarone* (1961), *55 Days at Peking* (1963), *The Fall of the Roman Empire* (1964) and *The War Wagon* (1967). After the death of his wife, he moved to London and remarried. The final film he scored was *Great Katherine* (1968).

Select Discography

Alamo. Suite (Conducted by Stanley Black) London SP 44173

Lost Horizon and the Classic Film RCA ARL1–1669

Old Man and the Sea Columbia ACS 8013

Thing from Another World Suite (Conducted by Charles Gerhardt) RCA ARL 42005

Compact Discs

Fall of the Roman Empire (Original Sound Track.) Cloud Nine ACN7016

Friendly Persuasion (Original Sound Track) Movie Sound MSCD402

High Noon. Original Film Scores of Dimitri Tiomkin. (Berlin Radio Choir and Symphony Orchestra. Conductor Lawrence Foster) RCA Victor Red Seal 09026 6258–2

Lost Horizon. The Classic Film Scores of Dimitri Tiomkin (National Philharmonic Orchestra. Conductor Charles Gerhardt) RCA Victor GD81669

Western Film World of Dimitri Tiomkin (London Studio Symphony Orchestra. Conductor Laurie Johnson) Unicorn-Kanchana UKCD 20111

TOMLINSON, ERNEST

Ernest Tomlinson is a British composer and conductor who founded his own light orchestra in 1955. In 1969, he founded the Northern Concert Orchestra, which broadcast regularly from Manchester during the 1970s, specializing in performances of contemporary composers. Tomlinson has made many recordings for music publishers for film and television and has conducted concerts abroad. He has made compact disc recordings of his own works and the works of British light music composers such as HAYDN WOOD and RONALD BINGE.

Select Discography

British Light Music: Ronald Binge

British Light Music: Ernest Tomlinson Marco Polo 8223413, 8223513

British Light Music: Miniatures (Radio Television Concert Orchestra, Dublin) Marco Polo 8.223522

TORCH, SIDNEY (1908–16 July 1990)

Torch was born in London, educated at the Septimus Webb School and trained as an organist with Archie Parkhouse. He accompanied silent films at the Stratford Broadway cinema, East London, before obtaining a position in the early 1930s with Emmanuel Starkey's Orchestra. After assisting Quentin Maclean, he took over the Christie organ at the Regal, Marble Arch, London, from 1932 to 1934. He also played the organ at the Union Cinema and the Gaumont State Cinema, Kilburn. The first recording of his organ recitals was probably made at Marble Arch in 1932. He also recorded a succession of Columbia recordings at various London cinemas. He broadcast regularly during this period and made further records with the singer Les Allen, the saxophonist Howard Jacobs, violinist Albert Sandler and the Regal Virtuosi, who had originated with Emmanuel Starkey's Regal Cinema Orchestra.

After serving in the Royal Air Force during World War II, he gave up organ playing and concentrated on composing, arranging and conducting. He led the Queen's Hall Light Orchestra and subsequently joined BBC Radio. After 1946, Torch collaborated with Harry Alan Towers who set up his own radio production company, known as Towers of London. Torch supplied much of the music for the company, which made and distributed programs for sale overseas and was linked to IBC and Radio Luxembourg.

Torch's first recording with his own forty-piece orchestra appeared on Parlophone in January 1947. This was the 'London Fantasia' by CLIVE RICHARDSON, with the composer at the piano. The first of Torch's own compositions to be released was 'Samba Sud'.

Columbia Records released 78 rpm recordings of Torch conducting the Queen's Hall Light Orchestra. He also recorded for the CHAPPELL library and conducted the New Century Orchestra for Francis, Day and Hunter. In addition, he made a number of recordings for the American Lang–Worth library of New York, which produced many transcription discs for radio and television use.

In 1953, he devised the program *Friday Night Is Music Night.* He conducted the BBC Concert Orchestra and contributed many original arrangements and compositions. He also recorded pieces such as 'The Dambusters March', 'Canadian Capers', 'The Petite Waltz', 'Domino' and the first recording of the Jose Belmont composition, 'Ecstasy', which became a best-seller. In the later 1950s, his commercial recording output decreased in quantity. He made a few recordings for Decca in 1963, which included his 'Soft Shoe Shuffler' and 'Trapeze Waltz'.

He retired from the BBC in 1972 but his name was perpetuated in the program *Friday Night Is Music Night.* In 1985 he received an MBE. In 1989, a whole BBC program was devoted to Torch and his music. His compositions included 'The Trapeze Waltz', 'Cornflakes', 'On a Spring Note, 'Meandering', 'Shooting Star', 'Dance of the Marionettes', 'Hot Dog',

'Temptation Rag' and 'Twelfth Street Rag'. He also wrote the incidental music for radio shows such as *Much Binding in the Marsh*.

Select Discography

Columbia Records (With Queens Hall Light Orchestra)

Boulevardier, Jamaican Flirt DB 2421

Coronation Scot, Horse Guards—Whitehall DB2406

Nell Gwynn (Edward German): **Overture** DB2867

Pale Moon, Song of Capri DB2564

Petite Suite de Concert (Coleridge-Taylor) DB2479–80

Portrait of a Flirt, Music in the Air DB2436

Shooting Star, Dance of an Ostracized Imp DB 7456

Wellington Barracks, Wayfarer's Song DB2498

Long-Playing Records

Sidney Torch Programme 10" PMDJ 1008

Compact Discs

Sidney Torch (Compilation of Light Orchestral recordings) EMI CD: CDHMV 2, Cassette: TCHMV 2

THREE SUNS. *See* NEVINS, AL

TOYE, GEOFFREY (1889–1942)

Geoffrey Toye was born in Winchester and studied at the Royal College of Music, London. After the end of World War I he became a conductor, first with the D'Oyly Carte Opera Company and later at the Old Vic and Sadler's Wells.

Toye also conducted symphonic music and served for a while as managing director of the Royal Opera House Company. He was responsible for the revival of the Gilbert and Sullivan opera *Ruddigore* in 1921, for which he rewrote the overture. He returned to the D'Oyly Carte Opera and adapted, produced and conducted the film version of *The Mikado* in 1939. He also wrote a radio opera *The Red Pen*, in collaboration with A. P. Herbert. His first ballet was for Ninette de Valois's *Douanes*. This was followed by *The Haunted Ballroom* in 1939.

TROTTER, JOHN SCOTT

John Scott Trotter, an American conductor and arranger, was educated in the classical tradition at North Carolina University. He subsequently joined the Hal Kemp Band at the Manger Grill in New York and did arrangements for the singer, Skinnay Ennis. He came to the attention of Bing Crosby, who persuaded Trotter to become his musical arranger in 1937 and conduct the backing orchestra for the Kraft radio show. Trotter remained with the show for more than three hundred sessions. He finally left in 1945, when Crosby's association with the show ended. He continued to be associated with Crosby on his radio and TV shows and also arranged the music for Bing Crosby's records, including the backing for the original recording for Decca of 'White Christmas' (1942) from the film *Holiday Inn* and 'Swinging on a Star' (1944) from the film *Going My Way*. Trotter remained with Crosby for seventeen years and subsequently recorded for Warner Brothers as an arranger and conductor.

Select Discography

Escape to the Magic Mediterranean Warner W1266

John Scott Trotter's Music Hall Warner W1333

A Thousand and One Notes Warner W1223

V

VAN DER LINDEN, DOLF (born David Gysbert) (b. 22 June 1915)
Dolf van der Linden was born in the Dutch fishing village of Vlaardingen. He was the son of a music dealer, who owned several shops of musical instruments. Under the tuition of his father, he started violin lessons at the age of seven. He showed little academic inclination and left school at an early age to enter his father's business as an aspiring piano tuner.

He went on to study the art of composition at an academy, where he continued his violin and piano lessons. Later, in Rotterdam, he studied instrumentation, composition and harmony under Henri Zagwijn. From the outset, he was interested in light symphonic music and jazz and especially in improvisation.

Music dominated his every action, and he spent holidays traveling through the country as a street musician. At this period of his life he also began to compose. Van der Linden longed to conduct his own orchestra and collected a number of musicians together from local bands, forming an orchestra that played at local events. At the age of sixteen, he obtained a position as organist at a theater in his birthplace, where he remained for a number of years. During the 1930s, he experienced extreme difficulties in pursuing his musical career. He served as an arranger for a touring dance orchestra. Between 1936 and 1939, he became a regular arranger for various radio orchestras.

In 1939, he wrote a lengthy paraphrase on a well-known theme and submitted it to Radio Hilversum. An engagement as arranger-composer followed, and his career seemed secured. However, the Second World War

Dolf van der Linden

broke out, during which he was captured by the Germans and forced to do hard labor in Germany. He escaped and reached Holland after several months and spent the rest of the war in hiding.

After the liberation, van der Linden played with a small ensemble in a club for Canadian officers in a street called Parklaan. This was the origin of his distinctive signature tune 'Parklane Serenade', which became internationally famous. Before long, he was approached by the local broadcasting authorities Herryzen Nederland (Rising Netherlands) and asked to form an orchestra of thirty-two musicians, specializing in light music. The name Metropole Orchestra was chosen at the suggestion of one of the musicians.

The orchestra's emphasis is on quality and originality, in no small measure because van der Linden combined his enthusiasm and aspirations with the outstanding technical qualities of the orchestra.

The Metropole Orchestra has for many years consisted of seventeen violins, five violas, four cellos, two double basses, one harp, two percussions, one bass, one drum, two flutes, one oboe/English horn, one French horn, five saxes, four trumpets, four trombones, one piano and one synthesizer, fifty-two musicians in all.

Unlike many other conductors, composers and arrangers, van der Linden has always been under contract to the Dutch National Radio System. He has never freelanced, thus depriving himself of the opportunity to have complete freedom in the choice of compositions and arrangements. Although he was invited to create the Metropole Orchestra and served as its chief conductor, the State Radio and Broadcast Systems were his bosses. Even to this day, Metropole Orchestra is still kept alive by the State organization named Nederlands Omroep Stichting (NOS). In 1980, at age sixty-five, van der Linden had to step down as principal conductor, but the Radio Management and members of the orchestra insisted that he continue for another five years, which he completed.

Musical Achievements

Dolf van der Linden made a number of successful guest appearances with the British Broadcasting Corporation, the Swedish, Norwegian, Danish, Belgian, French and Dutch radios, and in Israel. Here the radio authorities asked him to form an orchestra similar to the Metropole Orchestra, and he achieved this in about six weeks; the orchestra has recently been dissolved. Van der Linden was also regularly invited to England. During the Nord Ring Festival in 1974, he won an award (given once only) for the best conductor. Also at a Nord Ring Festival, in September 1981, he conducted the BBC Radio Orchestra in Jersey where the Dutch team won first prize and was named festival winner.

Metro Music has been in existence for almost thirty years, during many of them, a coproduction between the BBC in England and NOS. It was jointly financed for seven years by both radio companies, but more recently the Dutch Radio has financed the program on its own. The cream of British and American soloists were often featured in the program, with van der Linden as accompanist. They included, among others, Mark Murphy, Bill Evans, Phil Woods, Bud Shank, Frank Wess, Toots Thielemans, Bob Cooper, Bill Perkins and Al Cohn. Recordings were made for Philips, Columbia (U.K.), Capitol (U.S.) as well as Paxton (London) and Brull (London), the latter two, often of film music.

During the first twenty years of the Metropole's existence, the principal arrangers were, besides van der Linden himself, Manny Oets (his first pianist), Tony van Hulst (his first guitarist), Bert Paige (a Belgian musician whose real name was Albert Lepage, and who was a former trumpeter of the famous Dutch Orchestra, the Ramblers), Joop Elders (who arranged mostly semiclassical music), Rob Pronk (the main arranger for some ten to fifteen years and one of the principal conductors succeeding van der Linden in 1985), Lex Jasper (an important arranger), Pi Scheffer (in the early years) and Jerry van Rooyen (who conducted the orchestra occasionally after van der Linden left).

Dolf van der Linden used a number of pseudonyms during the course of his recording career, which included Van Lynn and Daniel de Carlo (both on the Decca label), Gerard Blene (on the Jubilee label), Alex Pinto (on HMV 78s), Paul Franklyn, David Johnson and Guy Brain (on 78s). Brain was actually the pseudonym of a wealthy Hollander called Van Beuningen, who made his fortune in the oil business. He paid van der Linden handsomely for composing and conducting, while he, himself, listened and smoked cigars during recording sessions.

Van der Linden composed some 180 compositions, many of which were published. He also wrote music for several Dutch films, numerous radio plays, lyrical dramas and operettas. His own views on the nature of his music are revealed in the sleeve notes for Ongetrouwd Man Kamer. 'I try to find the way to the heart of everyone', he wrote to Capitol Records. 'My great love is my orchestra—my music—and I envisage music as being a combination of wonderful colors. I like the natural sound of musical instruments—I detest technical tricks—and only music that comes to you healthy and clean can speak directly to your heart. This is language without words'.

Van der Linden, known for years as the Kostelanetz of Western Europe, deserves to be known as a superb maestro in his own right, of the same genre and caliber as PERCY FAITH, MORTON GOULD and ANDRE KOSTELANETZ. He is a landmark figure in the world of popular orchestral music.

Published Compositions by Dolf van der Linden

Ardmore & Beechwood, Ltd.: By Starlight (also known as Little Star)
Brull: Mambingo; Adios, Guidiano; Blow the Horn; Jamaica Road; Forest Fantasy; Bouncing Boy; Palais de Dance; Pennsylvania Dutch; Marionette March
Chacksfield: Four A.M.; Bolero Taludo; Leblon
De Wolfe: Souvenir
Francis Day: Terra Del Fuego; Entre Rios
Melodia Amsterdam: Pobre Tonto; Land of Promise
Metro Music: Parklane Serenade
Modern Stuttgart: Concertino for Orchestra
Paxton: Four Playing; Fanfares; Bal Masque; Remembrance; Temple Bar; State Occasion; Hyde Park; Carnival Time; Table Talk; The Dancing Jack; Vampire (Man from Mars); Leicester Square Dance; Sagé-Brush; Hora Hurray; Utopia Road; South Winds; My Lady's Lorgnette (Face a Main); Pop Squeak; Morning Light; Final Line; Storm and Stress; Top Drawer; High Treason—Hill Top—Oceans—

Undercover; Grand Strategy—Court Jester—Thunder Bird; Peter Pan; Tragico; Grand Canyon; Valse Melancolique; Horn Pipe; Miniature Overture—Tension; Factory on Wheels—The Jug and the Bottle—Motor Races—Parade of the Bottles

Prop Antwerp: The Bells Are Singing; Dancing Feet

Southern Synchro: Coffeebean Calypso; Automotive—Power Plant

Wolters Groningen: Ferdinant; Hab Mich Lieb

World Music: Love Affair; Little Romance; Spanish Dance; Prima Ballerina; Tides (Marees); Slavia; Song of Spain; Les Danseurs Mondains; Blues; Librations Rhapsody; Prima Ballerina

Note: Van der Linden also wrote unpublished music, music for several Dutch films, numerous radio plays, lyrical dramas and operettas. In total, this results in approximately 180 compositions.

Select Discography (under various pseudonyms)

BLENE, ***Gerard***

Moment of Desire Jubilee

Time for Love Jubilee

DE CARLO, ***Daniel***

Moonlight Madness Decca DL 8452

One Night of Love Decca DL 8447

This Is Romance Decca DL 8488

LYNN, ***Van***

Candlelight Melodies Decca DL 8062

Escape Brunswick LAT 8080

Listening Pleasure Brunswick LAT 8165, Decca DL 8066

My One and Only Love Decca DL 8094

One Night of Madness Decca DL 8065

South American Contrasts Brunswick LAT 8074, Decca DL 8064

Whispering Moonlight Decca DL 8063

Select Discography (under own name)

A Carol Symphony (Composed by Victor Hely Hutchinson) Paxton. LPT 1002 (10" LP)

Casino on the Riviera Camden CAL 259

Claire de Lune Philips 78 rpm

Dutch Moonlight Capitol T 10070

Dutch Sax Capitol T 10061

Golden Violins Epic LN 3296

Listen to Nature Camden CAL 260

Moto Perpetuo P 010095

Ongetrouwd Man Kamer! (Bachelor's Apartment) Capitol T 10058

Seductive Saxophone Columbia, Britain 33SX1056

Starlight Reverie Columbia, Britain 33SX1156

String Serenade South African Philips P 10013 R. 10" LP

Notes: 'Casino on the Riviera', 'Listen to Nature', 'Candlelight Melodies' and 'Whispering Moonlight' all feature compositions by Dutch and Belgian composers promoted by van der Linden's manager and publisher Jack Kluger, who owned World Music.

The Jubilee label was distributed by World Music, and the composers are mostly the same as those on the Van Lynn and Daniel de Carlo LPs listed in this discography. Jack Kluger issued these two LPs without van der Linden's knowledge.

The biographical information was mainly obtained from interviews with Dolf van der Linden. For this, the authors are indebted to Robert van Camp.

VAN HEUSEN, JAMES (JIMMY) (born Edward Chester Babcock) (26 January 1913–6 February 1990)

James van Heusen was born in Syracuse, New York, and educated at Casenovia College and Syracuse University. He showed a keen interest in music, playing the piano and attempting to write songs in high school. At the age of sixteen he started work as a radio announcer on station WSYR, Syracuse, where he changed his name for professional purposes from Babcock to Van Heusen.

HAROLD ARLEN brought Van Heusen to New York to assist him in writing for the Cotton Club Revues. Subsequently, he worked as a demo pianist for a publishing house and in 1938 met bandleader Jimmy Dorsey. Dorsey liked one of Van Heusen's tunes and wrote lyrics for it; it became the successful 'It's the Dreamer in Me'. He also wrote several numbers with bandleader and songwriter Eddie de Lange, including 'Deep in a Dream' (1938), followed by 'All This and Heaven Too' and 'Heaven Can Wait', both in 1939. Van Heusen and de Lange also wrote the music for the Broadway show *Swingin' the Dream.*

At this time Van Heusen met Frank Sinatra, who had just joined the Tommy Dorsey Orchestra, and lyricist Johnny Burke, who was to replace Eddie de Lange. One of the earliest Van Heusen-Burke songs was 'Polka Dots and Moonbeams', made into a hit by the Tommy Dorsey Orchestra, with vocals by Frank Sinatra. From then onward, Sinatra became an enthusiastic supporter of Van Heusen's compositions and contributed to his success.

In 1940, Van Heusen was invited to write the score for the film *Love Thy Neighbor*. This was followed by the Bing Crosby–Bob Hope film *Road to Zanzibar* (1941). For both of these productions, the lyricist was Johnny Burke. From then on, Van Heusen wrote the music for some eighteen films starring Bing Crosby. He became a composer of the most popular songs of all time, including such numbers as 'Moonlight Becomes You' (from *Road to Morocco*, 1942); 'Personality' (from *The Road to Utopia*, 1945); 'Swingin' on a Star' (from *Going My Way*, which earned an Oscar, 1944); 'Aren't You Glad You're You?' (from *The Bells of St. Mary's*, 1945) and 'Sunshine Cake' (from *Riding High*, 1950).

From 1954 onward, Van Heusen worked with lyricist Sammy Cahn. Together they produced the score for the Frank Sinatra film *The Tender Trap* (1955), closely followed by 'Love and Marriage', first heard in a television show and later given an Emmy Award. The Van Heusen-Cahn team received three Oscars for songs they wrote for Frank Sinatra. These included 'All the Way' from *The Joker Is Wild* (1957); 'High Hopes' from the movie *A Hole in the Head* (1959) and 'Call Me Irresponsible' from *Papa's Delicate Condition* (1963). Other memorable songs are 'Pocketful of Miracles' (1961), 'My Kind of Town' (1964) and 'The September of My Years' (1965), which won a Grammy Award.

Additional Readings

Ewen, David. *American Songwriters*. New York: H. W. Wilson, 1987. pp. 403–08.

Ewen, David. *Great Men of American Popular Song*. Englewood Cliffs, NJ: Prentice-Hall, 1970. pp. 321–39.

Select Discography

Faith, Percy. **It's So Peaceful in the Country: Music of Jimmy van Heusen and Alec Wilder** Columbia CL 779 [Also on CD]

Heart Strings (Conductor not named) **Moonlight Becomes You: Music of Jimmy van Heusen** Jubilee 1019

VARDI, EMANUEL

Emanuel Vardi was born in Jerusalem and came to the United States at the age of four. He studied music at Juilliard and established himself as a leading violist. He played with many major orchestras and gave recitals at home and abroad. He also achieved fame as a conductor with a repertoire ranging from baroque to contemporary works. He recorded both as arranger and conductor and served as producer for the Kapp Medallion Record Company in New York. He became identified with Stravinsky's 'Histoire du Soldat', which he performed on television.

Vardi served as musical director and conductor of the Chatham Sinfonietta and the West Hempstead Symphony Orchestra of Long Island. He also worked on the Broadway stage as associate conductor for Gian Carlo

Menotti's production of *The Saint of Bleeker Street* and conducted at Carnegie Hall. As conductor of the Concert Masters of New York, he recorded a series of string concerts for Decca Records. Vardi also had great artistic abilities as a painter. He studied art in the United States and abroad, and his paintings were exhibited in leading galleries and museums.

Select Discography

Can This Be Love? RCA Camden CAL 372

Great Movie Hits of the Thirties KAPP Medallion Records MS-7530 (S)

Holiday in South America Brunswick LAT 8112

Love Dances of Brazil (With Bernardo Segall at the piano) Decca DL 78764

Maggie's Theme KAPP Medallion ML-7527

More Sounds of Hollywood KAPP KS-3289

Sound of Hollywood (With the Medallion Strings) KAPP Medallion ML-7513

Voice of the Strings KAPP 9059

VAUGHN, BILLY (12 April 1919–14 September 1991)
Billy Vaughn was born in Kentucky and began his career with the vocal group the Hilltoppers in 1952. He worked as musical director for Dot Records and as an arranger and conductor for Pat Boone, the Fontaine Sisters, Gale Storm and other Dot artists. His hits of the 1950s include 'Melody of Love' and 'The Shifting, Whispering Sands'. He was also able to play eight or nine musical instruments, and his arrangements varied from his 'twin sax' trademark, as in his album *Golden Saxophones*, to the gentle strings and voices of his *Billy Vaughn Plays Stephen Foster*.

Select Discography

Big 100 Dot DLP 10500

Billy Vaughn Plays Dot DLP 3156

Billy Vaughn Plays Stephen Foster Dot DLP 3260

Billy Vaughn Plays the Million Sellers Dot DLP 3119

Christmas Carols Dot DLP 3148

Blue Hawaii Dot DLP 3165

Golden Hits Dot DLP 3201

Golden Instrumentals Dot DLP 3016

Golden Saxophones Dot DLP 3205

Instrumental Souvenirs Dot DLP 3045

Linger Awhile Dot DLP 3275

Look for a Star Dot DLP 3322

Melodies in Gold Dot DLP 3064

Music for the Golden Hours Dot DLP 3086

La Paloma Dot DLP 3140

Sail Along, Silv'ry Moon Dot DLP 3100

Sweet Music and Memories Dot DLP 3001

Theme from 'A Summer Place' Dot DLP 25276

VINTNER, GILBERT (1901–1969)

Gilbert Vintner was born in Lincoln in England, and sang in the local choir. He joined the Lincolnshire Regiment and studied bassoon and cello at the Royal Military School of Music, Kneller Hall. In 1927, he commenced studies of bassoon and composition at the Royal Academy of Music, later becoming a professor at this institution.

During World War II, he joined the Royal Air Force and conducted various bands, where he performed his own compositions and arrangements. From 1945 to 1955, Vinter was employed successively with the BBC Midland Orchestra and the BBC Concert Orchestra. After leaving the BBC, he founded his International Concert Band.

Vintner was a prolific composer and arranger. His compositions included three ballets. He was fond of telling a story through his music, as is evident in *The Legend of Cracow*. He scored effectively for brass bands, with several works such as *The Trumpets* with soloists and chorus. He was also interested in music from other parts of the world. He wrote twenty fantasias on the indigenous music of different countries, including Bulgaria and Iceland. An example of such a composition is *Portuguese Party*.

Select Discography

World of Light Music HMV CSD 1588 [LP]

W

WARREN, HARRY (born Salvatore Guaragna) (24 December 1895–22 September 1981)

Harry Warren was the son of U.S. emigrants from Italy and was born in New York. He was educated at public schools, and his only formal musical training was as a choirboy at the local Catholic church. He taught himself to play the accordion and piano and worked as a stagehand at the Loew Theatre on Liberty Avenue in Brooklyn. He also took on a job at the Vitagraph film studios and played the piano at the silent movie houses.

During World War I Warren enlisted in the navy, where he was put in charge of entertainment at Long Island. Here he first started improvising tunes for shows that he produced. After the war he returned to piano playing for silent movies and wrote his first song, 'I Learned to Love You When I Learned My ABCs'. This song was never published, but it found him a job as song plugger for the publishers Stark and Cowan.

In 1922, he produced his first published song 'Rose of the Rio Grande'. This was followed by 'Back Home in Pasadena' (1924, with lyrics by Edgar Leslie). He became staff composer at the Shapiro Bernstein publishing company. His next big hit, 'Nagasaki', appeared in 1928. He began to write songs for Broadway revues, such as *Sweet and Low* in 1910 and for Billy Rose's *Crazy Quilt* in 1931. For this latter show, he wrote 'I Found a Million Dollar Baby', which was popularized by Bing Crosby. Also in 1931, he wrote 'You're My Everything', which appeared in the show *The Laugh Parade* and became a standard popular song. Another success in

1931 was 'By the River Sainte Marie', made famous by the singer Kate Smith. A later show was *Shangri-La*, produced in 1956.

Harry Warren is best remembered as a composer of movie hits, particularly in collaboration with lyricist Al Dubin. After 1945, Warren worked with other lyricists such as Mack Gordon and Johnny Mercer and Leo Robin. His films included the following titles: *42nd Street* (1933); *Gold Diggers of 1933; Moulin Rouge* (1934); *Twenty Million Sweethearts* (1934); *Dames* (1934); *Gold Diggers of 1935*; *Go into Your Dance* (1935); *Broadway Gondolier* (1935); *Star over Broadway* (1935); *Gold Diggers of 1937; Jezebel* (1938); *Garden of the Moon* (1938); *Down Argentine Way* (1940); *Tin Pan Alley* (1940); *That Night in Rio* (1941); *Orchestra Wives* (1942); *Ziegfeld Follies* (1946); *The Jolson Story* (1946); *Pagan Love Song* (1949); *The Belle of New York* (1952); *Artists and Models* (1955); *An Affair to Remember* (1957).

Some of Warren's greatest songs are 'I'll String Along with You' (from *Twenty Million Sweethearts*, 1934); 'I Only Have Eyes for You' (from *Dames*, 1934); 'At Last' 'Serenade in Blue' (from *Orchestra Wives*, 1942) 'There Will Never Be Another You' (from *Iceland*, 1942); 'The Boulevard of Broken Dreams' (from *Moulin Rouge*, 1943) and 'The More I See You' (from *Billy Rose's Diamond Horseshoe*, 1945).

Additional Readings

Ewen, David. *American Songwriters*. New York: H. W. Wilson, 1987. pp. 417–22.

Ewen, David. *Great Men of American Popular Song*. Englewood Cliffs, NJ: Prentice-Hall, 1970. pp. 310–20.

Thomas, Tony. *Harry Warren and the Hollywood Musical*. Secaucus, NJ: Citadel Press, 1975.

Select Discography

Phillips, Woolf. Lullaby of Broadway: Music of Dubin and Warren. London LL 1426

Winterhalter, Hugo. I Only Have Eyes for You: Music of Harry Warren RCA LPM/LSP 2645 [Also on CD]

WAXMAN, FRANZ (born Wachsmann) (24 December 1906–24 February 1967)

Franz Waxman was born in Konigshutte, Germany, and studied at the Dresden Music Academy and the Berlin Conservatory. He played the piano in a jazz orchestra called the Weintraub Syncopators, who performed the sound track for Marlene Dietrich's film *Der Blaue Engel* (*The Blue Angel*) in 1930. Waxman orchestrated and conducted Friedrich Hollander's score. His first original score was for Fritz Lang's French film, *Liliom* (1933).

In 1934, he moved to Paris and then to Hollywood as music director of Erich Pommer's film production *Music in the Air*, featuring the music of

JEROME KERN. Waxman's score for *Bride of Frankenstein* (1935) was considered a significant development at that time and led to his appointment as music director for Universal Studios. In 1937, he was given a seven-year contract at MGM. He was loaned out to David O. Selznick in 1940 to compose the music for *Rebecca*, which firmly established his reputation.

From 1943 to 1947, he worked for Warner Brothers. After this period he began to freelance and be more selective about film assignments. He founded the Los Angeles Music Festival and conducted the concerts, arranging premieres of outstanding contemporary works, and introducing guest artists.

His film scores included *Dr. Jekyll and Mr. Hyde* (1941), *Suspicion* (1941), *Woman of the Year* (1942), *Objective Burma* (1945), *Humoresque* (1946), *Sunset Boulevard* (1950), *A Place in the Sun* (1951), *The Silver Chalice* (1954), *The Nun's Story* (1959), *Taras Bulba* (1962) and *Lost Command* (1966).

Select Discography

The Nun's Story Stanyan SRQ 4022

Peyton Place RCA ARL-42005

The Silver Chalice (Conducted by Elmer Bernstein) Filmmusic Collection FMC-3

The Spirit of St. Louis Entr'acte ERS 6507

Sunrise at Campobello (Conducted by Fred Steiner) Entr'acte ERS 6506

Sunset Boulevard and The Classic Film Scores of Franz Waxman RCA ARL1–0708

Compact Discs

Bride of Frankenstein. The Invisible Ray (Westminster Philharmonic Orchestra. Conductor Kenneth Alwyn) Silva Screen FILMCD135

Legends of Hollywood, Volumes 1–3. (Queensland Symphony Orchestra. Conductor Richard Mills) Varese Sarabande VSD5242, VSD5257, VSD5480.

Rebecca (Bratislava Radio Symphony Orchestra. Conductor Adriano) Marco Polo 8.223399

Sayonara. Orchestral Suites. (Berlin Radio Symphony Chorus and Orchestra. Conductor Elmer Bernstein) RCA 09026 62657–2

Sunset Boulevard. The Classic Film Scores of Franz Waxman (National Philharmonic Orchestra. Conductor Charles Gerhardt) RCA Victor GD80708

WEILL, KURT (2 March 1900–3 April 1950)

Kurt Weill was born in Dessau, Germany, and studied with Albert Bing before attending the Berlin Hochschule fur Musik and Berlin University. During his student days he played the piano in beer cellars, gaining an introduction to popular music. From 1919 to 1920, he worked as repetiteur at the Dessau Hofoper and then became a theater conductor in Ludenscheid. At the end of 1920, he was accepted at the Akademie der Kunste,

Germany, in a composition master-class held by Ferruccio Busoni. From 1921 to 1923, he composed various classical works and by 1925 completed his first major stage work, *Der Protagonist.*

In the late 1920s, Weill became caught up in the German Zeitkunst Movement (Music for the People) and under the influence of Bertolt Brecht began to apply popular techniques to opera writing. This was clearly apparent in his ballad opera *Die Dreigroschenoper* (*Threepenny Opera*, modeled on John Gay's *Beggar's Opera*), performed at the Theater am Schliffbauerdamm, Berlin, in August 1928. It contained the song 'Mack the Knife', whose strains appeared in much of Weill's subsequent music.

With the triumph of Nazism in Germany, Weill and his wife, the actress Lotte Lenya, left Berlin for France. In Paris he wrote *Die Seiben Todsunden* (*The Seven Deadly Sins*), *Der Weg der Verheissung* and *Marie Galante*, which contained the song 'I Wait for a Ship', used by the Resistance during World War II. In September 1935, they went to London, where *A Kingdom for a Cow* was performed. They then sailed to New York.

His first piece for the American theater was *Johnny Johnson* (1936). He applied for American citizenship in 1937 and in 1938 collaborated with Maxwell Anderson on *Knickerbocker Holiday*, in which 'September Song' appeared. Subsequent Broadway productions included *Lady in the Dark* (1941); *One Touch of Venus* (1943); *The Firebrand of Florence* (1945); *Street Scene* (1947); *Down in the Valley* (1948); *Love Life* (1948) and *Lost in the Stars* (1949). In 1963, a revue entitled *The World of Kurt Weill in Song* was staged in New York.

His music is distinctive in that it covered both classical and popular styles. In the pre-American period it was extremely individual and contained political and social undertones. After 1940, he relinquished the style of *The Threepenny Opera* and adopted a more sophisticated, popular form of music that appealed more to the audiences of the time.

Additional Readings

Ewen, David. *American Songwriters.* New York: H. W. Wilson, 1987. pp. 426–31.

Jarman, Douglas. *Kurt Weill: An Illustrated Biography.* London: Orbis Publishing, 1982.

Kim H. Kowalke, ed. *New Orpheus: Essays on Kurt Weill.* New Haven, CT: Yale University Press, 1986.

Sanders, Ronald. *The Days Grow Short: The Life and Music of Kurt Weill.* London: Weidenfeld & Nicolson; New York: Holt, Rinehart and Winston, 1980.

Schebera, Jurgen. *Kurt Weill: An Illustrated Life.* New Haven, CT: Yale University Press, 1995.

Taylor, Ronald. *Kurt Weill: Composer in a Divided World.* New York: Simon & Schuster, 1991.

Paul Weston

Select Discography

Gould, Morton. The Two Worlds of Kurt Weill RCA LMP/LSC 2863

Levine, Maurice. Speak Low: The Great Music of Kurt Weill (Arranged by David Terry) Warner W/WS 1313

WESTON, PAUL (12 March 1912–20 September 1996)
Paul Weston was born in Springfield, Massachusetts, and grew up in Pittsburgh. He was educated at Dartmouth College and led a Dartmouth dance band called the Green Serenaders, for whom he did the arranging.

While doing graduate work at Columbia University, he sold some arrangements to Joe Haymes's orchestra, which were heard by Rudy Vallee. He joined Vallee's *Fleischman Hour* on radio as an arranger and also wrote arrangements for Phil Harris's orchestra. In the fall of 1935, Tommy and Jimmy Dorsey decided to break up their band and go their separate ways. Tommy took over the Haymes's band. For the next five years, Weston worked with the Tommy Dorsey orchestra on arrangements such as 'Song of India', 'Stardust', 'Night and Day' and 'Who?'.

In 1940, Weston decided to branch out as a conductor and freelance arranger, and his first job was a Lee Wiley album for Liberty Records, followed by arranging and conducting some of the first recording sessions of a relatively unknown singer, Dinah Shore.

Weston also did some arrangements for the Bob Crosby orchestra and at their invitation came to Hollywood in the summer of 1940. He continued as Dinah Shore's arranger for records and radio and in 1941 did his first motion picture arranging for the Crosby band for *Holiday Inn*, with Bing Crosby and Fred Astaire. This led to other work at Paramount Pictures with Crosby, Bob Hope, Betty Hutton and others. While at Paramount, Weston met Johnny Mercer, who was about to form Capitol Records with Glenn Wallichs and Buddy de Sylva.

Mercer offered Weston the position of musical director at Capitol, making his own albums in a style that was to be called mood music, and accompanying Capitol artists like Mercer, Jo Stafford, The Pied Pipers, Betty Hutton, Margaret Whiting and later Gordon MacRae and Dean Martin.

In 1943, Mercer went on the radio with the *Johnny Mercer Music Shop*, and for the next seven years Weston divided his time between records and radio, working with Mercer, Joan Davis, Duffy's Tavern, and others. Finally he spent three years as conductor for the *Jo Stafford Chesterfield Supper Club*. During this period, he followed his first Capitol album, *Music for Dreaming*, with similar albums. In a *Coronet* magazine article he was dubbed 'Master of Mood Music' for his distinctive style, which combined melodic strings with a big band sound, featuring jazz instrumental solos by Ziggy Elman, Eddie Miller, Paul Smith, Barney Kessel and others.

In 1950, Weston switched over to Columbia Records, where he continued to make his instrumental albums, functioned as Columbia's West Coast Director of Artists and Repertoire and with his orchestra accompanied singers Doris Day, Rosemary Clooney, Jo Stafford, Frankie Laine and others. After a CBS radio series, *The Paul Weston Show*, in 1951 and 1952 he appeared regularly on television with the *Jo Stafford Show* in 1954.

In 1957, Weston was chosen to conduct *Crescendo*, TV's first big musical spectacular, and thereafter spent five years as a musical director for NBC-TV, doing Chevy Shows with Roy Rogers and Dale Evans, specials for Texaco and DuPont, the U.S. Steel show with Sid Caesar, the award-winning *Peter and the Wolf Show* with Art Carney, the original *Laugh-In Show* with Dick Rowan and Dan Martin, and in 1961, a year with the Bob Newhart comedy show. In 1963, he commenced a four-year stint as musical director on the Danny Kaye TV show, followed by two years with Jonathan Winters and two with Jim Nabors on CBS. During these years, he continued his recording and radio work, doing seven years of *Christmas*

Sing with Bing on radio with Bing Crosby and recordings with Judy Garland and Sarah Vaughan, and a two-album set with Ella Fitzgerald.

As a composer, Weston is responsible for such pop songs as 'Day by Day', 'I Should Care', 'Shrimp Boats', 'Autumn in Rome', 'When April Comes Again' and many others. He has written two symphonic suites 'Crescent City Suite', which has been performed many times in New Orleans and elsewhere, and 'The Mercy Partridge Suite'. With Marilyn and Alan Bergman, he wrote 'The Bells of Santa Ynez', a choral work that has been performed for many years in the Santa Ynez Valley. He has also written religious music, including two Masses published by the Gregorian Institute of America and many hymns.

He was a founder and first national president of the National Academy of Recording Arts and Sciences and received a Grammy Award for his *Jonathan and Darlene in Paris* album, a comedy album recorded with his wife, Jo Stafford. Jonathan and Darlene have recorded four albums and have a devoted following dedicated to the appreciation of inept musicianship.

After retiring from television, he served as musical director for *Disney on Parade* for three years. During the 1990s, he became president of Hanover Music Corporation and Corinthian Records. Corinthian released Jo Stafford and Paul Weston albums made for Columbia and Capitol, which enjoyed sales throughout the world. In 1971, the Trustees of the National Academy of Recording Arts and Sciences gave its trustees' award to Paul Weston.

Select Discography

Bells of Santa Ynez Capitol

Carefree Capitol T/ST 1261

Caribbean Cruise Columbia CL 572, CL 6266

Columbia Album of Jerome Kern Columbia C2L2 (2 records) [Also on CD]

Columbia Album of Sigmund Romberg Columbia C2L14 (2 records) [Also on CD]

Crescent City Columbia CL 977

Dream Time Music Columbia CL 528

Floatin' Like a Feather Capitol T/ST 1153

Hollywood Columbia ASF 1028 (South Africa)

Love Music from Hollywood Columbia CL 794; Philips BBL 7085 (U.K.) [Also on CD]

Melodies for a Sentimental Mood Columbia CL 6204 (10")

Melodies for Moonlight Columbia CL 6191 (10")

Melodies for Sweethearts Columbia CL 6192 (10")

Mood for Twelve Columbia CL 693

Mood Music Columbia CL 527

Moonlight Becomes You Columbia CL 909

Music for a Rainy Night Columbia CL 574 [Also on CD]

Music for Dreaming Columbia H 222 (10"); Capitol T/ST 1154

Music for Easy Listening Columbia H 195 (10"); Capitol T/ST 1154

Music for Jennifer Capitol T/ST 1222, Columbia H225 (10")

Music for Memories Columbia H225

Music for My Love Capitol T/ST 1563

Music for Quiet Dancing Columbia CL 659

Music for Reflection Columbia H 287 (10")

Music for Romancing Columbia H 153; Capitol T/ST 1223

Music for the Fireside Columbia H245 (10"); Capitol T/ST 1192

Music from Hollywood Columbia

Solo Mood Columbia CL 879

Sound Stage Columbia CL 612

The Sweet and the Swingin' Capitol T/ST 1361

Whispers in the Dark Columbia CL 6232

Note: There are also albums accompanying Doris Day, Jo Stafford, Dean Martin, Gordon MacRae and Bing Crosby. A later release was *Man of La Mancha*, accompanying Jim Nabors and Marilyn Horne.

Compact Discs

Columbia Album of Jerome Kern Sony 4786

Crescent City Corinthian 116

Columbia Album of Jerome Kern Sony AK 47861

Music for Easy Listening Corinthian 102

Music for Memories and Music for Dreaming Capitol CDP 7–92091–2

Orquestras Spectaculares CBS 464011

WHITE, EDWARD (TEDDY) (1910–1994)

Edward White was born in London and received little formal musical education. He served first as a violinist in a trio and subsequently as a performer in various dance bands from 1930 onward, including the Palais Band at Streatham Lacarno, with Lou Praeger at Romano's in the West End and then with the Ambrose Octet. During World War II White joined the air force and was enrolled in the Felix King Group. He was also involved in playing and arranging for light orchestral shows in Bristol. After the war, he formed his own ballroom orchestra in Bristol, at the Grand Spa Hotel.

During the war period he was much involved with composing and produced pieces such as 'Caprice for Strings' and 'Runaway Rocking Horse'.

He subsequently received commissions from BBC Television and found a ready market for mood music. His light orchestral pieces include 'Puffin Billy', which became the signature tune in the 1950s of the BBC Children's program *Children's Favourites.*

WILDER, ALEC (born Alexander LaFayette Chew Wilder) (16 February 1907–23 December 1980)

Alec Wilder was a composer, author, arranger and musical director whose career was equally devoted to classical and popular music. He composed popular ballads, illustrative works, jazz and classical pieces.

He attended Collegiate School, New York, and studied privately at the Eastman School of Music. He became an active composer in 1930 and wrote several hundred popular songs, including 'It's So Peaceful in the Country', 'While We're Young' 'I'll Be Around' and 'Goodbye, John'. Among his serious works are sonatas, concertos, quintets and trios, all for various musical instruments, piano works, operas, ballets and several unorthodox pieces.

He wrote several books, including a landmark analysis of American popular song, 1900–1950. This has become a definitive work of reference and is of great musicological value.

Additional Readings

Balliett, Whitney. 'The President of the Derriere Garde: Alec Wilder', in his *American Singers: Twenty-Seven Portraits in Song*. New York: Oxford University Press, 1988. pp. 3–20.

Demsey, David, and Ronald Prather. *Alec Wilder: A Bio-bibliography*. Westport, CT: Greenwood Press, 1993 (Includes a comprehensive discography on pp. 111–44).

Stone, Desmond. *Alec Wilder In Spite Of Himself: A Life of the Composer.* New York: Oxford University Press, 1996.

Select Discography

Faith, Percy. It's So Peaceful in the Country: The Music of Alec Wilder and Jimmy van Heusen Columbia CL 770 [Also on CD]

WILLIAMS, CHARLES (8 May 1893–7 September 1978)

Charles Williams was one of Britain's most prolific light music composers. He pioneered the music of the first all-sound film made in Britain, Alfred Hitchcock's production of *Blackmail* (1929). Williams scored for numerous British films during the 1930s and 1940s. He was also largely responsible for establishing the CHAPPELL MOOD MUSIC LIBRARY, which supplied films, newsreels, radio and television with background music and signature tunes of good quality.

Williams recorded with his own concert orchestra and also conducted the Queen's Hall Light Orchestra. He scored for over twenty films and was musical director on various occasions. He did not always receive screen credit for his work. His most notable titles were *The Thirty-nine Steps* (1935); *Will Hay* comedies, *Kipps* (1941); *The Night Has Eyes* (1942); *The Way to the Stars* (1945, with NICHOLAS BRODSKY); *This Is Britain*, documentary series (1945); *The Noose* (1946); *Night Boat to Dublin* (1946); *While I Live* (1947, from which came the famous 'Dream of Olwen'); *Flesh and Blood* (1951) and *The Apartment* (1960, which made use of 'Jealous Lover' as its title theme).

Among Williams' best-known light orchestral works are 'Devil's Gallop' (signature tune of *Dick Barton, Special Agent*); 'Voice of London' 'Rhythm on Rails', 'The Starlings', 'A Quiet Stroll', 'Sleepy Marionette', 'Side Walk', 'The Old Clockmaker' and 'Girls in Grey'.

WILLIAMS, JOHN (b. 8 February 1932)

John Williams was born in New York and in 1948 moved with his family to Los Angeles, where he attended the University of California, Los Angeles. He studied composition privately with Mario Castelnuovo-Tedesco and later attended the Juilliard School of Music, where he studied piano with Madame Rosina Lhevinne.

After returning to Los Angeles, Williams began his career in the film studios, working with composers such as BERNARD HERRMANN, ALFRED NEWMAN and FRANZ WAXMAN. His first score was for the film *I Passed for White* in 1960. He wrote music for many television programs in the 1960s, winning two Emmys for his work. His television scores include the productions *Heidi, Jane Eyre* and *The Screaming Woman*. In 1985, he was commissioned to construct themes for NBC news stories, which resulted in compositions such as 'The Sound of the News', 'The Pulse of Events' and 'Fugue for Changing Times'. Williams has composed the music and served as music director for more than seventy films, including *Home Alone*, *Presumed Innocent*, *Born on the Fourth of July*, *Indiana Jones and the Last Crusade*, *Empire of the Sun*, *Indiana Jones and the Temple of Doom*, *Star Wars*, *Return of the Jedi*, *Raiders of the Lost Ark*, *The Empire Strikes Back*, *Superman, Close Encounters of the Third Kind*, *Jaws* and *Goodbye, Mr. Chips*. He has received twenty-eight Academy Award nominations, four Oscars and fifteen Grammys, as well as several gold and platinum records. His Academy Awards have been for his adaptation of the film score for *Fiddler on the Roof* (1971) and the scores of *Jaws* (1975), *E. T. The Extraterrestrial* (1982) and *Schindler's List* (1993). He has also written many concert pieces including two symphonies and concertos for flute, clarinet and violin.

In 1980, he succeeded ARTHUR FIEDLER as conductor of the BOSTON POPS ORCHESTRA and regularly played and recorded with this orchestra until

1993. Many of his film scores have been recorded, including the sound track to *Star Wars*. The first recording by John Williams and the Boston Pops Orchestra was *Music of the Night*, released on the Sony label in 1990. They have also recorded a collection of marches for Sony entitled *I Love a Parade* and an album *The Spielberg/Williams Collaboration*, consisting of Williams's music for the Steven Spielberg films.

Compact Discs (Unless otherwise stated, all recordings are with Boston Pops Orchestra.)

Aisle Seat Philips 411 037–2

By Request Philips 420 178–2

Close Encounters of the Third Kind Varese Sarabande VSD5275

Dracula (London Symphony Orchestra) Varese Sarabande VSD5250

Empire of the Sun Warner Brothers 7599–25668–2

E.T. The Extraterrestrial MCA MCLD19021

The Fury (London Symphony Orchestra) Varese Sarabande VSD5264

Green Album Sony SK 48224

Home Alone Sony MK46595

Home Alone 2: Lost in New York Arista 20th Century Fox 11002–2

Hook Epic ED48888

Indiana Jones and the Last Crusade Warner Bros 925 883–2

Indiana Jones and the Temple of Doom Edel TCS102–2

Jaws MCA MCLD19281

Jaws 2 Varese Sarabande VSD5328

Jurassic Park MCA MCD10859

Music for Stage and Screen Sony Classical SK64147

Night and Day Sony SK 47235

Pops by George: Music of George Gershwin Philips 426 404–2

Pops in Space Philips 412 884–2

Raiders of the Lost Ark Silva Screen RAIDERS001

Salute to Hollywood Philips 422 385–2

Schindler's List MCA MCD10969

Space and Time Spectrum 550 106–2

Star Wars Polydor 800096

Star Wars Trilogy. Complete Soundtrack Anthology Arista 20th Century–Fox 11012–2 (four discs)

Superman: The Movie Warner Bros 3257–2

That's Entertainment Philips 416 499–2

Unforgettable Sony SK 53380

Very Best of the Boston Pops Philips 432802.2

WILSON, STANLEY

Stanley Wilson originally embarked on a medical career but changed to music while still at college. He studied arranging and composition while playing the trumpet in jazz bands for three years. At the age of twenty-five, he became the arranger for Freddy Martin's orchestra and for a number of top radio shows.

Wilson obtained employment with MGM, doing arrangements for musicals featuring Jeanette MacDonald, Jimmy Durante and Lauritz Melchior. He rose to musical director at Republic Pictures and music director of Revue Studios. In the 1960s and 1970s he was music director of Universal Films, where he signed on a pool of leading musicians and displayed a sincere interest in finding and sponsoring young, promising talent. These included DAVE GRUSIN, Quincy Jones, Oliver Nelson, Lalo Schifrin and Billy Goldenberg. His television credits included writing and conducting the theme music for the *Alfred Hitchcock Show*, *G.E. Theater*, *Wells Fargo* and *M-Squad*.

Select Discography

The Great Waltz TIME 52041

Themes to Remember: Top TV Themes and Background Music Decca DL 4481

WINTERHALTER, HUGO (15 August 1909–17 September 1973)

Winterhalter was born in Wilkes-Barre, Pennsylvania. He studied music as a boy and his parents encouraged his musical ambitions. He was educated at Mt. St. Mary's College in Emmitsburg and the New England Conservatory. He played in various orchestras after graduation, principally in the woodwind section. He taught for several years. In the mid-1930s he commenced his musical career and played with several bands, including that of Larry Linton, for whom he arranged his best-selling record of 'Stardust'. In the 1940s he acted as arranger for Count Basie, Will Bradley, Tommy and Jimmy Dorsey, Vaughn Monroe and Claude Thornhill and for the singers Billy Eckstine, Eddie Fisher, Dinah Shore, Kate Smith and Kay Starr. He was always fond of the violin but did not get a chance to write for strings until 1944, when he arranged for Tommy Dorsey. He was musical director for MGM Records from 1948 to 1949, Columbia from 1949 to 1950, RCA Victor from 1950 to 1963 and Kapp in 1963. He also recorded under his own name and favored an orchestra producing the lush sound of many strings.

Winterhalter's earliest mood music LPs were several 10" discs on the RCA Victor label. These clearly demonstrated that he was ahead of his

Hugo Winterhalter

time as an arranger. 'Music by Starlight' and 'Reminiscing' are good examples of his arranging art in the earlier years.

Among the Winterhalter discs that appeared regularly in the 1950s were a series of musical journey LPs set in different parts of the world, including (by titles) Hawaii, Continental Europe, Latin America and South of the Border. The best of these was the gypsy album, which was highly acclaimed by Joe Pasternak.

Winterhalter was also a remarkably fine composer. Clear evidence of his talent is provided by such items as 'The Back of Her Head' (included on the *Gypsy* LP) and Brasilia Romantica (included on the *South of the Border* LP.)

In the years immediately preceding his death, Winterhalter recorded a number of LPs for the Musicor label. These discs show the distinct influence of the commercial pop market, featuring a heavy beat, and are entirely different in concept from the fine discs made for RCA Victor. Winterhalter died of cancer at the age of sixty-four in Greenwich, Connecticut.

Musical Achievements

Winterhalter played a major part in shaping the development of popular orchestral music in the years following World War II and in the 'Golden Fifties', when he was considered the equal of such artists as MORTON GOULD, PERCY FAITH, ANDRE KOSTELANETZ and PAUL WESTON.

There was something very distinctive about a Winterhalter arrangement. He admitted his debt to Frederick Delius, Jean Sibelius and Claude Debussy, whose influence is evident in his fine arrangements on his many LPs. Although he conducted both the Milwaukee and Washington Symphony orchestras, his finest work is often considered to be his mood music.

Two LPs deserve special mention. These are 'The Eyes of Love', a collection of great standards all referring to eyes, and the first side of 'Two Sides of Winterhalter'. His arrangement of 'Spring Is Here' (on the LP *A Season for the Beloved*) is an outstanding example of the haunting and sonorous Winterhalter sound. Another is his superb scoring of 'Take Me to Your World', which is featured on the LP *Nashville Strings Play Country Hits*, volume 1). (The entire LP was arranged by Winterhalter.)

Select Discography

All-time Movie Greats Musicor 3160

Always RCA LPM 1179

Applause Musicor 3190

Best of Hugo Winterhalter RCA LPM/LSP 3379

Best of 1964 Kapp 1407/3407

Big and Sweet with a Beat Camden CAL 443

Big Hits of 1965 Kapp 1429/3429

Christmas Magic Camden CAL 449

Classical Gas Musicor 3170

Eyes of Love RCA LPM 1338

Eyes of Love Good Music Company DMC 2–1420/159921 (A 2-CD compilation entirely different from the similarly titled LP.)

Favorite Broadway and Hollywood Musicor 3184

Goes Continental RCA LPM/LSP 2482

Goes Gypsy RCA LPM/LSP 2167

Goes Hawaiian RCA LPM/LSP 2417

Goes Latin RCA LPM/LSP 1677

Goes South of the Border RCA LPM/LSP 2271

Golden Hour of Hugo Winterhalter Musicor 3232

Grand Canyon Suite/Rhapsody in Blue RCA LPM 1429

Great Themes in Television RCA LPM 1020

Happy Hunting RCA LPM 1400

Hits from "Peter Pan" and "Hans Christian Andersen" RCA LPM 3101

I Only Have Eyes for You RCA LPM/LSP 2645 [Also on CD]

Isham Jones for Dancing RCA LPM 20

Latin Gold (Reissue of previous Latin LPs) RCA Camden S 2546

Love Story (Also titled: **Love at First Sight**) Musicor 3196

Magic Touch Camden CAL 379

Motion Pictures Hit Themes Musicor 1040

Music by Starlight 12" RCA LPM 1185 10" RCA LPM 3051

Music, Music, Music Harmony 7078

Nashville Strings Play Great Country Hits (vol. 1) Columbia CS 9646

Reminiscing RCA LPM 3050

Romancing and Danceable Musicor 3168

Season for My Beloved ABC/ABC S 447

Semiclassical Favorites Kapp 1426/3426

Two Sides of Winterhalter RCA LPM/LSP 1905; RCA 74321 35750 2 (Compact Disc)

Winterhalter Magic RCA LPM 3100

Winterhalter Strings Columbia CL 2537

Wish You Were Here RCA LPM/LSP 1904

WOOD, HAYDN (25 March 1882–11 March 1959)

Haydn Wood, the British composer and violinist, was born in Slaithwaite, Yorkshire. He studied at the Royal College of Music and in Brussels. He composed both serious and popular light music. The latter includes his suites 'London Cameos' and 'London Landmarks', various orchestral pieces and works for military and brass bands. He wrote many songs, the most famous of which are 'Roses of Picardy' (1916, lyrics by Fred E. Weatherly); 'Love's Garden of Roses' (1914, lyrics by Ruth Rutherford); 'A Brown Bird Singing' (1922, lyrics by Royden Barrie) and 'Homeward at Eventide' (1931, lyrics by A. Harvey Lang-Ridge). He also contributed to a musical comedy entitled *Dear Love* (1929).

Y

YORKE, PETER (4 December 1902–2 February 1966)
Peter Yorke was born in London and educated at Trinity College of Music and was an organist at the age of sixteen. He developed an interest in dance music, both as a pianist and arranger. He worked for Peter Mackey in 1927 and also recorded for HMV with a group known as the Rhythm Band. In the 1930s he became known as one of the finest dance band orchestrators in England. He played with Jack Hylton and LOUIS LEVY and formed his own orchestra in 1937.

During World War II, he served in the Royal Air Force, mostly with service orchestras. After the war, he became well known for his radio series and the Columbia recordings with his Concert Orchestra, which featured the alto saxophone playing of Freddy Gardner. Songs he recorded include 'I'm in the Mood for Love', 'I Only Have Eyes for You', 'Roses of Picardy', 'These Foolish Things', 'Body and Soul' and 'Valse Vanité'. Yorke also recorded one of his compositions 'Sapphire and Sables', which he used as his theme music. He wrote much light orchestral music and items for brass band. His compositions include 'Melody of the Stars', 'Dawn Fantasy', 'Quiet Countryside', 'Carminetta', 'Faded Lilac', 'Fireflies', 'Flyaway Fiddles', 'Golden Melody', 'Oriental Bazaar', 'In My Garden', 'Midnight in Mexico', 'Parade of the Matadors', 'Royal Mile', 'Highdays and Holidays', 'Brandy Snaps', 'Miss in Mink', 'Lazy Piano' and 'Ladies' Night'. From 1957 to 1967, 'Silks and Satins' was used to close the popular British television series *Emergency Ward 10*.

Most of Yorke's music was written for various London mood music libraries, including CHAPPELL; Francis, Day and Hunter; Bosworth; Harmonic; Conroy; Paxton; Southern and Josef Weinberger. He also conducted several albums of popular song.

Select Discography

Melody Lingers On: The Music of Irving Berlin and Victor Herbert Decca DL 8240

Mood for Love EMI-World Records 1979

Music for Sweethearts—Romantic Compositions of Victor Herbert Decca DL 8242 (The Victor Herbert melodies on Melody Lingers On and Music for Sweethearts are entirely different selections.)

Sapphires and Sables—Music in the Peter Yorke Manner Delyse-Envoy VOY 9141

YOUMANS, VINCENT (27 September 1898–5 April 1946)

Youmans received his first piano lessons at the age of four, and his musical talents were clearly evident from his childhood days. Upon the completion of his schooling, he entered the world of finance and business but before long preferred to take a job as a song plugger. He served in the U.S. Navy in World War I. After the war, he resumed his career as a song plugger.

He reached the apex of his stage career with *No, No, Nanette* in 1925. This became the first musical to circle the globe, and it earned Youmans half a million dollars.

From 1933 onward, Youmans faced a series of serious personal and professional setbacks from which he never recovered. He divorced his wife, and his business affairs went from bad to worse. The Vincent Youmans publishing company went into bankruptcy in 1934. The same year, he also lost the Cosmopolitan Theater. His health failed. Stricken by tuberculosis, Youmans moved to Colorado Springs in 1935, where he married for the second time. He filed for bankruptcy in 1935, with liabilities exceeding half a million dollars and only negligible assets.

Despite this adversity, he retained his zest for life and enjoyed parties. In 1946, Youmans and his second wife were divorced. He died in his Park Lane, Denver, hotel suite on 5 April 1946. He had overindulged in alcohol in his earlier years, and his subsequent downfall was due to neglect of his health. On 9 May 1983, Youmans was posthumously elected to the Theater Hall of Fame in New York, a richly deserved tribute to a great songwriter.

Musical Achievements

A consummate craftsman who used his notes economically but always to full effect and a magician in evoking sounds with impeccable taste, Youmans left a rich and durable repertory of songs, not great in number but unquestionably superior in quality. JEROME KERN paid tribute to Youmans as one of the greatest of all American melodists.

Youmans's output as a composer was small in quantity but great in quality. Fewer than a hundred of his songs were published, and his Broadway output consisted of twelve scores, while his Hollywood contribution comprised just two original film scores. Youmans's first great song was 'Bambalina', which was included in the show *Wildflower* (1923). Two years later, in 1925, the show *A Night Out* included 'Sometimes I'm Happy', a loose, uncluttered song, with no harmonic complexity. This rhythm ballad was later used in the score of *Hit the Deck* (1927), where it became a hit. Also in 1925 came *No, No, Nanette*, and in it was featured one of the phenomenal hits of the century, 'Tea for Two'. This was undoubtedly one of Youmans's biggest hit songs, and it became an enduring standard.

The well-known Youmans's song 'I Know That You Know' was included in *Oh, Please* (1926). This was a rousing rhythm song, based on an unusual device, which is sometimes criticized as being monotonous. *Hit the Deck* (1927) had one of Youmans's best scores. It included 'Hallelujah', first performed in 1918. It is a declamatory song, set up by a long, strong verse and rousing chorus.

Great Day (1929) was a Youmans show that was considered a failure. It included, however, three great standards: the rousing title song 'Great Day', 'More Than You Know', which ranks among the best of popular music and 'Without a Song'. In 1930, in the show *Smiles*, which ran for only sixty-three performances, there was another famous Youmans song, 'Time on My Hands'. This has a gentle, persuasive melody and excellent lyrics. The failed show of 1932, entitled *Through the Years*, included the song 'Drums in My Heart', which had enjoyed semistandard status through the decades since its first publication. The title song from the show *Through the Years* was Youmans's own personal favorite.

Youmans's last major effort was the highly successful score for the film *Flying Down to Rio* (1933). It was undoubtedly his most consistent theatrical score, highlighted by the unforgettable presence of Fred Astaire and Ginger Rogers. Nearly all the songs in this score showed a marked Latin American influence and style. 'Carioca' was the big production number in the show. 'Orchids in the Moonlight' from the same show is a very well-written Latin song that has become a standard.

Arrangements for Orchestra

Among the best recordings of 'Bambalina' are those of REG OWEN on the LP *Deep in a Dream* and Richard Jones with the Pittsburgh Symphony Strings on the LP *Songs for Strings*.

REG OWEN's LP recording *Deep in a Dream* also contains a superb arrangement of 'Sometimes I'm Happy', which has also been recorded to excellent effect by PERCY FAITH. ANDRE KOSTELANETZ's tribute to Youmans includes notable arrangements of 'Tea for Two', 'I Know That You Know', 'Hallelujah', 'More Than You Know', 'Drums in My Heart', 'Without a Song', 'Time on My Hands', 'Through the Years', 'Carioca' and 'Orchids in the Moonlight.' He appears to be the most prolific in arrangements of Youmans's music. Superb arrangements of 'Tea for Two' have also been made by MORTON GOULD and by Johnny Arthey in the MOODS ORCHESTRAL version. Percy Faith excels in his version of 'More than You Know' from the show *Great Day*. 'Time on My Hands' has been recorded by several fine orchestras, including Morton Gould, Peter Knight (Moods Orchestral) and, as mentioned, Kostelanetz.

The BOSTON POPS ORCHESTRA under ARTHUR FIEDLER produced a good arrangement of 'Through the Years'. Several excellent versions of 'Orchids in the Moonlight' have been recorded, including those of Morton Gould, Andre Kostelanetz and Richard Jones (Pittsburgh Symphony Orchestra).

Additional Readings

Bordman, Gerald. *Days to be Happy, Years to be Sad: The Life and Music of Vincent Youmans*. New York: Oxford University Press, 1982.

Ewen, David. *American Songwriters*. New York: H. W. Wilson, 1987. pp. 446–50.

Ewen, David. *Great Men of American Popular Song*. Englewood Cliffs, NJ: Prentice-Hall, 1970. pp. 123–43.

Wilder, Alec. *American Popular Song: The Great Innovators*. Oxford: Oxford University Press, 1972. Reprinted 1990. pp. 292–312.

Selected Discography

Camerata. I want to Be Happy: Music of Vincent Youmans

Farnon, Robert. Music of Vincent Youmans [Also on CD]

Kostelanetz, Andre. Music of Vincent Youmans Columbia ML 4382; CL 734 [Also on CD]

YOUNG, VICTOR (8 August 1900–10 November 1956)

Young was born in Chicago and was an accomplished violinist by the age of six. He moved to Warsaw at the age of seven, when his mother died, and lived with his grandmother. He studied music at the Warsaw Conservatory and made his concert debut with the Warsaw Philharmonic Orchestra at the age of seventeen. He toured Europe and returned to Chicago in 1921 to become musical director of the Central Park Theater. His first close contact with film music was during an engagement as conductor in a cinema in Los Angeles. He joined Ted Fiorito's orchestra as violinist and arranger. He also conducted and supervised vaudeville productions, eventually becoming assistant musical director of the Balaban and Katz theater chain. From the late 1920s to 1935, he worked as conductor and arranger on radio programs in New York. He played solo violin on the first recording of 'Stardust'.

In 1935, he formed his own orchestra for film work in Hollywood, where he was under contract to Paramount. He remained active in this field for the rest of his career. He made many light orchestral recordings and also recorded with singers.

For the theater he wrote *Blackbirds* (1933–34) and *Pardon Our French* (1950). His film scores between 1933 and 1944 include *Murder at the Vanities*, *Fatal Lady*, *Wells Fargo*, *Way Down South*, *Golden Boy*, *Raffles*, *Heritage of the Desert*, *All Women Have Hearts*, *And Now To-Morrow*, *Dancing on a Dime*, *A Night at Earl Carroll's*, *Caught in the Draft*, *The Outlaw*, *Reap the Wild Wind*, *Beyond the Blue Horizon*, *The Glass Key*, *The Palm Beach Story*, *For Whom the Bell Tolls*, *Frenchman's Creek*, *Ministry of Fear* and *The Uninvited.*

His films from 1945 to 1956 included *Love Letters*, *To Each His Own*, *The Night Has a Thousand Eyes*, *The Paleface*, *Sands of Iwo Jima*, *My Foolish Heart*, *The Quiet Man*, *Shane*, *Three Coins in the Fountain* and *Around the World in Eighty Days*, for which he won a posthumous Oscar.

Young produced some memorable theme tunes and songs between 1944 and 1956, including 'Love Letters', 'Golden Earrings', 'To Each His Own', 'Unconquered', 'My Foolish Heart', 'Samson and Delilah', 'Our Very Own', 'September Affair', 'The Greatest Show on Earth', 'The Quiet Man', 'Shane', 'Johnny Guitar', 'The Conqueror', 'Around the World in Eighty Days', 'Written on the Wind', 'Buster Keaton Story', 'Omar Khayyam', and 'The Run of the Arrow'. He wrote for a total of about 350 films.

His other songs included 'Sweet Sue, Just You', 'Falling in Love with You', 'Can't We Talk It Over', 'Street of Dreams', 'I Don't Stand a Ghost of a Chance with You', 'Love Me Tonight', 'Lawd, You Made the Night Too Long', 'Waltzing in a Dream', 'Any Time, Any Day, Anywhere'.

Select Discography

Music Conducted by Victor Young

After Dinner Music Decca DL8350

April in Paris Decca DL 8243

Cinema Rhapsodies Brunswick LAT 8029

Gypsy Magic Brunswick LAT 8033

Hollywood Rhapsodies Decca DL 8060

Imagination Decca DL 8278

Love Themes from Hollywood Decca DL 8364

Night Music Decca DL 8085

Pearls on Velvet Decca DL 8285

Soft Lights and Sweet Music Decca DL 8789

Sugar and Spice Decca DL 8466

Victor Young Conducts Victor Young AEI 2107

Film Music

Around the World in 80 Days (Conducted by Victor Young) Decca DL 9046

For Whom the Bell Tolls (Conducted by Ray Heindorf) Stanyan SRQ 4013

For Whom the Bell Tolls. Suite (Conducted by Stanley Black) London SP 44173

For Whom the Bell Tolls (Conducted by Victor Young) Decca DL 8481

Music of Victor Young, Conducted by Other Conductors

Hayman, Richard. Great Motion Picture Themes of Victor Young Mercury SR 60012

Kaufman, Richard. Shane: A Tribute to Victor Young (With New Zealand Symphony Orchestra) Koch International Classics 37365–2 [CD]

Love, Geoff. Our Very Own: Melodies of Victor Young Columbia 33SX1069

Mancini, Henry. Concert Sound of Henry Mancini. Includes: **Tribute to Victor Young** RCA LPM/LSP 2897

Ornadel, Cyril. Forever Young: The Music of Victor Young (With Starlight Symphony Orchestra) MGM E/SE 4432 [Also on CD]

Compact Discs

Around the World in 80 Days MCA MCAD31134

Quiet Man (Dublin Screen Orchestra. Conductor Kenneth Alwyn). Scannan Film Classics SFC1501

Rio Grande Varese Sarabande VSD 5378

Z

ZACHARIAS, HELMUT (b. 1920)
Helmut Zacharias was born in Germany, the son of a professional violinist. Helmut followed in his father's footsteps and at the age of seventeen won a Fritz Kreisler Award. He formed his own orchestra, which became popular throughout Europe. One of his earliest hits was 'When the White Lilacs Bloom Again', which was also released in the United States in 1956. In the late 1950s, Zacharias settled in Ascona, Switzerland, and in the early 1960s produced many albums that gained popularity in Britain. These included *Strauss Waltzes*, *Golden Award Songs*, *On Lovers Road*, *Candlelight Serenade*, *The Best of Everything* and *Hi-Fi Fiddle*.

Some items appeared under the title 'With Orchestra' and others 'With Magic Violins'. One of his most popular compositions was 'Love Is like a Violin' (1960). This was followed in 1964 with 'Tokyo Melody', written with Heinz Hellmer and Lionel Bart. This became the theme tune for the 1964 Olympic Games, held for the first time in Asia. Zacharias used a mixture of contemporary popular music and light classics, played in a relaxed style in which the violins predominated. His album *Greatest Hits* contained numbers such as 'Cherry Pink and Apple Blossom White', 'Under the Linden Tree' and his own composition 'Blue Blues'.

Select Discography

Le Disque d'Or de Helmut Zacharias. Polydor 2418158

Happy-Go-Lucky Polydor LPHM 46048

Hello, Scandinavia Polydor LPHM 46064

Hi-Fi Fiddle Polydor LPHM 46018

Hi-Fi Fiddler's Delight Decca DL8822/ Polydor LPHM 46081

Holiday in Spain Polydor LPHM 46096.

Magic Violins Decca DL 8431; Polydor 2482161

Million Strings (Coupled with Selections by Werner Muller Orchestra) Decca DL 8382

On Lovers' Road Polydor LPHM 46234

Portrait of Helmut Zacharias Polydor 2418 084

Rendezvous for Strings Decca DL 8982

Romantically Yours Polydor SLPHM 237627

Songs of Old Russia Polydor LPHM 46326/237 526

Strauss Waltzes Decca DL 8985

Strings, Moonlight and You Decca DL 85491; Polydor LPHM 46035

Themes Decca DL 4083

Two Million Strings (Coupled with Selections by Werner Muller Orchestra) Decca DL 8926; Polydor LPHM 46091

World of Helmut Zacharias Polydor 2418095

Zacharias Hi-Fi Show Polydor LPHM 46308

Select Discography of Conductors Not Included in the Main Biographical Sequence

This discography relates to conductors about whom it has not proved possible to find biographical information. Record manufacturers' names and numbers have been included in the discographies wherever possible; we regret that this has not always been feasible.

Abravanel, Maurice (American Conductor)

Porgy and Bess: Symphonic Picture/Themes from Show Boat: Scenario for Orchestra (With Utah Symphony Orchestra). Vanguard VCS 10023

Fiddle Faddle: Leroy Anderson Favorites. Vanguard VCS 10016

Acquaviva, Nick (American Conductor)

Exciting Sound. Decca DL 7445

Music of Acquaviva. MGM SE 3226

Albeniz, Jose (Spanish Conductor)

Your Musical Holiday in Spain. Brunswick LAT 8127

Alguero, Augusto, Jr. (Portuguese Conductor)

Holiday Abroad in Lisbon. RCA LPM 1596

Alvarez (Spanish Conductor)

Spanish Inferno (With the International Pop Orchestra). London LMS 9

Ambassador Strings (Conductor not named)

Night Was Made For Love: Music of Jerome Kern. Compose Records 98018 [Contents and arrangements identical to Eric Drucker's Best of Jerome Kern, p. 299.]

Amore, Don

Latin Holiday. RCA RAL 1006

Armengol, Mario Ruiz (Mexican Conductor)

Most Beautiful Music in the World (With Living Strings). RCA Camden CAS 687

Music to Help You Stop Smoking (With Living Strings). RCA Camden

One Night in Acapulco. RCA LPM 1292

Songs That Will Live Forever (With Living Strings). RCA Camden CAL/CAS 821

Arnold, Harry (Swedish Conductor)

All-time Favorites of Cole Porter and Richard Rodgers. Mercury MG 20279

Best of Noel Coward. Mercury MG 20278 [Also on CD]

Girls of My Dreams (With Frank Barclay, piano). ATCO 33–127

In the Still of the Night: Cole Porter Melodies. NIXA NPT 19001

Isn't It Romantic: Richard Rodgers Melodies. NIXA NPT 19000

Moon and the Stars. Mercury SR 60088.

29 Strings and Then Some. RCA LPM 1457.

Arraujo, Severino (Brazilian Conductor)

Teleco Teco en Cordas. Continental SLP 7005

Ashley, Robert (American Conductor)

Concerto for Lovers MGM E 3354

Music from Italian Films. MGM E 3485

Music for Your Solitude. MGM E 3355

Symphonic Pictures of 'Porgy and Bess', 'Oklahoma' and 'Kiss Me, Kate' MGM E 3131

Symphonic Pictures of 'South Pacific' and 'Showboat'. MGM E 256

Ayres, Mitchell (American Conductor)

Romantic Ballads For You. Everest SDBR 1016

Baker, Tony (Conductor)

50 Academy Award Winners (With the Radio Orchestra [3LPs]) Lucky LTV 8

Barati, George (American Conductor)

Music from the Majestic Islands (With the Honolulu Symphony Orchestra). Decca DL 79104

Barrier, Georges (French Conductor)

Passeggiata a Parigi. Riviera POP 14

Bassman, George

Gershwin: From Broadway to Hollywood. Decca DL 4468

BBC Film Orchestra (Conductor not named)

The Hollywood Musical. Object OP 0042 [CD]

Bentley, Robert (British Conductor)

Hits from Broadway. Reader's Digest RDS 6037. (U.K. entitled: Curtain Up. Reader's Digest RDM 2037)

Interlude for Strings. Reader's Digest RD 56032

Boosey and Hawkes Mood Music

The Archive Collection [CD] CAV CD 32137

Borland, John Henry (Conductor)

For You . . . With Love. Sonia 77001 (Germany)

Botkin, Perry (American Conductor)

Great Motion Picture Themes from Jean Harlow Films. World Artists WAM 2007

Oldies but Goldies (With Hollywood Strings). Capitol T 2564

Bregman, Buddy (American Conductor)

Lovely Afternoon. Verve MGV 2068

Brigman, Norman (French Conductor)

Siempre Paris. Stereo 7.002 (South Africa)

Brott, Boris (Canadian Conductor)

Hooray for Hollywood (with Toronto Festival Pops Orchestra) Pro Arte CDD 422 [CD]

Busch, Lou (American Conductor and Pianist)

Lazy Rhapsody. Capitol ST 1072

Romantic Themes for Piano and Orchestra. Capitol ST 1833

Cacavas, John (American Conductor)

Moonstruck. DOT DLP 25269

Touch of Plush. Golden Crest CRS 4080

Velvet Is the Beat. Gallery GS 6201

Calvi, Pino (Italian Conductor and Pianist)

Autumn in Rome. Capitol T 10027

Music from Great Italian Motion Pictures. Capitol SP 8608

Cambridge Strings (Conductor not named)

Blue Strings. Decca LK 4532

12 Great Movie Themes. Decca ACL 1087

Campbell, Bruce (British Conductor and Composer)

Lovelight. MGM E3460

Carpenter, Gary (British Conductor)

British Light Music: Billy Meyerl Marco Polo 8223514

Carribean, Jose (Conductor)

Fire and Romance of Lecuona. Stereo Dynamic PSD 1017

Case, Russ (American Conductor)

Gypsy Moods. 'X' RCA LXA 1027

Oklahoma. Pickwick SPC 3114

Castaway Strings (Conductor not named)

Peter, Paul and Mary Songbook. Vee-Jay VJ-1115

Songs of Andy Williams. Vee-Jay VJ-1114

Challet, Pierre (French Conductor and Composer)

Strings in Hi Fi. Mercury SR 60066

Chante, André (French Conductor)

A Musical Setting for the Midnighters. DOT DLP 3019

Passport to Dreamland. DOT DLP 3022

Clegg, John (British Conductor)

And Still I Love You. RCA LPM/LSP 1916

Music for Nervous People. RCA LPM/LSP 1732

Coates, Harold (Conductor)

Musical Spellbinders. RCA Camden CAL 181

Waltz Time. RCA Camden. CAL 149

Coles, Jack (British Conductor)

Music of Jack Coles. Columbia TWO 126

Comissiona, Sergiu (American Conductor)

Celebrate America (With Houston Symphony Orchestra) Pro-Arte SPL 263

Corner, Ted (Conductor)

Famous Melodies of Irving Berlin, Richard Rodgers and Cole Porter (With New Pacific Orchestra) Sonia 77140 [CD]

Corp, Ronald (British Conductor)

British Light Music Classics (With New London Orchestra) [CD] Hyperion CDA 66818

Costa, Don (American Conductor and Arranger)

Days of Wine and Roses. HS 11147

Echoing Voices and Trombones. United Artists WWS 8501

The Golden Touch. United Artists UAL 7001

Fifteen Hits. ABC 362

Hits! Hits! Hits! Columbia CS 8841

Hollywood Premiere. Columbia Cl 1880; CS 8680

Music to Break Sub-Lease. ABCS 212

Simon & Garfunkel. SR 61177

Cugat, Xavier

The Beautiful New Sound of Strings. Musicor M 253179

Delgado, Robert (German Conductor)

Romance in Venice. Polydor LPHM 46090

De Oliveira, Renato

Hi-Fi Pops Concert. Harmony OK 5029

Drucker, Eric (American Conductor) (With the Magic Violins)
Note: All LPs were released on the Magic Violins label.

Be My Love. 2514/DS 2514

Best of Broadway. 2509/DS 2509 [Also see Ambassador Strings]

Best of George Gershwin. 2508/DS 2508

Best of Jerome Kern. 2500/DS 2500

Enchantment of Rodgers and Hammerstein. 2502/DS 2502

Many Sides of Lerner and Loewe. 2505/DS 2505

Memories of Victor Herbert. 2507/DS 2507

Movie Themes. 2506/DS 2506

Musical Pattern of Leroy Anderson. 2501/DS 2501

Say It With Music (With Twin Pianos). 2503/DS 2503

Strings in Motion. 2512/DS 2512

Dumont, Cedric (German Conductor)

Musical Cocktail Party. Polydor LPHM 46047

Durand, Paul (French Conductor)

Souvenir de Paris. Polydor 48822

Duval, Ramon (American Conductor)

Music from the Movies. 1958

Dvorak, Joseph (American Conductor, Composer and Arranger)

Golden Strings (With Hollywood Film City Orchestra). Amano D-3000

Edelhagen, Kurt (German Conductor)

Ballroom in Paris. Polydor LPHM 46357

Concerto. Polydor SLPHM 237630

Holiday in Brazil. Polydor SLPHM 237 534

Holiday in Italy. Polydor SLPHM 237565

Esquivel (Mexican Conductor)

Exploring New Sounds. RCA LSP 1978

Four Corners of the World. RCA LSP 1749

Genius of Esquivel. RCA LSP 3697

Other Worlds, Other Sounds. RCA LSP 1753

Strings Aflame. RCA LSP 1988

European Concert Orchestra (Conductor not named)

European Favourites. EMI EURO 1

Fantastic Strings Vol. 1 (Conductor not named but is George Melachrino) Laserlight 15176. [CD]

[Note: Subsequent CDs in this series were not conducted by Melachrino]

Farnon, Dennis (British Conductor)

Enchanted Woods. RCA LSP 1897

Magoo in Hi Fi. RCA LPM 1362

Felère, Pierre (French Conductor)

Music for a French Dinner at Home. RCA LPM 195

Feller, Sid (American Conductor)

Music for Expectant Mothers. ABC Paramount 123

Feyer, George (American Conductor and Pianist)

Jerome Kern. VOX VX 25500

Fitzgerald, Mark (Conductor)

Music of the Movies (With RIAS Jugendorchester). 2 vols. Milan CH 03718 [CD]

Fontanna (American Conductor)

Music for Expectant Fathers. Remington Musirama (Not numbered)

Forsythe, Kevin (British Conductor)

London Romance. Coral CRL 57075

Music from London. Coral CRL 57076

Francis, David (British Conductor)

Sound of Strings. Invicta INV 197 (U.K.)

Franconi, Dean (American Conductor)

Lerner and Loewe's 'Camelot'. KM Corp. KS 153

Music from Award-Winning Films. KM Corp. KS 150

Music from 'Show Boat' and 'Roberta'. KM Corp. KS 157

Franks, Gordon (British Conductor)

Orchestral in the Night. Deram DML/SML 701

Strings in the Night. Deram DML/SML 706

Frontiere, Dominic (Conductor and Composer)

Love Eyes. Columbia CS 8224

Gamley, Douglas (British Conductor, Composer and Pianist)

Irving Berlin's Broadway. Diplomat DS 2287

Love. Marble Arch MAL 693

Gerhardt, Charles (American Conductor)

Casablanca: Classic Film Scores of Humphrey Bogart. RCA ARLI-0422

Giovannini, Caesar (American Conductor)

Caesar Plays. Columbia CS 40

My Fair Lady and Gigi (With Radiant Velvet Orchestra). Concert-Disc CS 23

Satin Strings. SA Stereo Sounds SA-7

Silk, Satin and Strings. Columbia CS 36

Gordon, Jay (American Conductor)

Music for a Lonely Night. TOPS L1524

Greene, Norman (American Conductor)

Body and Soul. Decca DL 8377

Romantic Moods. XMGM E 160

Greger, Max (German Conductor)

Ballroom in Rome. Polydor SLPHM 237555

Hagen, Hans (European Conductor)

Movie Cocktails. VOX VX 660

Hause, Alfred (German Conductor)

Blue Tango. Polydor 237579

La Violetera. Polydor 184170

On a Tropic Night. Polydor 1222 102

Tango der Welt. Polydor 833138; Teldec 826196 [CD]

Tango Notturne. Polydor 237544

Tango Party. Polydor 237658

Henderson, Joe (Conductor and Pianist)

Secret Love and Other Unforgettable Hits of the 50s. Columbia TWO 369

Hermann, Jurgen (German Conductor)

Fascination. Decca ND 176 (Germany)

World of Popular Serenades. Decca SPA.R131 (U.K.)

Herron, Joel (Conductor and Pianist)

The Way You Look Tonight and other Jerome Kern Favorites. Westminster WP 6074

Hertzman, Franz (German Conductor)

Music for a German Dinner at Home. RCA LPM 1935

Hollywood Orchestra (Conductor not named)

Music From the Films. Hollywood Records LPH 104

Horlick, Harry (American Conductor)

Jerome Kern Melodies. Decca DL 5078 (10")

Hruby, Victor (Austrian Conductor)

Franz Lehar: A Musical Portrait in Hi-Fi. VOS VX 25.560

Hunter, Frank (American Conductor)

Dancing Cheek to Cheek. Medallion MS 7502

Great Melodies. KAPP K 1099S (Stereo)

Great Melodies from the Motion Pictures. London ZA.K.5545

Just a Minute. PA 203/4

Sound of Strings, vol. 2. Medallion ML/MS 7509

Sounds of Hunter. Jubilee LP 1020

Sweet Sound of Strings. KAPP MS 7502

International Pop Orchestra (Conductor not named. Probably Don Costa)

One Hundred and Ten Men. Columbia 33 SX 1427 (U.K.)

12 Greatest Songs Ever Written. Cameo SC 2003

International Symphony Orchestra (Conductor not named)

Magnificent Movie Themes. Ronco SR 028

Irving, Joseph (American Conductor and Arranger)

And Then I Wrote Cole Porter. Time S 2114

Ivanoff (British Conductor)

Stardust and Other Romantic Tunes. Presto PRE 659

Jaffa, Max (British Conductor and Violinist)

Music From the Palm Court. Columbia 33 S 1104

Prelude to Romance. Valentine VAL 8051

Serenades of Yesterday for Sweethearts of Today. Columbia 33 SX 1116 (U.K.) Released in the U.S. as By Candlelight. Capitol ST 10220

Violin and Voices (With the Bill Shepherd Chorus) Columbia 33 S 1120

Johnson, Eric (British Conductor)

Blue Skies: Music of Irving Berlin. Westminster WP 6098

Glamorous Nights: Music of Ivor Novello. Westminster WP 102

With a Song in My Heart: Music of Richard Rodgers. Westminster WGM 8284

Jones, Leslie (British Conductor)

Best of Robert Farnon. PYE GH 601

Jones, Richard (American Conductor and Arranger)

Moonlight and Violins (With Pittsburgh Symphony Orchestra Strings) Capitol T 534 [Also on CD]

Music in the Night (With Pittsburgh Symphony Orchestra Strings). Capitol T 690 [Also on CD]

Songs for Strings (With Pittsburgh Symphony Orchestra Strings). Capitol T 419 [Also on CD]

Stringtime (With Pittsburgh Symphony Orchestra Strings). Capitol T 890 [Also on CD]

Jupp, Eric (British Conductor)

Magic Memories. EMI 8133722 (Australia) [CD]

Memories Are Made of These: Songs That Sold a Million. PYE GGL 0063

Romantic Magic. EMI (Australia) SREG 30116

Music for Sweethearts.

Kaye, Sammy (American Conductor)

Dreamy Dancing. Columbia ASK 3005

Keating, John (British Conductor)

Ireland (With Royal Philharmonic Orchestra). Decca PFS 4200

Keith, Priam (American Conductor and Pianist)

Do Not Disturb. DOT DLP 3020

Kingsway Strings

Music for Skaters. Stereo Fidelity SF 28200

Knight, Peter (British Conductor and Pianist)

Best of Noel Coward and Ivor Novello. Pye GGL 0173 (U.K.)

Musicals Collection (With London Symphony Orchestra). Cadenza CDCC125 (2 vols.) [CD] Also released under title: Musical Fantasy. David Gresham Records DGR 1068 [2LPs] South African issue.

La Salle, Guy (French Conductor)

Rendezvous for Two. MGM E3570

Lanchberry, John (Australian Conductor)

Music of Eric Coates (With Sydney Symphony Orchestra) HMV ESD 7062

Laredo, Roger (Italian Conductor)

Italy. Decca PFS 34015

Lars, Eric (Conductor with Briarcliff Strings)

Academy Award Hits. Harmony HS 91216

Favorite Songs from the Movies. Harmony HS 11151

Great Themes from Great Movies. Harmony HS 11278

Hits of Sinatra. Harmony HS 11213

Music from the Movies. Harmony HS 11315

Plays. Harmony HS 11404

Some Enchanted Evening. Harmony HS 11165

Leaper, Adrian (Conductor)

British Light Music: Robert Farnon (With Czechoslovak Radio Symphony Orchestra). Marco Polo 8223401

British Light Music: Haydn Wood. Marco Polo 8223402

British Light Music: Frederic Curzon. Marco Polo 8223425

British Light Music: Roger Quilter. Marco Polo 8223444

Lecussant, Maurice (French Conductor)

Under Paris Skies. Omega OSL 30; Bestseller BNL 7004

Leighton, Michael (American Conductor)

Sound of Strings. Medallion MS 7502

Levine, Maurice (American Conductor)

Speak Low: The Great Music of Kurt Weill. Warner WS 1313

Light, Enoch (American Conductor)

Familiar Songs From Foreign Lands (2 LPs) Command RSSD 9762

Show Spectacular. Grand Award GA 228

Sound 35 mm (2 LPs) Command RS 82/831

Spanish Stings. Project PR 5000

World's Most Precious Violins. Command RS 804

Lin Will, Bob (Chinese Conductor)

Music for a Chinese Dinner at Home. RCA LPM 1936

Lockyer, Malcolm (British Conductor and Arranger for Knightsbridge Strings)

Lazy Afternoon. RCA RAL 1008

Seasons of Love. Mercury MG 20205

We're Having a Party. RCA RAL 1012

Loges, Henry (German Conductor)

Romantic Waltzes Around the World. Polydor 2310053

Tanz Tee. Karussell 635004

London Pops Orchestra (Conductor not named)

Music for You and Me. Bestseller BNL 7008

London Theatre Orchestra (Conductor not named)

Best From Broadway. Hallmark 300492 [CD]

Loss, Joe (British Conductor)

The Loss Concertium. EMI Q4 TWO 352

Luboff, Norman (American Conductor and Choir Leader)

Choral Spectacular (With RCA Victor Symphony Orchestra and Chorus). RCA LPM/LSP 2522

Luxemburg Pop Orchestra

Glenn Miller Symphony (Conductor not named, but probably Norrie Paramor). Polydor 2310006 [Also on CD]

Magnante, Charles (French Conductor)

Magnante . . . In Concert ABC Records GA 2685

Moods for Moderns. Grand Award GA 33–413

Magne, Armand (French Conductor)

Paris. Belair 7065

Malneck, Matty (American Conductor)

As I Hear It: Dramatic Themes from the Great Motion Pictures of William Holden (Arranged by Warren Barker) Warner B1247

Maltby, Richard (American Conductor)

Hello, Young Lovers. CBS ALD 6339 (S.A.)

Maltby with Strings Attached. VIK LX 1074

Mann, Roberto (British Conductor)

Accordion Sounds. Deram DML.SML 1016

Go, Go, Go. Deram DML/SML 1011

Great Love Themes. Deram DML/SML 1019

Great Waltzes. Deram CML/SML 1010

World of Waltzes. 2 vols. Decca PA/SPA 23, 180

Marino, Richard (American Conductor and Arranger)

Out of this World. Liberty LSS 14007

Martinelli, Dino (American Conductor)

South Pacific. Harmony OK 5026

Martini, Julio (Conductor)

Sweetest Sounds. NAXOS 8.880032 [CD]

Maxwell, Robert (American Conductor and Harpist)

Anytime. Command SCOM 108

McGlinn, John (British Conductor who has set out to record on compact discs the scores of original Broadway shows)

Gershwin, Kern and Porter Overtures; (Gershwin Overtures with New Princess Theatre Orchestra; Porter Overtures with London Sinfonietta; Kern Overtures with National Philharmonic Orchestra). EMI 72435685892 3 [CD]

Jerome Kern Overtures (With National Philharmonic Orchestra). EMI CDC 7 49630.2 [CD]

Meynard, Raoul (European Conductor)

American Film Favorites. Warner W/WS 1440

Carte Blanche Continentale. Warner B 1370

Continental Host. Warner W 1424

Continental Visa. Warner W 1215

Continental Visa Renewed. Warner B 1320

Passport to Pleasure. Warner WS 1469

Strolling Mandolins. Warner W 1405

Michael, Patrick (Conductor)

For Lovers: Good Night Sweetheart. DET MDG 2012

Michaels, Daniel (American Conductor)

Candlelight and Wine. Reader's Digest from Album *Mood Music for Listening and Relaxation* RDS 6090

Migiani, Armand (French Conductor)

Play a Song of Paris. Polydor LPHM 46107

Milano (Conductor)

I'll Always Be in Love with You: Songs by Sammy Stept. MGM E.3184

Mitchell, Parris (American Conductor)

Dancing in the Dark. Pickwick SPC 5006

From Paris with Love. Pickwick SPC 5002

From Rome with Love. Pickwick SPC 5001

From Spain with Love. Pickwick SPC 5003

Night and Day and Other Great Songs of Love. Pickwick SPC 5005

Monese, Gianni (Italian Conductor)

Cook's Tour of Venice. VOX VX 25120

Neapolitan Gold. Columbia WL 118

Monet, Charles (French Conductor)

When the Day Draws To a Close. Intercord INT 892.692

Montero, André (French Conductor)

Something in the Wind. URAMA UR 9007

Moonlight Strings (Conductor not named)

Love After Midnight. Columbia Musical Treasures DS 441

Moonlight Becomes You. Columbia Record Club DS209

Muller-Lampertz, Richard (Conductor)

Holiday Abroad in Vienna. RCA LPM 1598

Munro, Ronnie (British Conductor)

Music of Victor Herbert. Richmond B20009

Nabarro, Malcolm (British Conductor)

Music of Eric Coates. [CD] ASV WHL 2053, 2075

Robin Hood Country. [CD] ASV WHL 2069

Neubrand, Heinz (European Conductor)

Made in Italy. Bestseller BAM 7012

Newell, Norman (British Record Producer)

Falling in Love. EMI Studio Two 217

More than Memories. EMI Studio Two 148

The Onedin Line and Other Wonderful Themes Philips 6308.094

Nirenberg, Henrique (Conductor of the Magic Strings)

Broadway Yesterday. Musidisc M 6012

Ogden, Ronnie (Conductor)

Hits from Hollywood. RCA RAL 1003

Orquesta Violines de Oro (South American Orchestra. Conductor not named)

Boleros. Capitol T 20

Ortolani, Riz (Italian Conductor and Composer)

Made in Rome: Themes from Great Films. United Artists UAS 6360

Mondo Cane. United Artists UAS 5105

Otis, Clyde (American Conductor)

Here Comes the Showboat. Mercury SRW 16221

Love Letters. Mercury MG 20571/SR 60230

Paige, Raymond (American Conductor)

Classical Spice Shelf. SDBR 3027

Love's Several Faces. RCA Camden CAL 278

Music Hall Bon-Bons. Everest LPBR 5024; SDBR 1024

Showplace of the Nation. Roulette R 25008

Star Dust Melodies. RCA Camden CAL 135

Parker, John

The Sound of Conversations in Music. Medallion ML/MS 7504

Paxton Music Library

Everyday Events AA CD2 [CD]

Showtime AA CD6 [CD]

Social Life and Events AA CD 4 [CD]

Payne, Jack (British Conductor)

Say It with Music. His Master's Voice CLP 1160 [Also on CD]

Penny, Adrian (Conductor)

British Light Music: Archibald Joyce. Marco Polo 8223694 [CD]

Peretti, Hugo (American Conductor and Arranger)

And So to Sleep: The Music of Harry Revel. Mercury MG 21079

Phillips, Woolf (British Conductor)

Lullaby of Broadway: Music of Dubin and Warren. London LL 1426

Piesker, Rudiger (German Conductor)

Fascination Strings. MPS 12009

Prince, Robert (American Conductor and Arranger)

Orchestral Moods of a Western Sunset. Warner W 1259

Pro Arte Orchestra

British Light Music of the Twentieth Century. Leroy Anderson's Greatest Hits. Maxiplay 8011 [CD]

Prowse, Keith Mood Music

Archive Series. KPM 81/84 [3 CDs]

Vintage Themes. KPM 223 [CD]

When the Lights Are Low. DOT DLP 3018

Rafael, Sergio

Moon River. Marvel MARC 434 [CD]

Ramsay, Harlan (American Conductor)

Portfolio for Easy Listening (With the Cosmopolitan Orchestra). RCA Camden CAL 130

Reisman, Joe (American Conductor)

All-time Instrumental Favorites. Roulette R 25082

Great American Waltzes. Roulette R 25089

Robinson, Harry (American Conductor)

Moody and Magnificent. Riverside RLP 7528

Romaine, David (American Conductor)

It's Just the Gypsy in My Soul. Mercury MG 20361

Sack, Al (American Conductor)

Concert Favorites. Gramophone 20116

Salinger, Conrad (American Arranger and Conductor)

Lovely Afternoon. Verve MGV 2068

Sandauer, Heinz (Austrian Conductor and Pianist)

George Gershwin: Musical Portrait in Hi Fi. VOX VX 25130

Sannell, Andy (American Conductor)

The Girl Friend. Everest LPBR 5005

Sarbek, Boris (French Conductor)

Symphonie Sur Paris. Philips B 680001 L

Saunders, Jack (American Conductor)

Mike Todd's Broadway. Everest LPBR 5011

Say, Jack (American Conductor)

Girl That I Marry. RCA Camden RAL 1009

Hits from The Most Happy Fella. RCA Camden CAL 319

Irving Berlin Hits. TOPS L919 (10")

Sbarra, John (American Conductor)

All My Best [CD]. Fairfield JS 001

Movie Themes of Tomorrow [CD]. Fairfield JS 003

Scott, Francis (American Conductor)

Moods for Candlelight

Moods for Firelight. Capitol LC 6589 (10")

Selinsky, Vladimir (American Conductor)

Dinner Music. Columbia CL 6036 (10")

Senati, John (American Conductor)

Flower Drum Song and Rodgers and Hammerstein Musical Showcase. (With Bravo Pops Symphony Orchestra). KM Corp KS 120

Music for a Listening Mood. KM Corp KS 143

Music from 'Can-Can' and Other Cole Porter Favorites. KM Corp KS 144

Music of Around the World in 80 Days and The King and I (With Bravo Pops Symphony Orchestra). KM Corp KS 102

Music of South Pacific and Oklahoma (With Bravo Pops Symphony Orchestra). KM Corp KS 103

My Fair Lady and Gigi. (With Bravo Pops Symphony Orchestra). KM Corp KS 104

Porgy and Bess and Rhapsody in Blue. (With Bravo Pops Symphony Orchestra) KM Corp KS 119.

Rodgers and Hammerstein's Sound of Music. KM Corp KS 139

Tribute to George Gershwin (With Bravo Pops Symphony Orchestra). KM Corp AK 158

Shaw, Roland (British Conductor and Arranger)

Mexico. Decca PFS 34027; London SP 44030

Under Latin Skies. Decca DGS 18

Westward Ho. London SP 44045

Silberman, Benedict (Austrian Conductor)

Dark Eyes: Songs of the Steppes. Columbia WL 118

International Souvenirs. Philips P 10043 R

Sinatra, Frank (American Singer and Conductor)

Music from Pictures and Plays (Arrangements by Harry Sukman) Reprise R 6045

Singing Strings (Conductor not named; probably William Hill Bowen)

Dream Along. RCA CPM 108/CSP 108

Siravo, George (American Conductor and Arranger)

And Then I Wrote Richard Rodgers. Time S 2115

Rodgers and Hart: Percussion and Strings. Time S 20F

Seductive Strings. Time S 2019

Smith, Pete (British Conductor)

Great Songs of Irving Berlin. Fontana STL 252

Snell, David (British Conductor)

Magic of the Waltz. Sunset SLS 50346

Snyder, Bill (American Conductor)

Music for a Moonlight Rendezvous. Bestseller BSU 7003

Somerset Strings (Conductor not named)

Because I Love You. Epic LN 3254

Dinner Music. Epic LN 3147

Far Away Lands. Epic LN 3161

Look for the Silver Lining. Epic LN 3236

Music for Washing and Ironing. Epic LN 3084

Wanting You. Epic LN 3099

Will You Remember? Epic LN 3255

Sommers, Pierre (French Conductor)

Holiday Abroad in Paris. RCA LPM 1600

Spencer, Herbert (American Conductor)

Magic of the Caribbean. Decca DL 9080

Steele, Eric (American Conductor)

Instrumental Selections from Porgy and Bess and Showboat. Mercury MG 20394

Steinberg, William (American Conductor)

Symphonic Picture of My Fair Lady and The Sound of Music (With Pittsburgh Symphony Orchestra). Command CC 11041 SD

Symphonic Story of Jerome Kern/A Commemoration Symphony: Stephen Foster. Everest 3063

Stellari, Gian (Italian Conductor and Arranger)

Great Songs from Italian Films. Philips PSK 3019 (S.A.)

Stevens, Jay (American Conductor)

In the Blue of Evening. TOPS L 1553

Stockholm String Orchestra (Conductor not named)

The Best of Victor Herbert. Somerset P 400

Stradivari Strings (Conductor not named)

Sound of Gershwin

Rodgers and Hammerstein. Pirouette RFM 42

Stratford Strings (Conductor not named)

Music from The Sound of Music. Decca DL 78975

Surrey Strings (Conductor not named)

Made in Hollywood. SS 1011

Made in London. SS 1036

Thompson, Benjamin

Music of Irving Berlin and Cole Porter. Stardust STACD 030

Trendler, Robert (Conductor)

George Gershwin. NIXA XLPY 155

Jerome Kern. NIXA XLPY 154

Trent, Ronnie (British Conductor)

Magical Melodies of Ivor Novello (With the Palace Players). Variety PMEM 6012

Trovajoli, Armando (Italian Conductor and Pianist)

Champagne for Dinner. RCA LPM 1122

Controluce. VIK KLVP 143

Musical Nightcap. RCA Camden CAS598

One Night in Naples. RCA LPM 1755

One Night in Rome. RCA LSP 1920

Un Notte a Venezia. RCA A12 P0015 (Italian)

Valentino (Italian Conductor and Pianist)

Around the World. Jacklyne JPR 1056 (U.K.)

Prelude to a Kiss: Valentino Plays Duke Ellington. ABC Paramount ABC 169

Stairway to Paradise: Popular Themes from the Classics. ABC Paramount 217

Strauss in Hi-Fi. ABC Paramount ABC 143

They Say It's Wonderful: Irving Berlin Melodies. ABC Paramount ABC 142

Valentino. Columbia Studio Two 248

Van Hoof, Harry

Strings by Candlelight. Philips STAR 5086

Villard, Michel (French Conductor)

Music from the Films of Charlie Chaplin. Vogue VGC 7096

Walker, Bill (Conductor)

Bouquet of Roses (With Living Strings). RCA Camden CAL/CAS 2154

Wayland, Newton

Sophisticated Ladies (With Utah Symphony Pops Orchestra) Pro-Arte CDD421

Weldon, George (British Conductor)

British Concert Pops (1970) EMI SXLP 30123; 1978 Reissue EMI SCLP 30243

British Light Music of the 20th Century. HMV CSD 1503

Whitaker, David (British Conductor)

Latin in the Night. Deram SML 703

White, Robin (British Conductor)

Edwardian Echoes: British Light Music. Chandos 9110

Grand Tour: The Ballet Music of Noel Coward (With City of Prague Philharmonic Orchestra). Silva KD 6007

Whitehall, David (American Conductor)

Love's Several Faces. RCA Camden CAL 278

Hi-Fi Portraits of Italy (With Symphony Orchestra of Rome). RCA Camden CAL 298

Moonglow and Music. RCA Camden CAL 271

Young, Leon (British Conductor and Arranger)

Ellington for Strings. EMI OU 2094; Columbia 33 SX1601 (U.K.)

Liverpool Sound. Atco 33–163

Sound of Strings. Golden Guinea GGL 0147

Zarzosa, Chucho (Mexican Conductor)

Hit Motion Picture Themes (With Living Strings). RCA Camden CAL/CAS 673

Salute to Glenn Miller (With Living Strings). RCA Camden CAL/CAS 688

South of the Border (With Living Strings). RCA Camden CAL/CAS 682

Souvenir of Italy (With Living Strings). RCA Camden CAL/CAS 696

Select Bibliography

The bibliography consists of sources consulted by the authors in the compilation of this book. Numerous other sources were also consulted, but only the most useful and substantial of these have been included in the bibliography.

There are a great number of books, especially biographies and articles, which cover the lives and work of the composers, who ranged from the giants of American and British popular music (such as Jerome Kern, George Gershwin, Cole Porter, Richard Rodgers, Irving Berlin, Harold Arlen, Noël Coward and Ivor Novello) to film and mood music composers (such as Robert Farnon, Eric Coates and Charles Williams).

No useful purpose would have been served to duplicate what has already been admirably achieved in the existing literature of popular music by such authors as David Ewen and others. The authors have tried instead to guide the reader to existing literature through additional readings at the end of respective articles.

The notes given on the backs of record sleeves/covers proved an especially useful source of biographical information in respect to many of the conductors included in this book.

DISCOGRAPHICAL SOURCES

Erlewine, Michael, and others, eds. *All Music Guide: The Best CDs, Albums and Tapes. The Expert's Guide to the Best Releases from Thousands of Artists in All Types of Music.* San Francisco: Miller Freeman Books, 1994.

Gramophone Musicals Good CD Guide. Harrow, Middlesex: General Gramophone Publications, 1997.

Gramophone Popular Catalogue: 1955–1987. Harrow, Middlesex: General Gramophone Publications.

Harris, Steve. *Film, Television and Stage Music on Phonograph Record: A Discography*. Jefferson, North Carolina: McFarland, 1988.

Hodgins, Gordon W. *The Broadway Musical: A Complete L.P. Discography*. Metuchen, N.J.: Scarecrow Press, 1980.

Hummel, David. *The Collector's Guide to the American Musical Theater*. Metuchen, N.J.: Scarecrow Press, 1984. 2 vols.

Jazz 'n Pops: A Complete Catalog of Popular and Jazz Longplay Records. Vol.1, 1957–Vol. 3, 1959. New York: Long Player Publications.

Limbacher, James L. *Film Music: From Violins to Video*. Metuchen, NJ: Scarecrow Press, 1974.

———. *Keeping Score: Film Music 1972–1979*. Metuchen, N.J.: Scarecrow Press, 1981.

———. *Keeping Score: Film and Television Music 1980–1988*. Metuchen, NJ: Scarecrow Press, 1991.

Long Player: A Complete Catalog Listing Long Playing Records. Vol. 1, 1952–Vol. 4, 1955. New York: Long Player Publications.

Murrells, Joseph. *Million Selling Records From the 1900s to the 1980s: An Illustrated Directory*. London: Batsford; New York: Arco, 1984. Includes useful biographies of artists and conductors whose recordings exceeded a million or more copies.

Raymond, Jack. *Show Music on Record*. New York: Frederick Ungar, 1981.

Schwann, Opus. Albany, New York: Schwann Publications. Quarterly. A guide to classical recordings.

Schwann Spectrum. Albany, New York: Schwann Publications. Quarterly. A reference guide to popular music.

Schwann Long Playing Record Catalog, Vol. 1, 1948–. Boston: W. Schwann.

POPULAR MUSIC

Burton, Jack. *Blue Book of Tin Pan Alley: A Human Interest Anthology of American Popular Music*. New York: Century House, 1950.

———. *Blue Book of Broadway Musicals*. New York: Century House, 1952

———. *Blue Book of Hollywood Musicals*. New York: Century House, 1953.

Clarke, Donald, ed. *Penguin Encyclopedia of Popular Music*. London: Penguin Books, 1990.

———. *Rise and Fall of Popular Music*. London: Penguin Books, 1995.

Ewen, David. *All the Years of American Popular Music*. Englewood Cliffs, NJ: Prentice-Hall, 1977.

———. *American Popular Songs*. New York: Random House, 1966.

———. *American Songwriters*. New York: H. W. Wilson, 1987.

———. *The Life and Death of Tin Pan Alley: The Golden Age of American Popular Music*. New York: Funk & Wagnalls, 1964.

———. *Panorama of American Popular Music*. Englewood Cliffs, NJ: Prentice-Hall, 1957.

———. *Popular American Composers*. New York: H. W. Wilson, 1962.

Gammond, Peter, comp. *Oxford Companion to Popular Music*. Oxford and New York: Oxford University Press, 1991.

Green, Benny. *Let's Face the Music: The Golden Age of Popular Song.* London: Pavilion Books, 1989.

Hamm, Charles. *Yesterdays: Popular Song in America.* New York: W. W. Norton, 1979.

Hardy, Phil and Dave Laing. *Faber Companion to 20th Century Popular Music.* 2nd ed. London: Faber & Faber, 1995. First published in 1990.

Hemming, Roy. *The Melody Lingers On: The Great Songwriters and Their Movie Musicals.* New York: Newmarket Press, 1986.

Hischak, Thomas S. *The American Musical Theatre Song Encyclopedia.* Westport, Connecticut: Greenwood Press, 1995.

Hitchcock, H. Wiley and S. Sadie. *New Grove Dictionary of Popular Music.* London: Macmillan, 1986. 4 vols.

Hyland, William G. *The Song Is Ended: Songwriters and American Music, 1900–1950.* New York: Oxford University Press, 1995.

Jablonski, Edward. *The Encyclopedia of American Music.* New York: Doubleday, 1981.

Jacobs, Dick, and Harriet Jacobs. *Who Wrote That Song?* 2nd ed. Cincinnati, Ohio: Writer's Digest Books, 1994. First published in 1988.

Jaques Cattell Press. *ASCAP Biographical Dictionary.* New York: R. R. Bowker, 1980.

Journal into Melody. London: Robert Farnon Society, no. 1, 1956–. The periodical continues to be published. Nos. 1–128 were the issues consulted by the authors. An invaluable and indispensable source of information for almost half a century on light and popular orchestral music, universal in scope. Published by the Robert Farnon Society, with a focus on Robert Farnon, the contents of this publication have a wealth of information on light and popular orchestral composers, conductors and recordings. A detailed index concerning the contents of nos. 1–105 (1956–91), compiled by Reuben Musiker, is available from the publishers (Stone Gables, Upton Lane, Seavington, St Michael, Ilminster, Somerset TA190PZ, England).

Kennedy, Michael. *Concise Oxford Dictionary of Music.* 4th ed. Oxford and New York: Oxford University Press, 1996. Based on the full Oxford Dictionary of Music (revised edition), which was published in 1994. Includes numerous entries on popular music.

Kinkle, Roger D. *The Complete Encyclopedia of Popular Music and Jazz, 1900–1950.* New Rochelle, NY: Arlington House, 1974.

Lanza, Joseph. *Elevator Music: A Surreal History of Muzak, Easy-Listening and Other Moodsong.* New York: Picador, 1995.

Larkin, Colin, ed. *Guinness Encyclopedia of Popular Music,* Revised edition. Middlesex, England: Guinness Publishing, 1996. 6 vols. First published in 1992 in 4 vols.

———. *Guinness Encyclopedia of Popular Music.* Concise Edition. Middlesex, England: Guinness Publishing, 1993.

Lax, Roger, and Frederick Smith. *The Great Song Thesaurus.* New York: Oxford University Press, 1984.

Lissauer, Robert. *Lissauer's Encyclopedia of Popular Music, 1888 to the Present.* New York: Paragon House, 1991.

Palmer, Tony. *All You Need is Love: The Story of Popular Music.* London: Weidenfeld and Nicolson and Chappell, 1976.

Paymer, Marvin E. *Facts Behind the Songs: A Handbook of American Popular Music From the Nineties to the 90's.* New York: Garland Publishing, 1993.

Spaeth, Sigmund. *A History of Popular Music in America.* New York: Random House, 1948.

Stambler, Irwin. *Encyclopedia of Popular Music.* New York: St. Martin's Press, 1965. Succeeded by *Encyclopedia of Pop, Rock and Soul*, Revised edition. New York: St. Martin's Press, 1989.

Suskin, Steven. *Show Tunes, 1905–1985.* New York: Dodd, Mead, 1986.

White, Mark. *You Must Remember This: Popular Songwriters, 1900–1980.* London: Frederick Warne, 1983.

Wilder, Alec. *American Popular Song: The Great Innovators, 1900–1950.* New York: Oxford University Press, 1972. Reprinted, with new introduction by Gene Lees and minor revisions, 1990.

Wilk, Max. *They're Playing Our Song: From Jerome Kern to Stephen Sondheim.* New York: Atheneum, 1973; London: W.H. Allen, 1974.

FILM MUSIC

Evans, Mark. *Soundtrack: The Music of The Movies.* New York: Da Capo Press, 1979.

Gramophone Film Music Good CD Guide, 2nd ed. Harrow, Middlesex, England: Gramophone Publications, 1997. Includes extensive biographical articles on film music composers. First published in 1996.

Huntley, John. *British Film Music.* London: Skelton Robinson, 1947.

Karlin, Fred. *Listening to Movies: The Film Lover's Guide to Film Music.* New York: Schirmer Books, 1994.

Limbacher, James, ed. *Film Music from Violins to Video.* Metuchen, NJ: Scarecrow Press, 1974.

———. *Keeping Score: Film Music, 1972–1979.* Metuchen, NJ: Scarecrow Press, 1981.

———. *Keeping Score: Film and Television Music, 1980–1988.* Metuchen, NJ: Scarecrow Press, 1991.

Palmer, Christopher. *The Composer in Hollywood.* London and New York: Marion Boyars, 1990.

Thomas, Tony. *Film Score: The Art and Craft of Movie Music.* Burbank, California: Riverwood Press, 1991. An enlarged and revised edition of *Film Score: The View from the Podium.* New York: Barnes, 1979.

Index

About the Authors

REUBEN MUSIKER is Professor Emeritus at the University of the Witwatersrand in Johannesburg, South Africa, where he was Professor of Librarianship and Bibliography and University Librarian. He is an inveterate collector of popular orchestral music and has contributed many articles on the subject to music journals.

NAOMI MUSIKER is a freelance book indexer of some seventy-five books by leading South African publishers. She has assisted her husband in the compilation and indexing of this book.